Inspector of Irish Fisheries

Inspectors of Irish Fisheries report, 1872

Inspector of Irish Fisheries

Inspectors of Irish Fisheries report, 1872

ISBN/EAN: 9783741104688

Manufactured in Europe, USA, Canada, Australia, Japa

Cover: Foto ©ninafisch / pixelio.de

Manufactured and distributed by brebook publishing software
(www.brebook.com)

Inspector of Irish Fisheries

Inspectors of Irish Fisheries report, 1872

REPORT

OF THE

INSPECTORS OF IRISH FISHERIES

ON THE

DEEP SEA, COAST, AND INLAND FISHERIES OF IRELAND,

FOR

1872.

Presented to both Houses of Parliament by Command of Her Majesty.

DUBLIN:
PRINTED BY ALEXANDER THOM, 87 & 89, ABBEY-STREET,
FOR HER MAJESTY'S STATIONERY OFFICE.

CONTENTS.

REPORT

OF THE

INSPECTORS OF IRISH FISHERIES

ON THE

DEEP SEA, COAST, AND INLAND FISHERIES OF IRELAND, FOR 1872.

TO HIS EXCELLENCY JOHN POYNTZ, EARL SPENCER, K.G.,

LORD LIEUTENANT-GENERAL AND GENERAL GOVERNOR OF IRELAND.

MAY IT PLEASE YOUR EXCELLENCY,

In conformity with the 112th sec., 5 & 6 Vic., cap. 106, we beg to submit our Report for the year 1872, being the fourth since our appointment.

We desire to explain to your Excellency that, consistently with furnishing all necessary information, it was quite impossible for us to present this Report at an earlier period, and that, for the reasons we will submit, our future Reports cannot be presented to Parliament before April.

At the time the Act was passed there were no Boards of Conservators in Ireland. Since then Boards throughout the country have been formed, who furnish statistics, and whose accounts are made up to the 31st December in each year. The Inspecting Commanders of Coast-guard in the thirty divisions into which the coast of Ireland is divided, also furnish statistics with regard to the sea fisheries. In both instances the returns are made up to the 31st of December.

Being particularly anxious to get the Report for this year out as soon as possible, we forwarded the usual queries to Conservators and Inspecting Commanders of Coast-guard early in December, earnestly requesting them to furnish replies not later than the first week in January of the present year.

The utmost difficulty was experienced, as usual, in obtaining returns from the Boards of Conservators, especially with regard to their receipts and disbursements. In many instances repeated applications had to be made before they were forwarded. In one case eight letters had to be written in succession before the return was made on 25th March.

Some of the Coast-guard returns were not received until the 31st of March, although a special circular was addressed to the Inspecting Commanders, stating that "as it was of importance that the Report of the Inspectors should be laid before Parliament soon after its opening, they would feel obliged by the returns being completed and transmitted the first week in January."

As our own Report is founded on the information contained in the replies to the queries sent to the Conservators and Coast-guard officers, we could not complete it until the first week in April, when it was placed in the printer's hands.

The statistics were sent to be printed as they came in. A good deal of delay was involved in having some of these returns corrected by the Coast-guard. Owing to the voluminous appendices, they occupied a month in printing.

To show that the same difficulty was experienced by our predecessors, we append the dates of their Reports since the formation of the Boards of Conservators:—

1850,	7th June, 1851.	1860,	4th July, 1861.
1851,	8th August, 1852.	1861,	17th June, 1862.
1852,	20th May, 1853.	1862,	24th July, 1863.
1853,	30th June, 1854.	1863,	1st September, 1864.
1854,	31st October, 1855.	1864,	21st April, 1865.
1855,	7th June, 1856.	1865,	9th June, 1866.
1856,	31st March, 1857.	1866,	22nd May, 1867.
1857,	1st June, 1858.	1867,	15th June, 1868.
1858,	1st June, 1859.	1868,	18th May, 1869.
1859,	20th July, 1860.		

The Sea Fisheries.

We believe that the statistics prepared this year with regard to the craft and crews engaged in the sea fisheries, will convey a more accurate idea of their number than the figures we were able to furnish in our preceding Reports. Having reason to believe that there were inaccuracies in the Coast-guard returns, with regard to the boats that came properly under the denomination of fishing boats, and also with regard to the number of men and boys partially engaged in fishing, we addressed a circular to the Inspecting Commanders, requesting that greater care would be observed in ascertaining the required particulars, and pointing out where we considered the errors lay. We also requested that the craft and crews should be ascertained in the unguarded portions of the coast, undertaking to pay the expenses of the men while engaged on this duty.

The returns furnished to us show that in 1872 the number of vessels and boats wholly and partially engaged in the fisheries was 7,914, and men and boys, 31,311, against 9,099 craft and 38,650 crews in 1870–71, showing an apparent falling off since our last Report of 1,185 vessels and boats, and 7,339 men and boys.

We should remark that owing to an error in the Coast-guard returns for 1870–71, the craft appeared as 8,999, and the crews 38,629, instead of the correct figures now given above.

As will be seen by Appendix No. 3, the number of boats registered by the Collectors of Customs was 8,534, and men and boys 35,838; being 620 boats and 4,527 men and boys in excess of the number returned to us by the Coast-guard.

The only way that we can account for the discrepancy is, that many boats were registered by the Collectors of Customs which did not properly come under the denomination of fishing boats, and that the owners, in making a return of the crews, stated the number required to man the boat, without mentioning the fact—which we found frequently occurs with regard to boats only partially engaged in fishing—that the same persons often furnish crews to two or three boats in the same locality.

From the particular directions which we addressed to the Coast-guard, to avoid falling into the error of returning any fishing boats which really could not be considered as such, and to ascertain the actual number of persons engaged in fishing, not by calculating the crews required for the existing boats, we venture to think that the figures we submit may, for the reasons we have stated, be relied on as being likely to be the most correct.

The 6,116 boats partially engaged in fishing are usually occupied in cutting sea-weed and conveying goods, turf, manure, and passengers. Their crews of 22,747 do not fish altogether a month in the year on an average.

As stated in our last Report—

"This arises from the following causes:—The tempestuous nature of a great part of the coast, especially the northern and western portions—the number of days that even good-sized and well-found boats could venture out being much less than in any other part of the kingdom; the unsuitability of many of the boats to encounter storm, and the inadequacy of the gear; the distance from markets, and deficiency in many places of the means of transport."

The following shows the decrease in the number of fishing craft and crews since the famine:—

NUMBER of VESSELS and BOATS, MEN and BOYS, EMPLOYED in the COAST FISHERIES, from 1846 to 1872, inclusive.

Year.	Vessels and Boats.	Men and Boys.	Year.	Vessels and Boats.	Men and Boys.
1846	19,883	113,073	1860	13,483	55,630
1848	19,652	81,717	1861	11,845	48,624
1849	18,100	71,505	1862	11,590	50,220
1850	15,247	68,380	1863	11,375	48,601
1851	14,756	64,612	1864	9,300	40,946
1852	11,789	58,863	1865	9,455	40,802
1853	12,381	49,208	1866	9,444	40,663
1854	11,079	49,327	1867	9,332	38,444
1855	11,251	47,854	1868	9,184	39,339*
1856	11,069	48,774	1870 } 1871 }	9,099	38,650
1857	12,758	53,673			
1858	11,823	52,101	1872	7,914	31,311
1859	11,881	50,115			

* There must be some error in this return. An increase of 827 men is set forth at Clifden, and only 19 vessels; this would give an average of nearly 44 men to each of the additional vessels.

Thus it will be seen that the vessels and boats are now less than half as compared with 1846, and the crews reduced to less than a third.

The return showing the falling off in the number of boats and men returned in 1872 as compared with 1870 and 1871, is, no doubt, attributable to some extent to our directions to the Coast-guard having caused them to be more particular in ascertaining the number of fishermen really on the coast, as the greatest diminution appears amongst those only partially engaged in fishing—26,374 in 1871, as against 22,747 in 1872. Many of this class often appeared as belonging to two boats, and until our late instructions to the Coast-guard, were returned twice over. However, from our own observations along the coast, we believe there has been a very large decrease since 1871.

It will be seen from the foregoing that there has been a rapid decrease since the famine years of 1846–47–48. That direful period gave the great blow to fishing industry in Ireland as regarded the humbler coast fishermen. Many were totally annihilated. Others made a desperate and too often unsuccessful effort to hold on to their pursuits; but as boats and gear got out of repair or were lost, they were too poor to restore them. In the course of a few years thousands were compelled to seek other occupations or to emigrate; and now, as we stated in our preceding Report, "in many places the coast may be traversed for miles, even where good shelter exists and fish abound, without a boat being seen."

If the same means had been adopted to sustain the distressed Irish fishermen during the famine, or even after it, that we understand was done for a similar class in Scotland about the same period, much suffering would have been saved, and the Irish fisheries on many parts of the coast would now probably present a much more prosperous appearance.*

One of us, when visiting the Scotch fisheries last summer, learned that in 1845 and 1846, when distress prevailed amongst the fishermen of the Hebrides and other western parts of Scotland, the Board of Fisheries at Edinburgh had placed at their disposal funds to aid the necessitous fishermen with loans, and that advances were made to many of them on their own notes, and which they were never afterwards called on to repay.

Thus were preserved to Scotland many amongst her fishermen who would otherwise, like the Irish fishermen, have succumbed to the visitation of Providence. The sons of those men are to-day some of the finest fishermen in the kingdom.

No loans were made to our fishermen at the same period, nor indeed for many years before.

A few thousand pounds out of a charitable fund raised by private contributions to relieve distress which prevailed in Ireland many years before, were expended on curing-houses, which proved most useful, but were unfortunately given up prematurely. It is to be regretted that a sum of money offered from the same source to the Irish Fishery Department in 1844, to be employed in loans, was declined.

So many erroneous statements have been made with regard to the amount really given to the Scotch Fishery Board, that we deem it well to state for your Excellency's information what we believe to be the facts.

It has been asserted that the amount paid for branding fees, and which is handed over to the Treasury, nearly covers the expenses of the Scotch Board, and that Scotland really receives little more than Ireland for the promotion of her sea fisheries. This is not so, as the following extracts from official documents will prove. According to the last published Report of the Scotch Fishery Board (1871), the sum expended was £13,312; the amount received back for branding fees was £5,807, which was remitted to the Treasury, and probably paid nearly all the salaries. The balance, £7,505, was retained and expended by the Board for the various purposes connected with the department, amongst them the annual outlay for fishery piers and harbours, £3,000. Assuming that a similar amount is expended for same purpose in Ireland, Scotland has still a considerable advantage over this country, even making the most liberal allowance for the proportion that ought to be charged to the sea fisheries for offices, staff, and travelling expenses, &c.

Besides the sum just stated, Scotland received in 1871 a special grant, voted by Parliament, of £7,000 towards the completion of the repairs of the east pier of the fishery harbour of Anstruther.

It is impossible to estimate the vast good that has been accomplished for the fisheries of Scotland through the instrumentality of its Fishery Board. When this great industry, which has added so much to the wealth and importance of the country, was in its

* Mr. Blake is responsible for the paragraphs referring to the Scotch Fisheries, as they have been framed upon investigations and calculations made by him.

infancy, the numerous officers of the department, zealous and well-informed, did much in instructing the people in the proper mode of cure. Their rigid examination of the condition of the fish, the salting, packing, &c., in the barrels submitted to be branded, insured the requisite care in the process, and the brand secured a ready sale and a price for the fish in the foreign, English, and even Irish markets; while a country like Ireland, denied the benefit of the branding system, was placed at so enormous a disadvantage that it was useless to attempt competition, and after a few efforts the curing trade was abandoned.

Although the Fishery Board of Scotland has fully accomplished the object for which it was established, and there are some now who contend that the Scotch fisheries could get on without it, still, if the branding system, which is its principal function, were discontinued, it would deal a very severe blow on the smaller curers who may not yet have established a sufficient reputation for their own brand to enable them to compete with the large curers, to whom many of them would, if the Government brand was abolished, be compelled to sell at lower prices than they can obtain now that the brand puts on equal footing all who cure up to the required standard of excellence.

The following figures will show how the fisheries of Scotland have progressed under the Board.

The published statistics commence with 1810. In that year the total quantity of herrings cured was 90,185 barrels; of these, 34,701 were branded, and 35,848 exported. In 1871, the number cured was 825,475 barrels; of these, 346,633 were branded, and 502,534 exported. As the number of barrels branded increases, there is a proportionate diminution in the sum received from the Imperial Exchequer; but if, owing to any cause, such as a bad fishing, the receipts for branding decline, the amount from the Treasury for the maintenance of the Board must be augmented. Thus the sum voted in 1867–8 for the Scotch fisheries was £14,544, exclusive of superannuations.

Scotland has received since the Union upwards of a million sterling for the promotion of her fisheries more than Ireland. Long before bounties and loans were extended to the latter the Scotch fishermen were in the enjoyment of them; and when the Irish Fishery Board was practically abolished for years, and the fishermen left at a most critical time to shift for themselves, the Scotch Board continued in full operation, having, amongst other things, a grant for the repairs of poor fishermen's boats.

This year we have only to repeat what we said last year and the year before, that—

"Another year's experience fully confirms the opinion which we have already expressed to your Excellency, that 'no great improvement can be looked for in the sea fisheries until loans are advanced to a portion of the fishermen for the repair and purchase of boats and gear.'

"Having visited every part of the coast, and fully informed ourselves of the condition of the fishermen, we unhesitatingly pronounce that if much longer time is allowed to pass without our suggestions being carried out, fishing industry will nearly expire on half the coast. Every day's delay will add enormously to the difficulty of restoration, as boats and gear get out of repair, and the owners abandon the pursuit—in many instances their little tracts of ground become absorbed in the larger farms near them—and there is less opportunity for the youthful portion of the sea-coast population becoming acquainted with the mode of managing boats or capturing fish.

"Already in many places the coast may be traversed for miles, even where good shelter exists and fish abound, without a boat being seen. This deplorable state of things is certain to increase if a helping hand be not extended to save this important industry from perishing. Ten or twenty thousand pounds, judiciously expended now—not as a gift, but as a loan—would do far more good than a million given away in half a dozen years hence. Indeed no amount of money, if things be suffered to take their present course, could in that time accomplish what might now be done by the outlay of a few thousands, certain to be again nearly all refunded to the State.

"Numerous instances have come to our knowledge of industrious fishermen being prevented from adequately pursuing their calling for want of a little money to procure materials, for which they could give satisfactory security.

* * * * * * *

"That loans could be easily and inexpensively administered, and that little or no loss would be likely to be incurred if due care were observed by the department charged with their administration in obtaining proper security, is fully proved by the operations of the 'Society for bettering the Condition of the Poor of Ireland.'

"To free grants we would be strongly opposed, and consider that much of the benefit likely to result from loans would be marred unless their repayment was strictly enforced.

"According to a Report lately issued by the 'Society for bettering the Condition of the Poor of Ireland,' a sum of £24,981 was lent by them during the last seven years to the fishermen on different parts of the coast. Great good appears to have been done and no losses to the Society seem to have occurred."

We have ventured to repeat our statements of preceding years, as we believe they contain elements of the most vital importance to the fisheries; and as it is the only industry in the country which the Government may be said to have particularly in its charge, and therefore has responsibilities with regard to it that do not exist with respect to any other, we deem it incumbent on us to call attention to its rapid decline around the greater part of the coast, and the means by which we believe, without appreciable loss to the Exchequer, great and lasting good might be effected.

Unless our suggestion be adopted, we must continue, as at present, almost powerless to accomplish anything of value for the sea fisheries. Every day's delay, as we have before stated, will increase the difficulties of resuscitation.

It has often been urged by those not having an intimate acquaintance with the coast of Ireland, that there is sufficient capital to induce private enterprise to do whatever is necessary for the development of the fisheries. This holds good with regard to those parts of the coast where large shoals of fish come in at fixed periods. For instance, as regards the herring fishery on the east coast, and the mackerel on the south, private enterprise has done much, and very likely will continue to do all that is necessary for the prosecution of fishing industry on these portions of the sea-board, as there are other favouring circumstances in addition to the almost certain influx of the shoals of fish at regular periods. The extent of coast occupied by the chief herring and mackerel fisheries does not, however, exceed 300 miles out of a coast line of 2,500.

Around the greater part of the coast, however, the case is very different. Take, for example, long stretches of the coasts of Donegal, Mayo, Galway, Clare and Kerry, where the fishing can only be carried on at uncertain periods, owing to the stormy character of the coast.

There, the fisherman (who, unless he combines farming with fishing, cannot live by it, and would be in a state of enforced idleness for the greater part of the year,) carries on his operations necessarily on so small a scale that there is no inducement to invest capital in his petty enterprise. His neighbours are either too poor or too cautious; and we regret to say that on the part of the landlords we see no evidence of a desire to afford material aid to promote fishing industry.

The humble individual fisherman who prosecutes his calling has to do so often under serious difficulties. He has to shift for himself. Be he ever so skilful, honest, and industrious, the loss of a boat or nets will, in numerous instances, necessitate his abandoning the employment, with many chances against his ever again being able to return to it. This is not alone a loss to himself, but also to the immediate community he lives amongst, deprived of the opportunity of obtaining through him occasionally a change of food.

To the State every man under existing circumstances abandoning the pursuit is a serious loss. First, there is so much food lost to the public, as the farmer fisherman not only obtains from the land he cultivates all that can be produced, but draws from the sea what otherwise would, for the most part, go to waste. Secondly, he performs an important part in maintaining a valuable nursery for the mercantile and royal navy.

It has been often urged, as an argument against aiding the fishermen, that if the landlords would do certain things, and the opulent portion of the mercantile community also aid, all that is required would be accomplished. This is quite true, but neither class will give the very slightest help. We have found the landed proprietors occasionally willing to lend their moral influence to improve the condition of the fishermen on their estates, but unwilling to afford any other aid. Amidst all this indifference it is gratifying to us to be enabled to record one instance—unfortunately the only one—of a generous desire to assist the struggling fishermen. Mr. Benjamin Whitworth, of Manchester, late member for Drogheda, offered this year to give £2,000 to this department for their benefit, provided that a further sum of £8,000 would be contributed for the purpose. We much apprehend that a sufficient response from even the whole of Ireland cannot be expected, so as to enable his noble offer to be availed of.

The Inspecting Commanders of Coast-guard having so often reported on the subject of loans, we did not think it necessary this year to send out the usual queries on the subject.

On analyzing the replies for 1870-71 from the thirty divisions into which the coast is divided, we found according to those officers that in twenty loans would be beneficial; that security could be obtained in eight; that security would be doubtful in eleven; that it could not be obtained in one; that loans would not benefit the fishermen in six; that the benefit would be doubtful in three. From one district no return was made. It is singular that in some of the divisions in which the Coast-guard officers report that security would be doubtful or loans not likely to prove beneficial, the "Society for bettering the Condition of the Poor of Ireland" has made large advances without loss, and the fishermen have been much benefited.

It should be borne in mind that the seaboard of Ireland is 2,500 miles, and that in that large extent there are a number of fishermen who do not require loans, and many others who could not repay them. This department stated in the Report for 1869—"We agree with the Report of the Select Committee of the House of Commons (1867), that it would be unadvisable to make advances to fishermen unless on satisfactory security;" and in

1870 we reported—"To free grants we would be strongly opposed, and consider that much of the good likely to result from loans would be marred unless their repayment were strictly enforced." But we know very well that the small sum which we recommend should be advanced by way of loan for a few years could be lent to sufficient industrious fishermen on good security. The operations of the "Society for bettering the Condition of the Poor" is at once an answer to the objection urged with regard to the danger of the advances not being repaid.

The reports of the Inspecting Commanders of Coast-guard for this year represent the fishermen as most orderly, no conflicts having occurred between persons pursuing different modes of fishing, except at Galway, relative to trawling, to which we shall allude further on.

An analysis of the reports from the thirty Coast-guard divisions shows—that the fisheries are not improving in twenty-five, and improving in five. That fishing is usually combined with farming in twenty-eight. That no conflicts had occurred between persons pursuing different modes of fishing in twenty-nine. Fishermen peaceable and orderly in twenty-six—no remark on this point is made in three returns. Portions of coast unguarded in fourteen divisions. The meaning of this is, that owing to the decrease in the number of the Coast-guard, there are certain parts of the coast not visited at all. In some places the extent is considerable; for example, in the Sligo Division, sixty-one miles, and in the Clifden, 102 miles.

The difficulty in obtaining statistics from the unguarded parts has been considerable, and imposed a good deal of trouble on the Coast-guard and expense on this department for the travelling charges of the men employed on the duty.

We regret to state that the "South of Ireland Fishing Company," which carried on its chief operations at Kinsale for some years, to which it lately added herring fishing off Howth, has ceased to exist. Its vessels, &c., however, have been purchased by two or three private individuals, who it is to be hoped will succeed in making the undertaking more of a commercial success.

It affords one of the many instances in support of our view, that, as a rule, fishing companies in Ireland, will not prove successful.

Every fishing company, of the many started in Ireland from time to time, having Chairmen, Secretaries, Boards of Directors, and Managers, has in the end been obliged to be wound up, in almost every instance with great loss to the shareholders; whilst small enterprises, owned and managed by practical men understanding everything connected with boats and gear, and the capture, cure, and sale of fish thoroughly, have usually proved successful—for example, the boats belonging to Dublin, and the three or four small enterprises, now in most successful operation, at Dunmore, county Waterford.

A small company, known as the "Inishbofin Fishing Company (Limited)," has also been wound up this year. Its shareholders were chiefly at Belfast, and also the Board of Directors and Secretary, although its operations were off the Galway coast, and consisted in the purchase of fish.

There is now no joint stock fishing company in Ireland, properly speaking.

Any undertakings that exist, not altogether the property of individual owners, have not, we believe, in any instance more than three proprietors.

On many parts of the coast the fishermen have assured us that, as compared with former years there is a considerable falling off in fish, and that generally speaking they cannot be captured so close to the shore as they might have been thirty years ago.

We believe there is a good deal of foundation for these statements, and that many have been obliged to give up fishing in consequence of their boats being too small to seek for the fish in the deeper water that they now resort to.

Galway Bay.

The only exception during the year to the general good character of the fishermen as being peaceable and orderly is that of the Claddagh fishermen, who during the past year acted in a most violent and disorderly manner towards the men employed on board the trawlers. The Claddagh fishermen have always evinced a most determined hostility to trawling, and so bad was their conduct on the occasion referred to, that after an investigation by a very large bench of Magistrates, a number of them were returned for trial to the assizes.

We were obliged to apply to the Government for the aid of a gun-boat to protect the trawlers in their lawful avocations, and H.M.S. *Orwell* was at once sent to the spot, and remained there for some time.

We directed a public inquiry to be held at Galway into the question of trawling. A very lengthened investigation was held by one of us (Mr. Brady), and the allegations against this mode of fishing being principally that a large quantity of fry of fish and small fish were taken up in the trawl net, and that the most of them were dead when taken up, in consequence of the trawl being some hours down, and that spawn of fish was disturbed, Mr. Brady considered that no satisfactory conclusion could be arrived at from the evidence on oath of the witnesses who were more or less biased according to their prejudices, and more particularly as no evidence was adduced on the part of the trawlers to contradict or rebut the evidence of those against the trawling, the men engaged in this latter mode of fishing having made affidavits that their lives would be in danger if they attempted to come into court to give evidence.

He accordingly determined that before any decision should be come to experiments in trawling should be made all over the bay. These experiments were entrusted to the Inspecting Commander of the Coastguard at Galway, Lieutenant Drew, R.N., who most kindly consented to do everything in his power to carry out our wishes, and placed two of the most intelligent officers under his command on this special duty each month, the owners of two of the trawl boats giving us without any remuneration the use of their boats. To no public officer in Ireland more eminently qualified to carry out such experiments could they have been entrusted than to Lieutenant Drew, who had for a number of years been employed with the present Rear-Admiral Spratt, C.B., on scientific explorations of the sea and dredging, and when these investigations have been completed, Mr. Brady feels assured they will be the means of enabling a decision to be arrived at on this much vexed question, based on data more complete than on any inquiries heretofore adopted. Though however unsatisfactory that decision may be to any of the parties, it will be, it is hoped, a just and complete one.

Before Lieutenant Drew commenced these experiments the Claddagh fishermen, who are opposed to trawling, asked to be allowed to send one of their own body on board each trawler, and to this request Lieutenant Drew at once acceded, although against the wishes of the trawlers.

They remained on board however only a few days, when they wanted to know if they were to be paid, and having been answered in the negative they refused to accompany the trawlers any longer. Though the experiments are carried on each month, and will be so, for the whole year, none of the Claddagh men have since asked permission, or gone on board any of the trawlers, to satisfy themselves as to the correctness, or otherwise of their allegations.

The following is a copy of the instructions issued by Mr. Brady to the coastguard officers with regard to the investigations to be carried on.

GALWAY BAY.—EXPERIMENTS IN TRAWLING.

I. It is important to know in what parts of the bay the greatest quantity of fry or young fish are taken up.
II. In what quantities they are taken up.
III. The description of fish.
IV. The depth of water where most fry or young fish are taken.
V. The quantity of saleable fish taken.
VI. The different descriptions of saleable fish taken.
VII. The parts of the bay where the different descriptions of saleable fish are taken in *largest* quantity.
VIII. The depth of water they are taken in.

In order to carry out the above, it will be necessary that the bay be trawled in different sections—and inshore and in the different bays, and it would be important that the officer superintending the examination should make the following accurate notes in the diaries:—

1. The place to be marked on chart when trawl let down.
2. The course run when trawling.
3. The depth of water.
4. The time trawl let down.
5. The time trawl taken up.
6. The contents of trawl, most accurately detailing—

   a. Numbers of saleable fish.
   b. Different descriptions, numbers of each.
   c. Numbers and description, if possible, of unsaleable fish.
   d. Quantity and description, as far as possible, of the fry of fish.
   e. If any spawn, or anything resembling spawn taken up, and if so to preserve it in water in a vessel.

7. The wind and weather.
8. As full observations on every matter as the officer can make, detailing everything, no matter how minute.

Books are supplied for this purpose, and the officer is not to think of how much paper is taken up in his observations, but to write them as fully as possible.

He can write on one page the details of fish taken, and on the other his observations in full, as to what the trawl brings up, and in what state, and he had better devote a couple of pages of the book to each trawl, and not put the report of two scrapes on one page.

The Herring Fisheries.

The capture was considerably beyond that of the two preceding years; the prices, however, something lower than in 1871. At Howth 107,087 mease, at an average price of 18s. 1¾d., producing £96,855, were taken in 1872, against 50,915 mease, average price 19s. 8¾d., producing £49,197 in 1871; at Wicklow, 6,000 mease; Ardglass, 67,114 mease, producing £46,513 in 1872, against 15,495, producing £41,620, in 1871; Arklow, 20,000 mease in 1872, against 15,269 mease in 1871; Kilkeel, 13,500 mease, producing £6,200 in 1872, against 5,130 mease, producing £4,200 in 1871. The capture of herrings this year must have reached in value on the coast nearly a quarter of a million sterling. The smallest part of this, however, was realized by Irish boats, as will be seen by the following return of the highest number of boats that fished during the season off Howth, viz.:—Cornish, 120; Scotch, 100; Manx, 58; total 278, as compared with Irish, which were only 116.

Complaints having been made to us of injury arising from the reprehensible acts of some of the masters of fishing vessels, especially those from the Isle of Man, setting their nets before sunset—at our instance H.M.S. *Bruiser* was employed for some time to prevent the practice.

The Mackerel Fishery.

The capture was less than in 1870 and 1871. So far as can be ascertained it amounted to 6,000 tons or 60,000 boxes of six score each. The prices varied from 10s. to 25s. per 120 or six score.

The highest number of vessels of the following countries that fished was—Manx, 174; Irish 83; French, 83; English, 45; Scotch, 1. In 1871 the numbers were—English and Manx, 197; Irish, 70; French, 49.

The Pilchard Fisheries.

Large shoals appeared on the coasts of Cork and Kerry. But this fish is held in so little estimation that the fishermen usually prefer avoiding it on account of the small price to be obtained and the injury done to their nets by the quantity of oil exuded by the fish, the nets not being properly barked to resist the effects.

The return of pilchards again to the coast of Cornwall in large quantities has had the effect of preventing efforts which might otherwise have been made in Ireland to cure for foreign markets. As, however, the shoals appear off our shores often a month before they arrive on the Cornish coast, it is probable that an export to the Mediterranean ports from Ireland would prove profitable by anticipating the consignments from Cornwall, as there is a much larger price given for the new fish.

It has, however, been stated that the fish which are found off the Irish coast in the early season are too fat to be suitable for curing for foreign markets. Formerly large quantities were sent abroad from Ireland; but this uncertain fish abandoned the Irish coast for nearly fifty years, re-appeared again for a few years, and then almost totally disappeared for twenty years. A few years ago on the coast of Cornwall where the pilchard proved a great source of wealth, the shoals diminished so enormously that the exports decreased to less than a fourth as compared with former years; just at the same time the seas off the coast of Cork were swarming, and in some places every bay and creek was literally packed with them.

Having informed ourselves of the mode of capture and cure in Cornwall in 1871, we gave such information on the subject in various places along the coast as lay in our power, in the hope that some enterprises would be set on foot, which might have occurred only that at the end of the same season pilchards returned to Cornwall in such vast quantities that the prices fell so low as not to pay the cost of cure, and several cargoes could not be sold in the Continental markets at almost any price.

If during the period of the scarcity of the fish on the Cornish coast the opportunity had been availed of, it is impossible to say the amount that might have been realized on the coast of Cork alone.

As compared with the herring the home consumption of pilchards in Ireland is very small, notwithstanding the lower price, on account of the oily flavour when fresh. Some, however, that were prepared at Kinsale, under the immediate direction of two of the Inspectors, by a simple process which divests the fish nearly altogether of oil, which is preserved and brings a good price, were much relished by those who purchased them. By a little trouble the same thing could be done on a large scale, and this plentiful and wholesome fish more largely utilised.

TRAWLING.

During this year we did not repeal any of the By-laws against this mode of fishing, but have it in contemplation to hold inquiries into the subject, encouraged by the satisfactory results which have followed from the removal of the restriction since we came into office, in Lough Swilly, Belfast Lough, Kenmare Estuary, part of Donegal Bay, and Glandore Harbour.

We have already alluded to the dispute at Galway Bay relative to trawling, &c.

LINE FISHING.

Both long and short lines constitute a very important mode of fishing around the greater part of the coast, and is followed by the most numerous class of fishermen, especially those too poor to purchase good sized boats and nets. As already stated many fishermen have informed us that there is a considerable decrease in line fish as compared with former years, and that it is necessary to proceed further out to sea to capture them. For this purpose a large number of the existing boats are not sufficiently large, and the fishermen too poor to purchase ones of adequate size. It is in such instances that loans would prove most valuable, as the fishermen could at once obtain the required craft.

We could give numerous instances, when, if such accommodation existed, the advance could have been easily repaid in a few months.

OYSTER FISHERIES.

During the year we granted six new licences for the planting and cultivation of Oysters. Out of the 117 licensed beds, hardly a dozen can be said to be in a satisfactory position. In the majority of the licences we would be fully justified in withdrawing them, on ground that the conditions on which they were granted have not been fulfilled, viz., sufficient stocking and proper cultivation. In many cases there is not even a pretence of doing anything, the licensees contenting themselves with getting whatever Oysters they can off the beds for their private consumption. Some of the licences embrace hundreds of acres of foreshore and sea bottom (in one instance nearly eighteen hundred acres), in the aggregate 17,935 acres, from which the public are excluded from dredging or picking Oysters.

As we consider that this exclusion should not be continued, unless the conditions alluded to are complied with, we have, after due inquiry, warned some licensees that their licences will be withdrawn unless within twelve months they proceed to cultivate, and we intend, as other duties permit, to proceed with other inquiries for a like purpose.

The most successful undertaking has been that of Mr. Verschoyle, at Tanrego, in Ballisodaire Bay, County Sligo, carried out on the plan of enclosed ponds which was explained in the Report of the Royal Commission appointed through the instrumentality of the late Earl of Mayo, when Chief Secretary for Ireland, to report on the methods of Oyster culture in the United Kingdom and France.

We propose holding an inquiry at Wexford to inquire into the propriety of shutting up or buoying off a portion of the oyster beds from dredging, alternately, for the purpose of recovering from the exhaustion consequent on over-dredging.

The beds are now almost denuded of oysters, and hardly give occupation to one boat where over fifty formerly obtained remunerative employment. Carlingford, once so famous for its oysters, now only produces a few hundred pounds' worth a year.

The beds at Arklow and on the Galway coast are in a tolerably satisfactory position and afford the chief sources of supply.

At Tralee we have enacted stringent regulations to prevent the destruction of the beds by taking away small oysters.

We have made close investigations with regard to the spatting this year, and are in a position to state that the fall has been on the whole greater than for some years past.

HARBOURS.

During the year we only recommended the construction of two harbours, one at Courtmacsherry, county Cork, and the other at Glin, county Limerick.

We regret very much that a harbour we recommended at Giles'-quay, county Louth, is not likely to be proceeded with on account of certain conditions required by the Board of Works, and which we apprehend in this and in future instances will prove a serious if not a fatal obstacle to the construction of fishery harbours.

As we understand the case, on the estimate of the probable cost having been made by the Board of Works, and the sum to be contributed by the locality settled, Lord Clermont and J. P. Mulholland, esq., undertook to give the liberal sum of £633 6s. 8d. each, the barony contributing by instalments a like amount.

As tenders could not be obtained for constructing the harbour for the Board of Works estimate, the latter proposed to execute it on the condition that anything it might cost in excess should be made up by the other contributories. This proposal, we believe, was declined on the reasonable ground of the uncertainty of the amount that they might be called on to make up.

THE INLAND FISHERIES.

With a view of more efficiently and conveniently carrying out our duties, we arranged, shortly after our appointment, to divide Ireland into three divisions, assigning to each Inspector, as far as practicable, an equal part. All the duties relating to the sea and inland fisheries within those limits which could be performed by one Inspector (some inquiries must be attended by all three) have been discharged by us in our respective districts.

We propose to submit to your Excellency separate Reports for the divisions in our charge, with regard to the salmon fisheries, as we consider that in this form more detailed information, as to the state of the different districts, can be given.

Those Reports are given in the order in which we sign the Report this year addressed to your Excellency, and which varies every year.

MR. BLAKE'S REPORT.

Division extending seaward from Wicklow Head to Rossan Point, County Donegal, and embracing in whole or part the Counties of Wicklow, Dublin, Kildare, Meath, Westmeath, Louth, King's County, Monaghan, Down, Armagh, Antrim, Derry, Donegal, and including the Districts of Dublin, Drogheda, Dundalk, Ballycastle, Coleraine, Londonderry, and Letterkenny.

Dublin District.

Extends from Wicklow Head to Skerries, county Dublin, seaward, embracing portions of the counties of Wicklow, Dublin, Kildare, and Meath. The principal rivers frequented by salmon, taken in the order of their importance, are—the Liffey, Vartry, and Swords. The Liffey has many natural advantages for the production of salmon, which ascend nearly sixty miles to the Golden Water Cascade for the purpose of spawning. There are many good spawning tributaries, having excellent gravel bottom. In winter there is a large body of water to facilitate the ascent of the fish.

It suffers, however, from the following drawbacks:—A great reduction of the volume of water in summer, which has the effect, owing to the number of mill weirs (nearly twenty), of preventing the ascent of salmon until the autumn floods. A great injury in time of drought arises from the many pollutions to which the Liffey is subject, owing to sewage matter and gas and chemical works. The two latter injure at all seasons, but more especially in summer. Should the projected undertaking of conveying the sewage to the sea at the North Bull be carried out, and include also the conveying of the refuse of gas and chemical works, the productiveness of the river must be vastly augmented. The district suffers much from the insufficiency of funds, which prevents adequate means being taken for prosecuting parties for pellutions, the prevention of poaching and the sale of unseasonable salmon in the Dublin market.

As very little is done by the riparian proprietors for the preservation of the river, the funds for that purpose could be much increased if permission was more extensively given by them to anglers to fish in the upper waters, as it would offer a greater inducement than now exists to take out licences in the district.

The Vartry—previous to the impounding of half of the upper catchment basin of the river at Roundwood, by the Dublin Corporation, for the purpose of supplying the city with water—was, for its size, one of the best salmon producing rivers in Ireland. The principal capture was carried on by draft nets at the mouth and along a part of the coast at Wicklow. Since the completion of the Waterworks a vast diminution has taken place in the produce of the river, owing to the large amount of water abstracted.

The Swords.—Except at the mouth by draft nets, but few salmon are taken in this river; there is a good number of white trout. The preservation is more satisfactorily carried on than on the other rivers, owing to an angling club which gives a contribution for that object. Except, however, for purposes of sport, the quantity is unimportant. This river, like the preceding ones, affords good brown trout angling.

The Bray river, which is formed by the combination of the Cookstown, Glencree, and Dargle rivers, contains few salmon, but produces a fine quality of white trout.

The same want of protection exists here as throughout the rest of the district.

The capture of this district was not more than half that of the preceding year, owing to the floods and drought at inopportune times, as the same causes under favourable circumstances would produce opposite results.

Drogheda District.

Extends from Skerries to Clogher Head, embracing portions of the counties of Louth, King's County, Meath, Westmeath, and Cavan. On the whole, the capture in 1872 does not appear to have been much under that of 1871.

The principal rivers are the Boyne and Blackwater; the latter being, in fact, a tributary of the former, joining it at Navan, nearly twenty miles by water from the sea.

Salmon ascend about fifty miles to near Edenderry. Spawning grounds numerous and good. Most of the twelve tributaries are suitable for spawning for only a short distance above their junction with the Boyne.

The natural obstructions are few and unimportant, consisting of rocks across the bed of the river, but which can be easily surmounted in ordinary floods.

The artificial obstructions are numerous and formidable, consisting of weirs for navigation and milling purposes. Most of them have passes, but of a very inadequate character. They are, however, being gradually improved by the Board of Conservators as funds permit. The condition of the river has been steadily improving for some years, due to more active conservancy. The riparian proprietors also exhibit an increased desire to second the efforts of the Board.

Fish of greater size than formerly have been lately taken. Ten years ago fish exceeding 20 lbs. were rarely captured by either net or line; now the common run is 18 lbs. A number between 30 lbs. and 40 lbs. were taken last year, a few between 40 lbs. and 50 lbs., in one instance 54 lbs.

The principal capture takes place in the tidal waters by draft nets. There are two small weirs in the fresh-water portion. This district suffers much from flax-water, particularly in the remoter tributaries. This evil is, however, far below what is experienced from the same cause in the Ulster districts.

Both on the Boyne and Blackwater there are numerous eel weirs, which formerly proved most injurious from the number of unseasonable salmon taken. Latterly, owing to the more active supervision, these offences have much decreased.

Although it is most desirable to afford every facility for the capture of eels, as the descending fish never returns, still it is questionable whether the season for capture in this district is not too long, commencing as it does on 1st July and closing 10th January. The eels do not appear to run before August, and they usually stop on the appearance of frost.

It is doubtful, therefore, that for the very few likely to be taken in July and January, it is worth leaving those months open, on account of the risk involved of salmon being taken in the eel boxes and nets during these months.

The Blackwater is wholly an angling river and possesses numerous good spawning grounds. The obstructions are altogether artificial, arising from mill weirs, and the engines for the capture of eels already alluded to.

There has been more poaching on this river than any other in the district, but owing to the better disposition lately evinced by the riparian owners to contribute towards the expense of protection, this offence is decreasing.

This district, which extended from Skerries to Donaghadee, was divided in 1871, limiting its boundary from Skerries to Clogher Head, which proved most advantageous, as the former district was far too extensive to admit of being properly worked by a Board holding its meetings at Drogheda and Navan.

Dundalk District.

Extends from Clogher Head, in the county Louth, to Donaghadee, in the county Down, this portion being separated from the late Drogheda district, and comprises the entire or portions of the counties of Louth, Meath, Down, Armagh, Monaghan, and Cavan.

The principal rivers are the Dee, Glyde, Fane, Cully, Water, and Castletown, the two latter forming a junction a short distance above Dundalk.

There are some rivers northward of Dundalk possessing many natural advantages to render them excellent salmon rivers; but owing to the difficulty in preventing their being contaminated by flax-water the greater number of them are rendered almost valueless for either salmon or trout.

The Newry river, formerly much frequented by salmon, is now abandoned, owing to the flow into it of refuse matter from gas works.

The Kilbrony river, also well circumstanced, near Rosstrevor, has been injured in a similar manner by bleach works refuse.

The Whitewater, Causeway, Kilkeel, Annalong, Shimna, Comber, &c.,&c., have by flax-water been either wholly destroyed for fishing purposes or rendered so valueless that there is but little inducement to attempt preservation.

The vast quantity of flax steeped in the neighbourhood of these rivers, the great importance of the crop, and the reluctance of the landed proprietors to interfere with the farmers renders it almost hopeless to expect the adoption of effective means to place these rivers in a satisfactory condition. As they may be said to yield little or no revenue in the way of licence duties, there is no expenditure by the Board of Conservators for preservation, and on the part of the proprietors scarcely any. The capture in this district may, therefore, be said to be nearly confined to the three first-mentioned rivers in the neighbourhood of Dundalk—even their yield is not much. The take by nets unimportant. The capture by anglers is also small.

Fish passes could be advantageously erected in different places, but there does not appear to be a disposition to supplement the funds of the Conservators by private contributions for the purpose, without which these works cannot be undertaken, the funds raised from licence duties being hardly sufficient to provide for properly watching the rivers.

Product last year although less in number of fish captured was to a great extent compensated for by the number of fish taken of larger size than usual.

Ballycastle District.

Extends from Donaghadee to Portrush, embracing portions of the counties of Down, Antrim, and Derry.

Owing to heavy floods the capture in this district was below that of 1871.

The Bush is the only river of importance, owned altogether by one proprietor. The upper portion is well preserved and affords considerable angling. The lower waters are fished by draft nets, and three bag nets outside.

Artificial breeding has been successfully carried on by Sir Edmund MacNaghten.

There are many more bag nets on the coast of this district (fourteen) than in any other.

The remaining rivers, Glenarm, Glencloy, Glenariffe, Cushendall, Cushendun, Ballycastle, &c., afford some angling, but the proceeds, in a commercial point, are of little importance. In some of these streams salmon are rarely seen. Flax-water exercises the same destructive influence as in the rest of the north.

To class some of the streams in this and other districts which formerly abounded with fish—but which now, owing to the baneful effects of this destroyer, hardly contain a single one—amongst salmon-producing rivers, would only serve to convey a very erroneous idea.

Coleraine District.

Extends from Portrush to Downhill Boundary, embracing portions of the counties of Monaghan, Armagh, Down, Antrim, and Derry.

The product this year was below that of the previous one.

The Bann and its tributaries constitute the entire of this district.

Pollen, a species of fresh-water herring, found in few other places, abound in Lough Neagh; and the eel fisheries commencing at Toome Bridge yield a large income to the proprietors.

The Irish Society claim the river from Lough Neagh to the bar mouth. Their lessees fish it by a weir and fixed and moving draft nets. Draft net fishing also from bridge of Portglenone to Lough Neagh. An angling club rent a large portion of the river and do much towards preservation.

As the income of the district, considering its size, is considerable, there are ample funds for conservancy.

Much good could be accomplished by having better fish-passes constructed on some of the navigation weirs, especially at Carnroe, where the ladder is quite insufficient to allow fish to pass up at low water.

This district also suffers much from flax-water being allowed to flow into the rivers, although great efforts are made by the Conservators to prevent it. Owing to the great floods this year, the evil has been less than during some preceding ones.

Londonderry District.

Extends from Downhill Boundary to Malin Head, embracing portions of the counties of Derry, Donegal, and Tyrone.

The capture in 1872 below that of 1871.

The Foyle, the river of the greatest importance in the district, has several good tributaries. Their value is, however, much lessened, owing to flax pollution.

In addition to the 100 water-bailiffs employed by the Board of Conservators, the lessees of the Irish Society also have about ninety in their pay. Their watchfulness is, however, unfortunately insufficient to prevent considerable destruction from this cause.

The culpability of the offending parties is the greater from the fact that much of the evil might be diminished by a little care and outlay on their part.

. The most important portion of the seventy-two miles of the river (having an area of catchment basin equal to 212 square miles) is the property of the Irish Society, together with the whole of Lough Foyle. Their lessees carry on their fishing operations from near Strabane to their limits in Lough Foyle. With the exception of three stake nets the capture is accomplished by fixed and running draft nets.

Outside of Greencastle the public fish about thirty draft nets.

The other rivers—Roe, Faughan, Culdaff—with the exception of some netting at the mouths, are chiefly valuable for angling and breeding.

Considerable destruction of salmon and fry having, it is alleged, taken place in the head and tail races of mills in this district, the enactment requiring gratings on same at the points of divergence from and return to the rivers has, as elsewhere, been enforced, but only in such instances where it was manifest that with the exercise of ordinary care on the part of the mill-owners substantial injury would not be inflicted.

Letterkenny District.

Extends from Malin Head to Rossan Point, and embraces the greater portion of the county Donegal.

The take of salmon this year below that of 1871.

Notwithstanding the numerous rivers in this district, their commercial importance is comparatively insignificant. Their chief value consists in the sport afforded to anglers.

Along the north-west portion there are several streams which might be made very productive, if the obstructions to the ascent of salmon to places suitable for spawning were removed, some fish-passes constructed, and means adopted for the preservation of the fish during the breeding season.

As few of these rivers yield revenue, and the funds of the district are very limited, there is no attempt at preservation in the majority.

There is some poisoning from flax-water, but considerably less than in the four preceding districts.

The Lennane River opens for fishing in the tidal portion on 1st of January, being earlier than any of the rivers in the seven districts composing this division. The owner of the fishery has urged that without disadvantage to the river the opening might commence even earlier.

In all the other rivers in this district—some apparently similarly circumstanced—the opening does not take place for more than a month later. But this is only one of the many instances of the unsolved mystery as to the cause of difference of season in rivers.

CONCLUSION.

The aggregate length of the rivers with their catchment basins, a matter of very simple calculation, in the foregoing seven districts, has not been given, as it would convey a very erroneous idea, so far as this division is concerned, of the length of rivers available for salmon, on account of the natural obstacles which prevent the ascent of fish in many places, and the deadly effects of flax-water, bleach works refuse, and other pollutions, in nearly all the northern district.

The Liffey affords a good illustration as regards the effect of obstructions. Its length, according to the Ordnance Survey, is 82 miles, and its catchment basin 528½ square miles; the falls of Phoul-a-Phooka (over which fish passes are practicable if funds were available) now offer an insurmountable barrier to the further ascent of fish, thus shutting out upwards of thirty miles of good spawning ground on the main river alone. Numerous other instances of a like character might be given.

With regard to the rivers practically ruined by flax poisoning, especially in the county Down, there are some which at one time were most productive, but which are now only classed as salmon rivers from the circumstance of a few fish occasionally venturing up and surviving to reach some safe spawning bed; the chances, however, being considerably against either the parent fish or the fry ever descending to the sea.

The large floods this year will probably have the effect of bringing an amount of fish up some of those almost deserted rivers, greater than for many years before; but unless more aid can be obtained from the Constabulary authorities to compel farmers to desist from their inexcusable practice, with regard to flax-water, there can be no great result. While on the subject of the large floods of this year, it may not be out of place to remark that although they proved injurious so far as affecting the capture of fish, still beneficial effects are likely to follow as regards production, a number of salmon, probably greater than for some years past, having been enabled to reach the upper spawning beds; the only drawback being the probability that the ova has in many instances been deposited in such situations in the higher streamlets as may render it liable to exposure and destruction as the water subsides. The evil usually attendant on the flow of flax-water into the breeding streams in the northern Districts has undoubtedly been much diminished this year owing to the floods.

J. ALOYSUIS BLAKE.

MR. BRADY'S REPORT.

Salmon Fisheries.

As it had been considered by my colleagues and myself that it would tend to the advantage of all interests in the salmon fisheries if Ireland were divided into three divisions, and that each division should be under the superintendence of an Inspector, this arrangement was entered into, and Ireland was accordingly divided into the following :—

No. 1. That part of the coast and all the rivers flowing thereinto between Rossan Point in the county Donegal, and Wicklow Head in the county Wicklow.

No. 2. That part of the coast and all the rivers flowing thereinto between Wicklow Head and Dunmore Head in the county Kerry, and

No. 3. That part of the coast and all the rivers flowing thereinto between Dunmore Head in the county Kerry, and Rossan Point in the county Donegal.

That portion of the country mentioned in No. 3 division which embraces the salmon fishery districts of

Limerick,	Galway,	Ballinakill,	Bangor.
Ballina,	Sligo,	Ballyshannon,	

and contains 145 rivers frequented by salmon, embracing about 2,528 miles in length fell to my lot.

My colleagues having since decided that "each Inspector should write his own Report on the Salmon Fisheries of his District," it now becomes my duty to report on this division of the country and to give such an account of the fisheries as may be desirable for the information of your Excellency.

Although the arrangement referred to was made amongst ourselves for greater convenience, and as tending to a more systematic administration of the laws than could otherwise be obtained, it sometimes becomes my duty to accompany either or both my colleagues on many important inquiries into divisions not immediately under my own personal superintendence.

Some of the observations made in this report may therefore necessarily bear on matters which affect or concern other divisions as well as that allotted to me.

Limerick District

Extends from Dunmore Head in the county Kerry to Hags Head in the county Clare, and includes the Rivers Feohanagh, Owenafeana, Owenmore, Scorid, Owencashla, Derrymore, Lee, Shannon, Doonbeg, Annageeragh, Annagh, and Inagh, and their tributaries. Many of these rivers, though all are frequented by salmon, are only so during spawning season, and the fish only ascend short distances in them.

The principal river and from which very large commercial supplies of fish are obtained is the Shannon, 160 miles in length, and having a catchment-basin of 4,553 square miles. The Shannon is frequented by salmon from near its source to the sea. It has 25 tributaries more or less frequented by salmon. In many of these tributaries there exist obstructions to the free passage of the fish, which if overcome by proper Fish Passes would be the means not only of preventing much destruction of fish below them, but also of distributing more equably the fish over a more extended area, and of opening up a great extent of spawning ground.

There is about an equal number of tributaries not frequented by salmon.

In the Shannon itself the worst obstructions in the river are the navigation weirs at Tarmonbarry and Athlone. Although Fish Passes have been built on both these weirs in accordance with plans approved by the Special Commissioners appointed under the Act of 1863, yet these passes are not efficient—nor do they comply with the law which requires that all dams erected in rivers since 1842 shall be so built as to allow the free run of fish in one or more places at all periods of the year. In the last two reports reference was made to this matter in detail, and I have now only to state that nothing has since been done to improve the passage for fish over these two formidable obstructions.

In times of flood only are the fish enabled to pass these weirs. During the past year which was unusually wet, great quantities of fish are reported to have passed over them and to have got early access to the higher parts of the river. One proprietor on the banks of the river, high up the stream, is reported to have taken advantage of this circumstance, to have used nets for the capture of the fish; and application has been made for a By-Law to prohibit a practice which, it is stated, if continued, might prove seriously detrimental to the general interests of the Fisheries in the river. The inquiry, necessarily consequent on this complaint, will be held as soon as other business will permit.

The engines used in this district for the capture of salmon are—

37 Snap Nets,	129 Drift Nets,	33 Stake Nets,
69 Draft Nets,	20 Pole Nets,	1 Head Weir, and

9 Boxes or Cribs in a Fishing Weir, besides 204 Single Rods and 46 Cross Lines.

The Pole Nets are used in the upper or fresh waters. The Draft Nets and Snap Nets in both upper and lower or tidal, the Drift nets, Stake nets, Head weir, and Boxes, in the tidal waters exclusively.

Complaints have been made from time to time against the practice of drift net fishing in the Shannon, and several meetings have been held in Limerick and other places down the river, to inquire into the matter, but the evidence adduced at those inquiries was not such as would have warranted the prohibition of these nets in such a wide estuary as the Shannon, or such as, even if the urgent solicitations of many persons who complained of injury being done by these nets to the fish in the river had been complied with would have justified us in submitting for the approval of your Excellency a By-Law which would have had the effect, practically, of throwing probably 500 men out of employment. Of these nets there have been used in the Shannon during the past year 129, and 4 men may be taken as a fair average to work each net. In the estuary of the Forgus, however, which is a narrow channel as compared with the Shannon, their use was prohibited immediately on their introduction into that estuary on the ground that they would, particularly if increased to any extent, have had a damaging effect on the fisheries of that river, and the By-Law to that effect has received the sanction of the Privy Council.

In the estuary of the River Shannon, by the authority of the Court of Queen's Bench, and as the result of inquiries held by the late Special Commissioners, and subsequently by the Inspectors, there have been established thirty-three stake-nets. Out of this number the late Commissioners granted *Two* certificates. The Court of Queen's Bench held *Twenty* to have been legally erected, and after public courts of inquiry we held *Eleven* to have been legally erected under the decisions of the Court of Queen's Bench in the case of Stewart and Cubitt, and the Court of Common Pleas in the case of Williams and Boyd, *i.e.*, on the sites of bag-nets erected in 1862, but which were abolished by the 26th & 27th Vic., c. 114 as being in the estuary of the river.

The Boxes or Cribs are used in the Lax Weir.

The total revenue for the District during the year amounted to only £2,170, a sum totally inadequate to afford proper protection to the fish scattered over so extensive an area as is embraced in this district.

The system of protection afforded by the Board of Conservators has in my mind one serious drawback. There is not sufficient supervision over the bailiffs employed. In reality they have not one at present in many places to look after them, or see that they are doing their duty. It is true that a few of the Conservators, who have always taken a great interest in the fisheries of the river, impose on themselves this duty, but this is only in a few instances and places. As a rule the Bailiffs are not looked after, and in many places I have found that they may be either on or off duty as they pleased, no one apparently in the upper waters taking any interest in their proceedings.

In mentioning this matter I do not intend for an instant to reflect on or impute blame or neglect to the able Secretary and Inspector of the district who is a most efficient officer, and whose whole time must necessarily be more taken up in office in the direct management under the Board of so extensive and important a district. It is the system which I think defective. I am strongly of opinion that unless there be an active and constant supervision over men in the capacity of water bailiffs, duties which are most irksome, laborious, and dangerous will not be zealously performed.

Believing such, it was suggested to the Board of Conservators to appoint two or three Local Inspectors, whose duty should be to be constantly on the road and to visit the different stations and see that the Bailiffs were on duty, particularly during the spawning season. The Board gave a patient hearing to the suggestion, and after discussing the matter, the majority did not agree to it, principally I believe on the ground that the funds were not sufficient to warrant them in undertaking the expense. I cannot however but think that by such a system more efficient protection would be afforded and in the end that it would turn out to be more economical than the present one, and I am in hopes of seeing this carried out as soon as the new Board of Conservators is elected next October. There are about seventy Bailiffs employed by the Board in this district in the open season, and 135 in the close season; forty employed permanently at wages varying from 5s. to £1 a week.

There are some rivers in this district to which no protection whatever is at present afforded, the Board not receiving any, or if any, very little revenue from them. They are consequently neglected, and the fish becomes the prey of the poacher in every way. If the gentlemen resident on the banks of these rivers would take an interest in them and form themselves into a Board of Conservators, such portions of the district might be separated from the Shannon before the next general election and formed into a separate district to be managed by themselves. This, however, can only be done under the law on the application of the present Board of Conservators. I particularly allude to those rivers in the county Clare north of the Shannon. There are also some rivers in the county Kerry on the south side of the Shannon similarly circumstanced which might probably with advantage be attached to the Killarney district, but this would require an application from both Boards.

In other rivers formidable obstructions exist which with a little outlay might be overcome.

The past season's fishing has not been so good as the preceding one. The average weight of the fish captured has, however, considerably increased. The quantity of fish in the upper parts of the river, not only during the last spawning season, but all through the summer, is reported to have been much greater than for many years past. From this, with proper protection, good results must follow.

The Close Seasons fixed for this district in December, 1870, are as follow:—

Tidal Waters.—Between 15th July and 1st February, save rivers Cashen and Doonbeg, and rivers between Kerry Head and Dunmore Head. For Cashen, 13th August and 20th May; for Doonbeg, 31st August and 1st June; and for rivers between Kerry Head and Dunmore Head, 15th September and 1st April.

Upper Waters.—Netting and all other engines, save single rods, between 31st July and 1st February, save rivers Cashen, Doonbeg, and their tributaries, and save rivers between Kerry Head and Dunmore Head. For Cashen, Doonbeg, and rivers between Kerry Head and Dunmore Head same as in Tidal Waters.

Single Rods and Lines.—Between 30th September and 1st February, save Cashen and Doonbeg, and rivers between Kerry Head and Dunmore Head. For Cashen and Doonbeg and tributaries, between 30th September and 1st May, and for rivers between Kerry Head and Dunmore Head between 15th September and 1st April.

The By-Laws in force in this district are—

1. Prohibiting netting in that part of the Shannon between Wellesley Bridge and the Railway Bridge, between 1st June and 12th February.
2. Prohibiting, between the 20th July and 1st November in each year, the use of Draft Nets or any net having a foot-rope and leads or weights affixed thereto in that part of the Shannon between the Lax Weir and the western extremity of Graigue Island.
3. Prohibiting Draft Nets *for the capture of fish of any kind* of a mesh less than $1\frac{3}{4}$ inches from knot to knot in the tidal parts of the Shannon, or of rivers flowing into the Shannon.
4. Prohibiting the shooting of fish in that part of the Shannon between Portumna Bridge and Shannon Bridge, and also in the river Maigue.
5. Prohibiting fishing by any means whatsoever within twenty yards of Tarmonbarry Weir wall in the river Shannon.
6. Prohibiting fishing by any means whatsoever within twenty yards of Ennis Weir wall in the river Fergus.
7. Prohibiting the use of Draft Nets in the river Maigue, between Ferry Drawbridge and the old Bridge of Adare.
8. Prohibiting the use of all nets, except Landing Nets, in the river Maigue, above the Railway Bridge below Adare.
9. Prohibiting the use of Drift Nets in the tidal parts of the river Fergus.
10. Prohibiting having any net for capture of salmon or trout on board any boat, cot, or carragh, between the mouth of the Shannon and Wellesley Bridge, or in the tidal parts of any rivers flowing into the Shannon between said points, between 9 o'clock on Saturday morning and 3 o'clock on Monday morning, or between Wellesley Bridge and Killaloe Weir, between 8 o'clock on Saturday morning and 4 o'clock on Monday morning.
11. Permitting the use of nets in Lough Ree having a mesh of $1\frac{1}{4}$ inches from knot to knot.

Galway District

Extends from Hag's Head in County Clare to Slyne Head in County Galway, and embraces the rivers Kilcolgan, Clarin, Corrib, Furboe, Spiddle, Owenriff, Crumlin, Cashla, Screeb, Derinver, Ballinahinch, and Bunowen, and their tributaries, besides a number of other rivers not frequented by salmon.

The principal river is the Corrib. The modes of fishing are Draft nets and Boxes or Cribs in the Fishing Weir at Galway. There are few rivers in Ireland better protected than the Corrib and its tributaries, the expense of which protection being almost entirely borne by the enterprising Lessee of the fisheries in the tidal parts of the river. Good protection is also afforded to the extensive waters of Ballinahinch by the owners.

Formerly there existed fishing weirs in the Ballinahinch, Spiddle, and Furboe rivers, but since the Act of 1863 they have been discontinued.

In Screeb the proprietors have for several years carried on, very extensively, the system of artificial propagation of salmon, and have spared little expense in protecting and improving the spawning grounds, and removing obstructions. This river may be considered as only an angling one. No netting has been carried on for several years in the estuary, and of late in only a very limited manner, and yet the angling has not been good, though the river abounds with fish.

There are few obstructions to the free ascent of the fish in any of the rivers in this district. There is, however, a formidable one between Loughs Corrib and Mask, which bars the entrance of fish into the latter lake. If this were overcome, it would open up an extent of spawning ground fully equal to, if not greater than that at present in the tributaries to Corrib. There are, however, many difficulties in the way, but none so formidable that the enterprise of the various proprietors along the banks of the Lough and its tributaries could not overcome.

The amount of Licence Duty received in this district during the year was £385, a sum totally inadequate for proper protection. The lessee of the fishery in the tidal parts of the Corrib river expends about £700 a year in protection, in addition to the protection afforded by the Board of Conservators. There are over 200 water bailiffs in the district at salaries ranging from £3 to £17 10*s.* a year. Where such a small amount of salary is given to a bailiff, it should be remembered that he is only employed probably for a few weeks during the spawning season, and that he is living on the banks of the river. The remuneration for his short services is therefore not so small as one would be led to suppose at first sight.

There are no fixed nets used in this district. The fishing during the past season has not been so good as that during the preceding one. The fish, however, have increased in weight. The upper waters, during the past summer and spawning season, are reported to have been better stocked with fish than for many years past.

The Close Seasons fixed for this district in December, 1871, are as follow:—

Tidal and Upper Waters.—Netting and all other engines, save single rods, between 15th August and 1st February.

Single Rods and Lines.—Between 15th October and 1st February, save in Cashla and Doohulla rivers, between 31st October and 1st February.

The By-Laws in force in this district are as follow:—

1. Prohibiting the snatching or attempt to snatch in any tidal or fresh water with any kind of fish hook, covered or uncovered.
2. Prohibiting the use of nets in the Clare or Clare-Galway or Turloughmore rivers above the junction with Lough Corrib.

The Ballinakill District

Extends from Slyne Head, County Galway, to Pigeon Point, County Mayo, and embraces the rivers Westport, Owenee or Belclare, Bunowen or Louisburgh, Carrownisky, Bundorragha, Erriff, Culfin, Dawross, Traheen, and Derryherraun, and their tributaries, besides others not frequented by salmon.

The modes of fishing are Draft nets and one Pole net. The principal rivers are the Bundorragha and Erriff, in both of which there formerly existed Fishing Weirs with Boxes or Cribs; but they have long since been discontinued. With the exception of these two and the Dawross, all the rivers in the district are small, and can never be considered as commercial fisheries to any extent. There are obstructions in several of the rivers which prevent the free ascent of fish. The revenues derived from Licence Duties in 1872 amounted to £94, a sum totally inadequate for the protection *of even one river.*

The head waters of the Dawross, including Kylemore Lake and its tributaries, are protected to a considerable extent by the proprietors, as also are the Bundorragha, Erriff, and Louisburgh; but the system of protection afforded by the Board of Conservators is very deficient. There are about thirty water bailiffs employed by the Board of Conservators during the spawning season, at salaries varying from £1 10*s.* to £4, and about twelve by private individuals.

There are no fixed nets in this district. The fishing has been more productive during the past than during the preceding season.

The Close Seasons fixed for this district in June, 1872, are as follow:—

Tidal and Upper Waters.—For netting and all other engines save single rods, between 31st August and 16th February, save in Louisburgh and Carrownisky rivers and estuaries, which is between 15th September and 1st July.

For Single Rods and Lines.—Between 31st October and 1st February, save Louisburgh and Carrownisky rivers, which is between 31st October and 1st July.

There are no by-laws in force in this district.

The Bangor District

Extends from Pigeon Point to Benwee Head, and includes the rivers Moyour, Newport, Burrishoole, Owenduff, Munhim, Owenmore, Glenamoy, and Muignabo, and their tributaries.

The principal rivers in the district are the Owenduff or Ballyeroy, the Newport, Burrishoole, and Munhim rivers. In each of these rivers commercial fisheries to a considerable extent exist. There are no obstructions on these rivers of a formidable character. On the Newport a mill weir exists, on which a fish pass has been built. On this river there was formerly a Fishing Weir. Its remains are still in existence, but its use has been discontinued for a long time.

The modes of fishing in the district are Draft nets and Bag nets. Included in the term "Draft nets" are certain nets which were always considered, and commonly called and known only as Draft nets, but which were fished from time immemorial in the following manner :—" One end was fastened on the shore and the other to a buoy or boat anchored some distance off."

Although the 1st Section of the Act 13 & 14 Vic., c. 88 defines the words "fixed nets" to

"Extend to and include weirs, stake, bag, stop, and still nets, and all other engines or devices used for the like purposes of whatsoever construction or materials the same may be, or however known or styled, and whether fixed to the soil or held by hand, or made stationary in any other way."

Yet previous to the passing of the 26 & 27 Vic., c. 114, these nets were not considered or dealt with as fixed nets, but simply as ordinary draft nets. Even after the passing of that Act which imposed upon the Special Commissioners appointed thereunder the duty of inquiring into the legality of *all fixed nets* used for the capture of salmon in Ireland, they were still considered nothing more than ordinary movable draft nets until a case arose in the north of Ireland, when the magistrates decided that a net used in the manner described was a fixed net. On the hearing of the appeal in that case the Court of Queen's Bench expressed their opinion that "the justices decided as is now admitted to be right and fairly, that the net was fixed."

From thenceforward such nets were held to be fixed nets, and in consequence of the provisions of the 16th section of the 32 & 33 Vic., c. 92, which imposed a penalty of £50 on any person using a fixed net without having obtained a certificate therefor from the Special Commissioners under the Act of 1863, or from the Inspectors in regard to such fixed net, it became necessary for the owners and lessees of such nets to demand a certificate to enable them to exercise rights which had, in many cases, existed as long as living memory. Many of these nets were used in estuaries of less breadth than three-quarters of a mile, and the 22nd section of the 5 & 6 Vic., c. 106 enacts, that—

"In such parts of any estuary, or the mouth or tidal part of any river, where the breadth of the channel at low water of spring tides is less than three-quarters of a mile statute measure, it shall not be lawful (anything herein contained to the contrary notwithstanding) for any person, save and except the proprietor of a several fishery in the whole of such estuary and river to erect any such stake weir, stake net, bag net, fixed net, or contrivance for placing or erecting a net."

The 23rd section, however, of the same Act provides—

"That nothing herein contained shall be construed to render illegal any stake weirs or other contrivances for placing or erecting nets *which have been established for* 20 *years or upwards before the passing of this Act* in any estuary or portion of a river within a tideway of less than three-fourths of a mile at low water of spring tides."

And the 24th section provides—

"That nothing herein contained shall be construed to render illegal any stake weirs, ebb and flood weirs, and other contrivances for placing or erecting nets *which have been established for ten years or upwards before the passing of this Act within the limits of a several fishery* in any estuary or portion of a river within a tideway of less width than three-fourths of a mile at low water by any person legally possessed of or entitled to such several fishery by charter, grant, patent, prescription, or Act of Parliament."

Before granting any certificates for fixed nets, public inquiries were held in the districts, notices thereof having been first given, and at such inquiries all persons were heard either for or against the application. In this district certificates were granted for the use of eight of these engines, all being used in channels of less breadth than three-quarters of a mile. These were all granted on proof of a several fishery existing in the *locus in quo* and that the nets had been used for ten years before 1842 and in the year 1862. As it may be of some importance to know exactly the grounds of our decision in such cases, I submit, for your Excellency's information, extracts from a judgment delivered by me during the past year in a case analogous to those in this district.

Extracts from Judgment delivered at on the in the case of an Application for Certificate to use Fixed Draft Nets in Channel of less width than three-quarters of a mile.

"In this case the application is for a fixed net in the estuary of river. A claim has been made to a several fishery in this place. Taking the old documents and leases which have been put in in evidence into consideration, together with the uninterrupted user of over sixty years (as has been proved by two witnesses) there is such evidence as will justify us in coming to a decision that there is a several fishery in the place in question. We sit here as jurors, and we think we are bound, as such, by the language of Lord Chief Justice Erle, in 'Gan. and Johnstone' (412):—'Every presumption is to be made in favour of long usage, and though the evidence only went back to 1770, yet it has been repeatedly laid down that, when a continuous user has been shown for a much shorter period, in the absence of anything to the contrary, a jury will be warranted in inferring its existence beyond the time of legal memory.' Then, with regard to the absence of any evidence to the contrary, there has been proof of exclusive user of over sixty years given; so that we are justified, as jurors, in inferring its existence beyond legal memory. With respect to the use of the fixed net in this place, we think the evidence quite sufficient to entitle us to come to the conclusion that the net is legal. Whatever we may feel about the use of such a fixed engine in a narrow estuary, we have not to consider that question. It is an exercise of a right of property, and we are bound, when a party comes forward and proves a title to a fixed net, legally erected in 1863, to grant—and we think we have no alternative—but to grant a certificate. With respect to fixed engines in narrow channels, it is quite true that the 22nd section of the 5th and 6th Vic., c. 106, provides that where the breadth of the channel at low water of spring tides is less than three-quarters of a mile statute measure, it shall not be lawful for any person, *save and except the proprietor of a several fishery in the whole of such estuary and river to erect any fixed net* or contrivance for placing or erecting a net. But then the 23rd section of the same Act enacts 'that nothing herein contained shall be construed to render illegal any stake weirs and other contrivances for placing or erecting nets *which have been established for twenty years before the passing of this Act*, in any estuary or portion of a river within a tideway of less width than three-fourths of a mile at low water of spring tides', and the 24th section further provides that nothing shall be construed to render illegal any such fixed nets in such places, if they have been established in a several fishery for ten years or upwards, before the passing of the Act. Here we have two sections taking fixed-nets, established in these narrow channels for certain periods, out of the penal consequences provided for the erection of such engines by a former section—in the first case, if they have been established *for twenty years* before 1842—and in the second case, *for ten years* before 1842 *in a several fishery*. Now, what is the meaning of these sections, and how are we enabled to give the certificate (without which since the passing of the 32nd & 33rd Vic., c. 92, no person can use a fixed engine) mentioned by the 6th section, 26th & 27th Vic., c. 114, or the 10th section, 32nd & 33rd Vic., c. 92?

"The 6th section, 26 & 27 Vic., c. 114, provides that when a fixed net other than a bag-net prohibited by the Act is in use at the time of the passing of the Act, and any person claims to have erected it in pursuance of the provisions of the Act 5 & 6 Vic., c. 106, the Commissioners may, on proof being given to their satisfaction that such fixed *engine has been erected in pursuance of said provisions*, certify to that effect. There may be cases where a fixed net has been established for twenty years *before* 1842, which could hardly be said to have been *erected in pursuance of the Act 5 & 6 Vic., c. 106, passed twenty years afterwards* in 1842. Are the parties who own such property therefore to be debarred from exercising their rights because of the 10th section of the 32nd & 33rd Vic., c. 92, which prohibits the use of such engines without such a certificate? We think not. The words of this latter section are, 'any person who shall fish with, make use of, or erect any fixed engine for the capture of salmon without having obtained a certificate from the Special Commissioners for Irish Fisheries, *under the provisions of the 'Salmon Fishery Ireland Act*, 1863,' (*the 26th and 27th Vic., c. 114, s. 6*), *or a certificate* from the Inspectors acting in execution of this Act, *in regard to such fixed engine*, shall forfeit such fixed engine,' &c. This section, in our mind, relieves us from any difficulty in the matter, and in the case of a fixed net established for twenty years before 1842, which might not be erected in pursuance of the Act of 1842, we would only have to give a certificate *in regard to such fixed engine*; in other words to certify that it was legal, if we found it to be so. But we have decisions with regard to the meaning of these sections sufficient to guide us. In the case of the Queen *v.* Ryan, Baron Pennefather says:—'The question then is, supposing the weir to have been established for twenty years before the passing of the Act, does the Act make it legal? It does not. It merely says, it shall not be illegal by virtue of anything contained in the Act, and leaves it as if the Act was not made. After mature consideration this is the construction which in my opinion the Act ought to receive. Then this weir is to be dealt with as if this Act had not passed. The 10th Charles I., has been repealed and leaves this weir as at common law.'

"Again he says:—'By the 23rd section of the Fishery Act, 5 & 6 Vic., c. 106, weirs would have a protection after a continued existence for twenty years and upwards, although in point of fact, the party using the weirs could not prove the existence of the right.'

"And again he says, the same case:—'The meaning of the 23rd section is that a weir should be established for twenty years immediately before the passing of the Act, but an interruption by force is not to alter a title, and in my opinion this weir must be considered as established for twenty years before the Act. A weir being thus excepted from the prohibitionary enactment contained in the 22nd section is left as it would be at common law, and is to be justified by the common law.'

"In that case the weir was declared a common nuisance to the public right of fishery, and therefore ordered to be abated. In this case no public right was ever exercised, and we find the place where the net was used is a several fishery, and that being so, under the decision of Baron Pennefather in the case I have quoted, this net is legal.

"Again we have a more recent case decided by the Court of Queen's Bench—the case of the Sheel weir in the river Blackwater—R. M'Sweeney, appellant. In that case the weir was erected in a channel of less width than three-quarters of a mile and its legality was claimed on the ground of being erected for twenty years before 1842. The Special Commissioners condemned the weir as being illegal, but on appeal the Court of Queen's Bench reversed the decision of the Commissioners, and in consequence we gave a certificate for its use. Other cases of fixed engines in narrow channels have also been decided to be legal, notwithstanding the provisions of the 22nd section of the 5th & 6th Vic., c. 106, and it can only be under the interpretation put upon the meaning of the 23rd & 24th sections of the Act—that is, that if they are erected for twenty years in the one case, or ten years in the other in a several fishery, and that they are not in either case injurious to navigation, or in the former a nuisance to the public right of fishing, there is nothing to render them illegal; and that being so that we are bound on these conditions being proved to us to decide that they are legal, and to give our certificate *in regard to them*.

"Then as to the question who is the party entitled to receive our certificate, we do not consider that title of that kind is a material point in the case, because we think if we grant the certificate to the person we find in possession of the several fishery we comply with the provisions of the Act of Parliament, and we do not commit an act of injustice by doing so, because if any other person is entitled thereto, the person so aggrieved has the other tribunals of the country to go to, to obtain possession of the property to which he may lay claim. In the language of Judge Fitzgerald in another case:—'The question before us is not whether A. B. has a good title or not, but whether the net in 1863 had a legal existence.'

"To sum up therefore, we find—

"1. That this fixed net has been established for twenty years before the passing of the Act 5 & 6 Vic., c. 106, and that it is not injurious to navigation or the public rights of fishing;

"2. That it has been established for ten years before the passing of the 5th & 6th Vic., c. 106, within the limits of a several fishery;

"3. That this fixed net was legally erected for catching salmon and trout during the open season of 1863;

"4. That   is entitled to a certificate in regard to such fixed engine;

and that we will grant our certificate accordingly.

"In conclusion I have only to say that if any person feels aggrieved at our decision—that this is a several fishery, or that this net is legal—they have the right of appeal under 14th section of the 26th & 27th Vic. We will be most happy to facilitate that appeal in every way in our power. Notice of appeal should be given seven days after the delivery of our decision. Any party, therefore, feeling aggrieved by our decision has a right of appeal within the next seven days.

"It is quite right that every one should know that our certificate will not protect against fishing in an illegal manner, for if he does anything against a statutable enactment, our certificate would not save him from the penalties. It protects him merely from the penalty of fishing without a certificate. He must only use a net of   yards, and use it in a legal manner."

Against this an appeal was invited in order that the opinion of the Court of Queen's Bench on the very nice points of law that arose might be obtained. No appeal was, however, taken, and the certificate was issued under which the parties have since been exercising their rights.

There are 17 bag-nets in this district. Our predecessors granted a certificate for 1, and during the past year certificates have been issued for 16 more, 2 of them being on the property of Sir Francis A. K. Gore, bart., 2 on the property of William Pike, esq., and 12 on the property of the Trustees of the Achill Mission on Achill Island. These certificates were granted after a lengthened inquiry in the locality at which eminent counsel attended, both to support and oppose the claims of the proprietors, who proved that the nets were legally erected under the 19th section of the Act 5 & 6 Vic., c. 106, and had been used in 1862 and that they were not injurious to navigation, or a nuisance to the public rights of fishing. Notice of appeal against two of these decisions was given, but the appeal was not proceeded with.

In the Owenmore and Munhim rivers there formerly existed Fishing Weirs, but since the passing of the Act of 1863 they have been abandoned.

The amount of revenue received from licence duties in this district during the past year was £139. This is quite inadequate for the proper protection of the rivers. In fact the amount allocated by the Board does not pay one-fourth the cost of protection, the remainder is subscribed by the persons holding fisheries in the tidal waters. The revenue in this district will in future be considerably increased by the licence duties on the bag-nets lately sanctioned, and more ample protection than heretofore can thus be afforded. An unprecedented amount of poaching, which even the Royal Irish Constabulary, with the utmost vigilance, could hardly restrain, has been carried on in parts of this district.

There are hardly any obstructions to the free passage of fish in any of the rivers in this district, which generally are capable, if properly managed and protected, of producing a large quantity of fish. There are about eighty water bailiffs employed in the district, but the funds collected by the Board not being sufficient to pay the number of bailiffs required, the difference, being the largest portion of the salaries, is paid by the owners or lessees of the tidal fisheries.

The fishing has not been as good during the past as during the preceding season. The fish, however, are increased in size. The quantity of fish in the upper waters during the summer and the last spawning season has been greater than for many years past.

The close seasons fixed in June, 1872, for this district are as follow:—

TIDAL AND UPPER WATERS FOR NETS AND ALL OTHER ENGINES SAVE SINGLE RODS AND LINES.—Between 31st August and 10th February save Newport and Glenamoy rivers and estuaries. For Newport river and estuary, between 31st August and 1st May, and for Glenamoy river and estuary, between 15th September and 1st May.

FOR SINGLE RODS AND LINES.—Between 30th September and 1st May, save in Burrishoole, Owenmore, Munhim, and Owenduff or Ballycroy, which are between 30th September and 1st February.

The by-laws in force in this district are as follow:—

1. Prohibiting the removal of gravel or sand from the Owenmore River where the spawning of salmon may take place.
2. Permitting the use of nets of one and a half inches, from knot to knot, in so much of the rivers Owenduff or Ballycroy, Owenmore and Munhim as lies above the mouth as defined during June, July, and August.

THE BALLINA DISTRICT

Extends from Benwee Head in the county of Mayo to Coonamore Point in the county Sligo, and embraces the rivers Belderg, Ballinglen, Cloonaghmore, Moy, Leaffoney and Easkey and their tributaries. The modes of fishing are Draft-nets, Drift-nets, Bag-nets, and Boxes or Cribs in a Fishing Weir. The principal river in the district is the Moy. It is sixty-three miles in length and has a catchment basin of over 800 square miles, and twenty-one tributaries, all more or less frequented by salmon.

The estuary of this river is fished by means of Draft nets such as I have already described in the neighbouring district, and for nine of which, on proof being given of a several fishery, and that they had been so used for ten years before 1842, and in 1862, the necessary certificates were issued. At the top of the tideway, but in the fresh waters, a fishing weir having Boxes or Cribs is situated. Previous to the Act of 1863 no free gap existed in this weir. In the year 1864, however, under the provisions of the statute 26 & 27 Vic., c. 114, a free gap of 37½ feet was opened, and since then the capture of fish in the weir has very materially diminished. Up to that period no nets were used in the fresh water portions of the river; but soon after the opening of the gap some of the proprietors of property along the banks of the river let their rights of fishing and netting, for the first time commenced. Since then it has been carried on extensively in about nine miles of the upper waters of the river. It can hardly be imagined that at the time the Legislature compelled, by the Act of 1863, the opening of free gaps in all weirs without compensation, it intended merely that the property should be transferred from the proprietor of the weir to the proprietor of lands adjoining the river above the weir. Its object certainly was that these latter proprietors should have a greater interest in the fisheries than heretofore, principally for the sport of angling, and that the quantity of fish that would escape through the free gap would in time so increase that eventually ample compensation would be afforded to the weir owner for any loss he might in the first instance sustain by reason of opening the gap. Such, however, in this river has not been the case. The result has been merely a transfer of property from one proprietor to several. Nor has it had even the effect of stimulating these latter proprietors to afford greater protection to the fish during the spawning season. The only amounts subscribed for this purpose by the majority of them are simply the amounts of licence duty payable under the Act on each net used, although the quantity of fish taken by nets at five different fishing stations within those nine miles in extent of the upper waters of this river has been for the last few years very considerable. On this subject I beg to refer to my general remarks on protection. The Drift nets are used in the bay outside the river. There are five Bag-nets in the Bay of Killala, two being on the county Mayo, and three on the county Sligo side of the bay. These Bag-nets were condemned by our predecessors as illegal for want of title, but on appeal to the Court of Queen's Bench that decision was reversed and the circumstances under which they have been since re-erected are detailed in the last Annual Report.

The licence duties paid on these bag-nets formed a considerable revenue for the protection of the rivers nearest them, but, during the time between their condemnation and their re-erection, the river in the county Mayo nearest to them, which may be considered as merely a breeding river, few fish entering it until very late in the season, was left wholly unprotected for want of means to employ water bailiffs, and so, during that time, a great loss was sustained by the public.

The protection in the river Moy and its extensive tributaries is carried on at a very large cost (I am informed nearly £1,000 a year) by the proprietors of the fisheries in the tidal waters of the river.

Some of the smaller rivers in this district, such as the Leaffoney, the Ballinglen, the Belderg, and others, though possessing great capabilities and being good spawning rivers, are not protected. The proprietors along their banks take little or no interest in them, and the fish consequently become the prey of the poacher. It could hardly be expected that the Board of Conservators not receiving any revenue from these rivers could allocate any portion of their funds derived from, and more urgently required for, other more important rivers for the purpose. In other rivers there are some slight obstructions, but nothing, except perhaps in one instance, of such a formidable character as to prevent fish ascending to the spawning beds.

The total amount of revenue from Licence Duties in this district is only £326.

There are about fifty Water Bailiffs employed by the Board of Conservators, 250 by the Lessees of the Tidal Fisheries, and about three by the Upper Proprietors.

The Close Season fixed for this district in December, 1870, is as follows:—

TIDAL WATERS.—Between 12th August and 16th March, save Cloonaghmore and Easkey rivers, which is between 31st August and 1st June.

UPPER WATERS.—Nets and all other engines, save single rods, between 31st July and 1st February, save Cloonaghmore and Easkey rivers, which is between 31st August and 1st June.

FOR SINGLE RODS AND LINES.—Between 15th September and 1st February, save Cloonaghmore and Easkey rivers, which is between 30th September and 1st June.

The only By-Laws in force in this district are as follow:—

1. Prohibiting angling for trout during April and May in each year in the river Moy and its tributaries; Loughs Cullen and Conn excepted.
2. Permitting the use of Nets with meshes of one and a quarter inches from knot to knot, or five inches in the round.

THE SLIGO DISTRICT

Extends from Coonamore in the county Sligo to Mullaghmore in the county Sligo, and embraces the rivers Dunneill, Dunmoran, Ballisodare, Garvogue or Sligo, and Drumcliffe, and their tributaries.

The principal rivers are the Ballisodare and Sligo. The Ballisodare is discharged over a series of precipitous falls about 60 feet in height into the sea at Ballisodare; the lower fall being about 20 feet high. Previous to the building of fish passes over these falls the river was inaccessible to salmon. According to tradition one or two salmon were seen a great many years ago above the lowest fall, but none were ever seen as far as the bridge of Ballisodare.

Below the bridge is another fall surmounted by flat flagstones, and again in the Owenmore river at the village of Colloney, about half a mile above the junction of the rivers Arrow and Owenmore, which are discharged into the Ballisodare river, is a fall of greater height than those at Ballisodare. Hence there was a necessity for three passes being built. In 1852, the lowest pass was completed, and six fish were taken above this pass and put up above the upper fall of Ballisodare. In 1854 the fish came up the lower pass without difficulty, and numbers were taken and put in above the upper fall, on which the pass was not then completed. In 1855 the upper pass was completed and the fish had free run up the river. In 1856 a large quantity of fry were seen in the river, and one spent fish, which had been marked the year before, and which would probably have weighed about 14 lbs. if in good condition, was captured. The largest that had been marked the year before was 8 lbs. In April, 1857, the river seemed full of fry about four inches long and some were marked. In that year grilse were first seen at the lowest fall, and were very plentiful. In December of that year two fish about 4 lbs. each, that had been marked in April, 1856, were got, but none of the fry that were marked in the spring of 1857. In 1857 the river between Ballisodare and Colloney was well stocked, salmon being seen in almost every deep hole, and a number being congregated between Colloney bridge and the hole under the fall. The fish passes that had been built at the several falls being governed by sluice-gates at their mouth or entrance, experiments by means of shutting the sluices were now made to ascertain if the fish were ascending the passes, and the following was the result:—

October	3,	Seven salmon in ladder—five being females.
"	13,	Twenty-seven—majority females.
"	28,	Three male fish.
"	30,	Four male and two female fish.
November	3,	Sixteen male and eight female fish.
	4,	Ten fish.
"	5,	Nine fish.
"	6,	Seven fish.
"	7,	Eleven fish.
"	9,	Twenty-four male and fifteen female fish.
"	23,	Twenty-five male and twenty female fish, some of them 14 and 15 lbs. weight.
December	3,	Thirty-six male and forty-five female fish.

In 1858 the spawning beds in the river were first seen, and on the 1st July of that year the netting for fish was first regularly commenced, though a few had been taken during February, March, April, May, and June. During July, 568 salmon were taken by the nets, and up to the 20th of August, 530 more; the average weight being very little more than 4 lbs. each.

One of the fish taken in February of that year and weighing 9 lbs. was a fry marked in 1856. And among the fish taken in July, seven were fry that had been marked the year before and they weighed 5½ to 6 lbs. each.

In September of 1858, the passes are reported to have been "literally full of fish," and the run of fish fully two months earlier than the year before. In October, the Colloney pass is reported "to resemble a steeplechase, as the fish was seen clearing the steps in pairs." In one hour one of the water-keepers reports having seen 267 salmon ascending this pass. In December of same year the experiments were continued, and at one time 256 fish were in the pass ascending. On another occasion, when the water was turned off, the pond in the pass was "actually alive with fish, in general larger and fresher from the sea than those of the day before;" 246 fish were put up and then there must have been left still in the pond from 300 to 400 fish.

The foregoing is a short summary taken from the report of the then proprietor of the river, who had these passes built at his own expense. I have thought it desirable, and perhaps it may be interesting to some, to enter into these details, to show the vast importance of having passes built over natural or artificial obstructions in rivers, so as to enable salmon to have free access to the spawning beds, and with the further view of considering how far many of our rivers now wholly unproductive, either from obstructions barring the ascent of the fish, or from the several interests therein being too much divided, might not be made, like the Ballisodare river, a source of wealth, not only to the proprietor, but to the country at large. This matter must form the subject of another and subsequent report.

The Ballisodare river has still continued to advance in prosperity, and is now a valuable salmon fishery property. The fishing has not been so good, however, during the past as during the preceding season; but the fish taken has increased considerably in weight. There are no fixed nets used, and the manager is, I believe, most careful that over-netting does not take place.

The Sligo river is one of the earliest in the country. Salmon in its finest condition is found in the estuary of this river in winter. In 1871 after two public inquiries, at one of which we all attended, and at the other one of my colleagues with me, it was decided on adopting, as far as possible, the season for fishing recognised previous to the Act of 1842, which fixed a uniform season for all rivers, and netting and angling were permitted to commence in the tidal parts of this river on the 1st of January. An outcry was raised against this decision, on the ground that it would be destructive to the angling interests in the river. I am happy, however, to state that the result has not proved this to be the case, for the angling in the upper waters during the past season is reported to have been as good as during any year preceding the change. Indeed one gentleman, who is an ardent follower of the sport, admitted to me he had a very good season. On this subject I refer to my general remarks.

The protection of the fish in the upper waters is carried out by the lessee of the tidal fisheries of the river; the funds derived from licence duties, £67, being wholly inadequate for the purpose.

The modes of fishing in the district are Draft-nets and Bag-nets. Of the former, four are what I have already described in my remarks on the Bangor District, viz.: fixed draft-nets, two of them being certified for as legal in the estuary of the Sligo river, one in the estuary of the Drumcliffe river, and one on the sea coast on the site of a bag-net which had been legally erected in 1862, but which had been abolished by the provisions of the Act of 1863, as being within three miles of the mouth of a river frequented by salmon. No appeals were brought against the decisions declaring these nets legal, though the illegality of the nets was strongly contended for by eminent counsel at the hearing of one of the cases. On this subject I beg to refer to some further observations in my general remarks.

The two bag-nets were certified for as legal by the late Special Commissioners.

The Close Season fixed for this district in April, 1871, is as follows:—

IN TIDAL WATERS.—Between 19th August and 4th February, save tidal parts of Sligo River, which is between 15th July and 1st January.

IN UPPER WATERS, NETS AND ALL OTHER ENGINES SAVE SINGLE RODS.—Between 19th August and 4th February.

FOR SINGLE RODS.—Between 30th September and 1st February, save in the tidal parts of Sligo river, which is between 30th September and 1st January, and save also Drumcliffe river and Glencar Lake, which is between 19th October and 1st February.

The By-Laws in force in this district are as follows:—

1. Prohibiting the snatching or attempt to snatch salmon in the Sligo river, with any kind of fish-hook, covered or uncovered.
2. Permitting the use of nets in Lough Doon with meshes of half an inch from knot to knot.

THE BALLYSHANNON DISTRICT

Extends from Mullaghmore to Rossan Point in the county Donegal, and embraces the following rivers:—

The Duff or Bunduff, Bundrowes, Erne, Ballintra, Eak, Eanny or Inver, Oily, Bungosteen, and Teelin or Glen, and their tributaries.

The principal river in the district is the Erne, which is sixty-four miles in length, has a catchment basin of 1,689 square miles, and thirteen tributaries, nearly all of them having good spawning grounds, besides a great chain of lakes. A large commercial fishery exists in the lower waters, which is carried on by means of one Stake-net, three Boxes or Cribs, and Draft-nets, three of the latter being fixed, and for which certificates were granted after public inquiry, and proof being given that they were situated in a several fishery, and had been so for ten years before 1842, and were so used during the year 1862.

The upper waters of this river contain some of the best angling in Ireland. A very extensive system of protection is carried out over the whole of the river and its tributaries, by the proprietors of the lower parts of the river, who spare no expense in their endeavour to improve the fisheries.

In the Bundrowes, a valuable early fishing formerly existed in the weir near the mouth of the river, but owing to the provisions of the Act of 1863 which directed gaps in all weirs to be opened, this portion of the property has become so deteriorated as to be hardly worth fishing. It is now stated by some that the angling in the upper waters and lake has not proportionately improved. In the Duff river complaints have been made of the erection of a dam for supplying water to a mill. This has been lately made the subject of a public inquiry.

The Oily river was formerly frequented by salmon, but owing to the erection of mill-dams they have become nearly extinct. As two of these obstructions have been placed in the river since 1842, the law directs the owners of the mills to build such fish passes thereon as may be approved by the Inspectors. To effect this, surveys of the weirs and designs for passes have been made, and during the coming summer I hope to see them completed, and that fish will once more have free access to the spawning grounds of this river.

The river Inver is fished by Draft-nets and two fixed Draft-nets in the estuary, for which certificates were granted on the same grounds as those referred to in former cases. In this river there formerly existed a fishing weir, but it has been discontinued for some years.

The Esk has been for several years left unprotected, but as the fishing has been leased to a gentleman who has for many years taken a great interest in fisheries, it is hoped he will reap all the advantages to be derived from a proper system of protection which he is adopting. The estuary of this river is fished by draft-nets. Formerly there existed a fishing weir on the river, but it has been for many years discontinued.

Along the coast of this district, more particularly on the north shores of Donegal bay, the poorer classes of the fishermen who exercise their common law or public rights of fishing in the sea had been from time immemorial in the habit of fishing for salmon by means of what are called "Half Trams," or in other words "fixed draft-nets," such as I have described before, the difference between the two modes of fishing being hardly worth noticing. Since the decisions referred to in the case of Stewart and Cubitt, they have been unable to follow this mode of fishing, not being able to bring themselves within the provisions of the 19th section of the Act of 1842 as persons entitled to use fixed nets. The consequence is, that unless by stealth or in the absence of the local authorities they are now virtually prohibited from fishing in the open sea for salmon, the ordinary draft-net, unless fixed as described, being practically useless on such a wild coast.

Great complaints have been made to me from time to time by these poor fishermen of the hardship of being prevented taking salmon in the sea in the only way available for them, and the way in which salmon had, until the passing of the Act 32 & 33 Vic., c. 92, been taken from time immemorial, but I have explained that there is no power to grant any certificate, without which they cannot use a fixed net, to any person save those mentioned in either the 18th or 19th section of the Act of 5 & 6 Vic., c. 106.

Certificates have been issued for three of such nets on this coast, to the proprietors of land adjoining the sea, under the provisions of the 19th section of the Act.

Some of the rivers in this district are not frequented by salmon though no obstructions to their free ascent exists, while in others there are many obstructions which I hope in time to see overcome by fish passes. A large portion of upper waters in which there is apparently good spawning ground is not frequented by salmon.

The fishing in this district has not been so good during the past as during the preceding season. The fish have, however, increased in weight. The upper waters of most of the rivers in the district had an abundance of fish through the summer, and the spawning grounds during the past winter have been amply stocked.

There are about 200 water bailiffs employed by the Board of Conservators—the revenue of the district being largely supplemented by the proprietors of the lower waters of the river Erne—and eight by private individuals.

The Close Season fixed for this district in November, 1871, is as follows:—

TIDAL AND UPPER WATERS, NETS AND ALL OTHER ENGINES, SAVE SINGLE RODS.—Between 20th August and 1st March.

FOR SINGLE RODS AND LINES.—Between 9th October and 1st March, save Bunduff, Bundrowes, and Erne rivers. For Bunduff, between 30th September and 1st February; Bundrowes, 30th September and 1st January; Erne and tributaries, 30th September and 1st March.

The By-Laws in force in this district are as follow:—

1. Prohibiting the use of nets for the capture of fish of any kind with meshes less than one inch from knot to knot on that part of the Coast of Donegal inside lines drawn from Rossan Point to Teelin Head, from Teelin Head to Carrigan Head, and from Carrigan Head to Muckross Point.
2. Prohibiting the use of the Spoon Bait, or any instrument of like nature or device, in that part of the Erne River between the Falls of Belleek and the west point of Castlecaldwell Demesne.
3. Permitting the use of nets, with meshes of one inch from knot to knot, in the tideway of the River Erne.
4. Permitting the use of nets, with meshes of one inch from knot to knot, in the River Inver, above its mouth as defined.

GENERAL REMARKS.

The total amount of revenue received by these seven fishery districts for licence duties in 1872 was £3,694, being an increase over that received in 1871 of £202 11s. 3d. The total amount of revenue received in Ireland amounted to £8,998 1s., so that these seven districts, which embrace some of the largest commercial fisheries in the country, received nearly three-sevenths of the entire amount of the twenty-two districts. If this sum had not been so largely supplemented by the proprietors of the lower fisheries, in such rivers as the Galway, Ballina, Ballisodare, Sligo, Erne, and smaller rivers, it would have proved totally inadequate to afford the necessary protection, even during the spawning season. It is to be regretted that, *as a rule, in Ireland*, the upper proprietors contribute so little to the protection of the fisheries, no matter how large their interests. In very few instances do they contribute more than the amount of licence duty imposed by Act of Parliament on the engines used in their fisheries. The greater bulk even of the licence duty is derived from engines used in the tidal waters. So far as the districts I have now reported on are concerned, the following is the result, and it may be taken, I think, as a fair criterion of the country in general:—

		£	s.	d.
In LIMERICK DISTRICT the amount of licence duty paid	by lower proprietors in 1872, .	1,671	0	0
" "	by upper proprietors " .	58	10	0
In GALWAY DISTRICT the amount of licence duty paid	by lower proprietors in 1872, .	90	0	0
" "	by upper proprietors " .	9	0	0
In BALLYNAKILL DISTRICT the amount of licence duty paid	by lower proprietors in 1872, .	54	0	0
" "	by upper proprietors " .	0	0	0
In BANGOR DISTRICT the amount of licence duty paid	by lower proprietors in 1872, .	114	0	0
" "	by upper proprietors " . .	9	0	0
In BALLINA DISTRICT the amount of licence duty paid	by lower proprietors in 1872, .	192	0	0
" "	by upper proprietors " . .	48	0	0
In SLIGO DISTRICT the amount of licence duty paid	by lower proprietors in 1872, .	55	0	0
" "	by upper proprietors " . .	0	0	0
In BALLYSHANNON DISTRICT the amount of licence duty paid	by lower proprietors in 1872,	190	0	0
" "	by upper proprietors " .	4	0	0

So that in these seven districts the total amount received by licence duties for salmon fishing from the owners or lessees of lower fisheries was £2,366, while there was only received from the same source from the upper waters the sum of £128 10s. This does not, of course, include rod licences, which in these seven districts amounted to £637.

To the sum of £2,366 received from the lower waters may be added the contributions of the owners of fisheries in the lower parts of certain rivers to which I have referred, of at least £2,500, which will leave £5,866 contributed by the tidal fisheries as against £765 10s., including rod licences, contributed by the upper or fresh water fisheries.

It may however be said that the upper proprietors employ water bailiffs themselves in addition to those employed by the Conservators.

I have caused a series of queries on this subject to be issued to each district in Ireland, and I now give the substance of the replies received from these seven districts.

The queries submitted were as follow:—

1. Do any of the upper proprietors employ or pay any water bailiffs for protection in addition to those employed and paid by the Board of Conservators, and if so, where and by whom?

The replies to this query from three districts are "They do not." From two districts "There are eight;" from another district "There are five;" from another district "Three;" total sixteen.

This does not of course include the number of bailiffs who are employed by persons owning both tidal and upper water fisheries.

2. Do any of the upper proprietors subscribe anything towards protection in addition to the licence duties they have to pay, and if so state amount and by whom?

The replies to this query from six districts out of the seven, are "They do not;" from one district the reply is, "One gentleman subscribes £1, and he is the only instance in the whole district."

3. Do any of the lower proprietors employ or pay any water bailiffs for protection in addition to those employed and paid by the Board of Conservators, and if so, where and by whom?

The replies are, from one district—"Yes; a very large number in addition to the few employed by the Board. This observation applies to all the rivers in this district." From another district—"The amount allocated by the Board of Conservators to each river does not pay one-fourth the cost of protection. The remainder is subscribed altogether by the tidal fishers." From another district—"The lower proprietors employ all the water bailiffs required. The money supplied by licences does not in any instance, except one, suffice to pay their salaries." From another district—"The proprietors of the estuary fishings employ over 200." From another district—"There are fifty-one employed by the owners of fisheries in the tidal waters, one of them being also owner of the upper waters." From another district—"Yes, six;" and from another district—"No."

Nothing could show more clearly the little interest taken by upper proprietors in Ireland, no matter how large their interests, *and in many cases they are very considerable*, towards protecting the fish during the close season, and that without the aid contributed by the tidal fisheries, the salmon fisheries of the country would be at a low ebb, and the public suffer materially.

It is hardly necessary for me to say that there are some exceptions in Ireland to this state of things, but they are few in number.

Close Season.

This is probably one of the most embarrassing and difficult subjects with which we have to deal. It is really the vital question relating to this important portion of the industrial resources of the country, and in dealing with it I think the following rules should be our guidance:—

1. That the public good is to be the object of paramount importance, and is to be effected by adopting only that system which will raise the salmon fisheries to their maximum state of permanent productiveness of the fish in the best condition as an article of food.

2. That the salmon fisheries should be considered with reference to their commercial value, and not merely with reference to private or local convenience or interests.

3. That the salmon fisheries on the sea coast and tideways comprise, and must always comprise, almost the entire of the commercially valuable or marketable fisheries of the country.

4. That the quantity of fish in the best condition taken in the upper waters must always form but a small proportion of the whole.

5. That as much time previous to the period of spawning should be made a close season as will allow a sufficient supply of fish to ascend to stock the rivers for breeding.

6. That the spent fish should be carefully protected, and permitted to return safely to the sea, without which there cannot be a supply of large fish.

These are some of the propositions put forward many years ago, and are, in my mind, in dealing with this question, those entitled to the best consideration.

The legislature of old recognised these principles, and adapted the laws to the peculiarities of each river, and did not attempt to make the peculiarities of the river adapt themselves to the laws.

It made differences in the legal seasons to be observed in different rivers, according as they were either "late" or "early" rivers—*i.e.*, according to the time at which salmon were found in their finest condition—and this continued until the Act of 1842 fixed a uniform season for all rivers. It is well known that the seasons fixed by that Act, not only deprived the public of that article of food when it was in its primest state, but actually deprived some men of their property in fishing; the only valuable time in which salmon could be taken in many fisheries having been made the close season, within which all fishing was prohibited.

The error of this legislation was soon discovered, and successive Acts of Parliament recognised a different principle, and conferred on the Commissioners appointed to carry them out, power to vary the close season in localities—though, indeed, it would appear that the Legislature was doubtful of the wisdom of the uniform season, for it provided by the same Act that the Commissioners should have power to alter it.

In the inquiries into this subject in these districts, I have kept in view the principles here set forth, believing, and indeed feeling assured, that they are the best for the promotion and welfare of all interests in the salmon fisheries, and that in a short time they will be found productive of great benefit to the public.

Fixed Nets.

In my report on the several districts I stated the reasons and circumstances under which we felt coerced to grant certificates for fixed nets, and that on each occasion, in public court, appeals against our decisions from persons who opposed the claims were invited by us. None, however, were ever brought, though notices in two cases were given, but were afterwards withdrawn.

As the law at present stands no person can fish with fixed nets for salmon in Ireland, no matter how good his title may be, unless he has received a certificate either from the Special Commissioners or from the Inspectors in regard to such fixed net. To obtain this certificate he must prove in public court the following—

5 & 6 Vic., c. 106, ss. 18, 19. 1stly. That there is a good title to erect the net under either the 18th or 19th section of the Act 5 & 6 Vic., c 106.

13 & 14 Vic., c. 88, s. 17. 2ndly. That the engines had not been ordered to be abated and removed by any order or decision of any Judge of Assize, heretofore made, or by any order or any decision of any court whatsoever, which latter includes orders or decisions

32 & 33 Vic., c. 92, s. 20. of the Special Commissioners for Irish Fisheries.

26 & 27 Vic., c. 114, s. 4. 3rdly. That they had been legally erected for catching salmon during the open season of 1862.

Ib., s. 5. 4thly. That they are not injurious to navigation; and

Ib., s. 6. 5thly. That they are not a nuisance to the public right of fishing, or otherwise in violation of any Act of Parliament.

He must, often at great expense, defend his claim against any person opposing it. When this has been done, he must, if necessary, be prepared to defend it on appeal before the Court of Queen's Bench. And after he has succeeded through all the processes of law, he finds out that the certificate is really of no value to him. He may be summoned before a bench of magistrates who may take a different view of the law to that taken by us, and find he has no redress. This is not an imaginary case. It has occurred in Ireland, and may occur in any of the cases I have mentioned in these districts, where by far the greatest number of fixed nets in Ireland are used, and where some of them involve properties of large commercial value. It is hardly fair for an opposing party in the court below to refuse taking an appeal against the decision, and then be enabled by a provision in the law to put the claimant to the expense of defending himself again before magistrates, thus indirectly bringing an appeal against the decision before the latter tribunal, instead of before the Court of Queen's Bench, as provided by the statute. Under the statute, any person feeling aggrieved has the right of appeal to the Court of Queen's Bench. If no appeal be brought, the certificate should be made final. No injustice can be done by this, while great and manifest injustice may and has been done by the present state of the law.

I am, therefore, strongly of opinion the law should be altered in this respect.

In the appendices will be found a schedule of the inquiries held on this subject and the decision in each case.

While on this subject I cannot help expressing my conviction that to no tribunal whatever, without the right of appeal, should a power be given to condemn any engine on any grounds. This power is practically given to the Commissioners under the present law, the Court of Queen's Bench having declined to hear an appeal from their decision in the case of injury to navigation, the law giving them the power to "abate and remove all fixed nets erected or used for catching salmon or trout in Ireland that are *in their judgment* injurious to navigation."

I am convinced that it would be much more satisfactory to the public, as I know it would be to myself as one of the judges bound to come to some decision on this nice question of fact, if an appeal could be brought on this as well as on all matters of law, and that the court should have the power, if they desired, to send such a question of fact for trial before a jury, if necessary.

No such provision in the law as that to which I have referred exists in England or Scotland.

I am led to make these observations as the result of long experience, and from a consideration of the nature of some of the cases of this description on which I was obliged during the past year to come to some conclusion, more particularly of one in which I had the misfortune to differ in opinion with my colleagues, and respecting which I then made the following remarks in coming to my decision:—

"It is true that the statute 26 & 27 Vic., c. 114, s. 5, provides that, '*Subject to such appeal as is hereinafter mentioned*, the Commissioners shall abate and remove all fixed nets erected or used for catching salmon or trout that *are in their judgment* injurious to navigation.'

"But I think that these words *in their judgment* cannot mean that the Commissioners or Inspectors were to have the power capriciously of stating that *in their judgment* a weir was injurious, and that it should thereupon be removed.

"I think *the judgment* must be governed by the evidence and principles of law on the subject, and that the injury should be a *common annoyance*, and that that annoyance must, as Lord Hardwicke says, 'be of a *real and substantial nature*, and that the fears of mankind, though they may be reasonable, will not create a nuisance.' In fact, as Mr. William O'Connor Morris, the late Legal Commissioner of Fisheries, expresses it in one of his Judgments, 'You must show that the obstruction is a nuisance—*nocumentum commune*—*a substantial and appreciable injury, in fact, to the navigation in the locality*.'

"Now, is this not such? It has been erected since 1854. Mr. ——, who always worked these nets, has sworn that he never knew or heard of this net being in the way, or that any accident ever occurred at it. Mr. ——, the gentleman who occupied the position of Commissioner of Fisheries for over forty years, says he devoted his attention to this question of navigation for over twenty years—that he knows the sites of these nets—that the only one he considered might be an obstruction was a net belonging to another proprietor, which had been formerly erected on the north side near ——, that from the character of the shore off which these nets are fished, being rocky, boats must be kept a long way out—that upon such a shore it would be necessary for boatmen to keep a sharp look-out to avoid the rocks rather than the nets, and that from his own observation of these nets he does not think any of them injurious, even to a row boat; the Chief Officer of Coast-guard, who was stationed for over twelve years at ——, states the net is not, in his opinion, injurious, and that during his time no complaint was ever made of it, nor did any accident ever, to his knowledge, occur at it. Two fishermen who fish in the locality are produced, and they say the net is not injurious. *The only evidence on which we are asked to condemn this net* is that of a pilot who said that *on one occasion* he got entangled with it, and had to unship his rudder, and that his boat half filled with water—that he was piloting for about twenty years, *and that was the only time he got foul of the net, and that he never was put to inconvenience by it but then*.

"Now, it must be remembered that a bag-net is an engine only in the water during fishing season—that it is wholly removed during the close season in winter, and during the close season every week from Saturday morning at six o'clock to Monday morning at six o'clock; and on this evidence of a single very slight accident, on uncorroborated testimony, have we any right or power to say that this net is *a substantial and appreciable injury, in fact, to the navigation of the locality*?

"I cannot think that the law is such as to enable us to say, under such circumstances and on such evidence —'In *our judgment* the net is injurious to navigation.'

"If the law be such, then I can only say that that law may work a confiscation of property. And as I am strongly of opinion that it is not competent for us to say (on such evidence as has been brought before us in respect to this net) *that it is in our judgment injurious to navigation*, and to refuse to grant a certificate for it, I hope this question, which has not yet been decided by the Superior Court, may be brought under their consideration, by which we may obtain some decision on the point to govern us in future cases."

Complaints have been frequently made to me during the past year, that the valuable assistance heretofore given by the Royal Irish Constabulary in protecting the fisheries and prosecuting offenders against the laws, has been materially restricted by orders recently issued to that Force. Previous to these orders, the Constabulary took cognizance of every infraction of the law that came under their notice, and rendered most valuable aid to the fisheries, particularly in preventing the flow of flax water, which is poisonous to fish, into rivers; and they prosecuted extensively for this offence. I have explained that the powers of the Constabulary to act in fishery cases are limited to the following:—

The observance and enforcement of the several periods fixed as the annual close seasons for the salmon, trout, eel, and oyster fisheries.

The observance of the free passage of fish during such annual close seasons, and requiring for that purpose the making and maintaining of openings, and the removal of obstructions, and directing certain acts, matters, and things to be done during and in relation to such annual close seasons.

The observance of the weekly close seasons, and of the free passage of fish during such, and requiring for that purpose the making and maintaining of openings, and the removal of obstructions, and directing certain matters, acts, and things to be done, and prohibiting other acts, matters, and things to be done, during and in relation to such weekly close seasons.

Wilfully taking, selling, purchasing, or having in possession the spawn, smelts, or fry of salmon, or trout, or eels, or in any way or by any device wilfully obstructing the passage of the said smelts or fry.

Injuring or disturbing any spawn or fry, or any spawning bed, bank, or shallow where the same may be.

Wilfully taking, killing, destroying, exposing to sale, or having in possession any red, black, foul, unclean, or unseasonable salmon or trout.

Placing, laying, setting, or drawing any net, grate, creel, or other engine, or using any means or device whatsoever (save and except rod and line), for the purpose of taking, destroying, or obstructing any salmon or other fish, or the fry thereof, in any works appurtenant to any mill or factory, or in any of the watercourses leading the water to or from such mill or factory.

Taking or suffering to be taken in any ebb weir any salmon or trout, or salmon or trout fry, or spent salmon.

Having or using any light or fire, spear, gaff, or strokehaul, or other such instrument, with intent to take salmon, in or on the banks of any lake or river between sunset and sunrise.

Chasing, injuring, or disturbing spawning fish or fish on spawning beds, or attempting to catch fish in such places (except with rod and flies only, within the lawful period).

Damming, or teeming, or emptying any river or mill-race, for the purpose of taking or destroying any salmon or trout, or the fry thereof.

The production of licence from any person using any engine, net, instrument, or device for the capture of salmon, or having the same erected, or in fishing order, or found in possession in or near any fishing place, or going to or returning from fishing.

As a rule, throughout Ireland the Royal Irish Constabulary were not unwilling to perform the duties expected from them formerly in connexion with the fisheries, and in a great many places their services, while on other duty, were most valuable.

It is to be regretted, therefore, that these services—so important to the salmon fisheries at all times—should be obliged to be curtailed in any way or season, so long as they did not interfere with their other duties. I mention this matter merely as the opinion of most of those having an interest in fisheries, and not with the view of causing any change in the orders lately issued, which were only in accordance with the present provisions of the law.

In any new legislation I am strongly of opinion that the laws which are now extended over eight Acts of Parliament should be consolidated.

There are a few other matters of detail in the management of the salmon fisheries of Ireland, which I shall have the honour of submitting to your Excellency in my next Report.

THOS. F. BRADY.

MAJOR HAYES' REPORT.

In accordance with the arrangements previously referred to, I now beg to submit my Report of the division which has been especially under my supervision for the last three years.

This division extends coastwise from Slea Head, in the county of Kerry, the northern extremity of Dingle Bay, in the west, to Wicklow Head in the east, and contains all the rivers and lakes discharging into the sea between and southward of those points.

It is divided into eight fishery districts, viz. :—

No. 7. Killarney.	No. 5. Cork.
No. 6². Kenmare.	No. 4. Lismore.
No. 6³. Bantry.	No. 3. Waterford.
No. 6¹. Skibbereen.	No. 2. Wexford.

These districts possess an aggregate of fifty-eight rivers discharging direct into the sea—their total length considerably exceeding 1,100 miles—besides their principal tributary rivers, of an almost equal length, and very many valuable spawning streams which can scarcely be called rivers, but which are far too numerous to allow of their length being given even approximately.

The watershed or catchment basin of these rivers exceeds 8,400 miles, from which may be inferred, in some degree, the great extent of rivers and streams in a part of the country so well watered as this proverbially is.

I will now take the districts in their order of rotation.

1st.—No. 7, Killarney.

This district contains the following seven important salmon rivers :—

Maine.	Ferta.
Laune.	Inny.
Caragh.	Cummeragh.
Behy.	

The length of those principal rivers and their tributaries exceeds 200 miles, besides many lesser spawning streams—the catchment basin 722 miles; independently of which there are some lesser rivers, which at present are of little, if any, commercial value.

The Maine is an important river, having a length of about twenty-seven miles, with numerous tributaries, one of which (the Brown Fleck) is over nineteen miles in length.

The Laune, the most important in the district, is but a short river, as its length from the Killarney Lakes is but fourteen miles; but as it is the only outlet of the lakes and their numerous important spawning rivers, and drains a country with a catchment basin of 320 miles, its value may be understood to be great. This is a very early salmon river, spring salmon in finest condition being captured in it about the middle of January; whilst, strange to say, in the Maine, which discharges into the same estuary (Castlemaine Harbour), and within half a mile of it, they are not to be found before May.

The Caragh, with its lake and upper streams, a valuable early river.

The Behy, also early.

The Ferta or Valentia, and the Inny, both late rivers and much neglected.

The Cummeragh or Waterville, a very important salmon river, and one of the very earliest in Ireland—indeed it may be said that salmon in prime condition may be had in this river on almost every day in the year. In the month of November, 1870, being anxious to ascertain, if possible, by our own personal observation, the condition of the salmon at that season, the proprietor, Mr. Butler, at our request, kindly had a net drawn for my colleague Mr. Blake and myself. The haul was a large one. Most of the fish were black and unseasonable, but with them were several in as fine condition as fish could be; and I have been since informed by Mr. Butler that on 17th December, 1871, he observed a large run of spring salmon passing his weir.

There is very good angling in most of the rivers, as also upon the lakes; and in a commercial point of view the district is important, as it contributes a good deal of salmon—especially in the early season—to the English markets.

Notwithstanding the excessive wetness of 1872, the reports from the district are satisfactory, and the season is considered to have been a fair average one.

The quantity of spawning fish in the rivers is reported to have been far greater than in previous years.

Complaints have reached this department for a considerable time past as to the system of netting practised in the lower part of the Laune river, and which it is alleged has injuriously affected the upper fisheries. It is proposed to hold an inquiry, for the purpose of investigating this subject, during the present year, and, should it prove to be necessary, to adopt means by which any just complaint will be remedied.

Like in nearly if not all the districts in Ireland, insufficiency of funds to insure proper protection is the greatest difficulty under which Killarney labours. If proper protection could be secured the quantity of salmon would be, without doubt, very largely increased in a short time.

2nd.—No. 6[a], Kenmare.

In this district there are the following salmon rivers :—

Sneem.	Cloonee.
Blackwater.	Owenshagh.
Finnihy.	Croanshagh.
Roughty.	Kealincha.
Sheen.	

The length of these rivers exceeds eighty-six miles, and there are many tributaries of considerable extent, valuable as spawning ground.

The catchment basin is over 240 miles.

These are all late rivers, spring fish being seldom taken before June. Some of them afford excellent angling, but their commercial value is not great.

For some years past artificial propagation of salmon has been extensively and successfully carried on by Richard Mahony, Esq., of Dromore Castle, the proprietor of the Blackwater River. These operations commenced in 1867, and have been carried on up to the present time.

For the first three years the increase in the quantity captured in the immediate vicinity of the river was most remarkable, the gross take by all parties amounting in 1870 to 7,300 salmon, as compared with 3,600 in 1867. It is but right, however, to state that Mr. Mahony does not attribute this increase so much to the artificial breeding of salmon as to the opening up of new spawning beds. However, the fact remains that a very great increase actually took place.

In 1871 and 1872, however, the amounts captured fell off tremendously—even to less than half that in 1867; but I believe this may be accounted for by the boisterous nature of the seasons 1871 and 1872, and the excessive floods which prevailed, and which rendered netting difficult, if not at times impossible.

Large quantities of salmon have also been hatched artificially on the property of the Marquess of Lansdowne; but I regret to say that for the present, at any rate, this has been discontinued.

Unfortunately, in parts of this district a system of poaching prevails of the most destructive character. It is done by poisoning the streams and pools with some material which, though destructive to the life of fish, is not supposed to render them unfit for food. When a stream or pool has been thus poisoned, everything in the shape of salmon or trout coming within its influence becomes at once stupified, and in most cases dies, but in any case becomes an easy prey to the poacher. Thus not only the grown fish, but the fry—the stock of succeeding years—are all destroyed.

As may be supposed, the offence is one most difficult of detection, and being most fatal to the fisheries, deserves the severest punishment the law will allow. It is now punishable by a fine of not less than £5 nor exceeding £10. I am inclined to think that in a case of this kind, which involves the destruction of large quantities of valuable food, imprisonment without the option of a fine would be found more effective.

Insufficiency of funds to secure proper protection also prevails here, the amount received in 1872 and available for the purpose being only £91. Were it not that a number of additional bailiffs are employed by private individuals, the prospects of the district would not be encouraging; but from the fact that the heavy floods of last winter aided much in preservation, and the rivers having been exceedingly well stocked during the spawning season, I anticipate a more favourable report at the end of the present year.

3rd.—No. 6[2], Bantry.

This district contains the following salmon rivers:—

Adrigole.	Four-mile-water.
Ouvane or Ballylicky.	Glengarriffe.
Dunnemark.	Coomhola or Snave.

Their total length is about fifty-six miles, with a catchment basin of 118 miles; all small rivers, which afford excellent sport to the angler, and, considering their size, a fair amount of produce to the net-men; but commercially they cannot be regarded as very important in their present condition.

This district is capable of considerable improvement, if funds were forthcoming to secure thorough protection; but when the revenue derived from licence duties in 1872 amounted only to £17, it may be conceived that very little can be done in this way.

It is only surprising that the quantity of salmon captured should be as great as it is, under such circumstances.

The season of 1872 was, as in several other districts, less productive than the preceding year, in consequence of the excessive wetness of the season. The stock of breeding fish on the spawning beds much the same as in previous years.

In consequence of an application from the Board of Conservators for a change of season, a public inquiry was held at Bantry in October last. It was proved that the season opened at quite too early a period, which led to the destruction of large numbers of kelts or spent salmon; whilst by its closing so early for nets (15th September) it was believed that considerable quantities of good fish were lost to the public, as they were to be found at a period when it would be illegal to capture them.

In consequence of this the following changes were made, which I believe will be attended with good results:—Old season—angling, commenced 1st February, ended 1st November; nets and other engines, commenced 1st April, ended 15th September. New season—angling, to commence 16th March, to end 1st November; nets and other engines, to commence 30th April, to end 1st October.

This is a late district, few good fish being seen before March.

4th.—No. 6', Skibbereen.

In this district there are the following salmon rivers, viz.:—

Ilen.	Leamawadra.
Rowry.	Bawnaknockane.

The length of those rivers, including the Saivnose, the principal tributary of the Ilen, is about fifty miles; the catchment basin 155 miles.

The Ilen is the only considerable river in this district, having extensive and valuable tributaries, with a catchment basin of 116 miles.

It is very much to be regretted that night poaching prevails to a very serious extent, by means of lights and spears, during the spawning season. This is not suprising, when the funds of the district are capable of providing for the employment of only four water-bailiffs, and these not continuously throughout the year.

The pernicious system of poisoning rivers also prevails extensively here, as it appears that no less than nine convictions in the district for this offence took place during 1872.

Even under present circumstances the capture of fish by nets is very considerable, but with efficient preservation it might, in my opinion, be easily doubled.

There is excellent angling in the Ilen and Rowry, but quite late in the season.

In this district also, as in the Bantry, having last year received application to change the season, a public inquiry was held, at Skibbereen, and the same changes were made as in that district.

The quantity of fish captured in 1872 is reported to have been less than in the preceding year, the excessive rainfall of the season having prevented the successful working of the nets, the same as in the Bantry district.

5th. No. 5, Cork.

This district contains the following salmon rivers:—

Lee,	Owenacurra or Midleton,
Bandon,	Argideen.
Owenboy or Carrigaline,	

besides the Stock and Clashboy, which are of no importance.

The length of those principal rivers is over 170 miles, with tributaries of almost equal extent, and a catchment basin of 983 miles; the Lee alone possessing a length of fifty-five miles and tributaries of over 100 miles.

The Cork is an important and valuable district, and contributes considerably to the supply of salmon for the English markets, independently of local consumption, which is considerable, and it affords excellent sport to the angler.

As an angling river the Lee possesses a very high character, and in the tidal waters it affords means of subsistence to a considerable number of men who fish with nets, on their common law rights.

For some miles below Cork those nets may be seen constantly at work during the open season, and I regret to say also at times when not permitted by law, although every effort is made by the Board of Conservators to prevent the illegality. Want of funds to employ a sufficient staff of water-bailiffs prevents this being effectually done.

Complaints have been made of two weirs in the vicinity of Cork impeding the passage of salmon to the upper waters during the angling season, except in floods; these are the Waterworks weir and Carrygrohane. On the former a fish ladder was erected at an expense of £315 in 1868, under the superintendence of the late Special Commissioners, but unfortunately up to the present time it has proved of little value, as the salmon will not use it, whether from its being faulty in form or from the entrance to it being situated in the tail-race of Cork Waterworks and close to one of the wheels used for the purpose of pumping water for the supply of the city, it is difficult to determine. I fear, myself, that it can never be made a satisfactory salmon pass; but I am not without hope that before long those interested in the upper fisheries will make some efforts to have a fish ladder constructed on another part of the weir which will prove more successful, and which I believe can be accomplished without very great expense. I hope also that funds may be soon provided for the construction of a ladder in Carrygrohane weir.

Although the funds of the district are not at all sufficient to secure proper preservation, yet, as far as they would admit, every effort has been made by the Conservators to effect this object, and in this they have been aided considerably by an association, established in 1870, called the Cork Anglers' Club, got up by the resident gentry on the river, and mainly supported by them.

This society has expended considerable sums in payment of additional water-bailiffs, &c., &c., but one of the most useful works it has accomplished, out of its own funds, has been done during last summer, viz., hitching the various places on the upper waters, wherever it would be possible to take salmon by nets. This was, of course, done by permission of the riparian proprietors. Although these gentlemen neither used nor permitted the use of nets on the fresh water, yet hauls were frequently made by poachers; and it is believed large quantities of salmon have been thus illegally captured at all seasons of the year at night. The hitching it is expected will prevent this. I should explain that hitching is accomplished by piling very heavy stones in considerable heaps in the drafting pools, which prevents the successful working of nets, and I am informed that this has been done throughout the entire length of the Lee, which will give some idea of the work done. It is to be hoped that they will be carefully watched and kept in order.

Through the liberality of many of the proprietors on the Lee, the Anglers' Club offers to the general public excellent angling at a comparatively nominal cost; thus a stranger by taking out his licence in the Cork district for a single rod may have, by payment of £1 in addition, eight days' salmon fishing; sixteen days' for £2, and so on up to one month. The fishing, under the club rules, is limited to Tuesdays, Thursdays, and Fridays, the other days being reserved by the proprietors.

The Bandon River, next in importance in the district to the Lee, is a charming river, and produces considerable quantities of salmon. Up to the year 1866 the river was netted as far up as the town of Bandon, a distance of seventeen and a half miles from the sea, and including about four miles of the fresh-water portion of the river.

In that year, in consequence of the alleged great decrease in the stock of salmon in the river taking place year by year, and which it was believed was caused by over-netting, the late Special Commissioners made a by-law prohibiting the use of nets, for a period of three years, above a part of the river about seven miles below Bandon. At the end of that period an inquiry was held on the subject, and it was considered desirable to extend its operation for a further period of three years, which was done, and at the present moment a by-law is in progress further extending it for two years more; at the end of which time it will have been fully tested whether the by-law has had all the effects anticipated, and it should be easy to decide what course to adopt for the future.

In my opinion, although the principal part of the netting ground has been closed by the by-law, the capture of salmon is increasing year by year, and the quantity finding their way to the upper waters above Bandon has been very much greater since it came into operation; but I fear the preservation is by no means as satisfactory as it should be in the upper waters. The funds of the district are insufficient for the purpose; but with valuable rod fisheries extending for many miles above Bandon, it is surprising that means have not been taken in some way to supplement the funds—even the formation of an anglers' club, as on the Lee, would, I believe, prove successful if the same privileges were accorded to its subscribers as on that river, and the funds of the district might be thus considerably supplemented.

The Argideen and the other rivers in the Cork District at present are not of great importance, although it is possible that much might be done for their improvement if funds were available.

In consequence of an application for change of season, public inquiries were held last year at Cork, Macroom, Bandon, Kinsale, and Timoleague. It was specially requested that the quality of the salmon in the month of January should be tested, as it was alleged that they were then in fine condition; and in consequence my colleague, Mr. Blake, and I attended to see the nets drawn at the Brickfields in the river Lee below Cork, on 9th January, 1872. Six drafts were made, but not a fish was captured. The net-men urged that we should attend again on the following day, as they asserted that the condition of the water was then unfavourable. This request we complied with, but with the like results.

It was clearly shown at the inquiries that up to the middle of February the average number of good seasonable fish captured by rods was as one to eight or ten spent fish—in the latter part of the month the proportion of old fish would not be quite so great; and it was also proved that considerable quantities of old fish were captured by nets in February. It is well known in the district that both on the Bandon and Lee it was the general practice amongst anglers to kill every fish they could, whether seasonable or not. At the same time, it is but just to say that a few gentlemen anglers—genuine sportsmen—did not kill the spent fish unless compelled to do so from the way in which they had been hooked.

After carefully considering all the information it was possible to obtain bearing upon the question, it was considered desirable to make the following alteration in the close season throughout the district:—

The old close season was as follows:—

Electoral divisions A and C, between Ballycottin and Barry's Head, for nets and all engines save rods and lines.—A, tidal, 15th August to 16th February; C, fresh-water, 15th September to 1st April; angling with cross lines, between 9th October and 27th March.

Electoral divisions B and D, between Barry's Head and Galley Head, for nets and all engines save rods and lines.—B, tidal, between 31st August and 1st March; D, fresh-water, between 31st August and 1st April; angling with cross lines, between 15th October and 2nd April; single rods throughout the district, between 1st November and 1st February.

The new close season order, which is dated 10th June, 1872, is as follows:—

Throughout the district—nets and all engines save rods and lines, between 16th August and last day of February; single rods, between 1st November and last day of February.

Although dissatisfaction has been expressed by a few anglers at the change postponing the rod fishing until 1st March—some of them even allowing themselves to be carried away so far as to take out their rod licences in other districts, thus depriving their own of a portion of its legitimate funds—I feel convinced that experience will show that the change will prove beneficial in every way.

The fishing season of 1872 is reported to have been very good as far as the tidal fisheries are concerned, but not so with regard to single rods. It is difficult to account for the latter, as it was almost universally admitted that there was abundance of salmon in the rivers throughout the season.

6th.—No. 4, Lismore.

It may be said that this district consists of the River Blackwater alone, with its many tributaries, there being only one other in the district discharging into the sea—the Womanagh, a stream of no great importance.

The length of the Blackwater is over 100 miles, with tributaries considerably over double that length, and with a catchment basin of 1,284 miles. It is one of the most important rivers in Ireland, and contributes large quantities of salmon to the English markets, but in my opinion its produce is as nothing compared with what it would be if the spawning streams were preserved efficiently. Unfortunately, however, here as in the other districts, insufficiency of funds renders this impracticable.

In consequence of the prevalence of illegal fishing in the tidal waters it has been found necessary to employ there more water-bailiffs than would be otherwise required, thus depriving the upper streams of the benefit of as much protection as the funds would otherwise permit, and as a natural consequence considerably lessening the produce of the river.

Were it not for the valuable assistance of the Coastguards, aided at times by the services of a gunboat, for the last four seasons, the fisheries would be in a lamentable state, but I am glad to be able to say that matters are improving, and I trust will continue to do so, and thus permit of the funds being more profitably employed in guarding the spawning streams than in watching the lower waters.

The tidal waters are fished by means of drift, draft, and snap nets, besides which there are three stake weirs, and, just above the junction of the tidal and freshwaters, a stone weir at Lismore—these are situated in proprietary or several fisheries. From the river's mouth at Youghal, almost to Cappoquin, a distance of eighteen miles, the river is fished principally by poor net-men. About 500 are so employed during the season.

From Lismore up, including some of the tributaries, there is excellent angling.

Looking at the value of these rod fisheries, extending over many miles, it is remarkable that scarcely anything is done by the proprietors for the protection of the river, beyond paying for their angling licenses. It is reported that only four water-bailiffs are paid for by private individuals. If the parties whose interest it should be to preserve the river thoroughly, would unite for the purpose, the results would speedily become apparent by the increased value of all the fisheries, and I believe the proprietors of the upper waters would especially reap the advantage by the increased rents they would obtain for their rod fisheries, or by the increased sport, if retained in their own possession. Unfortunately the feeling of jealousy so common between those interested in the upper and the tidal waters, also prevails here to a great extent, but I trust is less strong now than formerly, and that eventually they may all see, that there should be but one interest in common between all parties.

The fishing season of 1872, in the tidal waters, is considered by competent authority to have been a fair average one, but in the upper waters the angling was not good. The quantity of spawning fish in the beds is reported to have been greater than in previous years.

7th.—No. 3, Waterford.

This district is the second in importance in Ireland, possessing many valuable rivers, the most important being—

Suir.
Nore.
Barrow.

These rivers have a total length of upwards of 320 miles, and with their tributaries, exceed 800 miles, and possess a catchment basin of over 3,500 miles. Besides these there are in this district the—

Brickey,	Mahon,
Colligan,	Owenduff,
Dalligan,	Corock,
Tay,	

which possess together a length of 99 miles, and a catchment basin of 288 miles.

Although immense quantities of salmon are annually captured, most of them being exported to England, yet, as in the preceding districts, the produce is not by any means commensurate with the producing power of the district, which will never be attained until sufficient funds are provided to secure more protection. A reference to the returns of salmon and trout conveyed from Waterford by two lines of steamers, at pages 68 and 69, will show that no less than 420 tons of salmon were shipped in 1872 for England at that port.

On the Suir much good has been done by the exertions of an association called the Suir Preservation Society, which has aided much in protecting the rivers and tributaries; besides this, in 1870 the society provided funds for the erection of fish ladders on two weirs at and above Cahir, which offered serious obstructions to the passage of salmon up the Suir. These ladders were constructed under the authority and superintendence of this department, and have proved most efficient.

The ascent of salmon on these rivers is much impeded by mill and other weirs. Very great good would result if means could be provided for aiding salmon in their ascent over these obstructions, for in general, where constructions in the shape of fish passes have been provided they have proved to be insufficient. I fear there is but little prospect of this, unless by a revision of the scale of licence duties, the Legislature should provide means by which the funds may be considerably increased.

The tidal waters are fished by means of weirs and nets. Of the latter, 194 are snap nets, 19 draft, and 78 drift nets. The nets are generally worked by poor men who fish on the common law-right; and there are over 1,100 so employed during the fishing season, their tidal fishing ground extending on the Suir to the town of Clonmel; on the Nore to Inistioge; and on the Barrow to St. Mullins.

Reports having reached this department as to illegal netting having been carried on between Inistioge and New Ross by parties fishing without licence, and also by the non-observance of the weekly close season, the question was investigated publicly at Kilkenny in November last, and it was considered that the allegations in a great measure were substantiated. The result was communicated to the Board of Conservators, and they have been urged to take special steps to put a stop to the illegal practices, and which I believe they will use their best efforts to accomplish.

Although the other rivers of the district might be made to contribute considerably to the supply of salmon, if money were forthcoming to have them preserved, at present they do but little in that way; nor is it to be expected they will without more funds than they now have.

The fishing season of 1872 is reported not to have been as good as in that of 1871. It is believed that the wet, boisterous weather had much to do with this. However, the rivers were more abundantly stocked with spawning fish in the breeding season, which is encouraging.

8th.—No. 2, Wexford.

The seaward bounds of this district are Kiln Bay, east of Bannow, to Wicklow, and contains the following salmon rivers—the Slaney, the Ownavarragh, and two or three other smaller streams.

The Slaney may be regarded as the salmon river of the district, the others being of very minor importance. It has a length of seventy-three miles, and tributaries to the length of over 100 miles, its catchment basin amounting to 680 miles.

The tideway extends from the sea to the town of Enniscorthy, a distance of about twenty miles and as in two-thirds of this the breadth of the channel of the river is inconsiderable, great facilities for the capture of salmon exist and which are fully availed of, there having been no less than forty-seven draft nets used constantly upon it during the last season.

Many complaints have been made to this department that the tideway is over-netted. These complaints have been accompanied by applications to restrict the operation of the nets to a shorter portion of the river, and during the present season the subject will be carefully investigated.

Although in 1870 changes were made deferring the opening of the season to a later period than existed previously, representations have been again made by Conservators and other gentlemen interested in the fisheries, that even now the season opens too early, and requesting a further change, to prevent the great destruction of spent fish which still takes place, although the fishing only commences on 1st March for rods, and 9th April for nets. It is proposed at an early period to investigate this subject, and, if necessary, to make further changes.

The other rivers of the district are comparatively unimportant and much neglected, the funds available for preservation being, as in other districts, totally insufficient.

The Ovoca, which I have not referred to, was once a valuable salmon river; but since the refuse water from the mines has flowed into it, all the fish have been completely destroyed, and it is now useless. This is much to be deplored, for, with its numerous streams, the principal of which cover a length of sixty-five miles, besides lesser ones, most of them admirably adapted for the production of salmon, and draining some 250 miles of country, it is easily understood what a loss has been sustained in their being rendered unproductive.

It should be a subject of serious regret to the proprietors on the river that when the mines were first established they did not compel the companies working them to provide means for carrying off the refuse mine-waters to the sea, instead of allowing them to pollute the river and destroy its valuable fisheries, the more especially as it was quite practicable to do so, but of course at some expense. I am not without hope that this may yet be done, and that this beautiful river, situated as it is in the midst of charming scenery, should yet add to the attractions of the locality by affording good sport to the angler, whilst at the same time adding to our markets an additional supply of valuable food.

Concluding Observations.

In the course of the year 1872 I have made inspections in almost every part of the division under my supervision, making inquiries as to the state of the fisheries in each locality, and I am glad to be able to say that notwithstanding the exceptionally unfavourable weather prevailing almost throughout the fishing season, and which militated most seriously against the successful working of the nets in tidal waters, I consider the capture of salmon during 1872 to have been on the whole but little under that of an average year.

Had we been favoured with moderate weather I am satisfied that in this division the take would have been highly satisfactory.

Rod fishing in 1872 almost throughout Ireland was unsuccessful; but this should not be attributed to scarcity of salmon in the upper waters, as the rivers were generally well stocked. I am inclined to think it was caused by the constant floods keeping the fish supplied with some kind of sustenance which we know nothing of. I must confess that I am somewhat sceptical as to a prevailing theory, that salmon never feed in fresh water, having frequently witnessed their capture by means of bait of various kinds—bunches of worms, collies, shrimps, &c. That they swallow bait I am certain, for I have seen them killed by worm baits, and hooked far down in the intestines.

Some persons attribute the ill-success attending fly fishing to the practice now becoming common of using bait instead of artificial flies. They assert that when various kinds of bait are constantly used the salmon will not readily rise to the fly, and this may probably be true.

I have remarked in my observations on the different districts upon the difficulty of securing proper protection in consequence of the funds derived from licence duties being insufficient. It is impossible that I can too strongly comment upon this. I consider that even if doubled they would be insufficient. Money is not alone wanting to pay water bailiffs and other necessary officers, it is wanted to enable the conservators to secure that every weir or dam should have a thoroughly effective fish pass or ladder upon it, to remove obstructions, and to improve the spawning beds; the latter are capable of great improvement; they should be occasionally, when the water is low, cleansed and forked so as to loosen the gravel to a considerable depth, and I believe it would be easy in some places to add to their number by depositing gravel in suitable places, thus creating additional spawning beds.

If funds could be provided to secure this I am satisfied we should soon see the supply of salmon largely increased, if not doubled.

How this is to be accomplished it is difficult to say; a revision of the licence duties would do something, but much more than this is required. I can only express the hope that eventually means may be devised which will secure the desired ends.

Under existing circumstances I consider that our Inland Fisheries are as prosperous as we can expect—they are steadily increasing in value, which may be reasonably inferred by a glance at the following summary of the number of men employed (exclusive of Rod Fishers) and the amount received for licence duties for each year from 1862 to 1872 inclusive, viz. :—

	No. of Men	Amount of Licence Duty
1862,	7,229	£5,416
1863,	7,073	5,892
1864,	7,877	7,001
1865,	8,670	6,722
1866,	8,173	7,098
1867,	7,940	7,317
1868,	7,356	7,033
1869,	7,024	6,700
1870,	7,733	7,511
1871,	8,463	8,865
1872,	8,146	8,098

The size of the fish has largely increased in many districts, and is still increasing—in the Cork, Lismore, and Waterford districts especially.

This, together with the satisfactory reports received as to the stock of breeding fish in the spawning streams during the winter, I think fully justifies me in expressing the belief that we have every reason to anticipate a continuance of prosperity, although not at all to the extent to which our fisheries are capable if they were treated as they deserve to be.

JOS. HAYES.

As the foregoing contain all the necessary details respecting each district, we have only now in conclusion to say that we would again respectfully bring to your Excellency's notice the recommendation contained in our last report upon the subject of new legislation, as we consider it of importance in the interests of the salmon fisheries that they should be carried out.

The constabulary and coastguard have aided much in the preservation of the fisheries and in enforcing the laws. It is only to be regretted that the assistance of the former is now very much curtailed through a legal difficulty which we should much desire to see removed.

We have the honour to be,

Your Excellency's obedient servants,

J. ALOYSIUS BLAKE.
THOS. F. BRADY.
JOS. HAYES.

ALAN HORNSBY, *Secretary.*

Office of Irish Fisheries,
12, *Ely-place, Dublin,*
18*th April,* 1873.

APPENDIX.

APPENDIX,

STATE of the REGISTRY of FISHING VESSELS on the COAST

No.	Name of Division.	Boundaries.	Registering Officer.	1st Class employed in 1872.			2nd Class employed in 1872.			3rd Class employed in 1872.			Total employed in 1872.		
				Vessels.	Men.	Boys.	Vessels.	Men.	Boys.	Vessels.	Men.	Boys.	Vessels.	Men.	Boys.
1	Dublin, .	Howth to Greystones, .	J. F. Lemon, Commander, R.N.	93	388	91	72	303	29	56	183	19	221	874	139
2	Arklow, .	From the breaches three miles north of Five-mile-point Station, county Wicklow, to the sluices three miles south of Cahore Station, county Wexford.	Vincent Williams, Commander, R.N.	3	21	–	295	1,684	20	60	201	8	358	1,906	28
3	Wexford, .	Mizen Castle to Bannow, county Waterford.	Henry E. Stephens, Commander, R.N.	24	134	–	228	1,060	8	56	229	–	308	1,423	8
4	Waterford, .	From East Bank of Bannow Ferry, county Wexford, to Ballyvoile Head, north of Dungarvan Harbour, county Waterford.	William B. Stubbs, Commander, R.N.	11	34	10	141	460	5	48	137	1	200	631	16
5	Youghal, .	From Ballyvoile Bridge, county Waterford, to Garryvoe (in Ballycotton Bay), county Cork.	John H. B. Cooper, Commander, R.N.	7	30	3	110	394	18	64	258	–	181	682	21
6	Queenstown,	From Garryvoe (in Ballycotton Bay), westward to Ringabella Bay, including Queenstown Harbour, county Cork.	Thomas Hayes, Acting Divisional Officer.	8	41	1	81	320	8	107	306	35	196	667	44

No. 1.

of IRELAND from 1st January, 1872, to 1st January, 1873.

Total employed in 1871			Total Increase since 1871.			Total Decrease since 1871.			Substance of Observations made by Inspecting Commanders of Coast Guards, and other Registering Officers, up to the 1st January, 1873.	No.
Vessels.	Men.	Boys.	Vessels.	Men.	Boys.	Vessels.	Men.	Boys.		
237	1002	151	–	–	–	6	85	12	The fisheries in this district cannot be said to be improving, they are about at a stand-still. The descriptions of fish most largely captured are herrings and cod. When not employed fishing, the boats are generally laid up, except in some few cases where they are used as pleasure boats. No portion of coast unguarded. There are no public oyster beds in this division. Steps have been taken to mark the ground licensed for the establishment of private beds. The quality of oysters is very good, price about 6s. to 8s. a hundred, about £4,000 worth sold last year. There is a curing establishment at Howth, which has been successful. There is no curing carried on by individual fishermen. No instances of conflicts between persons pursuing different modes of fishing have occurred. The fishermen are generally very orderly. No spirit of emigration prevailing amongst the fishermen. They do not generally combine farming with fishing. The modes of fishing practised are drift net, trawling, and long line. The number of trawlers in this division is gradually increasing. The means of transit to market for sale of fish is good. Large shoals of herrings and mackerel appeared off this portion of the coast, and there were adequate means for their capture. Has no suggestions to offer with reference to the improvement of the fisheries.	1
232	1,436	34	10	70	–	–	–	6	No portion of coast in this division unguarded. No perceptible improvement in the condition of the fisheries. The principal fish captured are herrings, cod, and codling. Oysters are dredged in large quantities off Arklow, Kilmichael, Ballymoney, Courtown, and Cahore. Salmon and white trout are taken along the coast—sometimes in large quantities in Wicklow Bay, but last season not good. There are public oyster beds from Mizen Head to south extreme of division. Oyster fisheries are not improving. Cannot say whether spatting last year was better or worse than previous year. No new natural banks have been lately discovered. No private beds exist. Quality of oysters good; prices from 16s. to 20s. per barrel. Cannot ascertain amount realized by sales last year, as no general accounts kept, and buyers have left Arklow, where nearly all sales take place. At Courtown Harbour the following sales took place last year, viz.:—Oysters £376, herrings, £[illegible], and cod, £[illegible]. No curing establishments in this division. At Kilmichael and Ballymoney cure fish for their own consumption. At Courtown and Cahore there are some times large quantities cured by individual fishermen. No conflicts have occurred between persons pursuing different modes of fishing; the fishermen are generally very orderly. No spirit of emigration exists here, the fishermen prefer remaining at home if able to procure a livelihood. At Arklow and to the northward they combine piloting and coasting with fishing. South of Arklow—especially about Courtown and Cahore—fishermen farm small holdings. The modes of fishing practised are:—At Wicklow, herring fishing, long line for cod and codling, seines for salmon and white trout. At Kilmichael, herring fishing and oyster dredging. At Ballymoney and Courtown, herring fishing and oyster dredging, long line for cod and codling—cod fishing very successful at times, but not this year, the weather being unfavourable. At Cahore herring fishing, long line for cod and codling. The only trawling carried on in district is by Courtown fishermen, who occasionally trawl in from four to eight fathoms. The means of transit are very good, as there is direct communication with Dublin, Wicklow and Wexford Railway from all ports where fish are landed. Large shoals of herrings frequent coast from June to November. Fair means exist for their capture, but weather unaccountably bad last season and consequently fishery unsuccessful, as boats could not put to sea. Mackerel have been in Wicklow Bay this year in large quantities, but fishermen showed no energy in their capture, preferring long-line fishing for inferior codling. Pilchards have not appeared off coast. With regard to improvement of fisheries, may mention that the harbour of Arklow (being the principal fishery port) requires much repair; boats cannot enter it in unfavourable weather, and are obliged to run for Wicklow, away from their homes and fishing grounds, in consequence of bar and bad entrance. The piers of harbour require extending. The same state of things is applicable also to Courtown Harbour, which is in a very bad condition, boats are frequently prevented from entering it, and are obliged to go to Arklow with their fish, and find it difficult to get in there.	2
240	1,880	32	68	384	–	–	–	14	No portions of coast in the division unguarded. Condition of fisheries improving; but, owing to unfavourable weather, fishermen not successful. Descriptions most largely captured—turbot, sole, plaice, cod, pollock, bream, and herrings. Natural oyster banks exist at Wexford and Ballyteige, supply almost exhausted. Spatting last season much the same as previous year. No new natural banks have been discovered. No private beds in this division. Quality of oysters fair; price from 4s. to 10s. per hundred from public beds, amount realized by sales during year about £750. No curing establishments exist. No actual conflicts have taken place amongst persons pursuing different modes of fishing, but great dissatisfaction was caused by parties trawling in the herring season within the limits. Fishermen are generally orderly. No spirit of emigration prevailing. Many of coast fishermen hold on an average about three acres of ground each, those living in or near town have small gardens. Modes of fishing practised are—trawl, seine, long and hand lines, dredges, and nets. Number of trawlers not increased. Means of transit to market for sale of fish good. No large shoals of fish have appeared off this portion of coast during the year. Sixteen public oyster beds are in such an exhausted condition that it would be desirable to buoy or mark off a portion on which no fishing should be allowed for a time.	3
186	602	28	4	49	–	–	–	18	No portion of coast in division unguarded. No improvement in the general condition of fisheries. Descriptions of fish most largely captured—mackerel, soles, sprats, plaice, turbot, cod, and ling. No public oyster fisheries exist in district. Oyster fisheries not improving. No improvement in spatting last season. No new natural banks have lately been discovered. Not aware of any steps having been taken to mark ground licensed for establishment of private beds. General quality of oysters indifferent, prices from 6s. to 8s. per hundred. Cannot say what amount was realized by sales during past year. No curing establishments exist. Not aware of curing being carried on by individual fishermen. No conflicts have occurred between persons pursuing different modes of fishing. Fishermen are generally very orderly, when not employed fishing, generally engaged tilling their ground, collecting seaweed, &c. No spirit of emigration prevailing, fishermen would prefer remaining at home if able to follow fishing pursuits adequately. The modes of fishing practised are—hand-line, seine, drift net and trawling. The number of trawlers slightly increased. Means of transit to market for sale of fish good. Large quantities of mackerel appeared off coast during year. Considers adequate means exist for their capture. Has no suggestions to offer as to improvement of fisheries.	4
194	631	25	57	41	–	–	–	7	A portion of coast from Glenville to Ballycotton unguarded. No improvement in general condition of fisheries. Descriptions of fish most largely captured—salmon, cod, hake, ling, sprat, mackerel. No oyster fisheries in district. No curing establishments exist. Is not aware of curing being carried on by individual fishermen. No conflicts have occurred between persons pursuing different modes of fishing. The fishermen are generally orderly. A spirit of emigration still prevails, but fishermen would prefer remaining at home if able adequately to follow fishing pursuits. The modes of fishing practised—seining, trammel and salmon nets, hand lines and trawling. The number of trawlers increasing. Means of transit to market for sale of fish good. Shoals of herrings and mackerel have appeared off portions of coast. Means of capture inadequate. Fishermen require means to obtain proper gear and appliances for boats, &c.	5
189	705	28	7	–	16	–	35	–	No portion of coast unguarded. Condition of fisheries not improving. Descriptions most largely captured—hake, cod, ling, eel, bream, pollock, whiting, sole, plaice, sprat, and. Oyster fisheries in district not improving. Natural beds exist off East Ferry. Spatting worse last year than previous year. No new natural banks have been discovered. Steps have been taken to mark ground licensed for establishment of private beds. Quality of oysters good; price about 8s. per 100. Cannot ascertain amount realized by sales during year. No curing establishments exist. Fish all sold fresh. No conflicts have occurred between persons pursuing different modes of fishing. Fishermen generally orderly. A spirit of emigration still prevails, but fishermen would prefer remaining at home if able to follow fishing pursuits adequately. Modes of fishing practised—trammel, seine, long line, hand line, and trawling. Number of trawlers not increased. Means of transit to market for sale of fish good. Large shoals of sprat appeared off coast during year, but means of capture inadequate. Suggests the utility of a market or mole at Ballycotton, it being the principal fishing place in division.	6

STATE of the REGISTRY of FISHING VESSELS on the COAST.

No.	Name of Division.	Boundaries.	Registering Officers.	1st Class employed in 1872.			2nd Class employed in 1872.			3rd Class employed in 1872.			Total employed in 1872.		
				Vessels.	Men.	Boys	Vessels.	Men.	Boys	Vessels	Men	Boys	Vessels.	Men	Boys
7	Kinsale, .	From Myrtleville Point East, to Galley Head West, county Cork.	W. Nelson, Acting Divisional Officer	41	310	21	130	770	14	200	1,060	82	437	2,135	117
8	Skibbereen, .	From Galley Head to Snave Bridge at the head of Bantry Bay, county Cork.	E. H. Hartwell, Commander, R.N.	11	66	4	196	964	76	237	925	28	443	1,955	110
9	Castletown Berehaven.	From Snave Bridge, county Cork, to Kenmare Bridge, county Kerry.	William Vicary, Lieutenant, R.N.	1	3	1	6	30	–	260	1,173	26	267	1,206	27
10	Killarney, .	From Kenmare (S.), to Blennerville Bridge (N.), county Kerry.	P. Mahony, Divisional Officer	11	30	8	112	540	3	341	1,520	30	465	2,100	40
11	Ballyheigue,	From Blennerville Bridge, Tralee (S.W.), county Kerry, to Glin (E.), county Limerick.	Mr. W. Dalsh, .	1	3	–	35	96	2	114	422	2	150	521	4

No. 1—*continued.*

of Ireland from 1st January, 1872, to 1st January, 1873.

Total employed in 1871.			Total Increase since 1871.			Total Decrease since 1871.			Substance of Observations made by Inspecting Commanders of Coast Guards and other Registering Officers, up to the 1st January, 1873.
Vessels.	Men.	Boys.	Vessels.	Men.	Boys.	Vessels.	Men.	Boys.	
447	2,069	147	10	87	–	–	–	30	Portion of coast in this division unguarded extends from Flat Head (Oyster Haven, East) to Nohoval Cove, West, four miles. General condition of fisheries not improving. Descriptions most largely captured at various stations in division are—Robert's Cove, principally bream and cod; Oyster Haven—bream, cod, mackerel, and pilchards (occasionally). Upper Cove—hake and ling are most largely taken, except in [illegible] season when large quantities of the latter are captured, and there is sometimes a good catch of pilchards; Old Head—cod, hake, and bream, and sometimes large quantities of pilchards but fishermen have not means to provide tackle for capturing the latter, and have no knowledge of curing them. Garretstown—bream and cod, and occasionally sprats. Courtmacsherry—mackerel, sprats, ling, cod, plaice, soles, and pilchards; Barry's Cove—hake and bream principally. Dunny Cove—hake, bream, cod, ling, and pollock. Natural oyster banks exist at Bandon River; they are not improving. Has no idea as to whether spatting was better or worse this season than previous year. No new natural banks discovered. No private beds exist in division. Quality of oysters good. Price about 4s. per hundred at Kinsale only. Has no idea of amount realized by sale during year. A curing establishment exists at Courtmacsherry, none in any other portion of division. Fishermen cure a little for their own consumption. No conflicts have occurred between persons pursuing different modes of fishing. Fishermen generally very orderly and peaceable. In general a spirit of emigration does not prevail. Fishermen would prefer remaining at home if fully employed. They generally combine farming with fishing. Modes of fishing practised are, long and hand lines, seines, mackerel and herring nets, trammels, salmon nets and spillets. There are a few trawlers at Upper Cove and Courtmacsherry. Means of transit to market for sale of fish are, in general, good. Large shoals of fish appeared off this portion of coast during year. Means of capture inadequate, unless when fish very close to shore. States that some means should be adopted for compelling the owners of fishing boats to submit their registers for examination by Coast Guard, as directed by Order in Council. Generally speaking they do not comply with regulations, unless Coast Guard are continually calling upon them to do so.
927	3,441	233	–	–	–	184	1,480	123	A portion of coast of this division unguarded, viz.:—From Three Castle Head to Carbery Island in Dunmanus Bay, and the eastern shore of Bantry Bay from Sheep Head to Snave Bridge, including Whiddy Island. Condition of fisheries not improving. Hake and ling most largely captured, mackerel, cod, bream, pilchards, and herrings in lesser quantities. Lobsters and crayfish in considerable quantities. Cod, soles, turbot, very scarce, but the latter very fine. A few natural oyster banks exist in estuary of [illegible] River and [illegible] River. No improvement in supply. Spatting same as previous year. No new natural banks have been discovered. Dr. [illegible], of Durrus, has stocked some portion of the ground in Roaring Water Bay for which he obtained a license. Quality of oysters fair. Price 4s. per hundred from public beds. Quantity sold during year less than 10,000. No curing establishment exists. Not much curing carried on by individual fishermen. No conflicts have occurred between persons pursuing different modes of fishing. Fishermen generally orderly. There has been less emigration this year than last, probably owing to the new Land Act. Fishermen generally combine farming with fishing. Modes of fishing practised—seine and trammel nets, long and hand lines. Trawling is practised by those boats belonging to Bantry at [illegible] and Union Hall, to which places the Cork hookers sometimes resort for same purpose. The means of transit for the fish to market are bad. Large shoals of pilchards and mackerel, but not many herrings, have appeared off coast during year, but means of capture inadequate. Considers that with proper means and appliances for capture and curing of pilchards a fishery would be successful. These fish were taken in such quantities last year in Bantry Bay (even with the limited means at command for their capture) as to be frequently sold as low as 6d. a hundred. Considers that the erection of a light on Mizen Island would be of great benefit to the Mizen fishermen, when engaged fishing in the months of March, April, and May; their chief fishing grounds being off the Galley Head, the light would be of great use to them in making Crookhaven Harbour, when forced by threatening weather to seek refuge there, and thus save them a much longer run off their ground to Kinsale.
931	3,416	173	–	–	–	411	1,206	146	Portion of coast of this division unguarded, viz., from Snave Bridge to Mill Cove, and from Ardgroom to Kenmare Bridge. Condition of fisheries not improving. Description most largely captured are herrings. No oyster fisheries in this division. No curing establishments exist. No conflicts have occurred between persons pursuing different modes of fishing. Fishermen generally orderly. A spirit of emigration still prevails. Fishermen would not be likely to prefer remaining at home, even though they were able to follow fishing pursuits adequately. They generally combine farming with fishing. Herrings are taken with seine nets. No trawling carried on. Means of transit of fish to market [illegible] good. No large shoals of herrings, mackerel, or pilchards have appeared off coast during past year. Has no suggestions to offer as to improvements of fisheries.
367	1,032	174	96	576	–	–	–	134	Portion of coast of this division unguarded, viz., from [illegible] Head to [illegible] River, including Blasket Sound and Islands, Brandon Head to Blennerville Bridge, north shore of Castlemaine Harbour. This year's fishing of all kinds has been very bad, and the worst the fishermen have experienced for many years. Descriptions of fish most largely captured are—cod, ling, hake, pollock, cod, herrings, mackerel, pilchards, bream, whiting, eels, and plaice. One natural oyster bank exists in Kenmare River. The supply about the same as last year. Spatting about the same. No new natural banks have been discovered. Mr. R. Mahony, of Dromore, has purchased 100,000 oysters part of which are laid down on his licensed ground; and Mr. C. Bland, of Derreen, is also arranging to lay down a large quantity. Quality of oysters good, price 7s. per thousand. Amount realized by sale during year, up to 10th December, 1872—£273 17s. 6d. No curing establishments exist in the division. A large quantity is cured by individual fishermen, especially at Portmagee and Dingle. The farmer fishermen also cure a good deal for their own consumption. No conflicts have taken place between persons pursuing different modes of fishing. The fishermen are most orderly. The spirit of emigration is not now so great as in former years. It would be a strong inducement that would keep the fishermen at home if they had the means to be so. They all combine farming with fishing. The modes of fishing practised are—trawling, long and hand lines, trammel and seine nets. The number of trawlers has decreased three during the past year. The means of transit of fish to market are very indifferent. On a few occasions some large shoals of herrings, mackerel, pilchards, pollock, and cod have been seen during the year, but the weather was in general very unfavourable for going after them. The means of capture are inadequate for large quantities. A ready means of disposing of the fish in a fresh state by the formation of local companies with curing establishments would be an inducement to greater exertion, for there is plenty of room for improvement, and when large quantities are captured the greater part is left on the poor man's hands, who having to borrow money to purchase salt rather than lose the fish, their profits are lost, and consequently a "hand to mouth" system of fishing is the policy generally followed.
31	138	3	99	309	2	–	–	–	The unguarded portions of coast in this division extend from Blennerville Bridge to Spa (in Tralee Bay) [illegible] W. from [illegible] to [illegible], and from Leck Castle to Ballylongford. No improvement in general condition of fisheries. Descriptions of fish most largely captured—herrings, mackerel, cod, and whiting. Natural oyster banks exist at Tarbert, Clonderalaw Bay, [illegible] and Tralee Bay. Supply of oysters improving in Tralee Bay only. Spatting last season in Tralee Bay better than previous year. No new natural banks have been discovered. No steps have been taken to stock ground licensed for establishment of private beds. Quality of oysters good. Average price 4s. per hundred from public beds. There is no reliable source for ascertaining amount realized by sales during year. No curing establishments exist in this division. A slight altercation took place in Tralee Bay between the resident fishermen and a boat's crew from Cork, owing to the wish of the latter to work with a large dredge, winch and anchors. The Cork men have since returned home. Fishermen in the division generally orderly. A spirit of emigration still prevails. The fishermen would not be likely to prefer remaining at home, even though they could follow fishing pursuits adequately. They invariably combine farming with fishing. Modes of fishing practised—dredging for oysters; nets for mackerel, herrings and pilchards; hand lines and spillets for

APPENDIX,

STATE of the REGISTRY of FISHING VESSELS on the COAST

No.	Name of Division.	Boundaries.	Registering Officer.	1st Class employed in 1872.			2nd Class employed in 1872.			3rd Class employed in 1872.			Total employed in 1872.		
				Vessels.	Men.	Boys.	Vessels.	Men.	Boys.	Vessels.	Men.	Boys.	Vessels.	Men.	Boys.
12	Seafield, .	From Ballymacrevan Point, South, to Lackglass Head, North, county Clare.	W. H. Wright, Divisional Officer.	–	–	–	–	–	–	184	460	5	184	460	5
13	Galway, .	From Lackglass Head, county Clare, to Mace Head, county Galway.	John C. Drew, Lieutenant, R.N.	9	32	9	234	676	18	100	207	8	343	915	35
14	Clifden, .	From Mason Island, county Galway, to Roonagh, county Mayo.	James Pearson, Acting Divisional Officer.	31	64	1	384	801	11	824	2,363	10	1,220	3,228	22
15	Keel, . .	Doonbeg Head, East, to Deona Head, West, county Mayo.	Robert Geo. Gibbon, Inspecting Officer.	–	–	–	8	13	3	228	446	40	236	459	43
16	Belmullet, .	From Doohooma Head to Butter Point, county Mayo.	Duke Yonge, Lieutenant, R.N.	–	–	–	–	–	–	429	1,536	37	429	1,536	37

No. 1—*continued.*

of Ireland from 1st January, 1872, to 1st January, 1873.

Total employed in 1872.			Total Increase since 1871.			Total Decrease since 1871.			Substance of Observations made by Inspecting Commanders of Coast Guard and other Registering Officers, up to the 1st January, 1873.	No.
Vessels	Men	Boys	Vessels	Men	Boys	Vessels	Men	Boys		
									ground fish. Trawling not practised. Means of transit for fish to market good. Several large shoals of mackerel fish reported as seen off the coast of mouth of Shannon [illegible] as far up the river as Scattery Island. Adequate means do not exist for the capture of fish appearing in quantities off coast. The only suggestions he can offer for improvement of fisheries are those already stated in preceding years, viz., the adoption of some measures to enable the fishermen to increase the size of their boats, and to provide them with proper gear, and so allow them to prosecute their callings at a greater distance from their immediate residences. At present they are more farmers than fishermen.	
219	647	–	–	–	5	65	187	–	The unguarded portions of coast in this division extend from Kilkee to Loop Head, Poulnasherry Bay to Lough Donnell, Annagh Bridge to Green Island, Ballyvaughan, at Cape Craggan, to Lockstone Head. General condition of fisheries about the same as last year. Descriptions of fish most largely captured—ling, pollock, mackerel, pilchards, plaice, cod. A natural oyster bank exists extending from Aylevaroo Point to Bannerd Point, River Shannon. Supply of oysters not improving. Spatting worse last season than previous year. No new natural banks have been discovered. No steps have been taken to stock ground licensed for the establishment of private beds. Price of oysters 6s. a hundred. Amount realized by sales last year very small, as so few oysters taken, and those generally go to Limerick by steamer. No curing establishments exist in division. A few individual fishermen cure for their own consumption. No conflicts have occurred between persons pursuing different modes of fishing. Fishermen are generally very quiet and orderly. A spirit of emigration prevails generally in the spring; as this coast is so rough and exposed, and fishing pursuits consequently so uncertain, does not think fishermen could be induced to remain at home, many of them having already friends in America. The resident fishermen generally combine farming with fishing. Modes of fishing practised—nets and lines. No trawling practised. Means of transit for fish to market good. Fish generally bought on beach [illegible], and sold in the various towns. Off some parts of coast quantities of pilchards and mackerel have appeared during the year. Adequate means exist for their capture. Has no suggestions to offer for improvement of fisheries on this is such a dangerous coast in stormy weather.	12
306	1,308	36	–		–	24	288	1	The unguarded portions of coast in this division extend from Kinvarra to Galway, and from Greatman's Bay to Mace Head. Condition of fisheries not improving. Descriptions most largely captured are—herrings, mackerel, cod, hake, ling, and whiting. A natural oyster bank exists at Greatman's Bay; supply not improving. Does not know if spatting was better or worse last season than previous year. No new natural banks have been discovered. Steps have been taken to stock ground licensed for establishment of private beds. General quality of oysters fair; price about 5s. per hundred. Cannot correctly ascertain amount realized by sales during year. No curing establishments exist in this division, but on the Arran Islands individuals cure a good deal of fish. Conflicts have taken place between Claddagh fishermen and trawlers, the reason assigned being that the mode of capture practised by the latter destroys the spawn and young fry. Experiments are being carried on by Coast guard monthly to ascertain if trawling is injurious. Spirit of emigration still prevails. Does not think fishermen would remain at home even though fully employed. They generally combine farming with fishing. Modes of fishing practised are—hand lines, spillers, seine and drift nets. Number of trawlers not increased. Means of transit to market for sale of fish good. Large shoals of herrings and mackerel have appeared off this portion of coast. Means of capture [illegible]. Considers fisheries would be benefited by loans to fishermen to enable them to buy new boats and nets.	13
1,210	3,973	83	119	–	–	–	746	11	Unguarded portion of coast in this division about 162 miles in length, viz.:—[illegible] to [illegible] Bridge, twenty-one and a half miles; [illegible] Point to [illegible] Bridge, twelve and three-quarter miles; [illegible] Pier to Belmullet, seven miles; [illegible] Head to [illegible] Bay, twelve miles; [illegible] Bridge to [illegible] Island, six miles; [illegible] to [illegible] Bay, five miles; [illegible] Point to Croagh Island, four miles; Mouth of Killeries to [illegible] Head, [illegible] miles; [illegible] Head to [illegible], eight miles; and [illegible] to [illegible], [illegible] miles. Condition of fisheries not improving. Descriptions most largely captured are—cod, ling, bream, and pollock. Public oyster banks exist in Newport and Westport Bays; supply much the same as previous year. Spatting not so good this season as previous year. No new natural banks have been discovered. In some cases steps have been taken to stock ground licensed for establishment of private beds. Quality of oysters very good. States that Mr. [illegible] purchased 1,500 barrels from public beds, at £3 4s. per barrel, which he sent to England for stocking beds; he also purchased 1000 during this year for stocking his bed in Westport Bay. Mr. [illegible] also sent to England 700 barrels which he had bought at £3 4s. per barrel, he also purchased during the season 400 barrels from public beds at the same price, for stocking his bed at [illegible], in Newport Bay. About 3,000 bushels of oysters of very good description were sold from private beds at [illegible], at £1 10s. per bushel. A curing establishment exists on the island of Bofin, which has been pretty successful. No conflicts have occurred between persons pursuing different modes of fishing. Fishermen are generally orderly. A spirit of emigration still prevails. Does not think fishermen would remain at home even though they were able to follow fishing pursuits adequately. They generally combine farming with fishing. Nets and lines are the principal means of capture. No trawling practised. Means of transit to market for sale of fish in some cases very good, and in others the reverse. No large shoals of fish have appeared off this portion of coast during year. Considers adequate means exist for capture of such fish as appear in quantity. Has no suggestions to offer for improvement of sea fisheries.	14
251	903	44	–	–	–	15	234	1	Portion of this division unguarded, viz.—Clare Island, about eighteen miles in circumference. There are no fishermen on this island. No improvement whatever in the fisheries in this district. The descriptions of fish captured are—herrings, mackerel, gurnet, cod, and ling; but the quantities taken of each are very small. Public oyster banks exist in Achill Sound and near [illegible] Coast guard Station. There is a slight improvement in the supply this year. The spatting appears to have been a trifle better this season than previous year. No new natural banks have been discovered. No steps have been taken to stock ground licensed for the establishment of private beds. Quality of oysters indifferent; price about 3s. 6d. per hundred. About £1,000 realized by sales of oysters taken in Achill Sound within the year. No curing establishments exist, and only a small quantity of fish cured by individual fishermen. No conflicts have occurred between persons pursuing different modes of fishing. The fishermen are a quiet, orderly and inoffensive class. The spirit of emigration prevails to such an extent amongst fishermen and coast population, that it is doubtful whether full employment would induce them to remain at home; the want of means is all that keeps them from going. Modes of fishing, long and hand lines. Trawling not practised. Means of transit for fish to market are very bad in this locality. Several shoals of fish appeared off coast this year, but they were so far from shore that coast population were unable to capture them. Has no suggestions to offer for improvement of fisheries.	15
610	4,614	13	12	24	25	–	–	–	The unguarded portion of this division extends from [illegible] River to [illegible]—about two and a half miles. Condition of fisheries slightly improved. Descriptions of fish most largely captured—herrings, whiting, cod and [illegible]. Natural oyster banks exist at the following places, viz.:—Two in Tramore Bay, one in Broadhaven Bay, and two in [illegible] Bay, no improvement in supply. Spatting about the same as previous year. No new natural banks have been discovered. No steps have been taken to stock ground licensed for establishment of private beds. Price from £1 5s. to £1 10s. per barrel. Amount realized by sales during year about £1,300. No curing establishments in this division. All fish sold in local markets. No conflicts have occurred between persons pursuing different modes of fishing. Fishermen generally orderly. A spirit of emigration prevails, but fishermen would be likely to prefer remaining at home if able to follow fishing pursuits adequately. They generally combine farming with fishing. Modes of fishing practised—lines and nets. No trawlers in this division. Means of transit of fish to market for sale fair. No railway accommodation within forty miles. Large shoals of mackerel have appeared off coast during year. Adequate means exist for their capture. Considers that curing establishments would benefit the fisheries, as roads are so bad it takes a long time to send fish in a fresh state any distance.	16

State of the Registry of Fishing Vessels on the Coast

Boundaries.	Registering Officer.	1st Class employed in 1872.			2nd Class employed in 1872.			3rd Class employed in 1872.			Total employed in 1872.		
		Vessels.	Men.	Boys.	Vessels.	Men.	Boys.	Vessels.	Men.	Boys.	Vessels.	Men.	Boys.
From Brandy Point to Gap of Bartragh Island, county Mayo.	H. S. Mandeville, Lieut., R.N.	–	–	–	1	2	–	168	900	4	169	902	4
Bartragh Island, county Mayo, to Coney's Island, county Sligo.	R Bones, Divisional Officer.	–	–	–	–	–	–	56	270	–	56	270	–
Strandhill Barracks, co. Sligo, to Donegal Abbey, county Donegal.	George T. Merrell, Lieut., R.N.	1	5	–	56	266	15	136	690	23	193	961	38
Donegal-quay to Lower Ferry, East, co. Donegal.	Francis Osburn, Lieutenant, R.N.	–	–	–	91	476	66	188	973	101	279	1,449	167
Gweebarra Bar to Whale Head, Lough Swilly, county Donegal.	E. C. Ball, Divisional Officer.	–	–	–	106	447	15	169	334	42	277	781	57

No. 1—*continued.*

of IRELAND from 1st January, 1872, to 1st January, 1873.

Total employed in 1871.			Total Increase since 1871.			Total Decrease since 1871.			Substance of Observations made by Inspecting Commanders of Coast Guards and other Registering Officers, up to the 1st January, 1873.	No.
Vessels.	Men.	Boys.	Vessels.	Men.	Boys.	Vessels.	Men.	Boys.		
193	1,236	11	–	–	–	33	334	7	All portions of coast in this division guarded. Condition of fisheries about the same as previous year. Descriptions of fish most largely captured are—pollock, red and gray gurnet, soles, hake, and codling. During the autumn months some herrings and mackerel were taken with nets. No public oyster banks exist in this division. There are two private beds belonging to Sir A. K. Gore, situated at Moyne and Cortoon, but the oysters are not sold; and one at Kilcummin, the property of W. Little, Esq., which has been stocked, but not yet dredged. Ground licensed to Wm. M'Cormick, Esq., Summer hill, has not yet been stocked. No new natural banks have been discovered. No curing establishments in this division. Fish is chiefly sold in a fresh state, except when individual fishermen cure some for their own consumption. No conflicts have occurred between persons pursuing different modes of fishing. Fishermen are generally very orderly. A spirit of emigration prevails amongst the fishermen, who would, however, be likely to prefer remaining at home if able to follow fishing pursuits adequately. They generally combine farming with fishing. Modes of fishing practised—long lines and spillers, and nets for herring and mackerel. Only one trawler on this part of the coast, belonging to Galway [illegible], but he does not sell the fish, and only trawls occasionally for his own amusement. Fish always taken to local markets by fishermen themselves. Several shoals of herring and mackerel appeared off coast during year. More fish would have been caught if fishermen had better boats and nets. Considers fishermen would be benefited by loans, but fears they would have some difficulty in obtaining good security. They generally have small holdings of land adjacent to the shore, and only follow fishing when they cannot obtain work. In the winter months they very rarely go out, as their boats are small for this exposed part of the coast.	17
17	295	–	–	–	–	1	25	–	All portions of coast in this division guarded. Condition of fisheries not improving. Descriptions of fish most largely captured—salmon, herring, and horse mackerel, but weather during the season very unfavourable for boats having fishing. There is a public oyster bank at Tallorga, Ballysadare Bay. Supply not improving. Spatting last season about the same as previous year. No new natural banks have been discovered. Steps have been taken to mark ground licensed for the establishment of private beds. Quality of oysters very good, price from 6s. to 7s. a hundred. Current [illegible] realized by sales during year. No curing establishments in this division and not much curing by individual fishermen, except for their own consumption. No conflicts have occurred between persons pursuing different modes of fishing. Fishermen generally very orderly. No spirit of emigration prevailing amongst fishermen. They generally combine farming with fishing. Modes of fishing practised—nets and lines. No trawlers in this division. Means of transit to market for sale of fish good. Large shoals of herring and mackerel have appeared off this portion of coast during year. Means of capture inadequate. Has no suggestions to offer with reference to the improvement of fisheries.	18
221	1,397	60		–	–	39	306	19	About thirty-one and a half miles of coast in this division unguarded, viz., from Sligo Bridge to Streedagh Barracks (visited occasionally), six miles in length; Raughly Point, Lower, to Drumcliff Bridge, five miles; Rosslea Station to Mullaghmore (visited weekly by day patrol), seven miles; Streedagh to Roskeeragh Point (visited weekly by day patrol), seven and a half miles; Bunduff to Bundrowes, six miles; Ballyshannon to Donegal Abbey, twenty miles; and to Tullaghan, ten miles. Fishery improving, more productive in the take of herrings, with [illegible] about the same as previous year with other fish. Herrings sold at 3s. a hundred. Quantities taken at Poolday and in Sligo River. Several boats' crews made from £8 to £7 and £10 in two or three nights. One natural oyster bank in channel of Sligo River. About the same quantity dredged every year. Spatting last season has been considerably better, perhaps double that of previous years. No new natural banks have been discovered. Steps have been taken to mark ground licensed for establishment of private beds. Quality of oysters considered very good; price 7s. a hundred, for sale in Liverpool. An oyster bed in Drumcliff River has been stocked, but no oysters yet taken off it. The amount realized by sales within the year was between £[illegible] and £[illegible]. Dredging has been commenced on Captain Owen Wynne's private bed, which would increase the amount above stated by say £[illegible]. No curing establishments in this division, nor am I aware of any being carried on by individual fishermen. No conflicts have occurred between persons pursuing different modes of fishing. Fishermen generally orderly. At Raughly Station fishermen complain about fast nets being set in the rivers by farmers and others not fishermen. They say these nets [illegible] the herrings off in sea, and were a great injury to other fish. Several fishermen [illegible] drifting near these, of which they complain. A spirit of emigration prevails, and it is doubtful if the fishermen would be likely to remain at home even though they could follow fishing pursuits adequately. They generally combine farming with fishing. Modes of fishing practised are seine and long lines. Number of trawlers not increased; they have not been so successful as last year. Means of transit to market for sale of fish good. Large shoals of herrings have appeared off this portion of coast during the year. A good quantity would have been captured if fishermen had better boats and nets. With reference to the improvement of the sea fisheries, suggests that the Tidal Dock at Raughly be repaired and made a good harbour of refuge, as there are more men employed about there than on any other portion of the coast in this division.	19
192	1,843	167		–	–	13	93	20	No portion of coast in this division unguarded. Condition of fisheries not improving, except for sprats and herrings. Descriptions most largely captured—ling, sprat, salmon, herring, cod, bream, gurnet, and hake. Herrings, turbot, and bonnock are also caught in some quantities near Killybegs, but less this year than last, owing to the wet and stormy weather. The fish are generally in best condition at following periods, viz.:—salmon from May to August, mackerel and horse mackerel from August to October, whiting, gurnet, and bream, from September to November; herrings vary from September to January, and cod ling from November to February in each year. No oyster fisheries exist in this division. One curing establishment at Teelin West, but not successful. Fish generally sold in a fresh state. A good deal of curing of sprats and herrings, by salting, has taken place, almost universally, on the coast from Donegal to Teelin. Quantity unknown. No conflicts have occurred between persons pursuing different modes of fishing. Fishermen generally orderly. A spirit of emigration prevails amongst the fishermen. At Inver and [illegible] the sprat and herring fishing has been so productive that none of [illegible] the fishermen would now remain at home, should it continue. They mostly always combine farming with fishing. Modes of fishing practised are—herring nets and [illegible], drift, draft, and trammel nets, long and hand lines. The number of trawlers has not increased. Means of transit to market for sale of fish very bad. Large and good shoals of herrings and sprats have been seen in Donegal and Inver Bays; hundreds of tons of them have been captured and taken to Donegal, but much larger quantities would have been caught had the fishermen better and [illegible] boats. At present they can only go out in fine weather. Considers that money should be advanced to fishermen for repair and purchase of boats and gear. States that boats and nets are ruined, from no fault of the fishermen, but from want of proper boat harbours or sheds to protect them not only from rotting from exposure but also from the violent gales on the coast. Also suggests that some inducement should be given to the fish curers to venture out in bad weather. A small steamer would, in his opinion, be of great value for this purpose, and in summer time if not otherwise needed, this vessel could be used for conveying fish to a better market in Scotland or England.	20
473	1,499	270	–	–	–	196	711	119	Portions of coast in this division unguarded extend from Gweebarra Bar to Falmore, four miles; from Rosbeg to Glen [illegible] Point, three and a half miles; Horn Head Bridge to Horn Head two miles; and to Lackey Bridge, two and a half miles; Mulroy Bay to Fanad Light, nine miles. Condition of fisheries not improving. Descriptions most largely captured—cod, ling, haddock, and codling. No oyster fisheries exist in division. No curing establishments. Fish all sold in a fresh state. No conflicts have occurred between persons pursuing different modes of fishing. Fishermen generally orderly. A spirit of emigration still prevails, but fishermen would prefer remaining at home if fully employed. They generally combine farming with fishing. Modes of fishing practised—nets and long lines, between Gweebarra Bar and Fanad; in Lough Swilly trawling, nets, and lines. No increase in number of trawlers. A decrease in line fishing in Lough caused by the trawling. Means of transit good but slow. All fish sold in local markets, with the exception of salmon, which are sent to distant places. No shoals of fish of any description appeared off this portion of coast during year. Has no suggestions to offer for improvement of sea fisheries.	21

APPENDIX

STATE of the REGISTRY of FISHING VESSELS on the COAST

No.	Name of Division.	Boundaries.	Registering Officer.	1st Class employed in 1872.			2nd Class employed in 1872.			3rd Class employed in 1872.			Total employed in 1872.		
				Vessels.	Men.	Boys.	Vessels.	Men.	Boys.	Vessels.	Men.	Boys.	Vessels.	Men.	Boys.
22	Carn,	Inch Embankment, Buncrana, county Donegal, to Magilligan Point, south side of Lough Foyle, county Londonderry.	Arthur Salwey, Commander, R.N.	5	16	–	221	1,006	20	78	432	3	304	1,454	23
23	Ballycastle (Antrim).	Bann Mouth, co. Londonderry, to Red Bay, county Antrim.	Stratford Tuke, Commander, R.N.	–	–	–	116	365	–	47	140	–	163	505	–
24	Carrickfergus,	Jennings's Bridge, near Carron Point, to White Railings, near Belfast, county Antrim.	William G. England, Commander, R.N.	1	6	1	31	80	–	12	26	–	44	112	1
25	Donaghadee,	Tillysburn, near Belfast Lough (S.), co. Antrim, to Newcastle Quay, near Cloghy Bay, co. Down.	George Rivington, Commander, R.N.	20	143	9	83	158	7	7	4	2	110	305	18
26	Strangford, .	Newcastle Quay, North, near Cloghy Bay, to Sheepland Head, South, county Down.	James Pypor, Staff Commander, R.N.	9	5	–	34	71	3	3	4	–	46	80	3

No. 1—continued.

of IRELAND from 1st January, 1872, to 1st January, 1873.

Total employed in 1871.			Total Increase since 1871.			Total Decrease since 1871.			Substance of Observations made by Inspecting Commanders of Coast Guards and other Registering Officers, up to the 1st January, 1873.	No.
Vessels.	Men.	Boys.	Vessels.	Men.	Boys.	Vessels.	Men.	Boys.		
374	1,768	37	-	-	-	70	203	4	The only portions of coast in this division unguarded are those which are inaccessible and impracticable for boats to land at, extending from Malin Head Station and Culdaff to Leenan Bay, and from Magilligan Strand (south side of Lough Foyle) to Ballykelly; the few respectable creeks and boat ports are visited by the crews of adjoining stations. The condition of fisheries not improving, and much the same for the last three years. Some new boats have been added, but many of old boats falling into decay—their boats, nets, &c., are in very bad condition. Fishermen do not think their general prospects cheering, which they attribute to their uncertain means and the present high price of food, &c. Descriptions of fish most largely captured are—cod, ling, ray, hake, conger eels, soles, plaice, turbot, in their season. Small quantities of herrings appeared in Lough Foyle during October and November last. Natural oyster banks exist in nearly the entire of Lough Foyle, some of which are as follows, viz.:—Mr. Kennedy's bank, a [illegible] mile N.E. and S.W., Glen and Cloty bank, N. and S. four miles long, Rossford, N.E. and S.W. two and a half miles long and a quarter mile wide, &c. Supply not so plentiful as in former years, chiefly attributable to the [illegible] of the [illegible]. Considers trawling over beds improves them. Spatting much the same as previous year. Steps have been taken to stock natural beds belonging to Captain Hart and others at Lough Swilly by having oysters brought from the Foyle, Blacksod Bay, and Achill Sound, to propagate on their private beds. General quality of oysters very good, price from 5s. to 7s. per hundred from public beds. States the average quantity of oysters sold within the last year was as follows, viz.:—about 192,000 shipped to Liverpool and Glasgow, and 64,000 sold in local markets. No curing establishments exist now in division. The present Coastguard buildings at Culdaff Bay and boat-house [illegible]. Fish are generally sold in fresh state. In summer ice is used for packing it for English markets, where it arrives in excellent order, owing to the good packing and rapid transit. No conflicts have occurred between persons pursuing different modes of fishing. Fishermen are generally orderly and peaceable and industrious [illegible]. A spirit of emigration still prevails, but fishermen would prefer remaining at home if able to follow fishing pursuits adequately. Want of means and employment are the sole causes of their emigrating. Modes of fishing practised are—trawling, hand lines and herring nets. Lough Foyle abounds with salmon, and a great many are taken in the [illegible] River and at the mouths of [illegible]. The number of trawlers has not increased. A general complaint exists amongst them that their trawling is limited and prescribed in Lough Foyle. Means of transit good. No large shoals of fish have appeared off this portion of coast during the year. Considers adequate means do not exist for capture of herrings, mackerel, or pilchards. Suggests for improvement of fisheries, that [illegible] pier at Moville be raised and lengthened for the shelter of fishing craft and for the landing of fish. Suggests also that a small pier or quay at Culdaff would very much facilitate the landing of fish and render the approach to the beach less dangerous in stormy weather.	22
209	548	6	-	-	-	97	36	6	No portion of coast in this division unguarded where there are fishing boats, with the exception of Rathlin Island. Condition of fisheries not improving. Descriptions of fish most largely captured—glassan, gray gurnet, cod and ling. No oyster fisheries in district. No curing establishments exist. No conflicts have occurred between persons pursuing different modes of fishing. No [illegible] prevailing amongst fishermen. They generally combine farming with fishing. Modes of fishing practised—long and hand lines, and draft nets. Means of transit to market for sale of fish good. Shoals of mackerel have appeared off this portion of coast during the summer, but only a few captured. Has no suggestions to offer for improvement of the fisheries.	23
153	387	-	-	-	1	100	375	-	Portion of coast in this division unguarded extends from Larne Lighthouse to Magheramorne, eight miles in length. Condition of fisheries about the same as last year—no improvement. Descriptions of fish most largely captured are—cod, plaice, pollock, and herring, during summer months. No natural oyster banks exist off Holywood, Green Island, and Kilroot. Supply and quality about the same as last year. No new natural banks have been discovered. No [illegible] ground [illegible] for establishment of private beds. Quality of oysters good. Price varying from 8s. to 10s. a hundred. Amount realized by sales within the year about £300. No curing establishments exist in this division. Fish all sold in fresh state. No conflicts have occurred between persons pursuing different modes of fishing. Fishermen generally very orderly. As a rule the spirit of emigration does not prevail. A few fishermen would be inclined to go, if they had the means, but majority of them prefer remaining at home as they combine farming and gardening with fishing. Modes of fishing practised are—long and hand lines, trawling, and nets. Number of trawlers slightly increased. Means of transit for sale of fish good, as railway takes it to the best market when not disposed of locally. No large shoals of fish such as herrings, mackerel, pilchards, have appeared off this portion of coast during year. Should such appear, means of capture very limited. States fishermen would be benefited by loans for purchase of larger boats, with nets and gear in proportion. They could then pursue their occupations in deeper water, and follow up the shoals of herrings in Irish Channel.	24
349	886	24	-	-	-	139	588	6	No portion of coast in this division unguarded. Condition of fisheries slightly improved in some parts especially, herring fishing southwards. Descriptions most largely captured are—cod, ray, codling, herrings, pollock, flat fish and lobsters. One natural oyster bank exists, extending from Groomsport to the Copeland Islands. Supply not improving. Spatting about the same as previous year. No new natural banks have been discovered. No steps have been taken to stock ground licensed for establishment of private beds. Quality of oysters good, price from 7s. to 10s. a hundred. Has not sufficient information as to the amount realized by sales during the year; at Bangor alone it is supposed it reached about £25. No curing establishments in this division, and individual fishermen only cure for their own consumption. No conflicts have occurred between persons pursuing different modes of fishing. A spirit of emigration does not in general prevail, except about Cloghy, but fishermen would prefer remaining at home if fully employed. South of Ballywalter they combine farming with fishing, but not to the north. Modes of fishing practised are—drift nets for herrings, long and hand lines, seines, but only a few of the latter. The only trawling is at Groomsport. Number of trawlers decreasing, as owners unable to keep them up. Means of transit good from Donaghadee southwards, but not north of it. Large shoals of herrings only appeared off coast during year. Inadequate means exist for their capture in northern portion of division, while in south in port the means are ample. The only suggestion he can offer for improvement of fisheries is the erection of a pier or harbour at Cloghy, for the sheltering of fishing boats.	25
186	341	8	-	-	-	118	361	3	No portion of coast in this division unguarded. No improvement in condition of fisheries. Descriptions most largely captured are—cod, whiting and herrings. Natural oyster beds exist on the N.W. shore of Strangford Lough, between Killyleagh and Ballydorn. Supply diminishing. Spatting worse last season than previous year. A new natural bank was discovered within the last six weeks, it consists of a small patch of ground, about a boat's length each way in extent. Steps have been taken to stock ground licensed for the establishment of private beds. Quality of oysters good; price from 5s. to 7s. a hundred from public beds. Amount realized by sales within the year from £300 to £400. No curing establishments exist in this division. No conflicts have occurred between persons pursuing different modes of fishing. Fishermen generally very orderly. No spirit of emigration prevailing. The men employed fishing are mostly unfit for any other occupation, with very few exceptions, and these hire themselves as farm labourers. Modes of fishing practised are—long and hand lines and nets. No trawlers in this division. Means of transit good, but supply of fish readily sold in locality. Large shoals of fish, principally herrings, appeared off this portion of coast during year and were captured with draft nets by boats from other localities. Has no suggestions to offer for improvement of the fisheries.	26

APPENDIX,

STATE of the REGISTRY of FISHING VESSELS on the COAST

No.	Name of Division.	Boundaries.	Registering Officer.	1st Class employed in 1871			2nd Class employed in 1871			3rd Class employed in 1871			Total employed in 1871		
				Vessels	Men.	Boys.	Vessels	Men.	Boys	Vessels	Men.	Boys.	Vessels.	Men	Boys
27	Newcastle, .	Gun's Island, Strangford, North, county Down, to River Fool, Kilkeel, South.	Henry M Binghams, Commander, R.N.	26	168	12	68	223	12	47	170	16	141	561	40
28	Carlingford, .	From River Fool, Kilkeel, North, county Down, to Ballaghan Point, near Greenore, South, county Louth.	W. G. Gregory, Lieutenant, R.N.	18	125	15	118	501	6	134	347	–	263	973	21
29	Dundalk, .	Ballaghan Point, near Greenore, to Maiden Town, Drogheda, county Louth.	G. B. Bell, Lieutenant, R.N.	2	12	-	81	424	3	22	73	10	108	508	13
30	Malahide, .	Mouth of Boyne, county Louth, to Whip of the Water, Clontarf, county Dublin.	William Moriarty, Commander, R.N.	56	344	33	37	113	5	15	31	5	108	486	41
				373	2,000	210	3,091	12,206	368	4,451	15,095	327	7,914	30,197	1111

No. 1—*continued.*

of Ireland from 1st January, 1872, to 1st January, 1873.

Total employed in 1872.			Total Increase since 1871.			Total Decrease since 1871.			Substance of Observations made by Inspecting Commanders of Coast Guards and other Registering Officers, up to the 1st January, 1873.	No.
Vessels.	Men.	Boys.	Vessels.	Men.	Boys.	Vessels.	Men.	Boys.		
149	563	39	–	–	1	1	1	–	No portion of coast in this division unguarded. An improvement within the last year in the herring fishery at Ardglass also in cod, whiting, and haddock fisheries at Annalong and Leestone. Descriptions of fish most largely captured are—plaice and turbot in summer; cod, whiting, and ling in winter. The only oyster beds in this division are from three to four miles off Annalong, and they require working to remove the accumulations that have for years collected upon them. Supply not improving. Steps have been taken to stock ground licensed for establishment of private beds. No curing establishments exist in this division. No conflicts have occurred between persons pursuing different modes of fishing. Fishermen generally orderly. No spirit of emigration prevailing amongst fishermen. They would prefer remaining at home if fully employed. They generally combine farming with fishing. General mode of fishing practised—long lines. There are no trawlers in this division. Means of transit good at all seasons, except Annalong and Leestone. Large shoals of herrings and mackerel have appeared off this portion of coast during the year. Adequate facilities existed for their capture. Considers fisheries would be benefited if telegraph was extended from Newcastle to Annalong and Kilkeel.	27
308	1,140	18	–	–	3	83	107	–	No portion of coast in this division unguarded. There has been an improvement in the herring fishing during the last year. An oyster bed exists in the centre of Carlingford Lough. Supply not improving. Spatting has been the same as that of previous year. No new natural banks have been discovered. Steps have been taken to stock ground licensed for establishment of private beds. General quality of oysters good, price about £1 5s. per thousand from public beds. No curing establishments exist in the division. No conflicts have occurred between persons pursuing different modes of fishing. Emigration decreasing amongst fishermen; they would prefer remaining at home if able to follow fishing pursuits adequately. They generally combine farming with fishing. Modes of fishing practised are herring nets and oyster dredging. No trawlers in this division. Means of transit to market for sale of fish good. Shoals of herrings and mackerel appeared off this portion of coast during year, and large quantities of them were taken. Has no suggestions to offer as to the improvement of the fisheries.	28
291	897	15	–	–	–	113	318	2	No portion of coast in this division unguarded. No improvement in condition of fisheries. Descriptions most largely captured are—herrings, mackerel, whiting, cod, ling and flat fish, and salmon in summer. No oyster fisheries in this division. No curing establishments exist. No conflicts have occurred between persons pursuing different modes of fishing. Fishermen generally orderly. Considers if fishermen were fully employed, they would prefer remaining at home. They generally combine farming with fishing. Modes of fishing practised are—long lines, salmon and herring nets. No trawlers in this division. Means of transit to market (by horse and cart) very good. No large shoals of fish have appeared off this portion of coast during year. Herring fishing very bad. In Dundalk Bay mackerel are taken by lines from boats under sail. Fishermen are well provided with nets. Suggests for improvement of the fisheries the erection of the proposed harbour at Giles' Quay, and states that small harbour of Port Oriel, at Clogher Head, could also be improved for a small outlay; they are both badly required, as many days in the season fishermen are detained from going to sea, owing to the want of a place of refuge.	29
111	593	37	–	–	6	5	106	–	No portion of coast in this division unguarded. Condition of fisheries not improving. Descriptions of fish most largely captured are herrings during the season; cod, ling and congers are taken with long lines at Rush and Loughshinny. No natural oyster banks in this division. Steps have been taken to stock private oyster bed at Malahide, the property of Lord Talbot de Malahide. Quality of oysters fair. Price 6s. per hundred from bed at Malahide. Does not know amount realized by sales during year. Three curing establishments exist at Rush, and they have been very successful. Individual fishermen cure a number of ling and cod during the summer. No conflicts have occurred between persons pursuing different modes of fishing. Fishermen generally orderly. No emigration prevailing amongst fishermen. They generally combine farming with fishing. Modes of fishing practised are—long lines, herring nets, and trawls. Number of trawlers has not increased. Means of transit to market for sale of fish good. No large shoals of fish appeared off this portion of coast during past year. Has no suggestions to offer for improvement of sea fisheries, but states that if harbours at Baldoyle, Malahide and Rogerstown are reclaimed by Sewage Company for reclaiming the slob lands at the heads of those waters, there will be no places for fishermen to resort upon the coasts of this division.	30

Appendix No. 2.—Abstract of Returns from Coast Guard

No.	Name of Station.	Inspecting Officer.	Solely employed in Fishing: First Class			Second Class			Third Class			Chiefly altogether employed in Fishing: First Class			Second Class			Third Class			Only partially employed in Fishing: First Class			Second Class			Third Class			[illegible]		
[illegible]	[illegible]	[illegible]	[illegible]	[illegible]	[illegible]	[illegible]	[illegible]	[illegible]	[illegible]	[illegible]	[illegible]	[illegible]	[illegible]	[illegible]	[illegible]	[illegible]	[illegible]	[illegible]	[illegible]	[illegible]	[illegible]	[illegible]	[illegible]	[illegible]	[illegible]	[illegible]	[illegible]	[illegible]	[illegible]	[illegible]	[illegible]	[illegible]
		Total	[illegible]	[illegible]	[illegible]	[illegible]	[illegible]	[illegible]	[illegible]	[illegible]	[illegible]	[illegible]	[illegible]	[illegible]	[illegible]	[illegible]	[illegible]	[illegible]	[illegible]	[illegible]	[illegible]	[illegible]	[illegible]	[illegible]	[illegible]	[illegible]	[illegible]	[illegible]	[illegible]	[illegible]	[illegible]	[illegible]

APPENDIX No. 3.

RETURN showing the Number of Boats registered by the Collectors of Customs during the year 1872.

APPENDIX, Nos. 3, 4, & 5

Registered by Collector of Customs at	First Class. Boats.	Men.	Boys.	Second Class. Boats.	Men.	Boys.	Third Class. Boats.	Men.	Boys.	Total. Boats.	Men.	Boys.
Wexford,	21	124	.	725	1,069	6	56	330	.	392	1,603	8
Youghal,	1	18		47	324	8	88	247	5	88	658	11
Cork,	61	303	48	405	902	140	454	1,700	85	911	2,463	254
Westport,	.	.		57	78	2	505	2,186	81	572	2,234	84
Belfast,	43	387	14	187	848	8	43	181	1	274	1,048	38
Galway,	10	84	8	642	2,176	87	883	2,160	93	1,484	5,378	65
Skibbereen,	11	65	7	242	2,177	46	401	2,019	106	757	3,674	106
Waterford,	17	54	9	116	706	13	36	125	2	222	926	22
Drogheda,	1	5	.	46	249	2	12	34	9	65	288	11
Dublin,	155	607	114	565	1,880	42	124	486	14	541	3,359	201
Sligo,	1	5	.	146	824	128	397	2,086	125	588	3,088	181
Limerick,	.		.	.	.	.	76	920	.	76	930	.
Tralee,	18	42	7	146	884	5	455	2,118	60	625	3,043	65
Coleraine,	.	.	.	124	444	8	65	116	4	183	563	13
Londonderry,	7	34	.	473	1,932	89	379	486	18	618	2,486	72
Dundalk,	.	.	.	42	183	1	4	35	2	47	200	5
New Ross,	1	5	1	66	228	11	87	75	5	66	312	17
Newry,	64	327	40	187	640	28	103	501	6	294	1,554	68
Ballina,	.	.	.	1	3	.	100	1,194	.	101	1,197	.
Total,	384	2,082	216	3,686	14,818	583	4,368	17,868	611	8,534	34,637	1,391

APPENDIX, No. 4.

HOWTH.

ABSTRACT of Returns of Herring Fishing, between the 1st June, 1872, and the 9th November, 1872 furnished and authenticated by Chief Officer of Coast Guard at Howth.

Date. Week ending—	Average daily Number of boats employed. Cornish.	Scotch.	Manx.	Irish.	Number of Mease of 630 fish each.	Average price per Mease. £ s. d.	Gross Receipts. £ s. d.	Number of days Employed.	Observations.
1872.									
June 8,	—	17	—	1	48	1 8 11	68 10 6	4	Mixed fish.
" 15,	—	30	—	13	470	1 3 11½	563 18 6	3	Do.
" 22,	—	21	4	33	820	1 2 4	3,760 0 3	6	Do ; some good fish
" 29,	2	51	0	81	10,086	1 0 4½	10,648 0 0	6	Good fish
July 6,	34	70	15	79	10,080	1 1 9	11,130 6 6	6	Very good fish, but some of mixed quality.
" 13,	87	80	16	116	11,100	1 2 7½	12,843 6 6	6	Good fish
" 20,	116	100	26	109	13,100	1 6 3½	17,717 10 6	6	Do
" 27,	120	180	6	109	12,016	0 14 4½	8,089 15 6	4	Mixed quality ; some good fish.
August 3,	88	76	3	88	13,150	0 14 2½	9,248 10 0	6	Do do.
" 10,	87	66	17	08	10,300	0 11 11½	6,159 10 0	6	Do. do
" 17,	44	28	6	60	6,547	0 17 8½	5,624 18 6	6	Do. do.
" 24,	71	17	6	77	7,050	0 10 11	3,851 15 0	6	Do. do.
" 31,	22	16	3	45	1,873	0 12 6½	1,176 6 0	6	Do. do.
September 7,	17	6	1	22	986	0 16 0½	678 17 6	6	Good fish.
" 14,	18	21	3	39	682	1 1 4	862 18 6	6	Do.
" 21,	4	4	7	10	478	0 18 3½	436 11 6	6	Do.
" 28,	2	8	1	6	317	0 18 7½	262 8 6	5	Do ; some mixed
October 5,	3	2	2	13	440	1 8 0½	625 8 6	4	Bad, mixed, and some good fish.
" 12,	2	2	0	16	390	1 1 0½	420 10 0	4	Mixed fish.
" 19,	1	2	37	36	2,490	0 18 10	2,188 10 0	4	Small and mixed fish.
" 26,	1	2	45	21	2,149	0 12 1	1,830 10 8	6	Do do.
November 2,	3	1	66	36	360	0 14 2	254 18 6	5	Some good and some mixed fish.
" 9,	—	—	1	2	16	0 8 8	6 7 6	1	Mixed fish.
Totals,	—	—	—	—	167,087	0 18 1½	96,488 6 8	107	
Average numbers and amounts per day for the 107 working days,	22	33	18	47	1,500	0 18 1⅝	—	—	

APPENDIX, No. 5.

ARDGLASS HARBOUR.

ABSTRACT of Herring Fishing for Season 1872 (which commenced on 29th May and ended on the 15th October).

Month ending	Highest Number of Boats employed on any one Night, English, Irish, and Scotch.	Highest Number of Mease per Boat.	Total Caught for the Month.	Highest Price during the Month per Mease. £ s. d.	Average Price during the Month per Mease. £ s. d.	Total Amount realized. £ s. d.	Number of Days out.
May 31st,	8	8	17½	1 0 0	0 18 11	16 10 6	3
June 29th,	163	100	8,842½	1 4 0	0 16 10	7,450 11 6	15
July 31st,	300	110	40,373	1 2 0	0 14 0	28,388 10 0	22
August 31st,	145	118	14,638	1 2 6	0 11 6	8,400 6 0	23
September 30th,	109	97	3,318	1 3 6	0 8 10	2,296 17 8	14
October 15th.	1	30	86	1 0 0	0 18 10	84 1 0	2
Total for Season,			67,114			£46,518 16 6	

Appendix, Nos. 6, 7, 8, and 9.

Appendix, No. 6.

Wicklow.

Quantity of Herrings taken at Wicklow during the year ending 31st December, 1872.

Description of Fish.	Number of Mease taken	Average Price per Mease.
Herrings, . . .	6,000	From 8s. to 40s. each.

Appendix, No. 7.

Arklow.

Quantity of Herrings taken at Arklow during the year ending 31st December, 1872, furnished by the Chief Officer of Coast Guard at Arklow.

Description of Fish.	Number of Mease taken	Price per Mease
Herrings, . .	20,000	From 7s. to 35s per Mease.

Quantity of Oysters taken at Arklow during the year ending the 31st December, 1872.

Description of Fish.	Number of Barrels taken	Average Quantity in each Barrel.	Price per Barrel.	Total Price of Oysters taken.
Oysters, . .	16,000	450 (large and small)	18s.	£14,400

Appendix, No. 8.

Kilkeel.

Abstract of Returns of Herring Fishing in 1872, furnished and authenticated by the Chief Officer of Coast Guard at Kilkeel.

Date.	Number of Boats Employed.				Number of Mease.	Average Price per Mease	Gross Total.	Observations
	Cornish	Scotch	Manx.	Irish.				
1872.						£ s. d.	£ s. d.	
May 1st to 7th, . . .	–	–	–	6	30	1 10 0	45 0 0	The principal portion of the herrings captured off the Harbour of Kilkeel are landed at Kilkeel Pier, and thence carted away to different parts of the country to be sold; but, occasionally, a steamer calls off the Harbour to purchase a cargo for the use of the Liverpool Market.
" 7th to 14th, . . .	–	–	–	5	46	1 2 0	54 5 0	
" 14th to 21st, . . .	2	–	4	6	100	0 12 0	60 0 0	
" 21st to 28th, . . .	4	4	4	4	250	0 10 0	125 0 0	
" 28th to 4th June, . .	–	3	5	3	132	0 17 0	112 4 0	
June 4th to 11th, . .	2	–	3	8	142	0 15 0	106 10 0	
" 11th to 18th, . . .	–	–	4	8	112	0 17 0	97 13 0	
" 18th to 25th, . . .	8	6	2	21	700	0 12 0	430 5 0	
" 25th to 2nd July, . .	8	3	8	16	600	0 10 0	300 0 0	
July 2nd to 9th, . . .	2	2	4	10	675	0 7 6	253 2 6	
" 9th to 16th, . . .	–	4	7	18	482	0 7 0	168 14 0	
" 16th to 23rd, . . .	4	–	4	17	470	0 6 0	141 0 0	
" 23rd to 30th, . . .	4	3	9	19	760	0 5 0	190 0 0	
" 30th to 6th August, . .	10	2	8	33	1,100	0 6 0	331 10 0	
August 6th to 13th, . .	2	2	8	10	697	0 7 0	244 0 0	
" 13th to 20th, . .	–	–	6	25	885	0 18 0	783 10 0	
" 20th to 27th, . .	–	–	6	19	438	0 18 0	211 0 0	
" 27th to 3rd September,	–	–	7	24	654	0 10 0	333 5 0	
September 3rd to 10th, . .	8	3	6	18	545	0 8 0	218 0 0	
" 10th to 17th, . .	6	4	8	27	780	0 7 6	292 10 0	
" 17th to 24th, . .	6	4	9	27	1,514	0 8 0	605 12 0	
" 24th to 1st October,	5	3	6	35	918	0 10 0	459 0 0	
October 1st to 8th, . .	8	1	4	38	548	0 13 0	373 10 0	
" 8th to 15th, . .	6	4	–	32	535	0 14 0	374 10 0	
" 15th to 22nd, . . .	–	–	1	5	300	0 15 0	225 0 0	
" 22nd to 29th, . . .	–	1	–	5	80	0 17 6	70 0 0	
Total, . . .					12,530		6,290 14 6	

Appendix, No. 9.

Courtown Harbour.

Return of the Quantity of Herrings, Oysters, and other Fish captured and brought into Courtown Harbour during the year 1872, furnished by the Harbour Master at Courtown.

Landed—Herrings, 1,830 measses; Oysters, 675 barrels; Cod Fish, 30 dozen; Soles, 100 pairs.

APPENDIX, No. 10.

APPENDIX, No. 10.

LIST of STONE WEIRS in Ireland for SALMON FISHING, with their Breadth, and the size of the Queen's Gap or share maintained therein respectively.

Name of Fishery District.	Name of River.	Name of Weir.	Breadth of Stream.	Size of Queen's Gap previous to passing of 26 & 27 Vic., c. 114.	Observations.
			Ft. in.	Ft. in.	
Ballinakill,	Bundorragha,	Bundorragha,	about 60 0	10 0	Not used.
	Ass or Erriff,	Ashleagh,	,, 60 0	No gap,	Ditto.
Bangor,	Owenmore,	Goulamore,	,, 429 0	No gap,	Ditto.
	Munhin,	Munhin,	,, 34 0	No gap,	Ditto.
	Newport,	Newport,	158 4	. . .	Gap 15 feet 10 inches. Not used.
Ballina,	Moy,	Ballina,	341 6	No gap,	Do. 34 feet 2 inches.
	Ditto,	Foxford,	205 10	17 0	Do. 29 feet 7 inches, weir not used.
Sligo,	Sligo,	. . .	438 0	No gap,	Not used. A fishing mill-dam.
Ballyshannon,	Bundrowes,	Bundrowes,	68 4	No gap,	Gap 6 feet 10 inches.
	Erne,	Erne,	. . .	. . .	A fishing mill-dam.
	Inver,	. . .	about 195 0	No gap,	Not used.
	Ditto,	Eske,	,, 82 0	No gap,	Ditto.
Coleraine,	Bann,	The Cutts of Coleraine	455 0	18 0	A fishing mill-dam. Pass, 30 feet in breadth, opened.
Ballycastle,	Bush,	. . .	730 0	No gap,	Gap 12 feet 9 inches. Not used.
Drogheda,	Boyne,	Oldbridge,	210 0	23 0	Do. 24 feet.
	Ditto,	Rossnaree,	300 0	13 and 35	Do. 30 feet.
	Ditto,	Newgrange,	224 0	No gap,	Do. 10 feet.
Letterkenny,	Lennan,	Rathmelton,	150 0	No gap,	Two Gaps of 6 feet each.
	Lackagh,	Lackagh,	211 0	No gap,	Gap 20 feet. Not used.
	Owenea,	Owenea,	145 0	No gap,	Gap 14½ feet. Not used.
Londonderry,	Finn,	Killygordon,	about 183 0	No gap,	Do. 20 feet. Not used.
	Buncrana,	Buncrana,	190 0	No gap,	Do. 12 feet.
Waterford,	Nore,	Inistiogue,	173 0	60 0	Do. 60 feet.
	Ditto,	Reakslew,	90 0	78 0	Do. 78 feet.
	Ditto,	Jerpoint,	99 0	66 0	Do. 66 feet.
	Ditto,	Dysart,	93 0	47 0	Do. 47 feet.
	Suir,	Coolnamuck,	176 0	47 0	Do. 47 feet.
	Tay,	Woodhouse,	53 0	No gap,	Do. 6 feet.
Lismore,	Blackwater,	Lismore Weir,	313 0	No gap,	Do. 31 feet 6 inches.
Cork,	Lee,	"The North Lee Fishery Weir or "Hayes' Weir."	406 0	No gap,	A fishing mill-dam. Not used.
	Ditto,	The weir above Wellington Bridge.	780 0	No gap,	Ditto. Not used.
	Ditto,	"The Upper Gill Abbey Weir."	378 0	No gap,	Ditto. Not used.
	Ditto,	"The Sugar House Weir."	114 0	No gap,	Gap 11 feet 5 inches.
Killarney,	Carra,	Carra,	160 0	No gap,	Gap 16 feet.
	Waterville or Currane.	Waterville,	under 40 0	No gap,	Extension of weekly close season from noon on Friday to noon on Monday ordered instead of gap, stream being under 40 feet—26 & 27 Vic., c. 114, s. 11.
Limerick,	Shannon,	Lax Weir,	840 0	21 0	Gap 30 feet.
Galway,	Galway,	Galway Salmon Weir,	205 10	18 0	Do. 30 feet 7 inches.
	Owenmore or Great River.	Ballinahinch Trout and Salmon Weirs.	228 0	No gap,	Do. 23 feet. Not used.
	Spiddal,	Spiddal Salmon Weir,	varies greatly; 283 0 to 12 0	No gap,	Do. 13 feet. Not used.
	Furbough,	The Furbough Salmon Weir.	14 0	No gap,	Do. 3 feet. Not used.

APPENDIX,

RESULT of INQUIRIES held by the SPECIAL COMMISSIONERS of IRISH FISHERIES into the

No.	Where Fixed Net situated.	Description of Fixed Net.	Name of Person maintaining and using Fixed Net.	Name of Owner of Fixed Net, or of Land to which Net attached.	Name of Townland to which Net attached.	Parish.
1	Barrow, otherwise Ross, otherwise Nore and Barrow Rivers conjoined.	Head Weir,	Thomas Murphy,	John H. Glascott,	Dunganstown,	Whitechurch,
2	Barrow River,	Ditto,	Arthur Kavanagh,	Arthur Kavanagh,	Drummin,	St. Mullins,
3	Barrow, otherwise Ross River, otherwise Nore and Barrow Rivers conjoined.	Ditto,	Joseph Hunt,	W. M. Glascott,	Mountaungy,	Whitechurch,
4	Ditto,	Ditto,	Walter Sweetman,	Walter Sweetman,	Aunaghs	Shanbogh,
5	Ditto,	Ditto,	Michael and D. Cody,	—	Carrickcloney,	Kilmakevoge,
6	Ditto,	Ditto,	James Doody,	—	Great Island,	Kilmokea,
7	Ditto,	Ditto,	Samuel Bennett,	—	Ditto,	Ditto,
8	Ditto,	Ditto,	Richard Cashen,	—	Shanbogh, Upper,	Shanbogh,
9	Ditto,	Ditto,	John Sherlock,	—	Great Island,	Kilmokea?
10	Ditto,	Ditto,	P. Shanahan,	—	Ditto,	Ditto,
11	Ditto,	Ditto,	George Kent,	—	Ditto,	Ditto,
12	Suir,	Ditto,	John Lynch,	N. Power,	Faithlegg,	Faithlegg,
13	Ditto,	Ditto,	Hugh Treacey,	Ditto,	Ditto,	Ditto,
14	Ditto,	Ditto,	John Walsh,	—	Cheekpoint,	Ditto,
15	Suir, Nore, and Barrow Rivers conjoined.	Ditto,	John Lynch,	—	Coolbunnia,	Ditto,
16	Ditto,	Stake Weir,	Michael Dobbyn,	Marquess of Waterford,	Crooke,	Crooke,
17	Ditto,	Ditto,	Eliza Coghlan,	J. J. D. Coghlan,	Dromina,	Ditto,
18	Nore,	Head Weir,	W. F. F. Tighe,	W. F. F. Tighe,	Inistioge,	Inistioge,
19	Barrow, otherwise Ross River, otherwise Nore and Barrow conjoined.	Ditto,	Patrick Byrne,	R. W. Nunn,	Camlin,	Old Ross,
20	Barrow,	Ditto,	W. F. F. Tighe,	W. F. F. Tighe,	Kilconnelly,	The Rower,
21	Ditto,	Ditto,	John Elliot,	D. Burtchell,	Cochrney,	Ditto,
22	Barrow, otherwise Ross River, otherwise Nore and Barrow conjoined.	Ditto,	John Forrestal,	—	Carrickcloney,	Kilmakevoge,
23	Nore River,	Ditto,	John Hunt,	Mrs. and Miss Vicars,	Brownsford,	Dysartmoon,
24	Suir River,	Ditto,	Paul Anderson,	N. A. Power,	Gorteens,	Rathpatrick,
25	Ditto,	Ditto,	Cath. and P. Moroney,	N. Power,	Drumdowney, Upper,	Ditto,
26	Barrow, otherwise Ross River, otherwise Nore and Barrow conjoined.	Ditto,	Michael Irish,	Dr. J. Mackesy,	Ballyverneen,	Ballygurrim,
27	Ditto,	Ditto,	Thomas Murphy,	Col. Chas. Kearney,	Kearney's Bay,	Kilcolumb,
28	Ditto,	Ditto,	Joseph Hunt,	Peter Strange,	Rochestown,	Ditto,
29	Ditto,	Ditto,	P. Hanrahan,	Ditto,	Ditto,	Ditto,
30	Ditto,	Ditto,	J. Doyle,	J. Devereux,	Rosegville,	Ditto,
31	Ditto,	Ditto,	J. Holger,	Ditto,	Ditto,	Ditto,
32	Ditto,	Ditto,	W. Walsh,	Miss Bolton,	Drumdowney, Upper,	Rathpatrick,
33	Ditto,	Ditto,	J. Sullivan,	P. Hanrahan,	Ballinlaw,	Kilcolumb,
34	Ditto,	Ditto,	John Brien,	N. Power,	Drumdowney, Upper,	Rathpatrick,
35	Suir River,	Ditto,	David Bennett,	Ditto,	Ditto,	Ditto,
36	Barrow, otherwise Ross River, otherwise Nore and Barrow conjoined.	Ditto,	James Butler,	Samuel King,	Fisherstown,	Kilmokea,
37	Ditto,	Ditto,	Pierce Cox,	Ditto,	Ditto,	Ditto,
38	Ditto,	Ditto,	James Kavanagh,	—	Ditto,	Ditto,
39	Suir, Nore, and Barrow conjoined, otherwise Waterford Harbour.	Scotch Stake Weir	A. Ryan, or Hayes,	Lord Templemore,	Duncannon,	St James and Dunbrody.
40	Ditto,	Ditto,	M. Doyle,	Ditto,	Clonsharragh,	Ditto,
41	Ditto,	Ditto,	A. Stephens,	Ditto,	Ditto,	Ditto,
42	Suir,	Head Weir,	N. A. Power,	N. A. Power,	Gorteens,	Rathpatrick,
43	Shannon River,	Fly-Net,	Randle Borough,	Randle Borough,	Querrin,	Moyarta
44	Ditto,	Stake-Net,	S. M'Auliffe,	Ditto,	Shanganagh,	Ditto,
45	Ditto,	Ditto,	William Kennedy,	John Cox,	Clarefield,	Ditto,
46	Ditto,	Ditto,	D. M'Auliffe,	Francis Keane,	Scattery Island,	Kilrush,
47	Ditto,	Fly-Net,	Francis Connell,	Ditto,	Ditto,	Ditto,
48	Ditto,	Stake-Net,	S. M'Auliffe,	Benjamin Cox,	Clarefield,	Moyarta,
49	Ditto,	Ditto,	J. Connell and D. M'Auliffe,	Colonel Vandeleur,	Carrowncalla, S.,	Kilrush,
50	Ditto,	Ditto,	Francis Connell,	Francis Keane,	Scattery Island,	Ditto,
51	Ditto,	Fly-Net,	Ditto,	Ditto,	Ditto,	Ditto,
52	Ditto,	Ditto,	John Cummins,	Colonel Vandeleur,	Inishbig or Hog Island,	Ditto,
53	Ditto,	Ditto,	James Connell,	Ditto,	Ballynote, West,	Ditto,
54	Ditto,	Ditto,	John Slattery,	Ditto,	Ballymacrinan,	Killimer,
55	Ditto,	Ditto,	S. M'Auliffe,	Ditto,	Lakyle, South,	Killofin,
56	Ditto,	Ditto,	Ditto,	Ditto,	Ditto,	Ditto,
57	Ditto,	Ditto,	S. M'Auliffe and T. M'Namara,	Ditto,	Mount Shannon, West,	Ditto,
58	Ditto,	Stake-Net,	Maurice Sheehy,	Ditto,	Mount Shannon Wood,	Ditto,
59	Ditto,	Fly-Net,	Dennis M'Auliffe,	Ditto,	Clonkerry, West,	Ditto,
60	Ditto,	Stake-Net,	S. M'Auliffe,	Lord Leconfield,	Errinagh,	Killadysert,
61	Ditto,	Ditto,	S. Cunningham,	Ditto,	Ditto,	Ditto,
62	Ditto,	Ditto,	James O'Neill,	William Ashe,	Shanmuckinish,	Ditto,
63	Ditto,	Ditto,	John Griffin,	James Kelly,	Cahiracon,	Killadysert,
64	Ditto (Clonderlaw Bay),	Ditto,	Daniel Molony,	Lord Annaly,	Kilkerrin,	Killofin,
65	Ditto,	Ditto,	Ditto,	Ditto,	Ditto,	Ditto,
66	Ditto,	Ditto,	James Browne,	Ditto,	Lakyle, North,	Ditto,
67	Ditto,	Ditto,	D. Molony,	Ditto,	Ballina,	Ditto,
68	Ditto,	Ditto,	Ditto,	Ditto,	Kilkerrin,	Ditto,
69	Ditto,	Fly-Net,	Thomas M'Mahon,	Richard Barclay,	Ballyartney	Ditto,

Appendix, No. 11.

No. 11.

Legality or Illegality of Fixed Nets erected or used for catching Salmon in Ireland.

No.	Barony.	County.	Judgment of Commissioners.	Date of Judgment.	Whether Judgment of Commissioners Appealed against.	Result of Appeal in Court of Queen's Bench.
1	Shelburne, .	Wexford, .	To be abated, as being injurious to navigation, and erected without the title required by the 5th and 6th Vic., c. 106.	17 Oct 1863,	Appeal, . . .	Appeal withdrawn.
2	St. Mullin's,	Carlow, .	To be abated, not having been legally erected in 1862.	Ditto, .	No appeal.	—
3	Shelburne, .	Wexford, .	To be abated, as being injurious to navigation, and erected without the title required by the 5th and 6th Vic., c. 106.	Ditto, .	Appeal, . . .	Judgment affirmed.
4	Ida, . .	Kilkenny, .	Ditto, ...	19 Oct. 1863,	Ditto, . . .	Ditto.
5	Ditto, .	Ditto, .	Ditto, ...	Ditto, .	No appeal.	—
6	Shelburne, .	Wexford, .	Ditto, ...	Ditto, .	Ditto.	—
7	Ditto, .	Ditto, .	Ditto, ...	Ditto, .	Ditto.	—
8	Ida, . .	Kilkenny, .	To be abated, not having been legally erected in 1862,	Ditto, .	Ditto.	—
9	Shelburne, .	Wexford, .	To be abated, as being injurious to navigation and erected without the title required by the 5th and 6th Vic., cap. 106	Ditto, .	Ditto.	
10	Ditto, .	Ditto, .	To be abated, not having been legally erected in 1862,	Ditto, .	Ditto.	—
11	Ditto, .	Ditto, .	To be abated, as being injurious to navigation. .	20 Oct 1863,	Appeal, . . .	Judgment affirmed.
12	Gaultiere, .	Waterford, .	Ditto, and erected without the title required by the 5th and 6th Vic., c. 106.	21 Oct. 1863,	No appeal.	—
13	Ditto, .	Ditto, .	Ditto, ...	Ditto, .	Ditto.	—
14	Ditto, .	Ditto, .	Ditto, ...	Ditto, .	Ditto.	—
15	Ditto, .	Ditto, .	Ditto, ...	Ditto, .	Ditto.	—
16	Ditto, .	Ditto, .	Ditto, ...	22 Oct. 1863,	Appeal, . . .	Judgment affirmed.
17	Ditto, .	Ditto, .	Ditto, ...	24 Oct 1863,	Ditto, . . .	Ditto
18	Gowran, .	Kilkenny, .	To be abated, as injurious to navigation,	26 Oct. 1863,	Ditto, . . .	Ditto.
19	Bargy, .	Wexford, .	Ditto, and erected without the title required by the 5th and 6th Vic., c. 106.	Ditto, .	Ditto, . . .	Ditto.
20	Ida, . .	Kilkenny, .	Ditto, ...	Ditto, .	No appeal.	—
21	Ditto, .	Ditto, .	Ditto, ...	Ditto, .	Ditto.	—
22	Ditto, .	Ditto, .	Ditto, ...	Ditto, .	Ditto.	—
23	Ditto, .	Ditto, .	Ditto, ...	27 Oct 1863,	Ditto.	—
24	Ditto, .	Ditto, .	Ditto, ...	29 Oct. 1863,	Ditto.	—
25	Ditto, .	Ditto, .	Ditto, ...	10 Dec. 1863,	Ditto.	—
26	Ditto, .	Ditto, .	Ditto, ...	Ditto, .	Appeal, . . .	Appeal withdrawn.
27	Ditto, .	Ditto, .	Ditto, ...	11 Dec. 1863,	Ditto, . . .	Ditto
28	Ditto, .	Ditto, .	Ditto, ...	Ditto, .	Ditto, . . .	Ditto.
29	Ditto, .	Ditto, .	Ditto, ...	Ditto, .	No appeal.	—
30	Ditto, .	Ditto, .	Ditto, ...	Ditto, .	Ditto.	—
31	Ditto, .	Ditto, .	Ditto, ...	Ditto, .	Appeal. . . .	Judgment affirmed
32	Ditto, .	Ditto, .	Ditto, ...	Ditto, .	No appeal.	—
33	Ditto, .	Ditto, .	Ditto, ...	12 Dec 1863,	Ditto.	—
34	Ditto, .	Ditto, .	Ditto, ...	Ditto, .	Ditto.	—
35	Ditto, .	Ditto, .	Ditto, ...	Ditto, .	Ditto.	—
36	Shelburne, .	Wexford, .	Ditto, ...	Ditto, .	Appeal, . . .	Appeal withdrawn.
37	Ditto, .	Ditto, .	Ditto, ...	Ditto, .	No appeal.	—
38	Ditto, .	Ditto, .	Ditto, ...	Ditto, .	Ditto.	—
39	Ditto, .	Ditto, .	To be abated, as being injurious to navigation, .	16 Dec. 1863,	Appeal, . . .	Judgment affirmed.
40	Ditto, .	Ditto, .	To be abated, as being erected in narrow channel,	4 April, 1863,	No appeal.	—
41	Ditto, .	Ditto, .	To be abated, as being injurious to navigation, and being illegally erected—extending beyond low water mark.	23 Dec. 1863,	Appeal, . . .	Judgment affirmed.
42	Ida, . .	Kilkenny, .	To be abated, as injurious to navigation, and erected without the title required by the 5th and 6th Vic., c. 106.	Ditto. .	No appeal.	—
43	Moyarta, .	Clare, .	To be abated, as erected without the title required by the 5th and 6th Vic., c. 106.	1 Jan 1864,	Ditto.	—
44	Ditto, .	Ditto, .	Ditto, ...	Ditto, .	Ditto.	—
45	Ditto, .	Ditto, .	Ditto, ...	Ditto, .	Ditto.	—
46	Ditto, .	Ditto, .	Ditto, ...	Ditto, .	Ditto.	—
47	Ditto, .	Ditto, .	Ditto, ...	Ditto, .	Ditto.	—
48	Ditto, .	Ditto, .	Ditto, ...	2 Jan. 1864,	Ditto.	—
49	Ditto, .	Ditto, .	Ditto, ...	Ditto, .	Appeal, . . .	Judgment affirmed.
50	Ditto, .	Ditto, .	Ditto, ...	Ditto, .	No appeal.	—
51	Ditto, .	Ditto, .	Ditto, ...	Ditto, .	Ditto.	—
52	Ditto, .	Ditto, .	Ditto, ...	Ditto, .	Ditto.	—
53	Ditto, .	Ditto, .	Ditto, ...	Ditto, .	Appeal, . . .	Judgment affirmed.
54	Clonderlaw,	Ditto, .	Ditto, ...	Ditto, .	Ditto, . . .	Ditto,
55	Ditto, .	Ditto, .	Ditto, ...	4 Jan. 1864,	No appeal.	—
56	Ditto, .	Ditto, .	Ditto, ...	Ditto, .	Ditto.	—
57	Ditto, .	Ditto, .	Ditto, ...	Ditto, .	Ditto.	—
58	Ditto, .	Ditto, .	Ditto, ...	Ditto, .	Appeal, . . .	Judgment reversed.
59	Ditto, .	Ditto, .	Ditto, ...	Ditto, .	No appeal.	—
60	Ditto, .	Ditto, .	Ditto, ...	Ditto, .	Ditto.	—
61	Ditto, .	Ditto, .	Ditto, ...	Ditto, .	Ditto.	—
62	Ditto, .	Ditto, .	Ditto, ...	Ditto, .	Ditto.	—
63	Ditto, .	Ditto, .	Ditto, ...	Ditto, .	Ditto.	—
64	Ditto, .	Ditto, .	Ditto, ...	7 Jan. 1864,	Appeal, . . .	Judgment reversed
65	Ditto, .	Ditto, .	Ditto, ...	Ditto, .	Ditto, . . .	Ditto.
66	Ditto, .	Ditto, .	Ditto, ...	Ditto, .	Ditto, . . .	Judgment affirmed.
67	Ditto, .	Ditto, .	Ditto, and not having been legally erected in 1862.	8 Jan. 1864,	No appeal.	—
68	Ditto, .	Ditto, .	Ditto, ...	Ditto, .	Ditto.	—
69	Ditto, .	Ditto, .	Ditto, ...	7 Jan. 1864,	Ditto.	—

Appendix, No. 11

Result of Inquiries held by the Special Commissioners of Irish Fisheries into the

No.	Where Fixed Net situated.	Description of Fixed Net.	Name of Person maintaining and using Fixed Net.	Name of Owner of Fixed Net, or of Land to which Net attached.	Name of Townland in which Net attached.	Parish.
70	River Barrow, otherwise Nore and Barrow conjoined.	Head Weir,	Richard Hewitson,	M. W. Knox,	Kilmannock,	Kilmokea,
71	River Suir,	Ditto,	G. Giles,	G. Giles,	Kilmurry,	Rathpatrick,
72	Rivers Suir, Nore, and Barrow conjoined, otherwise Waterford Harbour.	Stake Weir,	James Ryan,	Lord Ely,	Dunmannon,	St. James and Dunbrody.
73	Slade Bay,	Bag-Net,	W. Breen,	Ditto,	Slade,	Hook,
74	Suir, Nore, and Barrow conjoined.	Head Weir,	J. Henlon and others,	Lord Templemore,	Nook,	St. James and Dunbrody
75	Ditto,	Ditto,	Anthony Wallis,	Ditto,	Ballyhack,	Ditto,
76	Ditto,	Stake-Net,	Arthur N. O'Neill,	Lord Carew,	Woodstown, Lower,	Crooke,
77	Ditto,	Ditto,	Ditto,	Ditto,	Knockaveelish,	Killea,
78	Suir, King's Channel,	Ditto,	Mary O'Neill,	Mary O'Neill,	Knockboy,	Ballygunner,
79	Ditto,	Ditto,	Ditto,	Ditto,	Ditto,	Ditto,
80	Suir, Nore, and Barrow conjoined.	Head Weir,	John Henlon & others,	Lord Templemore,	Saltmills,	St. James and Dunbrody.
81	Ditto,	Ditto,	Ditto,	Ditto,	Ballyback,	Ditto,
82	Shannon,	Stake-Net,	Stephen Cunningham,	Bryan O'Loghlen,	Ahrachag,	Killadane,
83	Ditto,	Fly-Net,	R. W. C. Reeves,	R. W. C. Reeves,	Poulnadarea,	Killimer,
84	Ditto,	Stake Net,	Ditto,	Ditto,	Barrane, Lower,	Ditto,
85	Ditto,	Ditto,	Ditto,	Ditto,	Ditto,	Ditto,
86	Ditto,	Ditto,	Ditto,	Ditto,	Ditto,	Ditto,
87	Ditto,	Ditto,	Michael Culhane,	Colonel Hickman,	Knock,	Kilmurry,
88	Ditto,	Ditto,	S. M'Auliffe & John Brooks,	Ditto,	Ditto,	Ditto,
89	Ditto,	Ditto,	Ellen Hednett,	Ditto,	Kilmore,	Ditto,
90	Ditto,	Ditto,	Ditto,	Ditto,	Ditto,	Ditto,
91	Ditto,	Ditto,	Ditto,	Ditto,	Ditto,	Ditto,
92	Ditto,	Ditto,	John Houlahan,	Ditto,	Carrowduane,	Ditto,
93	Ditto,	Ditto,	S. Pegum,	Rev. T. Butler,	Poulnadarea,	Killimer,
94	Ditto,	Ditto,	Ditto,	Ditto,	Ditto,	Ditto,
95	Ditto,	Ditto,	Henry S. O'Brien,	Henry S. O'Brien,	Partidrina,	Kilmacduane,
96	Ditto,	Ditto,	S. M'Auliffe,	T. R. Ross,	Shanakeelay,	Killofin,
97	Ditto,	Ditto,	T. Naughton & others,	R. T. Massy,	Ballymacasura,	Ballysteen,
98	Ditto,	Ditto,	M. Shaughnessy and others,	Lord Guillamore,	Courtbrown,	Askeaton,
99	Ditto,	Ditto,	R. M'Cauliffe,	Colonel Hickman,	Knock,	Kilmurry,
100	Ditto,	Ditto,	J. Browne,	Lord Monteagle,	Leahys,	Robertstown,
101	Ditto,	Ditto,	Ditto,	Ditto,	Durnish,	Shanagolden,
102	Ditto.	Ditto,	Ditto,	Ditto,	Foynes Island,	Robertstown,
103	Ditto,	Ditto,	Ditto,	Ditto,	Ditto,	Ditto,
104	Ditto,	Ditto,	Ditto,	Ditto,	Mount Trenchard,	Loghill,
105	Ditto,	Ditto,	Ditto,	Ditto,	Ditto,	Ditto,
106	Ditto,	Ditto,	P. Sheehan,	Lord Clare,	Ballynash (Clare),	Robertstown,
107	Ditto,	Ditto,	M. M'Namarra,	R. Bateson,	Loghill,	Loghill,
108	Ditto,	Ditto,	John Griffin,	Thomas Royse,	Carrowbuncheeg,	Ditto,
109	Ditto,	Ditto,	M. M'Namarra,	Earl of Clare,	Ditto,	Ditto,
110	Ditto,	Ditto,	J. Browne,	C. Mosdell,	Kilacolla,	Kilfergus,
111	Ditto,	Ditto,	Margaret Fitzhead and others,	Knight of Glin,	Coharagh,	Ditto,
112	Ditto,	Ditto,	Ditto,	Ditto,	Glin Demesne,	Ditto,
113	Ditto,	Ditto,	Ditto,	Ditto,	Ferrandallier,	Ditto,
114	Ditto,	Ditto,	J. Browne,	Elizabeth Standish,	Kilmacollia (Barker),	Ditto,
115	Ditto,	Fly-Net,	W. B. Barrington,	W. B. Barrington,	Ballyhoolahan,	Loghill,
116	Ditto,	Ditto,	J. Browne,	Rev. R. Fitzgerald,	Ballydonohoe,	Kilfergus,
117	Ditto,	Stake-Net,	P. J. Mayne,	P. J. Mayne,	East Aslon,	Aghavallin,
118	Ditto,	Ditto,	Ditto,	Ditto,	West Aslon,	Ditto,
119	Ditto,	Ditto,	J. Pim,	W. C. Hickey,	Cloonaman,	Ditto,
120	Ditto,	Ditto,	C. Sandes,	C. Sandes,	Carrig Island,	Ditto,
121	Ditto,	Ditto,	J. Pim,	R. Leslie,	Kilcolgan, Lower,	Kilnaughtin,
122	Ditto,	Ditto,	Alicia Wren,	Lord Listowel,	Carras and Sand Hills,	Kilconly,
123	Ditto,	Fly-Net,	Ditto,	Ditto,	Castlequarter,	Ditto,
124	Ditto,	Stake-Net,	Ditto,	Leslie Wren,	Kylestallen,	Ditto,
125	Ditto,	Ditto,	W. Sandes,	T. Sandes,	Carhoonakinneely,	Kilnaughtin,
126	Ditto,	Ditto,	Alicia Wren,	Leslie Wren,	Carrigane,	Aghavallin,
127	Sea off Coast of County Cork,	Bag-Net,	C. Desmond,	Samuel Hodder,	Kingsbella,	Tracton,
128	Ditto,	Fly-Net,	W. Atkinson,	Lord Ponsonby,	Redbarn,	Clonpriest,
129	Ditto,	Ditto,	N. T. Foley,	Murdock Green,	Summerfield,	Youghal,
130	Ditto,	Stake-Net,	J. Ronayne,	Ditto,	Ditto,	Ditto,
131	Ditto,	Fly-Net,	N. T. Foley,	D. L. Lewis,	Claycastle,	Ditto,

Legality or Illegality of Fixed Nets erected or used for catching Salmon in Ireland—*continued.*

No.	Barony.	County.	Judgment of Commissioners.	Date of Judgment.	Whether Judgment of Commissioners Appealed against.	Result of Appeal in Court of Queen's Bench.
70	Shelburne, .	Wexford, .	To be abated, as injurious to navigation, and as erected without the title required by 5 & 6 Vic., c. 106.	18 Mar 1864,	Appeal, . . .	Sent back for further inquiry as to partial abatement.—See No. 272.
71	Ida, . .	Kilkenny, .	Ditto, ...	14 Mar. 1864,	No appeal.	—
72	Shelburne, .	Wexford, .	To be abated, as erected without the title required by 5 & 6 Vic., c. 106	15 Mar. 1864,	Appeal, . . .	Withdrawn.
73	Ditto, .	Ditto, .	Ditto, ...	Ditto, .	No appeal.	—
74	Ditto,	Ditto, .	Legally erected, ...	16 Mar. 1864	—	—
75	Ditto. .	Ditto, .	To be abated, as injurious to navigation, .	Ditto, .	Appeal, . . .	Withdrawn.
76	Gaultiere, .	Waterford, .	To be abated, as erected without the title required by 5 & 6 Vic., c. 106.	17 Mar. 1864,	Ditto. .	Sent back for reconsideration.—See Nos. 251 to 254 inclusive.
77	Ditto, .	Ditto, .	Ditto, ...	Ditto, .	Ditto, .	
78	Ditto, .	Ditto, .	Ditto, ...	18 Mar 1864,	Ditto, . .	
79	Ditto, .	Ditto, .	Ditto, ...	Ditto, .	Ditto, . .	
80	Shelburne, . .	Wexford, .	To be abated, Lord Templemore consenting. .	Ditto, .	No appeal.	—
81	Ditto, .	Ditto, .	Ditto, ...	Ditto,	Ditto.	—
82	Clonderlaw,	Clare, .	Legally erected, ...	26 Mar. 1864	—	—
83	Ditto, .	Ditto, .	To be abated; not erected in 1862, . .	28 Mar 1864,	No appeal.	—
84	Ditto, .	Ditto, .	To be abated, as erected without the title required by 5 & 6 Vic., c. 106; and extending beyond low-water mark. The latter question to be tried by Commissioners when appeal on title decided.	29 Mar. 1864,	Appeal, . . .	Judgment reversed.
85	Ditto, .	Ditto, .	Ditto, ...	Ditto, .	Ditto, . .	Sent back.—See No. 263.
86	Ditto, .	Ditto, .	To be abated, as erected without the title required by 5 & 6 Vic., c. 106, and as being injurious to navigation.	Ditto, .	Ditto, . .	Judgment affirmed.
87	Ditto, .	Ditto, .	To be abated; not erected in 1862, . .	30 Mar 1864,	Ditto, . .	Ditto.
88	Ditto, .	Ditto, .	Ditto, ...	Ditto, .	No appeal.	—
89	Ditto, .	Ditto, .	To be abated, as injurious to navigation, and as erected without the title required by 5 & 6 Vic., c. 106	31 Mar 1864,	Appeal, . . .	Judgment affirmed.
90	Ditto, .	Ditto, .	To be abated, as erected without the title required by 5 & 6 Vic., c. 106.	Ditto, .	Ditto, . .	Judgment reversed.
91	Ditto, .	Ditto, .	To be abated; not erected in 1862, . .	Ditto, .	Ditto. . .	Judgment affirmed.
92	Ditto, .	Ditto, .	To be abated, as injurious to navigation, and as erected without the title required by 5 & 6 Vic., c. 106.	Ditto, .	Ditto, . .	Ditto.
93	Ditto, .	Ditto, .	To be abated by consent of Mr. Butler, . .	2 April, 1864,	No appeal.	—
94	Ditto, .	Ditto, .	Ditto, ...	Ditto. .	Ditto.	—
95	Bunratty Lr.	Ditto, .	To be abated, as being injurious to navigation, and to the public right of fishing.	4 April, 1864,	Appeal, . . .	New trial granted upon point of form, see No. 180.
96	Clonderlaw,	Ditto, .	To be abated, as erected without the title required by 5 & 6 Vic., c. 106,	Ditto, .	No appeal.	—
97	Kenry, .	Limerick, .	Ditto, ...	Ditto, .	Ditto.	—
98	Lower Connello.	Ditto, .	Ditto, ...	Ditto, .	Ditto.	—
99	Clonderlaw,	Clare, .	Ditto, ...	Ditto, .	Ditto.	—
100	Shanid, .	Limerick, .	To be abated, as injurious to navigation. .	5 April, 1864,	Ditto.	—
101	Ditto, .	Ditto, .	To be abated, as erected without the title required by 5 & 6 Vic., c. 106, and injurious to public right of fishing	6 April, 1864,	Appeal, . . .	Judgment reversed.
102	Ditto, .	Ditto, .	To be abated, as erected without the title required by 5 & 6 Vic., c. 106.	Ditto, .	Ditto, . .	Ditto.
103	Ditto, .	Ditto, .	Ditto, ...	Ditto, .	Ditto, . .	Ditto.
104	Ditto, .	Ditto, .	Ditto, ...	Ditto, .	Ditto, . .	Ditto
105	Ditto, .	Ditto, .	To be abated by consent; not erected in 1862,	Ditto, .	No appeal.	—
106	Ditto, .	Ditto, .	To be abated, as erected without the title required by 5 & 6 Vic., c. 106.	7 April, 1864,	Ditto.	—
107	Ditto, .	Ditto, .	Ditto, ...	Ditto, .	Ditto.	—
108	Ditto, .	Ditto, .	Ditto, ...	Ditto, .	Appeal, . . .	Judgment reversed.
109	Ditto, .	Ditto, .	To be abated, not having been erected in 1862,	Ditto, .	No appeal.	—
110	Ditto, .	Ditto, .	Legally erected, ...	Ditto, .	Appeal, . .	Judgment affirmed.
111	Ditto, .	Ditto, .	To be abated, as erected without the title required by 5 & 6 Vic., c. 106.	Ditto, .	Ditto, . .	Sent back.—See No. 265.
112	Ditto, .	Ditto, .	To be abated; injurious to navigation, . .	Ditto, .	No appeal.	—
113	Ditto, .	Ditto, .	To be abated, as erected without the title required by 5 & 6 Vic., c. 106.	Ditto, .	Ditto.	—
114	Ditto, .	Ditto. .	Ditto, ...	8 April, 1864,	Appeal, . . .	Appeal withdrawn.
115	Ditto, .	Ditto, .	Legally erected, ...	Ditto, .	No appeal.	—
116	Ditto, .	Ditto, .	To be abated, as erected without the title required by 5 & 6 Vic., c. 106, and not erected in 1862	Ditto, .	Ditto.	—
117	Iraghticonnor	Kerry, .	To be abated, not legally erected in 1862, and injurious to the public right of fishing.	11 April, 1864,	Appeal, . . .	Judgment affirmed.
118	Ditto, .	Ditto, .	Ditto, ...	Ditto, .	Ditto, . .	Ditto.
119	Ditto, .	Ditto, .	To be abated, as erected without the title required by 5 & 6 Vic., c. 106	Ditto, .	Ditto, . .	Judgment reversed.
120	Ditto, .	Ditto, .	To be abated; not erected in 1862, . .	Ditto, .	No appeal.	—
121	Ditto, .	Ditto, .	Ditto, ...	Ditto, .	Ditto.	—
122	Ditto, .	Ditto, .	To be abated, as erected without the title required by 5 & 6 Vic., c. 106.	Ditto, .	Ditto.	—
123	Ditto, .	Ditto, .	Ditto, ...	Ditto,	Ditto.	—
124	Ditto, .	Ditto, .	Ditto, and not erected in 1862, . . .	12 April, 1864,	Appeal, . . .	Judgment reversed.
125	Ditto, .	Ditto, .	Ditto, ...	Ditto, .	Ditto, . .	Judgment affirmed.
126	Ditto, .	Ditto, .	To be abated, as injurious to public rights of fishing.	Ditto, .	Ditto, . .	Judgment reversed; but public right of fishing preserved.
127	Kinalea, .	Cork, .	To be abated, as being within three miles of Carrigaline River mouth.	4 Aug. 1864,	Ditto, . .	Judgment reversed.
128	Imokilly, .	Ditto, .	To be abated, as erected without the title required by 5 & 6 Vic., c. 106,	6 Aug. 1864,	No appeal.	—
129	Ditto, .	Ditto, .	Ditto, ...	Ditto, .	Ditto.	—
130	Ditto, .	Ditto, .	Ditto, ...	Ditto, .	Ditto.	—
131	Ditto, .	Ditto, .	To be abated, as injurious to navigation, .	Ditto, . .	Ditto. .	

APPENDIX, No. 11.

RESULT of INQUIRIES held by the SPECIAL COMMISSIONERS of IRISH FISHERIES into the

No.	Where Fixed Net situated.	Description of Fixed Net.	Name of Person maintaining and using Fixed Net.	Name of Owner of Fixed Net or of Land to which Net attached.	Name of Townland to which Net attached.	Parish.
132	Sea off Coast of co. Cork,	Bag-Net,	John Walsh,	Roger Davis,	Knockadoon,	Youghal,
133	Ditto,	Ditto,	D. Sullivan,	M. Longfield,	Ballycotton,	Kilmahon,
134	Ballycotton Bay, co. Cork,	Ditto,	J. Lotton,	J. Lotton,	Ditto,	Ditto,
135	River Blackwater,	Stake-Net,	R. Power,	Trustees of Mrs. Osborne,	Pillpark,	Clashmore,
136	Ditto,	Ditto,	F. Kennedy and others,	Lord Stuart de Decies,	Tinnkock,	Ditto,
137	Ditto,	Ditto,	H. T. Dennehy,	Ditto,	Ardsallagh,	Ditto,
138	Ditto,	Ditto,	J. Ronayne,	Ditto,	Ditto,	Ditto,
139	Ditto,	Ditto,	Ditto,	Ditto,	Ditto,	Ditto,
140	Ditto,	Ditto,	M. B. Ronayne,	Ditto,	Ditto,	Ditto,
141	Ditto,	Ditto,	G. Crotty,	Ditto,	Coolbagh,	Ditto,
142	Ditto,	Head Weir,	G. Dalton,	Ditto,	Dromana,	Affane,
143	Ditto,	Stake-Net,	M. G. Adams,	Hon. C. W. M. Smythe,	Rincrew,	Templemichael
144	Ditto,	Ditto,	Hon. C. W. M. Smythe,	Ditto,	Ballynatray,	Ditto,
145	Ditto,	Ditto,	E. M'Sweeney,	—	Templemichael,	Ditto,
146	Ditto,	Ditto,	S. Allen & N. T. Foley,	Samuel Allen,	D'Loughtane,	[illegible]
147	Ditto,	Ditto,	P. Sliney & J. Hurley,	—	Newport, East,	Templemichael
148	Ditto,	Ditto,	P. Doolan,	Lord Huntingdon,	Ballynaclash,	Clashmore,
149	Ditto,	Ditto,	M. Ronayne,	Ditto,	Ditto,	Ditto
150	Ditto,	Ditto,	P. Mansfield,	J. Kiely,	Newport, East,	Kilcockan,
151	Ditto,	Ditto,	M. White & W. Murphy,	—	Scramcally,	Ditto,
152	Ditto,	Ditto,	M. White,	—	Carriglass,	Ditto,
153	Ditto,	Ditto,	R. Cotter,	Lord Stuart de Decies,	Tinnascart,	Aglish,
154	Ditto,	Ditto,	R. M'Sweeney,	—	Strad.	Templemichael
155	Ditto,	Ditto,	John Neil and W. Hennessy.	Rev. G. Gumbleton,	Sart,	Kilcockan,
156	Ditto,	Ditto,	R. Browne and Michl. M'Carthy	C. Musgrave,	Glenassy, or Glenasea,	Aglish,
157	Ditto,	Ditto,	J. Fitzgerald,	C. O'Mahony,	Ballyphillip, East,	Kilcockan,
158	Ditto,	Ditto,	R. Healy,	J. Hargrave,	Dromore,	Aglish,
159	Ditto,	Ditto,	William Collins,	Ditto,	Ditto,	Ditto,
160	Ditto,	Ditto,	Maurice Hickey,	Ditto,	Ditto,	Ditto,
161	Ditto,	Head Weir,	C. Ussher,	C. Ussher,	Camphire,	Lismore,
162	Ditto,	Ditto,	J. Rice,	—	Killahaly, East,	Ditto,
163	Ditto,	Ditto,	Sir R. Musgrave,	Sir R. Musgrave,	Town Demesne,	Ditto
164	Ditto,	Ditto,	Ditto,	Ditto,	Norrisland,	Ditto,
165	Bride,	Ditto,	M. Whelan,	C. Ussher,	Camphire,	Ditto,
166	Ditto,	Ditto,	J. M'Grath,	Ditto,	O'Kyle,	Ditto,
167	Ditto,	Ditto,	P. Walsh,	O. Smith,	Sapperborough,	Kilwatermoy,
168	Ditto,	Ditto,	J. Connell,	Duke of Devonshire,	Bridane, Lower,	Lismore,
169	Ditto,	Ditto,	R. P. Maxwell,	R. P. Maxwell,	Killanthony,	Kilwatermoy,
170	Ditto,	Ditto,	P. Keane,	R. Oliver,	Ballynarahs,	Lismore,
171	Ditto,	Ditto,	T. Hannigan,	Duke of Devonshire,	Kilnacarriga,	Ditto,
172	Ditto,	Ditto,	J. Barry,	Ditto,	Ballinvella,	Ditto,
173	Ditto,	Ditto,	R. P. Maxwell,	R. P. Maxwell,	Sapperton, North,	Kilwatermoy,
174	Ditto,	Ditto,	J. Mangan,	Duke of Devonshire,	Ballinvella,	Lismore,
175	Ditto,	Ditto,	J. Lealy,	Ditto,	Monatrim,	Ditto,
176	Ardmore Bay,	Bag-Net,	T. Healy,	E. O'Dell,	Duffcarrick,	Ardmore,
177	Ditto,	Ditto,	Ditto,	Ditto,	Dysert,	Ditto,
178	Castlemaine Harbour,	Stake-Net,	H. W. Dodd & others,	Tim M'Gillycuddy,	Killeenagh,	Ballinvoher,
179	Ditto,	Ditto,	M. Ashe,	Reps. Lord Ventry,	Inch,	Ditto,
180	Ditto,	Ditto,	H. W. Dodd & others,	E. Mahony,	Dooghs,	Killorglin,
181	Ditto,	Ditto,	Ditto,	Ditto,	Illaunstook,	Ditto,
182	Ditto,	Ditto,	M. De Moleyns,	Reps. Lord Ventry,	Cromane, Lower,	Ditto,
183	Ditto,	Ditto,	Sir R. Blennerhassett,	Sir R. Blennerhassett,	Douglas,	Ditto,
184	Ballinskelligs Bay,	Bag-Net,	W. Hester,	E. Reeves,	Dungeagan,	Prior,
185	Kenmare River,	Ditto,	M. O'Sullivan,	E. D. Hartopp,	Rath,	Kilcrohane,
186	Sea off Coast of co. Louth,	Ditto,	T. A. Newcomen,	Smith Darcy,	Glasspistol,	Clogher,
187	Ditto,	Ditto,	Arthur and Jane Newcomen.	Arthur Newcomen,	Callystown,	Ditto,
188	Ditto,	Ditto,	T. Kirk,	A. Godley,	Clogher,	Ditto,
189	Ditto,	Ditto,	Jane S. Newcomen,	Arthur Newcomen,	Callystown,	Ditto,
190	Ditto,	Ditto,	Ditto,	Ditto,	Ditto,	Ditto,
191	Ditto,	Ditto,	E. Jones,	Sir A. Bellingham,	Dunany,	Dunany,
192	Ditto,	Ditto,	John Jones,	Ditto,	Drakestown,	Ditto,
193	Ditto,	Ditto,	T. Kirk,	A. Godley,	Clogher,	Clogher,
194	Ditto,	Head Weir,	J. M'Keon,	Sir A. Bellingham,	Castlebellingham,	Gernonstown,
195	Sea off Coast of co. Antrim,	Bag-Net,	Charles Black,	Lord Antrim,	Portrush,	Dunluce,
196	Ditto,	Ditto,	Ditto,	Ditto,	Ditto,	Ditto,
197	Ditto,	Ditto,	Ditto,	Ditto,	Ditto,	Ditto,
198	Ditto,	Ditto,	Ditto,	Ditto,	Ditto,	Ditto,
199	Ditto,	Ditto,	Ditto,	Ditto,	Ditto,	Ditto,
200	Ditto,	Ditto,	Ditto,	Ditto,	Ditto,	Ditto,
201	Ditto,	Ditto,	Ditto,	Ditto,	Ditto,	Ditto,
202	Ditto,	Ditto,	John Ramsey,	Ditto,	Tow,	Culfeightrin,
203	Ditto,	Ditto,	N. D. Crommelin,	Ditto,	Ballyteerim,	Ditto,
204	Ditto,	Ditto,	A. M'Keegan,	Ditto,	Glebe,	Layd,
205	Ditto,	Ditto,	Lord Antrim,	Ditto,	Cornalough,	Ardclinis,
206	Ditto,	Ditto,	Ditto,	Ditto,	Townparks, Glenarm,	Tickmacrevan,
207	Ditto,	Ditto,	J. M'Intosh,	E. H. M'Neile,	Redbay,	Layd,
208	Ditto,	Ditto,	A. M'Keegan,	Charles Black,	Moneyvart,	Ditto,

Legality or Illegality of Fixed Nets erected or used for catching Salmon in Ireland—*continued.*

APPENDIX, No. 11.

No.	Barony	County.	Judgment of Commissioners.	Date of Judgment.	Whether Judgment of Commissioners Appealed against.	Result of Appeal in Court of Queen's Bench.
132	Imokilly,	Cork,	To be abated, being within three miles of mouth of Womanagh River.	8 Aug. 1864,	No appeal.	—
133	Ditto,	Ditto,	Postponed	—	—	—
134	Ditto,	Ditto,	Legally erected,	29 June 1863,	No appeal.	—
135	Drum-with-in Drum,	Waterford,	To be abated, as injurious to navigation,	12 Aug. 1864,	Ditto.	—
136	Ditto,	Ditto,	Ditto, by consent,	Ditto,	Ditto.	—
137	Ditto,	Ditto,	Ditto, ditto,	Ditto,	Ditto.	—
138	Ditto,	Ditto,	Ditto, ditto,	Ditto,	Ditto.	—
139	Ditto,	Ditto,	Ditto, ditto,	Ditto,	Ditto.	—
140	Ditto,	Ditto,	Ditto, ditto,	Ditto,	Ditto.	—
141	Ditto,	Ditto,	Ditto, ditto,	Ditto,	Ditto.	—
142	Drum-with-out-Drum,	Ditto,	Ditto, ditto,	Ditto,	Ditto.	—
143	Cashmore & Coshbride,	Ditto,	Ditto, ditto,	13 Aug. 1864,	Ditto.	—
144	Ditto,	Ditto,	To be abated, as injurious to navigation,	15 Aug. 1864,	Ditto.	—
145	Ditto,	Ditto,	Ditto,	16 Aug. 1864,	Ditto.	—
146	Drum-with-in-Drum,	Ditto,	To be abated, as erected without the title required by 5 & 6 Vic., c. 106.	Ditto,	Ditto.	—
147	Cashmore & Coshbride,	Ditto,	To be abated, as injurious to navigation,	Ditto,	Ditto.	—
148	Drum-with-in-Drum,	Ditto,	To be abated by consent of Lord Huntingdon,	Ditto,	Ditto.	—
149	Ditto,	Ditto,	Ditto,	Ditto,	Ditto.	—
150	Cashmore & Coshbride,	Ditto,	To be abated, as injurious to navigation,	Ditto,	Ditto.	—
151	Ditto,	Ditto,	Ditto,	Ditto,	Ditto.	—
152	Ditto,	Ditto,	To be abated by consent,	Ditto,	Ditto.	—
153	Drum-with-in Drum,	Ditto,	To be abated, as injurious to navigation,	17 Aug. 1864,	Ditto.	—
154	Ditto,	Ditto,	To be abated, as erected without the title required by 5 & 6 Vic., c. 106.	Ditto,	Appeal,	Sent back.—See 273.
155	Ditto,	Ditto,	To be abated so far as it extends beyond low water mark; legally erected as regards the rest	Ditto,	Ditto,	Judgment affirmed.—See 275.
156	Drum-with-in-Drum,	Ditto,	To be abated, as erected without the title required by 5 & 6 Vic., c. 106.	Ditto,	No appeal.	—
157	Cashmore & Coshbride,	Ditto,	Ditto,	Ditto,	Ditto.	—
158	Drum-with-in-Drum,	Ditto,	Ditto,	Ditto,	Ditto.	—
159	Ditto,	Ditto,	Ditto,	Ditto,	Appeal,	Sent back.—See 274.
160	Ditto,	Ditto,	Ditto,	Ditto,	No appeal.	—
161	Cashmore & Coshbride,	Ditto,	To be abated not erected in 1862,	Ditto,	Ditto.	—
162	Ditto,	Ditto,	To be abated, as injurious to navigation,	Ditto,	Ditto.	—
163	Ditto,	Ditto,	Ditto,	Ditto,	Ditto.	—
164	Ditto,	Ditto,	Ditto,	Ditto,	Ditto.	—
165	Ditto,	Ditto,	Ditto,	Ditto,	Ditto.	—
166	Ditto,	Ditto,	Ditto,	Ditto,	Ditto.	—
167	Ditto,	Ditto,	Ditto,	Ditto,	Ditto.	—
168	Ditto,	Ditto,	Ditto,	Ditto,	Ditto.	—
169	Ditto,	Ditto,	Ditto,	Ditto,	Ditto.	—
170	Ditto,	Ditto,	Ditto,	Ditto,	Ditto.	—
171	Ditto,	Ditto,	Ditto,	Ditto,	Ditto.	—
172	Ditto,	Ditto,	Ditto,	Ditto,	Ditto.	—
173	Ditto,	Ditto,	Ditto,	Ditto,	Ditto.	—
174	Ditto,	Ditto,	Ditto,	Ditto,	Ditto.	—
175	Ditto,	Ditto,	Ditto,	Ditto,	Ditto.	—
176	Drum-with-in-Drum,	Ditto,	To be abated, as erected without the title required by 5 & 6 Vic., c. 106.	Ditto,	Ditto.	—
177	Ditto,	Ditto,	Ditto,	Ditto,	Ditto.	—
178	Corkaguiny,	Kerry,	Ditto,	22 Aug. 1864,	Ditto.	—
179	Ditto,	Ditto,	Ditto,	Ditto,	Ditto.	—
180	Iveragh,	Ditto,	Ditto,	Ditto,	Ditto.	—
181	Ditto,	Ditto,	Ditto,	Ditto,	Ditto.	—
182	Ditto,	Ditto,	Ditto,	23 Aug. 1864,	Appeal,	Appeal withdrawn.
183	Ditto,	Ditto,	To be abated; not erected in 1862,	Ditto,	No appeal.	—
184	Ditto,	Ditto,	To be abated, within three miles of mouth of Inny River.	Ditto,	Ditto.	—
185	Dunkerron, S.,	Ditto,	Legally erected,	Ditto,	Ditto.	—
186	Ferrard,	Louth,	To be abated, as erected without the title required by 5 & 6 Vic., c. 106.	26 Aug. 1864,	Ditto.	—
187	Ditto,	Ditto,	Ditto,	Ditto,	Ditto.	—
188	Ditto,	Ditto,	Ditto,	Ditto,	Ditto.	—
189	Ditto,	Ditto,	Ditto,	Ditto,	Ditto.	—
190	Ditto,	Ditto,	Ditto,	Ditto,	Ditto.	—
191	Ditto,	Ditto,	Ditto,	Ditto,	Ditto.	—
192	Ditto,	Ditto,	Legally erected,	Ditto,	Ditto.	—
193	Ditto,	Ditto,	To be abated, as erected without the title required by 5 & 6 Vic., c. 106.	27 Aug. 1864,	Ditto.	—
194	Ditto,	Ditto,	Legally erected,	Ditto,	Ditto.	—
195	Lr. Dunluce,	Antrim,	Ditto,	29 Aug. 1864,	Ditto.	—
196	Ditto,	Ditto,	Ditto,	Ditto,	Ditto.	—
197	Ditto,	Ditto,	Ditto,	Ditto,	Ditto.	—
198	Ditto,	Ditto,	Ditto,	Ditto,	Ditto.	—
199	Ditto,	Ditto,	Ditto,	Ditto,	Ditto.	—
200	Ditto,	Ditto,	Ditto,	Ditto,	Ditto.	—
201	Ditto,	Ditto,	To be abated; injurious to navigation,	Ditto,	Ditto.	—
202	Carey,	Ditto,	Legally erected,	30 Aug. 1864,	Ditto.	—
203	Ditto,	Ditto,	To be abated; within 3 miles of mouth of Cushendun River.	Ditto,	Ditto.	—
204	Lr. Glenarm,	Ditto,	Ditto,	Ditto,	Ditto.	—
205	Ditto,	Ditto,	Ditto, ditto Glenarm River,	Ditto,	Appeal,	Judgment reversed.
206	Ditto,	Ditto,	Ditto; in Estuary of Glenarm River,	Ditto,	Ditto,	Judgment affirmed.
207	Ditto,	Ditto,	Ditto; within 5 miles of mouths of Cushendall and Glenariffe Rivers.	Ditto,	No appeal.	—
208	Ditto,	Ditto,	Ditto,	Ditto,	Ditto.	—

Appendix, No. 11.

Result of Inquiries held by the Special Commissioners of Irish Fisheries into the

No.	Where Fixed Net situated.	Description of Fixed Net.	Name of Person maintaining and using Fixed Net.	Name of Owner of Fixed Net, or of Land to which Net attached.	Name of Townland to which Net attached.	Parish.
209	Sea off coast of co. Antrim,	Bag-Net,	Thomas Tait,	A. Boyd,	Ballycastle,	Ramoan,
210	Ditto,	Ditto,	Ditto,	Ditto,	Ditto,	Ditto,
211	Ditto,	Ditto,	J. M'Gildowney,	J. M'Gildowney,	Clare park,	Ditto,
212	Ditto,	Ditto,	A. M'Quilkan,	J. K. Tonant,	Cromanboy,	Ditto,
213	Ditto,	Ditto,	S. Woodside,	Ditto,	Ditto,	Ditto,
214	Ditto,	Ditto,	H. Darlison,	G. E. Fullerton,	Carrick-a-rede Island,	Ballintoy,
215	Ditto,	Ditto,	H. Kelly,	Ditto,	Larrybane,	Ditto,
216	Ditto,	Ditto,	H. Stewart,	Sir E. M'Naghten,	Portbraddan,	Ditto,
217	Ditto,	Ditto,	Ditto,	J. E. Leslie,	Templastragh,	Ditto,
218	Ditto,	Ditto,	J. M'Alister,	K. M'Neale,	Carrylaskin,	Ditto,
219	Ditto,	Ditto,	P. Mills,	J. C. Anderson,	Portnacon - Feigh Mountain,	Dunseverick,
220	Ditto,	Ditto,	Ditto,	Ditto,	Ditto,	Ditto,
221	Ditto,	Ditto,	W. Gregg,	Sir E. M'Naghten,	Ardihennon,	Billy,
222	Ditto,	Ditto,	Ditto,	Ditto,	Bushfoot,	Dunluce,
223	Sea off Coast of co. Londonderry,	Ditto,	H. O'Neill,	A. Shuldham and Hon. Mrs. Campbell,	East Ballyguelagh,	Ballyaghran,
224	Ditto,	Ditto,	J. M'Keeman,	Sir H. H. Bruce,	Freehall,	Dunboe,
225	Sea off coast of co. Donegal,	Ditto,	C. M'Kinney,	Rev. S. Montgomery,	Glenagivney,	Lower Moville,
226	Ditto,	Ditto,	Ditto,	J. S. Nicholson,	Mossy Glen,	Ditto,
227	Ditto,	Ditto,	Ditto,	Anne Knox,	Ballymagaragh,	Ditto,
228	Ditto,	Ditto,	Ditto,	P. M'Clelland,	Ballyeharry,	Ditto,
229	Ditto,	Ditto,	B. Sheffry,	J. S. Nicholson,	Tirmacroragh,	Culdaff,
230	Ditto,	Ditto,	A. Maddison,	R. C. Stewart,	Horn Head,	Clondahorky,
231	Sea off Coast of co. Londonderry,	Ditto,	R. Stewart,	Sir H. H. Bruce,	Ballymaclary,	Magilligan,
232	Ditto,	Ditto,	Ditto,	Ditto,	Downhill,	Ditto,
233	Lough Foyle,	Stake-Net,	R. Allen,	Irish Society,	Granshaw,	Clondermott,
234	Ditto,	Ditto,	Ditto,	Ditto,	Ditto,	Ditto,
235	Ditto,	Ditto,	Ditto,	Ditto,	Ditto,	Ditto,
236	Ditto,	Ditto,	Ditto,	Ditto,	Ballynashallog,	Templemore,
237	Ditto,	Ditto,	Ditto,	Ditto,	Ditto,	Ditto,
238	Ditto,	Ditto,	Ditto,	Ditto,	Culmore,	Ditto,
239	Ditto,	Ditto,	Ditto,	Ditto,	Culmore Level,	Ditto,
240	Ditto,	Ditto,	Ditto,	Ditto,	Lower Campsey,	Faughanvale,
241	Ditto,	Ditto,	Ditto,	Ditto,	Coolkeeragh,	Clondermott,
242	Ditto,	Ditto,	Ditto,	Ditto,	Ditto,	Ditto,
243	Ditto,	Ditto,	Ditto,	Ditto,	Culmore,	Culmore,
244	River Inne,	Ditto,	Abram Shell,	Thomas Connolly,	Finner,	Inishmacsaint,
245	Sea off Coast of co. Sligo,	Bag-Net,	William Petrie,	Ormsby Jones,	Streedagh,	Ahamlish,
246	Ditto,	Ditto,	William Little,	R. Orme,	Carrowhubbock,	Kilglass,
247	Sea off Coast of co. Mayo,	Ditto,	M. Flynn,	Colonel Knox,	Castletown or Lacken,	Lackan,
248	Ditto,	Ditto,	William Little,	Rev. J. M'Naghten,	Ballinlena,	Kilcommon,
249	Ditto,	Ditto,	Ditto,	Rev. C. L. Thomas,	Ballyquery,	Ditto,
250	Shannon River,	Stake-Net,	H. S. O'Brien,	H. S. O'Brien,	Ferrulrine,	Kilrush,
251	Bantry Bay, Glengariffe Har.,	Bag-Net,	Lord Bantry,	Lord Bantry,	Mountmeenamodder,	Kilcaskin,
252	Ditto,	Ditto,	Ditto,	Ditto,	Ditto,	Ditto,
253	Ditto,	Ditto,	Ditto,	Ditto,	Ditto,	Ditto,
254	Bantry Bay, Adrigole Harbour,	Ditto,	Ditto,	Ditto,	Adrigole,	Ditto,
255	Sea off co. Mayo,	Ditto,	Alexander Hector,	William Pike,	Achilbeg,	Achill,
256	Ditto,	Ditto,	Ditto,	Ditto,	Ditto,	Ditto,
257	Sea off Achill Island,	Ditto,	Ditto,	M. M. Blacker,	Keem Net,	Ditto,
258	Ditto,	Ditto,	Ditto,	C. Bryan,	Gubrockeen,	Achill,
259	Ditto,	Ditto,	Ditto,	Ditto,	West Net,	Ditto,
260	Ditto,	Ditto,	Ditto,	Trustees Achill Mission,	Keel,	Ditto,
261	Waterford Harbour,	Stake-Net,	A. N. O'Neill,	A. N. O'Neill,	Woodstown,	Crook,
262	Ditto,	Ditto,	Ditto,	Ditto,	Knockaveelish,	Ditto,
263	River Suir, King's Channel,	Ditto,	A. N. O'Neill and Mary O'Neill,	A. N. O'Neill and Mary O'Neill,	Kilmokea,	Ballygunner,
264	Ditto,	Ditto,	Ditto,	Ditto,	Ditto,	Ditto,
265	River Shannon,	Ditto,	Jo. Jameson & others,	Knight of Glin,	Coberagh,	Kilfergus,
266	Ditto,	Ditto,	R. W. C. Reeves,	R. W. C. Reeves,	Burrane, Lower,	Killimer,
267	Lower Bunratty,	Head Weir,	Thomas Studdart,	Thomas Studdart,	Bunratty,	Bunratty,
268	Sea off the Coast of co. Sligo,	Bag-Net,	William Petrie,	Lady Palmerston and Hon. W. Cowper,	Mullaghmore,	Ahamlish,
269	Killala Bay,	2 Bag-Nets,	William Little,	R. Orme,	Carrowhubbock,	Kilglass,
270	Sea off Coast of co. Sligo,	Bag-Net,	William Petrie,	O. Jones,	Streedagh,	Ahamlish,
271	Sea off Coast of co. Londonderry,	Ditto,	Sir H. Bruce,	Sir H. Bruce,	Ballymaclary,	Magilligan,
272	Sea off co. Sligo,	Ditto,	Lady Palmerston and Hon. W. Cowper.	—	Mullaghmore,	Ahamlish,
273	River Blackwater,	Stake-Net,	E. M'Sweeny,	—	Stasi,	Templemichael,
274	Ditto,	Ditto,	William Collins,	J. Hargrave,	Dromore,	Aglish,
275	Ditto,	Ditto,	John Neill and W. Hennessey.	Rev. G. Gumbleton,	Scart,	Kilcockan,
276	River Barrow, otherwise Nore and Barrow conjoined.	Head Weir,	M. W. Knox,	M. W. Knox,	Kilmannock,	Kilmokea,
277	Sea off co. Donegal,	Bag-Net,	George Young,	—	Carthage,	Culdaff,
278	Shannon,	Stake-Net,	Daniel Moloney,	Lord Annaly,	Lakyle, North,	Kilrush,
279	Ditto,	Ditto,	Symon M'Auliffe,	Thomas Rice Hewson,	Shevaleeley,	Ditto,
280	Ditto,	Ditto,	R. W. C. Reeves,	R. W. C. Reeves,	Burrane, Lower,	Killimer,
281	Ditto,	Ditto,	Ditto,	Ditto,	Ditto,	Ditto,
282	Ditto,	Ditto,	Robert Leslie,	Robert Leslie,	Tarbert,	Kilnaughtin,
283	Ditto,	Ditto,	William Sandes,	William Sandes,	Ralappane,	Ditto,
284	Ditto,	Ditto,	Ditto,	Ditto,	Ditto,	Ditto,

Legality or Illegality of Fixed Nets erected or used for catching Salmon in Ireland—*continued.*

No.	Barony.	County.	Judgment of Commissioners.	Date of Judgment.	Whether Judgment of Commissioners Appealed against.	Result of Appeal in Court of Queen's Bench.
209	Cary,	Antrim,	To be abated; within 3 miles of Ballycastle River,	30 Aug 1864,	No appeal.	—
210	Ditto,	Ditto,	Ditto,	Ditto,	Ditto.	—
211	Ditto,	Ditto,	Ditto,	Ditto,	Ditto.	—
212	Ditto,	Ditto,	Ditto,	Ditto,	Ditto.	—
213	Ditto,	Ditto,	Ditto,	Ditto,	Ditto.	—
214	Ditto,	Ditto,	Legally erected,	Ditto,	Ditto.	—
215	Ditto,	Ditto,	Ditto,	Ditto,	Ditto.	—
216	Ditto,	Ditto,	Ditto,	Ditto,	Ditto.	—
217	Ditto,	Ditto,	To be abated, as erected without the title required by 5 & 6 Vic., c. 106.	Ditto,	Ditto.	—
218	Ditto,	Ditto,	Ditto,	Ditto,	Ditto.	—
219	Ditto,	Ditto,	Legally erected,	Ditto,	Ditto.	—
220	Ditto,	Ditto,	Ditto,	Ditto,	Ditto.	—
221	Ditto,	Ditto,	To be abated; within Estuary of Bush River,	Ditto,	Appeal,	Judgment affirmed.
222	Lr. Dunluce,	Ditto,	Ditto,	Ditto,	Ditto,	Ditto.
223	Coleraine,	Londonderry,	Legally erected,	31 Aug. 1864,	No Appeal.	—
224	Ditto,	Ditto,	To be abated; within three miles of mouth of Bann River	Ditto,	Ditto.	—
225	Inishowen,	Donegal,	To be abated, as erected without the title required by 5 & 6 Vic., c. 106.	3 Sept. 1864,	Ditto.	—
226	Ditto,	Ditto,	Ditto,	Ditto,	Ditto.	—
227	Ditto,	Ditto,	Ditto,	Ditto,	Ditto.	—
228	Ditto,	Ditto,	Ditto,	Ditto,	Ditto.	—
229	Ditto,	Ditto,	Ditto,	Ditto,	Ditto.	—
230	Kilmacrenan,	Ditto,	Ditto,	Ditto,	Ditto.	—
231	Keenaght,	Londonderry,	Ditto,	5 Sept. 1864,	Appeal,	Sent back on motion before hearing of appeal, to enable the court to make a case stated at first trial.—See No. 271.
232	Ditto,	Ditto,	To be abated; within Estuary of Foyle River,	Ditto,	No Appeal.	—
233	Tirkeeran,	Ditto,	Legally erected,	—	Ditto.	—
234	Ditto,	Ditto,	Ditto,	—	Ditto.	—
235	Ditto,	Ditto,	Ditto,	—	Ditto.	—
236	Coy & Muntirloney,	Ditto,	To be abated; injurious to navigation,	—	Ditto.	—
237	Ditto,	Ditto,	Ditto,	—	Ditto.	—
238	Ditto,	Ditto,	Ditto,	—	Ditto.	—
239	Ditto,	Ditto,	Ditto,	—	Ditto.	—
240	Tirkeeran,	Ditto,	Ditto,	—	Ditto.	—
241	Ditto,	Ditto,	Ditto,	—	Ditto.	—
242	Ditto,	Ditto,	Ditto,	—	Ditto.	—
243	Ditto,	Ditto,	Ditto,	—	Ditto.	—
244	Tyrhugh,	Donegal,	Legally erected,	8 Sept. 1864,	Ditto.	—
245	Carbury,	Sligo,	See No. 270.	—	—	—
246	Tireragh,	Ditto,	To be abated, as erected without the title required by 5 & 6 Vic., c. 106.	16 Sept 1864,	Appeal,	Sent back in consequence of the evidence at first trial being defective.—See No. 269.
247	Tyrawley,	Mayo,	Ditto,	13 Sept. 1864,	No Appeal.	—
248	Ditto,	Ditto,	Ditto,	Ditto,	Appeal,	Judgment reversed
249	Ditto,	Ditto,	Ditto,	Ditto,	Ditto,	Judgment affirmed.
250	Lr. Bunratty,	Clare,	To be abated, as injurious to navigation and public rights of fishing, and as erected on the site of a weir previously condemned. *Vide* sec. 17 of 13 & 14 Vic., c. 88.	17 Sept 1864,	Ditto,	Ditto.
251	Bere,	Cork,	To be abated; within Estuary of River,	8 May, 1867.	—	—
252	Ditto,	Ditto,	Ditto,	Ditto.	—	—
253	Ditto,	Ditto,	Ditto,	Ditto.	—	—
254	Ditto,	Ditto,	Abandoned,	Ditto.	—	—
255	Burrishoole,	Mayo,	To be abated, as erected without the title required by 5 & 6 Vic., c. 106.	13 July, 1865,	No Appeal.	—
256	Ditto,	Ditto,	Ditto,	Ditto,	Ditto.	—
257	Ditto,	Ditto,	Postponed for further evidence,	Ditto,	Ditto.	—
258	Ditto,	Ditto,	To be abated, as erected without the title required by 5 & 6 Vic., c. 106.	Ditto.	Ditto.	—
259	Ditto,	Ditto,	Ditto,	Ditto,	Ditto.	—
260	Ditto,	Ditto,	Legally erected,	Ditto,	Ditto.	—
261	Gaultiere,	Waterford,	(See 73 to 78 inclusive) Report made to Court of second trial.	No Judgment,	Set down on report,	Judgment reversed.
262	Ditto,	Ditto,		Ditto,	Ditto,	
263	Ditto,	Ditto,		Ditto,	Ditto,	
264	Ditto,	Ditto,		Ditto,	Ditto,	
265	Shanid,	Limerick,	Report made to Court,	Ditto,	Ditto,	Ditto.
266	Clonderalaw,	Clare,	Ditto,	Ditto,	Ditto,	Ditto.
267	Lr. Bunratty,	Ditto,	Legally erected,	16 Nov 1866,	No appeal.	—
268	Carbury,	Sligo,	Ditto,	14 Nov. 1866,	Ditto.	—
269	Tireragh,	Ditto,	Report made to Court,	—	—	—
270	Carbury,	Ditto,	Legally erected,	14 Nov 1867,	No appeal.	—
271	Keenaght,	Londonderry	Report made to Court,	21 Nov 1866,	Set down on report,	Judgment reversed
272	Carbury,	Sligo,	Illegal. Within 3 miles of mouth of Duff River,	15 June, 1867,	Appeal,	Judgment affirmed.
273	Decies-within-Drum.	Waterford,	Report made to Court,	No Judgment,	Appeal,	Judgment reversed.
274	Ditto,	Ditto,	Ditto,	Ditto,	Ditto,	Appeal withdrawn.
275	Ditto,	Ditto,	Legal,	4 Jan. 1868,	No appeal.	—
276	Shelburne,	Wexford,	Report to Court—That it is injurious to navigation—25th February, 1868.	No Judgment,	Set down on report,	Judgment affirmed.
277	Inishowen,	Donegal,	Legal,	6 Mar. 1868,	No appeal.	—
278	Clonderalaw,	Clare,	To be abated,	12 Nov. 1868,	Appeal,	Judgment reversed.
279	Ditto,	Ditto,	Ditto,	Ditto.	No Appeal.	—
280	Ditto,	Ditto,	Ditto,	Ditto.	Appeal,	Judgment reversed.
281	Ditto,	Ditto,	Ditto,	Ditto	Ditto,	Ditto.
282	Iraghticonnor,	Kerry,	—	17 Nov. 1868	—	—
283	Ditto,	Ditto,	To be abated,	Ditto.	—	—
284	Ditto,	Ditto,	Given up by Mr. Nelligan. Not erected or used either as Bag or Stake Net in 1862.	Ditto.	—	—

Appendix, No. 11.

RESULT of INQUIRIES held by the INSPECTORS of IRISH FISHERIES into the legality

No.	Where Fixed Net situated.	Description of Fixed Net.	Name of Person maintaining and using Fixed Net.	Name of Owner of Fixed Net, or of Land to which Net attached.	Name of Townland to which Net attached.	Parish
285	Sea off Coast co. Antrim,	Fixed Draft Net	Denis Black,	Denis Black,	Moneyvart,	Layd,
286	Ditto,	Ditto,	Archibald M'Keegan,	Earl of Antrim,	Glebe,	Layd,
287	Sea off Coast co. Cork,	Stake-Net,	Sampson French,	Sampson French,	Cuskinney,	Templebreedy,
288	Coomhola River (estuary),	Fixed Draft,	R. Vickery,	Earl of Bantry,	Dromkeal,	Kilmacomoge,
289	Ditto,	Ditto,	R. Warren,	Ditto,	Reenadesert,	Ditto,
290	Ouvane River,	Ditto,	William Sullivan,	Ditto,	Ditto,	Ditto,
291	Sea off Coast co. Cork,	Ditto,	Michael Murphy,	Ditto,	Reendonegan,	Kilmacomoge,
292	Dunamark River (estuary),	Ditto,	Ditto,	—	Stratenure and Newtown.	Ditto,
293	Shannon,	Stake-Net,	Thomas Sandes,	Thomas Sandes,	Cooleenoonagh,	Killnaughtin,
294	Sea off Coast co. Antrim,	Fixed Draft Net	Sir H H Boyd,	Sir H H Boyd,	Townparks,	Ramoan,
295	Ditto,	Ditto,	Archibald M'Keegan,	Earl of Antrim,	Glebe,	Layd
296	Ditto,	Ditto,	John Finlay,	John Finlay,	Ballyteerim,	Culfeightrin,
297	Ditto,	Ditto,	Henry H. M'Neill,	H H M'Neill,	Redbay,	Layd,
298	Ditto,	Ditto,	Edmund M'Neill,	Edmund M'Neill,	Curryabcklin,	Ballintoy,
299	Ditto,	Ditto,	Denis Black,	Denis Black,	Moneyvart,	Layd,
300	Ditto,	Ditto,	John M'Ildowney,	John M'Ildowney,	Clare,	Ramoan,
301	Ditto,	Ditto,	Robert Stewart,	James Leslie,	Templastragh,	Ballintoy,
302	Ditto,	Fixed Draft Net	Sir H H Boyd, bart,	Sir H. H Boyd, bart.,	Greggamboy,	Ditto,
303	Sea off Coast co. Londonderry,	Ditto,	John Cromie,	John Cromie,	North Mullaghacall,	Ballyaghran,
304	Ditto,	4 Ditto,	Henry O'Neill,	Arnold White and John P. Broughham.	East & West Tullaghmurray & Crossreagh	Ditto,
305	Ditto,	Fixed Draft Net	Sir H. H. Bruce, bt.,	Sir H. H. Bruce, bt.	Crossreagh.	Tamlaghtard,
306	Estuary of Inver River,	2 Ditto,	William Sinclair,	William Sinclair,	Ballymacalary,	Inver,
307	Eske River,	Fixed Draft Net	Earl of Arran,	Earl of Arran,	Inver Estuary, Eske River,	Donegal and Inver
308	Sea off Coast co. Donegal,	Ditto,	Marquis Conyngham,	Marquis Conyngham,		Killaghtee,
309	Ditto,	Bag-Net,	Ditto,	Ditto,	Ballyederlan,	Ditto,
310	Estuary of Leannan River,	2 Fixed Draft Nets,	R. Kelly,	Sir Jas Stewart, bt.,	Ditto, Leannan River,	Aughnish,
311	Sea off Coast co. Donegal,	1 Ditto,	W. R. Tredennick,	W. R. Tredennick,		Killaghtee,
312	Ditto,	Ditto,	Ditto,	Ditto,	Killalten,	Ditto,
313	Ditto,	Ditto,	S. Sheil,	S. Sheil,	Ballycroy, Magheracar,	Inishmacsaint
314	Ditto,	Ditto,	Mrs. S. M'Donnell,	Mrs. S. M'Donnell,		Killaghtee,
315	Ditto,	Ditto,	A. Hamilton,	A Hamilton,	Ballymagart,	Kilbarron,
316	Ditto,	Ditto,	Murray Stewart,	Murray Stewart,	Coolmore,	Kilcar,
317	Ditto,	Ditto,	Ditto,	Ditto,	Gortalia,	Ditto,
318	Ditto,	Ditto,	Ebenezer Bustard,	Ebenezer Bustard,	Muckros,	Killybegs,
319	Ditto,	Ditto,	James Hawkins,	—	Drumanoo, Ballybodonnell, &c.,	Killaghtee,
320	River Moy,	6 Ditto,	Mary Anne Little and Andrew Clarke.	Mary Anne Little and A. Clarke,	—	—
321	Ditto,	3 Ditto,	William Petrie,	John Wingfield Stratford,	Scurmore,	Castleconor,
322	Sea off Coast of Sligo,	1 Ditto,	J. Carney,	Richard G. Brinkley,	Stobeena,	Easkey,
323	River Owenmore,	3 Ditto,	William Petrie,	—	—	—
324	Tullaghan Bay,	7 Ditto,	Helen Little,	—	Tullaghan Bay,	Kilmore, &c.,
325	Blackwater,	Stake-Weir,	Hon C Wm. Moore-Smyth.	Hon. C. Wm. Moore-Smyth.	Ballynatray,	Templemichael
326	Shannon,	Ditto,	Capt. R Leslie,	Capt. R. Leslie,		Kilnaughtin,
327	Ditto,	Ditto,	Ditto,	Ditto,	Tarbert,	Ditto,
328	Ditto,	Ditto,	Thomas Sandes,	Thomas Sandes,	Kilpadogue,	Ditto,
329	Sea off Coast co. Sligo,	1 Fixed Draft Net.	James Hale,	James Hale,	Rathpeane, Killinacduff,	Easky,
330	Sligo River,	2 Ditto,	William Petrie,	Captain Martin,		Kilmacowen,
331	Erne River,	3 Ditto,	Ballyshannon Fishery Company.	—	Ballinacarrow and Cartron, Carrickboy and Townparks.	Kilbarron and Inishmacsaint
332	Teelin Estuary,	2 Ditto,	Mrs. Anne Hamilton,	Mrs. Anne Hamilton,	Kilcar and Glencolumbkill.	Glencolumbkill and Kilcar.
333	Sea off Coast co. Donegal,	1 Ditto,	Charles Stewart,	Charles Stewart,	Layatrenny,	Clondahorky,
334	Sea off Coast co. Londonderry,	Ditto,	G. M'Kinney,	Mary Ross and R. Deane,	Doughs,	Magilligan,
335	Ditto,	Ditto,	J. M'Gowney,	—	Lower and Middle Doughs.	Ditto,
336	Ditto,	Ditto,	William Lorton,	William Lorton,	Ditto,	Ditto,
337	River Foyle,	6 Ditto,	The Irish Society,	The Irish Society,	Clooghboy, Mountjoy, Ballydonaghy, Glenfad, Portball, Culmore and Coolkeeragh.	Donaghedy, Taughboyne, Leckpatrick, Clondermot, Templemore, and Glendermott.
338	Ditto,	2 Ditto,	Ditto,	Ditto,	Conspie & Coolattee,	[illegible] and [illegible].
339	River Bann,	4 Ditto,	Ditto,	Ditto,	Ballyaially, E. & W. Crossreagh.	Coleraine, Killowen, Dunboe, & Ballyaghran.
340	Sea off Coast co. Derry,	1 Ditto,	Earl of Antrim,	Earl of Antrim,	Portrush,	Ballywillin,
341	River Blackwater,	Stake-Weir,	Hon. C. W. Moore Smyth.	Hon C. W. Moore Smyth.	Ballynatray,	Templemichael
342	Sea off Coast co. Antrim,	1 Fixed Draft Net.	R. Hector,	Sir H. H. Boyd,	Ballycastle, Townparks, Portbrittas.	Ramoan.
343	Ditto,	Stake-Weir,	Denis Black,	Denis Black,	Moneyvart,	Layd,
344	Shannon,	Stake-Net,	Stephen Collis,	Stephen Collis,	Lower Kilcolgan,	Kilnaughtin,
345	Ditto,	2 Ditto,	Lord Annaly,	Lord Annaly,	Lakyle, North,	Kilfidu,
346	Ditto,	Ditto,	Colonel Vandeleur,	Colonel Vandeleur,	Ballynote, West,	Kilrush,
347	Ditto,	Ditto,	Ditto,	Ditto,	Carrowdotia, South,	Killimer,
348	Ditto,	Ditto,	Ditto,	Ditto,	Colmanstown,	Kilfidu,
349	Ditto,	Ditto,	Ditto,	Ditto,	Lakyle, South,	Ditto,
350	Ditto,	Ditto,	Ditto,	Ditto,	Carrowdotia, West,	Killimer,
351	Ditto,	Ditto,	R. H. Borough,	R. H. Borough,	Querin,	Kilfidu,
352	Ditto,	Ditto,	R. W. C. Reeves,	R. W. C. Reeves	Poulnaderna,	Killimer,
353	Ditto,	Ditto,	B. Cox,	B. Cox,	Clarefield,	Moyarta,
354	Ditto,	Ditto,	N. S. O'Gorman,	N. S. O'Gorman,	Ballynote, West,	Kilrush,

Illegality of Fixed Nets erected or used for catching Salmon in Ireland—*continued.*

APPENDIX, No. 11.

No.	Barony.	County.	Judgment of Inspectors.	Date of Judgment.	Whether Judgment of Inspectors Appealed against.	Result of Appeal in Court of Queen's Bench.
285	Lr. Glenarm,	Antrim,	See No. 210.	—	—	—
286	Ditto,	Ditto,	See No. 206.	—	—	—
287	Imokilly,	Cork,	Legal,	16 Feb. 1870.	—	—
288	Bantry,	Ditto,	Illegal, as erected without the title required by 5 & 6 Vic., c. 106.	24 Feb. ,,	—	—
289	Ibane,	Ditto,	Ditto,	Ditto.	—	—
290	Ditto,	Ditto,	Ditto,	Ditto.	—	—
291	Ditto,	Ditto,	Withdrawn,	Ditto.	—	—
292	Ditto,	Ditto,	Ditto,	Ditto.	—	—
293	Iraghticonnor,	Kerry,	Legal,	11 Mar. ,,	—	—
294	Cary,	Antrim,	Ditto,	10 May, ,,	—	—
295	Lr. Glenarm,	Ditto,	Ditto,	10 May, ,,	—	—
296	Cary,	Ditto,	Ditto,	Ditto.	—	—
297	Lr. Glenarm,	Ditto,	Ditto,	Ditto.	—	—
298	Cary,	Ditto,	Ditto,	Ditto.	—	—
299	Lr. Glenarm,	Ditto,	Ditto,	Ditto.	—	—
300	Cary,	Ditto,	Ditto,	Ditto.	—	—
301	Ditto,	Ditto,	Ditto,	Ditto.	—	—
302	Ditto,	Ditto,	Ditto,	Ditto.	—	—
303	N. E. Liberties of Coleraine.	Londonderry,	Ditto,	11 May, ,,	—	—
304	Ditto,	Ditto,	Ditto,	Ditto.	—	—
305	Keenaght,	Ditto,	Ditto,	Ditto.	—	—
306	Banagh,	Donegal,	Ditto,	13 May, ,,	—	—
307	Ditto,	Ditto,	Withdrawn,	Ditto.	—	—
308	Ditto,	Ditto,	Legal,	Ditto.	—	—
309	Ditto,	Ditto,	Illegal. Injurious to navigation,	Ditto.	—	—
310	Kilmacrenan,	Ditto,	Legal,	Ditto.	—	—
311	Banagh,	Ditto,	Withdrawn,	Ditto.	—	—
312	Ditto,	Ditto,	Ditto,	Ditto.	—	—
313	Tirhugh,	Ditto,	Illegal, as not having the title required by 5 & 6 Vic., c. 106.	Ditto.	—	—
314	Boylagh,	Ditto,	Ditto,	Ditto.	—	—
315	Tirhugh,	Ditto,	Ditto,	Ditto.	—	—
316	Banagh,	Ditto,	Legal,	Ditto.	—	—
317	Ditto,	Ditto,	Ditto,	Ditto.	—	—
318	Ditto,	Ditto,	Ditto,	Ditto.	—	—
319	Ditto,	Ditto,	Illegal, as not having the title required by 5 & 6 Vic., c. 106.	Ditto.	—	—
320	—	Mayo and Sligo.	Legal,	17 May, ,,	Appeal pending.	—
321	Tireragh,	Sligo,	Ditto,	18 May, ,,	Ditto.	—
322	Ditto,	Ditto,	Withdrawn.	—	—	—
323	Erris,	Mayo,	Legal,	18 May, ,,	—	—
324	Ditto,	Ditto,	Ditto,	Ditto	—	—
325	Coshmore & Coshbride.	Waterford,	No power to grant Certificate (see No. 341),	11 Jan 1871.	Appeal.	Order against weir to be no bar to granting a certificate.
326	Iraghticonnor	Kerry,	Legal,	16 Jan. ,,	—	—
327	Ditto,	Ditto,	Ditto,	Ditto	—	—
328	Ditto,	Ditto,	Ditto,	Ditto.	—	—
329	Tireragh,	Sligo,	Illegal, as not having the title required by 5 & 6 Vic., c. 106.	4 Feb. ,,	—	—
330	Erris,	Ditto,	Legal,	4 Feb. ,,	—	—
331	Tirhugh,	Donegal,	Ditto,	7 Feb. ,,	—	—
332	Banagh,	Ditto,	Illegal, as not having the title required by 5 & 6 Vic., c. 106.	Ditto.	—	—
333		Ditto,	Ditto,	Ditto.	—	—
334	Keenaght,	Londonderry,	Ditto,	14 Feb. ,,	Appeal.	Judgment Affirmed.
335	Ditto,	Ditto,	Legal,	Ditto.	—	—
336	Ditto,	Ditto,	Ditto,	Ditto.	—	—
337	Raphoe, Strabane, Lower, North-west Liberties of Londonderry, and Tirkeeran.	Ditto,	Ditto,	15 Feb. ,,	—	—
338	Omagh, East, and Raphoe	Londonderry and Donegal.	Illegal, not fished in 1862,	Ditto.	—	—
339	Ditto,	Londonderry,	Legal,	Ditto.	—	—
340	Lr. Dunluce,	Ditto,	Ditto,	Ditto.	—	—
341	Coshmore & Coshbride.	Waterford,	Not injurious to navigation,	24 May, ,,	—	Certificate granted.
342	Cary,	Antrim,	Adjourned (see No. 375).	19 July, ,,	—	—
343	Lr. Glenarm,	Ditto,	Legal,	Ditto.	—	—
344	[illegible], Lr.	Kerry,	Adjourned,	9 Nov. ,,	—	—
345	Clonderlaw,	Clare,	Legal,	10 Nov. ,,	—	—
346	Moyarta,	Ditto,	Ditto,	Ditto	—	—
347	Clonderlaw,	Ditto,	Ditto,	Ditto.	—	—
348	Ditto,	Ditto,	Ditto,	Ditto.	—	—
349	Ditto,	Ditto,	Withdrawn,	11 Nov. ,,	—	—
350	Ditto,	Ditto,	Ditto,	Ditto	—	—
351	Ditto,	Ditto,	Withdrawn,	Ditto.	—	—
352	Ditto,	Ditto,	Legal,	Ditto.	—	—
353	Moyarta,	Ditto,	Ditto,	Ditto.	—	—
354	Ditto,	Ditto,	Illegal, not fished in 1862,	Ditto.	—	—

RESULT of INQUIRIES held by the INSPECTORS of IRISH FISHERIES into the Legality

No.	Where Fixed Net situated.	Description of Fixed Net.	Name of Person maintaining and using Fixed Net.	Name of Owner of Fixed Net, or of Land to which Net attached.	Name of Townland to which Net attached.	Parish.
355	Sea off Coast co. Sligo,	3 Bag Nets,	W. Little,	R. Orme,	Carrowhubbock, Sth.,	Kilglas,
356	Estuary of Drumcliffe River,	Fixed Draft Net	William Petrie,	J. Obins Jones,	Court and Drumcliffe,	Drumcliffe,
357	Sea off Coast co. Mayo,	2 Bag Nets,	W. Pike,	W. Pike,	Dooega,	Achill,
358	Ditto,	Ditto,	Ditto,	Ditto,	Achill Beg,	Ditto,
359	Ditto,	4 Ditto,	Alexander Hector,	Trustees Achill Mission.	Slievemore,	Ditto,
360	Ditto,	3 Ditto,	Ditto,	Ditto,	Keel, East,	Ditto,
361	Ditto,	5 Ditto,	Ditto,	Ditto,	Doogort, West,	Ditto,
362	Ditto,	2 Ditto,	Ditto,	Ditto,	Doogort, East,	Ditto,
363	Ditto,	2 Ditto,	Ditto,	Sir F. A. Knox Gore, bart.	Cashlecka,	Ditto,
364	Ditto,	3 Ditto,	Ditto,	Ditto,	Dooghbeg,	Ditto,
365	Kenmare Estuary,	Bag Net,	R. Mahony,	R. Mahony,	Doon,	Kilcrohane,
366	Ditto,	Ditto,	Ditto,	Ditto,	Derreenafoyle,	Ditto,
367	Ditto,	Ditto,	Ditto,	Ditto,	Dromore,	Templenoe,
368	Ditto,	Ditto,	F. C. Bland,	F. C. Bland,	Derryquin,	Kilcrohane,
369	Ditto,	Ditto,	Ditto,	Ditto,	Ditto,	Ditto,
370	Ditto,	Ditto,	Marquis of Lansdowne.	Marquis of Lansdowne.	Cappahu,	Tuosist,
371	Ditto,	Ditto,	Ditto,	Ditto,	Clones,	Ditto,
372	Ditto,	Ditto,	Ditto,	Ditto,	Ardea,	Ditto,
373	Sea off Coast co. Louth,	Ditto,	A. Newcomen,	A. Newcomen,	Clogher,	Termonfeckin,
374	Ditto,	Ditto,	Ditto,	Ditto,	Ditto,	Ditto,
375	Ditto,	Ditto,	Ditto,	Ditto,	Ditto,	Ditto,
376	Sea off Coast co. Antrim,	Fixed Draft Net.	J. Finlay,	J. Finlay,	Sleans,	Layd,
377	Ditto,	Ditto,	R. Woodside,	R. Woodside,	Cregganboy,	Ramoan,
378	Ditto,	Ditto,	Sir H. H. Boyd, bart.	Sir, H. H. Boyd, bart.	Ballycastle, Town-parks, Port Britain.	Ditto,

or Illegality of Fixed Nets erected or used for catching Salmon in Ireland—*continued.*

No.	Fishery.	County.	Judgment of Inspectors.	Date of Judgment.	Whether Judgment of Inspectors Appealed against.	Result of Appeal in Court of Queen's Bench.
355	Tireragh,	Sligo,	Report made to Court,	—	—	Judgment of Commissioners reversed.
356	Carbury,	Ditto,	Legal,	27 Mar. 1872,	—	—
357	[illegible],	Mayo,	Ditto,	16 May, 1872,	—	—
358	Ditto,	Ditto,	Illegal,	Ditto,	—	—
359	Ditto,	Ditto,	Ditto,	Ditto,	—	—
360	Ditto,	Ditto,	Ditto,	Ditto,	—	—
361	Ditto,	Ditto,	Ditto,	17 May, 1872,	—	—
362	Ditto,	Ditto,	Ditto,	Ditto,	—	—
363	Ditto,	Ditto,	One illegal, not fished in 1862, and one legal,	Ditto,	—	—
364	Ditto,	Ditto,	Two illegal, not fished in 1862, and one legal,	Ditto,	—	—
365	Dunkerron, South.	Kerry,	Withdrawn,	15 June, 1872,	—	—
366	Ditto,	Ditto,	Postponed,	Ditto,	—	—
367	Ditto,	Ditto,	Ditto,	Ditto,	—	—
368	Ditto,	Ditto,	Ditto,	Ditto,	—	—
369	Ditto,	Ditto,	Ditto,	Ditto,	—	—
370	Glanarought,	Ditto,	Ditto,	Ditto,	—	—
371	Ditto,	Ditto,	Ditto,	Ditto,	—	—
372	Ditto,	Ditto,	Ditto,	Ditto,	—	—
373	Ferrard,	Louth,	Legal,	29 June, and 1st July, 1872.	—	—
374	Ditto,	Ditto,	Illegal,	Ditto,	Appeal pending.	—
375	Ditto,	Ditto,	Ditto,	Ditto,	Ditto,	—
376	Lower Glenarm.	Antrim,	Legal,	9 July, 1872,	—	—
377	Carey,	Ditto,	Ditto,	10 July, 1872,	—	—
378	Ditto,	Ditto,	Illegal—injurious to navigation,	Ditto,	Appeal pending.	—

Appendix, No. 12.

Appendix

Table showing the Close Seasons for Salmon and Trout in

No. and Name of District.	Boundary of District.	Tidal.
1. Dublin,	Skerries to Wicklow.	From Howth to Dalkey Island, between 31st July and 16th January. For remainder of District, between 31st Aug. and 16th Feb.
2. Wexford,	Wicklow to Kiln Bay, East of Bannow Bay.	Between 16th September and 10th April, both days inclusive.
3. Waterford,	Kiln Bay to Helvick Head.	" 1st September and 15th February, both days inclusive.
4. Lismore,	Helvick Head to Ballycotton.	" 1st September and 15th February, both days inclusive.
5. Cork,	Ballycotton Head to Galley Head	" 16th August and the last day of February, both days inclusive.
6¹. Skibbereen,	Galley Head to Mizen Head	" 1st October and 20th April, both days inclusive.
6². Bantry,	Mizen Head to Crow Head.	" Do. do. do.
6³. Kenmare,	Crow Head to Lamb Head.	" 16th September and 31st March, both days inclusive.
7. Killarney,	Lamb Head to Dunmore Head, including Blaskets	" 31st July and 16th January, save Rivers Maine, Ferta, or Valencia, Inny, and Waterville, and their Tributaries. Maine, Ferta or Valencia, Inny, and Tributaries, 15th September to 1st May. Waterville and its Tributaries, 16th July and 1st January.
8. Limerick,	Dunmore to Hags Head.	Between 16th July and 31st January, save Rivers Cashen and Doonbeg Rivers between Kerry Head and Dunmore Head, 16th September and 31st March, all said days inclusive. For River Cashen and tributaries, between 13th August and 19th May. For Doonbeg, 1st September and 31st May, all said days inclusive.
9. Galway,	Hags Head to Slyne Head.	Between 16th August and 31st January, both days inclusive.
10¹. Ballinakill,	Slyne Head to Pigeon Point.	Save in Louisburgh and Carrowniskey Rivers, between the 1st of September and the 15th of February, both days inclusive. For Louisburgh and Carrowniskey Rivers and Estuaries, between 15th of September and 30th June, both days inclusive.
10². Bangor,	Pigeon Point to Benwee Head.	Between 1st September and 15th February, both days inclusive, save in Newport and Glenamoy Rivers and Estuaries. For Newport River and Estuary, 1st September and 30th April; Glenamoy River and Estuary, 16th September and 30th April, all said days inclusive.
11. Ballina,	Benwee to Coonamore.	Between 13th August and 15th March, save Palmerston and Easkey Rivers, which is between 1st September and 31st May, all said days inclusive.
12. Sligo,	Coonamore to Mullaghmore.	" 20th August and 3rd February, save tidal parts of Sligo River, which is 16th July and 31st December, all said days inclusive.
13. Ballyshannon,	Mullaghmore to Rossan.	" 20th August and last day of February, both days inclusive.
14. Letterkenny,	Rossan to Malin Head	" 20th August and 3rd Feb., and one mile above Tideway, save Lennan River between 16th July and 31st December, all said days inclusive.
15¹. Londonderry,	Malin to Downhill Boundary.	" 31st August and 16th April.
15². Coleraine,	Downhill Boundary to Portrush.	" 20th August and 3rd February, both days inclusive.
16. Ballycastle,	Portrush to Donaghadee.	" Do. do. do.
17¹. Drogheda,	Skerries to Clogher Head.	" 20th August and 11th February, both days inclusive.
17². Dundalk,	Clogher Head to Donaghadee.	" 1st September and 31st March, save in Annagassan, Glyde, Dee, and Fane Rivers and Tributaries, both days inclusive. In Glyde, Dee, and Annagassan Rivers, between 20th August and 11th February; in Fane River between 20th August and 31st March, all said days inclusive.

Note.—The 61st section of the 26th & 27th Vic., c. 114, requires there shall not be fewer than 168 days Close Season in each Fishery.

Weekly Close Season.—By the 20th section of the 26th & 27th Vic., c. 114, no Salmon or Trout shall be fished for or taken in any way, except by Single Rod and Line, between six of the clock on Saturday morning and six of the clock on the succeeding Monday morning.

No. 12.

the different Districts in Ireland.

APPENDIX, No. 12.

Fresh Water.	Angling with Cross Lines.	Angling with Single Rod and Line.	Date of last change.	No. and Name of District.
From Howth to Dalkey Island, between 31st July and 1st Feb. For remainder of Dist. between 31st Aug. & 1st March.	15th October and 2nd March. 28th September and 16th March.	1st Nov. to 1st Feb.	10th Dec. 1861.	1. Dublin.
Same as Tidal.	30th September and 18th March	1st Oct. and last day of Feb., both days inclusive	18th Feb. 1870.	2. Wexford.
Same as Tidal.	Same as Netting.	15th Sept. and 31st Jan., both days inclusive	4th Nov. 1870.	3. Waterford.
Same as Tidal	Same as Netting.	1st Oct. and 31st Jan., both days inclusive	10th Dec. 1870	4. Lismore
Same as Tidal.	Same as Netting.	1st Nov. and last day of Feb., both days inclusive	10th June, 1872.	5. Cork.
Same as Tidal.	Same as Netting.	Between 1st Dec. and 16th March, both days inclusive.	30th Jan. 1873	6[1]. Skibbereen
Same as Tidal.	Same as Netting.		"	6[2]. Bantry.
Same as Tidal.	16th October and 31st March, both days inclusive.	1st Nov. and last day of Feb., both days inclusive.	7th Feb. 1856.	6[3]. Kenmare.
Same as Tidal	Same as Netting.	[illegible]		
Same as Tidal.	Same as Netting.	[illegible]	30th April, 1870.	7. Killarney.
Same as Tidal.	Same as Netting.	[illegible]		
Between 1st August and 31st January, save Rivers Cashen and Doonbeg and their Tributaries. Rivers between Kerry Head and Dunmore Head, 16th September and 31st March.* For Cashen and Tributaries, between 15th August and 16th May. Doonbeg and Tributaries, 1st September and 31st May, all said days inclusive.	Same as Netting in fresh water.	Between 1st Oct. and 31st Jan., save Cashen and Doonbeg Rivers. For Cashen and Doonbeg and Tributaries, 1st [illegible] April, all said days inclusive.	16th Dec. 1870	8. Limerick
Same as Tidal.	Same as Netting.	[illegible]	25th Dec. 1871.	9. Galway
Same as Tidal.	Same as Netting.	[illegible]	1st June, 1872.	10[1]. Ballinakill.
Same as Tidal.	Same as Netting.	[illegible]	1st June, 1872.	10[2]. Bangor.
Between 1st August and 31st January, save Palmerston and Easkey Rivers, which is between 1st September and 31st May, all said days inclusive.	Same as Netting in fresh water.	[illegible]	10th Dec., 1878	11. Ballina.
20th August and 3rd February, both said days inclusive.	Same as Netting in fresh water	[illegible]	24th April, 1871	12. Sligo
Same as Tidal.	Same as Netting.	[illegible]	24th Nov. 1871	13. Ballyshannon.
Between 20th August and last day of February, save Leannan River, between 16th July and 31st December, all said days inclusive.	Leannan, same as Netting. Between 15th August and 20th Sept.	1st Nov. and 1st Feb.	2nd Sept. 1857. 24th Feb. 1871.	14. Letterkenny.
Same as Tidal.	20th September and 15th April.	Do.	27th Jan. 1862.	15[1]. Londonderry.
Same as Tidal	20th September and 16th March.†	20th Oct. and [illegible] March, both days inclusive.	13th Dec. 1876 31st Mar. 1871.	15[2]. Coleraine
Same as Tidal.	20th September and 16th March.	1st Nov. and 1st Feb.	15th Dec. 1856	16. Ballycastle.
Same as Tidal.	Same as Netting.	15th Sept. and 31st Jan., both days inclusive.	20th Dec. 1871.	17[1]. Drogheda.
Same as Tidal.	Same as Netting.	[illegible]	8th July, 1872.	17[2]. Dundalk.

* Close Season for Fixed Engines for the capture of Eels, between the 10th January and 1st July save in the River Shannon, which is between the 31st January and 1st July, and in all other rivers in the Limerick District between 31st December and 1st July in year following.

† Pollen Fishing by Trammel Nets in Lough Neagh, between 31st October and 1st February.

Appendix. Nos. 13 & 14.

APPENDIX,

SCHEDULE of LICENCE DUTIES payable in each District

District.	1. Salmon Rods. £	s.	d.	2. Cross Lines. £	s.	d.	3. Snap Nets. £	s.	d.	4. Draft Nets. £	s.	d.	5. Drift Nets. £	s.	d.	6. Trammel Nets for Pollen. £	s.	d.	7. Pole Nets. £	s.	d.
1. Dublin,	1	0	0	2	0	0	1	10	0	5	0	0	3	0	0	1	10	0	2	0	0
2. Wexford,	1	0	0	1	0	0	0	15	0	5	0	0	1	10	0	0	15	0	1	0	0
3. Waterford,	1	0	0	2	0	0	1	10	0	5	0	0	3	0	0	1	10	0	2	0	0
4. Lismore,	1	0	0	2	0	0	1	10	0	4	0	0	3	0	0	1	10	0	2	0	0
5. Cork,	1	0	0	2	0	0	1	10	0	3	0	0	3	0	0	1	10	0	2	0	0
6¹ Skibbereen,	1	0	0	1	0	0	0	15	0	3	0	0	3	0	0	0	15	0	1	0	0
6² Bantry,	1	0	0	1	0	0	0	15	0	3	0	0	3	0	0	0	15	0	1	0	0
6³. Kenmare,	1	0	0	1	0	0	0	15	0	1	10	0	1	10	0	0	15	0	1	0	0
7. Killarney,	1	0	0	1	5	0	1	0	0	3	0	0	3	0	0	0	15	0	1	0	0
8. Limerick,	1	0	0	1	5	0	1	10	0	3	0	0	3	0	0	1	10	0	2	0	0
9. Galway,	1	0	0	2	0	0	1	10	0	3	0	0	3	0	0	1	10	0	2	0	0
10¹. Ballynakill,	1	0	0	2	0	0	1	10	0	3	0	0	3	0	0	1	10	0	2	0	0
10² Bangor,	1	0	0	2	0	0	1	10	0	4	0	0	3	0	0	1	10	0	2	0	0
11. Ballina,	1	0	0	2	0	0	1	10	0	3	0	0	3	0	0	1	10	0	2	0	0
12. Sligo,	1	0	0	2	0	0	1	10	0	3	0	0	3	0	0	1	10	0	2	0	0
13. Ballyshannon,	1	0	0	2	0	0	1	10	0	3	0	0	3	0	0	1	10	0	2	0	0
14. Letterkenny,	1	0	0	2	0	0	1	10	0	3	0	0	3	0	0	1	10	0	2	0	0
15¹. Londonderry,	1	0	0	2	0	0	1	10	0	3	0	0	3	0	0	1	10	0	2	0	0
15². Coleraine,	1	0	0	2	0	0	0	15	0	3	0	0	1	10	0	1	0	0	2	0	0
16 Ballycastle,	1	0	0	2	0	0	1	10	0	3	0	0	3	0	0	1	10	0	2	0	0
17¹. Drogheda,	1	0	0	2	0	0	1	10	0	3	0	0	3	0	0	0	15	0	2	0	0
17². Dundalk,	1	0	0	2	0	0	1	10	0	3	0	0	3	0	0	0	15	0	2	0	0

APPENDIX,

SCHEDULE of LICENCE DUTIES received by the BOARDS of

District.	Number and Description of Licences sold in 1871. 1 Salmon Rods.	2. Cross Lines.	3 Snap Nets.	4. Draft Nets.	5. Drift Nets.	6. Trammel Nets for Pollen.	7. Pole Nets.	8. Bag Nets.	9 Fly Nets.	10. Stake Nets.	11. Head Weirs.	12 Box, Crib, &c.	13 Gap, Eye, &c.	14. Snoops.	15. Coghills.	16. Loop Nets.	1871. Amount of Licence Duty. £	s.	d.	1871. Percentage on Poor Law Valuation. £	s.	d.	1871. Total Amount received. £	s.	d.	1871. Average No. employed.
1. Dublin,	154	1	–	15	–	–	–	–	–	–	–	–	–	–	–	–	201	0	0	—			201	0	0	246
2. Wexford,	66	–	–	49	–	1	–	–	–	–	–	–	–	–	–	–	221	15	0	—			221	15	0	349
3. Waterford,	234	24	214	81	70	–	–	–	–	4	1	4	23	–	–	–	1,084	0	0	3	12	0	1,088	12	0	1,090
4. Lismore,	240	16	87	6	63	–	1	1	–	6	–	2	–	–	–	–	731	10	0	12	0	0	743	10	0	946
5. Cork,	322	4	–	64	4	–	–	1	–	1	–	–	–	–	–	–	500	0	0	—			550	0	0	694
6¹. Skibbereen,	14	–	–	17	–	–	–	–	–	–	–	–	–	–	–	–	17	0	0	—			47	0	0	69
6². Bantry,	15	–	–	10	–	–	–	–	–	–	–	–	–	–	–	–	45	0	0	—			45	0	0	79
6³. Kenmare,	24	–	–	7	–	–	–	1	–	–	–	–	–	1	–	–	66	0	0	—			69	0	0	115
7. Killarney,	115	4	–	64	–	–	–	–	–	–	–	2	–	–	–	–	234	0	0	—			234	0	0	807
8. Limerick,	231	77	24	81	171	–	19	–	–	25	1	2	143	–	–	–	2,028	0	0	13	0	0	2,041	0	0	2,045
9. Galway,	179	12	–	12	–	2	–	–	–	–	–	4	10	–	–	–	324	0	0	60	0	0	384	0	0	826
10¹. Ballynakill,	37	–	–	24	–	–	2	–	–	–	–	–	–	–	–	–	104	0	0	—			104	0	0	169
10². Bangor,	23	–	–	29	–	–	–	1	–	–	–	–	–	–	–	–	66	0	0	—			93	0	0	147
11. Ballina,	71	1	–	24	21	–	–	2	–	–	–	1	7	–	–	–	285	0	0	—			285	0	0	[illegible]
12. Sligo,	23	–	–	14	–	–	–	12	–	–	–	–	11	–	–	–	102	0	0	—			102	0	0	144
13. Ballyshannon,	134	10	–	56	–	–	2	–	–	1	–	4	–	–	28	–	340	0	0	126	8	8	475	8	8	300
14. Letterkenny,	61	–	–	79	–	–	–	–	–	–	–	2	–	–	–	1	134	0	0	7	0	0	141	0	0	242
15¹. Londonderry,	70	7	–	22	28	–	3	4	–	3	–	–	–	–	–	–	400	0	0	94	0	0	494	0	0	454
15². Coleraine,	81	1	2	16	–	68	–	2	–	–	–	4	21	–	20	–	601	10	0	164	0	0	765	10	0	[illegible]
16. Ballycastle,	24	–	–	12	2	–	–	14	–	–	–	–	–	–	–	3	204	10	0	8	0	0	212	10	0	150
17¹. Drogheda,	57	7	2	50	–	–	–	1	–	–	1	4	46	–	–	–	447	0	0	14	10	0	461	10	0	[illegible]
17². Dundalk,	–	–	–	–	–	–	–	–	–	–	–	–	–	–	1	–	3	0	0	—			3	0	0	5
Total,	2227	124	280	622	346	80	26	28	–	57	3	40	275	1	60	10	8,364	5	0	501	10	0	8,865	15	0	10,0[illegible]

The estimate of the average number of

Salmon Rods,	1 man.	Draft Nets,	6 men.	Pole Nets,	3 men.
Cross Lines,	2 men.	Drift Nets,	5 do.	Bag Nets,	4 do.
Snap Nets,	4 do.	Trammel Nets,	2 do.	Fly Nets,	4 do.

APPENDIX, Nos. 13 & 14.

No. 13.

... Engines used for Fishing for Salmon, January, 1872.

8. Bag Nets.	9. Fly Nets.	10. Stake Nets.	11. Head Weirs.	12. Box, Crib, &c.	13. Gap, Eye, &c.	14. Sweepers.	15. Coghills.	16. Loop Nets.
£ s. d.	£ s. d.	£ s. d.	£ s. d.	£ s. d.	£ s. d.	£ s. d.	£ s. d.	£ s. d.
					1 0 0	—	—	—
					0 10 0	—	—	—
					1 0 0	—	—	—
					1 0 0	—	—	—
					1 0 0	—	—	—
					0 10 0	—	—	—
					0 10 0	—	—	—
					0 10 0	8 0 0	1 10 0	—
					0 10 0	—	—	—
					1 0 0	—	—	—
					1 0 0	—	—	—
10 0 0	20 0 0	20 0 0	6 0 0	10 0 0	1 0 0	—	—	—
					1 0 0	—	—	—
					1 0 0	—	—	—
					1 0 0	—	—	—
					1 0 0	—	—	—
					1 0 0	—	1 0 0	—
					0 10 0	—	—	1 0 0
					1 0 0	—	—	—
					1 0 0	—	1 0 0	—
					1 0 0	—	—	0 10 0
					1 0 0	—	1 0 0	—

No. 14.

CONSERVATORS for the Years 1871 and 1872.

District.	1. Salmon Rods.	2. Cross Lines.	3. Snap Nets.	4. Draft Nets.	5. Drift Nets.	6. Trammel Nets, for Pollen.	7. Pole Nets.	8. Bag Nets.	9. Fly Nets.	10. Stake Nets.	11. Head Weirs.	12. Box, Crib, &c.	13. Gap, Eye, &c.	14. Sweepers.	15. Coghills.	16. Loop Nets.	1872. Amount of Licence Duty. £ s. d.	1872. Percentage on Poor Law Valuation. £ s. d.	1872. Total Amount received. £ s. d.	1872. Average No. employed.	Increase in Amount. £ s. d.	Decrease in Amount. £ s. d.	Increase in Number employed.	Decrease in Number employed.
1	119	1	–	16	–	–	–	–	–	–	–	–	–	–	–	–	160 0 0	—	139 0 0	208	—	41 0 0	–	22
2	63	–	–	41	–	4	–	–	–	–	–	–	–	–	–	–	206 16 0	—	200 17 0	352	—	16 0 0	–	18
3	241	28	1,000	19	18	–	–	–	–	4	1	8	28	–	–	–	1,063 0 0	0 12 0	1,583 12 0	1,824	—	8 0 0	–	71
4	190	16	82	6	88	–	1	2	–	3	–	6	–	–	–	–	622 0 0	35 14 0	757 14 0	874	—	65 16 0	–	73
5	306	2	–	46	–	–	–	1	–	1	–	–	–	–	–	–	494 0 0	—	494 0 0	606	—	50 0 0	–	60
[illegible]	22	–	–	14	–	–	–	–	–	–	–	–	–	–	–	–	60 0 0	—	60 0 0	107	18 0 0	—	27	–
[illegible]	18	–	–	16	–	–	–	–	–	–	–	–	–	–	–	–	44 0 0	—	46 0 0	76	1 0 0	—	2	–
[illegible]	42	–	–	7	–	–	–	1	–	–	–	–	–	6	–	–	86 10 0	4 10 0	91 0 0	136	28 0 0	—	11	–
7	104	8	–	62	–	–	–	–	–	–	–	8	–	–	–	–	225 0 0	—	225 0 0	406	—	9 0 0	–	11
8	294	42	37	669	122	–	26	–	–	28	–	[illegible]	130	–	–	–	2,187 0 0	5 0 0	2,170 0 0	1,072	129 0 0	—	–	72
9	142	11	–	12	–	2	–	–	–	–	–	6	26	–	–	–	302 0 0	83 0 0	385 0 0	319	1 0 0	—	–	15
[illegible]	30	–	–	16	–	–	5	–	–	–	–	–	–	–	–	–	94 0 0	—	94 0 0	156	—	10 0 0	–	19
[illegible]	16	–	–	21	–	–	–	6	–	–	–	–	–	–	–	–	133 0 0	—	139 0 0	166	46 0 0	—	19	–
[illegible]	77	1	–	67	13	–	–	6	–	–	–	7	7	–	–	–	286 0 0	—	290 0 0	344	31 0 0	—	16	–
[illegible]	22	1	–	16	–	–	–	1	–	–	–	–	6	–	–	–	87 0 0	—	87 0 0	126	—	18 0 0	–	9
[illegible]	130	9	–	36	2	–	2	–	–	1	–	4	–	–	24	–	374 0 0	119 0 0	493 0 0	438	20 11 8	—	25	–
[illegible]	87	–	–	12	–	–	–	–	–	–	–	2	–	–	–	–	127 0 0	7 0 0	134 0 0	126	—	7 0 0	–	6
[illegible]	77	6	–	87	28	–	2	4	–	3	–	–	–	–	–	–	406 0 0	95 0 0	501 0 0	446	7 0 0	—	4	–
[illegible]	78	1	–	107	–	97	–	9	–	–	–	4	22	–	64	–	377 0 0	459 0 0	836 0 0	662	78 10 0	—	–	66
[illegible]	30	–	–	12	–	–	–	14	–	–	–	–	–	–	–	–	206 0 0	7 0 0	213 0 0	148	6 10 0	—	–	1
[illegible]	61	9	4	85	–	–	–	–	–	–	–	8	20	–	–	–	203 0 0	2 10 0	205 10 0	402	—	208 0 0	–	205
[illegible]	43	–	–	16	–	–	–	2	–	–	1	–	16	–	–	–	133 0 0	12 10 0	145 10 0	166	143 10 0	—	177	–
	2,404	131	[illegible]	1,656	338	[illegible]	27	37	–	45	2	40	355	8	86	4	8,360 [illegible]	[illegible] 16 0	9,368 1 8	10,290	490 1 2	357 15 0	294	734

... employed is made up as follows:—

Stake Nets, . . . 4 men.
Head weirs, . . . 1 man.
Box, crib, &c. (every 2) 3 men.

Gap, Eye, &c. . 2 men.
Sweepers, . . 6 do.

Coghills, ... 1 man.
Loop or Pound Nets, . 2 do.

* Increase in Licence duty in 1872 over 1871—£132 0s. 0d.

APPENDIX, No 15.—AMOUNT of LICENSE DUTY received for the different Fishing Engines for the Year 1872, in each District.

Single Rod.	Cross Lines.	[illegible]	[illegible]	Drift Nets.	Trammel Nets, or Draft Nets used as Fixed Engines	Pole Nets.	Bag Nets.	Fly Nets.	Stake Nets.	Head Weirs.	Box, Crib, &c.	[illegible]	[illegible]	Coghills.	[illegible]
£ s. d.	£ s. d.	£ s. d.	£ s. d.	£ s. d.	£ s. d.	£ s. d.	£ s. d.	£ s. d.	£ s. d.	£ s. d.	£ s. d.	£ s. d.	£ s. d.	£ s. d.	£ s. d.
[illegible]	[illegible]	–	[illegible]	–	–	–	–	–	–	–	–	–	–	–	–
[illegible]	–	–	[illegible]	–	[illegible]	–	–	–	–	–	–	–	–	–	–
[illegible]	[illegible]	[illegible]	[illegible]	[illegible]	–	–	–	–	[illegible]	[illegible]	[illegible]	[illegible]	–	–	–
[illegible]	[illegible]	[illegible]	[illegible]	[illegible]	–	[illegible]	[illegible]	–	[illegible]	–	[illegible]	–	–	–	–
[illegible]	[illegible]	–	[illegible]	–	–	–	[illegible]	–	[illegible]	–	–	–	–	–	–
[illegible]	–	–	[illegible]	–	–	–	–	–	–	–	–	–	–	–	–
[illegible]	–	–	[illegible]	–	–	–	–	–	–	–	–	–	–	–	–
[illegible]	–	–	[illegible]	–	–	–	[illegible]	–	–	–	–	–	[illegible]	–	–
[illegible]	[illegible]	–	[illegible]	–	–	–	–	–	–	–	[illegible]	–	–	–	–
[illegible]	[illegible]	[illegible]	[illegible]	[illegible]	–	[illegible]	–	–	[illegible]	–	[illegible]	[illegible]	–	–	–
[illegible]	[illegible]	–	[illegible]	–	[illegible]	–	–	–	–	–	[illegible]	[illegible]	–	–	–
[illegible]	–	–	[illegible]	–	–	[illegible]	–	–	–	–	–	–	–	–	–
[illegible]	–	–	[illegible]	–	–	–	[illegible]	–	–	–	–	–	–	–	–
[illegible]	[illegible]	–	[illegible]	[illegible]	–	–	[illegible]	–	–	–	[illegible]	[illegible]	–	–	–
[illegible]	[illegible]	–	[illegible]	–	–	–	[illegible]	–	–	–	–	[illegible]	–	–	–
[illegible]	[illegible]	–	[illegible]	[illegible]	–	[illegible]	–	–	[illegible]	–	[illegible]	–	–	[illegible]	–
[illegible]	–	–	[illegible]	–	–	–	–	–	–	–	[illegible]	–	–	–	[illegible]
[illegible]	[illegible]	–	[illegible]	[illegible]	–	[illegible]	[illegible]	–	[illegible]	–	–	–	–	–	–
[illegible]	[illegible]	–	[illegible]	–	[illegible]	–	[illegible]	–	–	–	[illegible]	[illegible]	–	[illegible]	–
[illegible]	–	–	[illegible]	–	–	–	[illegible]	–	–	–	–	–	–	–	–
[illegible]	[illegible]	[illegible]	[illegible]	–	–	–	–	–	–	–	[illegible]	[illegible]	–	–	–
[illegible]	–	–	[illegible]	–	–	–	[illegible]	–	–	[illegible]	–	[illegible]	–	–	–
[illegible]	[illegible]	[illegible]	[illegible]	[illegible]	[illegible]	[illegible]	[illegible]	–	[illegible]	[illegible]	[illegible]	[illegible]	[illegible]	[illegible]	[illegible]

APPENDIX, No. 16. — APPENDIX, No. 16.

LIST of RIVERS, the MOUTHS of which have been defined, one hundred and thirty-three in number.

Section 22 of 5 & 6 Vic., c. 106, enacts "That where the breadth of the mouth or entrance into the sea of any river, the inland "portion of which is frequented by Salmon, is less than half a mile, statute measure, at low water of spring tides, it shall "not be lawful for any person whatsoever (save and except the proprietor of a several fishery within the limits thereof) to "place or erect any stake weir or fixed net within one statute mile, seaward, coastwards, or inwards, from or on either "side of the mouth or entrance of any such river into the sea."

Section 44 of 13 & 14 Vic., c. 88, enacts "That it shall not be lawful for any person, save and except the owner of a several "fishery within the limits thereof, at any time to shoot, draw, or use any net for taking Salmon at the mouth of any river, "where the breadth of such mouth between the banks thereof shall not exceed a quarter of a mile statute measure; and "that it shall not be lawful for any person, save such owner as aforesaid, within such limits as aforesaid, to shoot, draw, "or use any net for taking Salmon within half a mile seaward, or half a mile inwards, or along the coast from the mouth "of any river."

Section 3 of 26 & 27 Vic., c. 114, enacts "That no bag net shall be placed or allowed to continue in any river, or the estuary "of any river, as such river or estuary has been defined by the Commissioners of Fisheries, or shall be defined by the "Commissioners under this Act, or within a distance of less than three statute miles from the mouth of any river, as "defined."

District.	Name of River.
Dublin,	Liffey
	Dodder.
	Bray
	Vartry.
Wexford,	Slaney.
	Owenavarragh or Courtown.
	Inch.
	Urrin.
	Boro.
Waterford,	Suir, Nore, and Barrow.
	Bannow.
Lismore,	Blackwater.
	Womanagh.
Cork,	Tramore or Douglas.
	Lee.
	Owenacurra or Midleton.
	Owenboy or Carrigaline.
	Argideen.
	Bandon.
Skibbereen,	Roury.
	Ilen,
Bantry,	Leamawaddra.
	Glengariffe.
	Coomhola or Snave
	Ouvane or Ballybakey.
	Mealagh or Dunnamark.
	Adrigole.
Kenmare,	Roughty.
	Sheen.
	Finnehy.
	Blackwater (Kerry).
	Cloonee
	Owenshagh.
	Crowanshagh.
	Sneem.
Killarney,	Currane.
	Inny.
	Carragh.
	Laune.
	Maine.
	Ferta or Valencia.
	Rosbehy.
Limerick,	Shannon.
	Ouhan.
	Deel or Askeaton.
	Fergus.
	Maigue.
	Bunratty.
	Doonbeg.
	Feeagh.
	Glenmahon.
	Scarid.
	Owenmore.
Galway,	Corrib.
	Furbogh.
	Spiddle.
	Screeb.
	Ballynahinch.
	Cashla.
	Invermore.
	Owengowla.
	Crumlin.
Ballinakill,	Carrownisky.
	Bundorragha.
	Erriff.
	Culfin.
Ballinakill,	Dawros.
	Derrysherrun.
	Ballinaboy.
Bangor,	Glenamoy.
	Owenmore.
	Owenduff.
	Owengarve.
	Burrishoole.
	Newport.
	Owenwee or Belclare.
	Bunowen or Louisburgh.
Ballina,	Easky.
	Moy.
	Cloonaghmore or Palmerstown.
	Ballinglen or Ballycastle.
Sligo,	Drumcliff.
	Sligo.
	Ballysadare.
	Dunmoran.
Ballyshannon,	Glen or Teelin.
	Ballyhoolee or Kilcar.
	Eany-water or Inver.
	Eske.
	Erne.
	Drowes or Bundrowes.
	Duff or Bunduff.
	Oily.
	Fintragh.
	Bungosteen or Loughead.
Letterkenny,	Crana or Buncrana.
	Mill.
	Leannan or Rathmelton.
	Swilly.
	Owenmarve.
	Gweebarra.
	Owenea.
	Owentocker.
	Bracky.
	Lackagh.
	Ray.
	Tullaghobegly.
	Glenna.
	Clady.
	Gweedore.
Londonderry,	Foyle.
	Roe
	Culdaff.
Coleraine,	Bann.
Ballycastle,	Glenarm.
	Glenariffe (Red Bay).
	Dall or Cushendall.
	Glendun or Cushendun.
	Margy or Ballycastle.
	Bush or Bushmills.
Drogheda,	Boyne.
Dundalk,	Glyde and Dee, or Annagassan.
	Fane.
	Castletown or Dundalk.
	Piedmont.
	Quoile.
	Dundrum.
	Shimna or Tullymore.
	Annalong.
	Kilkeel.
	Causeway Water.

APPENDIX, No. 17.

BY-LAWS, ORDERS, &c., made by the INSPECTORS of IRISH FISHERIES, up to 31st December, 1872.

District.	Places affected.	Nature of By-law, Order, &c.	Date.
Cork, . . .	Bandon River and Tributaries.	Prohibiting for three years the use of all nets (except landing nets, as auxiliary to angling with rod and line), for the capture of salmon or trout, in any part of, above a line drawn across the said river, at right angles with the river's course, from the northern point of the quay, at the mouth of the creek, between the townlands of Rockhouse and Kilmacsimon, to a point on the opposite shore, in the townland of Ahern.	2nd November, 1869.
Belfast Lough, . .	Lough of Belfast, . .	Repealing by-law prohibiting trawling, ...	27th November, 1869.
Lough Swilly, . .	Lough Swilly, . . .	Repealing by-law prohibiting trawling, ...	3rd December, 1869.
Ballycastle, . .	Bush River, . . .	Repealing the definition of the estuary of, . . .	28th February, 1870.
Sligo, . . .	Sligo River, . . .	Prohibiting snatching, ...	1st March, 1870.
Killarney, . . .	Fishing weir in Waterville River.	Regulating the width between the bars or rails of the inscales, and of the heck, or the up-stream side of the boxes or cribs in said weir.	7th March, 1870.
Bantry, . . .	Tidal portions of rivers, .	Permitting use of nets with meshes of 1½ inches from knot to knot	7th March, 1870.
Kenmare River, .	Kenmare River, . .	Repealing by-law prohibiting trawling in Kenmare, .	19th March, 1870.
Ballina, . . .	River Moy, ...	Permitting use of nets with meshes of 1½ inches from knot to knot.	21st May, 1870.
Ditto, . .	Cloonaghmore or Palmerstown River.	Re-defining the mouth and estuary of, ...	16th June, 1870.
Waterford, . .	River Coonck (above Wellington Bridge).	Permitting use of nets with meshes of 1 inch from knot to knot.	7th July, 1870.
Coleraine, . . .	District, ...	Prohibiting snatching, ...	17th October, 1870.
Wexford, . . .	Derrywater and River Derry,	Permitting the use of nets with meshes of 1 inch from knot to knot.	26th October, 1870.
Ditto, . . .	Pottire River, . . .	Ditto, ...	26th October, 1870.
Lismore, . . .	River Blackwater, . .	Limiting the length of drift nets to 220 yards, . .	2nd November, 1870.
Donegal Bay, . .	Donegal Bay, . . .	Repealing by-law prohibiting trawling; save so far as it relates to Inver Bay.	15th November, 1870.
Limerick, . . .	Fergus River, . . .	Prohibiting the use of drift nets, ...	10th December, 1870.
Ballina, . . .	Moy River, . . .	Prohibiting angling for trout in April and May, . .	11th February, 1871.
Ballyshannon, . .	Erne River, . . .	Permitting nets of 1 inch mesh in tideway, . . .	15th February, 1871.
Killarney, . . .	Waterville River, . .	Prohibiting netting in certain places and at certain times,	18th February, 1871.
Coleraine, . .	Lough Neagh, . . .	Permitting pollen to be taken by trammel nets of 1 inch from 1st February to 31st October.	20th February, 1871.
Londonderry, . .	Lough Foyle and tidal parts of river, . . .	Permitting use of nets with meshes of 1 inch from knot to knot.	28th February, 1871.
Limerick, . . .	Maigue River, . . .	Prohibiting use of nets above railway bridge below Adare,	1st March, 1871.
Sligo, . . .	Lough Dean, . . .	Permitting use of nets meshes ¾ an inch from knot to knot,	24th March, 1871
Cork, . . .	Lee River, . . .	Prohibiting use of nets in South Channel, . . .	21st April, 1871.
Londonderry, . .	Baronscourt Lakes and Streams.	Permitting nets with meshes of ½ an inch from knot to knot for capture of fish other than salmon or trout.	22nd April, 1871.
Bantry, . . .	Snave, Mealagh, Ouvane, and Carrigboy Rivers.	Prohibiting use of all nets in fresh water portions, . .	21st June, 1871.
Glandore Harbour, .	—	Repealing by-law, relative to trawling, dated 11th September, 1861, ...	11th November, 1871.
Limerick, . . .	Shannon, ...	Prohibiting nets on board any cot or curragh between mouth of Shannon and Wellesley Bridge, or in tidal parts of estuaries between said points, between Nine o'Clock on Saturday morning and Three o'Clock on Monday morning; also between Wellesley Bridge and Navigation Weir at Killaloe, between Eight o'Clock on Saturday morning and Four o'Clock on Monday morning, under £3 penalty.	1st March, 1872.
Dundalk, . . .	Between Clogher Head and Ballaghan Point.	Limiting length of nets to 500 yards, ...	20th April, 1872.
Ballyshannon, . .	River Erne, . . .	Prohibiting spoon-bait, &c., in certain portions of, . .	1st June, 1872.
Ditto, . . .	River Easky-water or Inver,	Permitting use of nets with meshes of 1 inch from knot to knot, above mouth as defined.	25th June, 1872.

APPENDIX, No. 18.

ABSTRACT of BY-LAWS, ORDERS, &c., in force on 1st January, 1873, relating to the FISHERIES of IRELAND.

Place affected by By-Law, and Date thereof.	Nature of By-Law
	TRAWLING.
Dublin, (18th Oct., 1843.)	Prohibiting Trawling inside lines drawn from the Bailey Light-house at Howth, to the Easternmost point of the rocks called the "Muglins;" thence by a straight line to the Southern point of Dalkey Island, thence by a straight line across Dalkey Sound, in the direction of the signal station on Killiney Hill.
East Coast, (14th Feb., 1851.)	Prohibiting Trawling within a line drawn from the Nose of Howth, to the Eastern point of St. Patrick's Island (Skerries), thence to Clogher Head; thence to Dunany Point, thence to Cranfield Point, in the County Down.
Dundrum Bay, &c., (3rd Dec., 1851.)	Prohibiting Trawling from Hellyhunter Rock, off Cranfield Point, to St. John's Point, both in the County Down.
Donegal Bay, (16th Feb., 1857.)	Prohibiting Trawling within a straight line from the Bun Rock, to a place called Doorin Point.
Galway Bay, (22nd March, 1843, and 8th Jan., 1854.)	Prohibiting Trawling within a line from Barna Pier to [illegible] Castle. Also when large shoals of Herrings shall have set in to the Bay, and while Boats are engaged in *Drifting* for Herrings or Mackerel, and when Boats shall commence Fishing for Herrings or Mackerel, that Trawl Boats shall keep at a distance of three miles from them.
Brandon Bay, (22nd Aug., 1850.)	Prohibiting Trawling within a line drawn from Brandon Point to Coosanea.
Bantry Bay, (27th March, 1856.)	Prohibiting Trawling within a straight line from Crowdy Point to Carrig-Aye Rock; and from thence to Rennavenny Point, on the North Shore of Whiddy Island.
	Prohibiting Trawling between sunset and sunrise.
Waterford Harbour, (2nd March, 1852, and 12th June, 1856.)	Prohibiting Trawling by Boats exceeding five tons measurement, within a line drawn from Creden Head to Temple Church.
Wexford Coast, (30th April, 1840.)	Prohibiting Trawling in all places where there are Boats engaged in Herring or Mackerel Drift Net Fishing; and that Trawl Boats shall keep at a distance of at least three miles from all boats fishing for Herrings or Mackerel, with Drift Nets. And whenever Herring or Mackerel Boats shall commence Drift Net Fishing in any place, on or off the Coast of Wexford, the Trawl Boats shall depart therefrom, and keep at least three miles distant from the Drift Net Herring or Mackerel Boats.
	TRAMMEL NETS.
Dungarvan Bay, (4th July, 1849.)	Prohibiting the use of Trammel and every other Fixed or Moored Net (except Bag or other Nets for the taking of Salmon) in Dungarvan Bay, within the limit formed as follows, namely, the space lying between a line passing due East and West, through the Northernmost point of Helvick Head, and a line passing due East and West through the Southernmost point of Ballinacourty Head, in the Co. Waterford; but to the North and East of the line through Ballinacourty Head, and to the South and West of the line through Helvick Head, such Trammel or Moored Nets may be set, and remain set in the water from Three o'Clock, p.m., of one day, until Nine o'Clock, a.m., in the following day, during January, March, October, November, and December in each Year; and from Five o'Clock, p.m., of one day, to Seven o'Clock, a.m., in the following day, during May, June, July, August, and September. Also prohibiting such Nets athwart or within 300 yards of any boat, which at the time of setting such net shall be moored, and the Crew thereof engaged in Line Fishing, and to every train of such Trammel or Moored Nets shall be attached at least one floating buoy or board, upon which shall be painted in legible characters not less than one inch in length, in white upon a black ground, the Letter of the District, and the name of the Owner to which such Net belongs.
Inver Bay, (24th Sept., 1860.)	Prohibiting the use of Trammel Nets within or to the North east of a line drawn from the Mouth of the Bonleghy River to Doorin Point.
Kenmare River Estuary, (31st Dec., 1854.)	Within the Estuary of the Kenmare River, in the County of Kerry, and eastward of a line drawn from the western point of Lamb's Head to the western point of Cod's Head, the use of Trammel and other Moored Nets for the capture of Sea Fish is authorized and permitted, from the hour of Three o'Clock in the Afternoon of any one day to the hour of Nine o'Clock in the Morning of the day next following, during the months of October, November, December, January, February, and March, in each year; and from the hour of Five o'Clock in the Afternoon of any one day to the hour of Seven o'Clock in the Morning of the day following, during the months of April, May, June, July, August, and September.
	OYSTERS.
Wexford Coast, (5th April, 1852.)	First.—All persons engaged in fishing for or taking Oysters off the said Wexford Coast, south of Raven Point, shall cull all such Oysters as may be taken or caught; and shall not remove from any Fishing Ground or Oyster Bed any Oyster of less dimensions than three inches, at the greatest diameter thereof, and shall immediately throw back into the Sea all Oysters of less dimensions than aforesaid, as well as all gravel and fragments of shells as shall be raised or taken while engaged in such fishing; and no person shall take from any Oyster Bed, Rock, Strand, or Shore, off said Wexford Coast, south of Raven Point, any Oyster of less dimensions than three inches, at the greatest diameter thereof; and any person offending in any respect against this By-Law, Rule, or Regulation shall, for each offence, forfeit and pay a sum of Two Pounds.
	Second.—All persons are hereby prohibited from throwing into the Sea, on any Oyster Bed, or Oyster Fishing Ground off the said Wexford Coast, the ballast of any boat, or any other matter or thing injurious or detrimental to the Oyster Fishery; and all persons acting contrary hereto shall, for each offence, forfeit and pay a sum of Two Pounds.
Cork Harbour, (28th Oct., 1853.)	First.—That between the 1st May and 1st September, no boat shall have on board any dredge or other implement for taking Oysters.
	Second.—Every fisherman shall, on the fishing ground, cull all Oysters, and shall not remove any Oyster of less dimensions than two and a-half inches at the greatest diameter thereof; and shall throw back into the Sea all gravel and fragments of shells as he shall raise while engaged in such fishing.
	Third.—All persons are prohibited from throwing into the Sea, on any Oyster Bed or Oyster Fishing Ground, the ballast of any boat, or any other matter or thing injurious to the Oyster Fishery.
	Fourth.—No person shall, between Sunset and Sunrise, dredge for, take, or catch any Oysters within the Harbour of Cork.

Appendix. No. 18. — Abstract of By-Laws, Orders, &c.

Appendix, No. 18—*continued*.

Abstract of By-Laws, Orders, &c., in force on 1st January, 1873, relating to the Fisheries of Ireland.

Place affected by By-Law, and Date thereof.	Nature of By-Law.
Tralee Bay.* (1st Nov., 1872.)	First.—That between the 10th day of March and the 1st day of November in any year, being the Close Season for Oysters in the said Bay of Tralee, no boat, in the said Bay of Tralee, shall have on board any dredge or other implement for the taking of Oysters, and if, between the periods aforesaid, there shall be on board any boat any such dredge or other implement for the taking of Oysters, the master or owner of such boat shall, for each such offence, forfeit and pay a sum of Two Pounds.
	Second.—All persons engaged in fishing for or taking Oysters in said Bay of Tralee, shall cull all such Oysters as may be taken or caught; and shall not remove from any fishing ground or Oyster Bed any Oyster of less dimensions than two inches and one-half, at the greatest diameter thereof, and shall immediately throw back into the Sea all Oysters of less dimensions than aforesaid, as well as all gravel and fragments of shells as shall be raised or taken while engaged in such fishing, and no person shall take from any rock, strand, or shore of said Bay of Tralee, any Oyster of less dimensions than two inches and one-half, at the greatest diameter thereof, and any person offending in any respect against this By-Law, Rule, or Regulation shall, for each offence, forfeit and pay a sum of Two Pounds.
Achill Sound, Clew Bay, & Blacksod Bay. (13th Dec., 1860.)	First.—That between the 1st day of April and the 1st day of October in any year, being the Close Season for Oysters in said Clew Bay, Achill Sound, and Blacksod Bay, no boat, in the said Clew Bay, Achill Sound, and Blacksod Bay, shall have on board any dredge or other implement for the taking of Oysters; and if, between the periods aforesaid, there shall be on board any boat any such dredge or other implement for the taking of Oysters, the master or owner of such boat shall for each such offence, forfeit and pay a sum of Five Pounds.
	Second.—All persons engaged in fishing for or taking Oysters in said Clew Bay Achill Sound, and Blacksod Bay, shall cull all such Oysters as may be taken or caught; and shall not remove from any Fishing Ground or Oyster Bed any Oyster of less dimensions than two inches and one half, at the greatest diameter thereof, and shall immediately throw back into the Sea all Oysters of less dimensions than aforesaid, as well as all gravel and fragments of shells as shall be raised or taken while engaged in such fishing; and no person shall take from any rock, strand, bed, or shore of said Clew Bay, Achill Sound, and Blacksod Bay, any Oyster of less dimensions than two inches and one-half, at the greatest diameter thereof, and any person offending in any respect against this By-Law, Rule, or Regulation shall, for each offence, forfeit and pay a sum of Two Pounds.
	Third.—All persons are hereby prohibited from throwing into the Sea, on any Oyster Bed, or Oyster Fishing Ground in said Clew Bay, Achill Sound, and Blacksod Bay, the ballast of any boat, or any other matter or thing injurious or detrimental to the Oyster Fishery; and all persons acting contrary hereto shall, for each offence, forfeit and pay a sum of Two Pounds.
	Fourth.—No person shall, between sunset and sunrise, dredge for, take, or catch, any Oysters within said Clew Bay, Achill Sound, and Blacksod Bay, and every person acting contrary hereto shall, for each offence, forfeit and pay a sum of Five Pounds.
Clew Bay, County Mayo. (1st April, 1866.)	That, for the sole purpose of replenishing and supplying licensed Oyster beds and other Oyster beds, the exclusive property of any person or persons within Clew Bay alone, in the County of Mayo, and for no other purpose whatever, it may be lawful for any person to dredge for and take Oysters from any natural public bed in the said Clew Bay lying below the level of the lowest water of spring tides, between the 1st and 13th April and the 20th June and 1st October in each year, such periods being respectively included within the Close Time at present fixed for the Oyster fisheries within the said Clew Bay: Provided always, that if
Clew Bay, County Mayo—*continued*.	any Oysters dredged or taken during such part of the Close Season shall be brought to shore, or sold or offered for sale, or be found in the possession of any person on land, or be used for any other purpose than the replenishing or supplying any such artificial or other bed as aforesaid, every person so offending shall forfeit all such Oysters, and be subject and liable to the same penalties and forfeitures as by said first recited Act (5 and 6 Vic.) prescribed in cases of offences against the provisions of the said first-recited Act for the observance of the Close Season in respect of Oysters.
Carlingford Lough. (17th April, 186[illegible].)	First.—That between the 1st day of March and 1st day of November in any year, it shall not be lawful for any person to dredge for, take, catch, or destroy any Oysters or Oyster Brood within the said Lough of Carlingford, or off or from any of the shores or rocks of said Lough, and any person offending against this By-Law shall, for each such offence, forfeit and pay a sum of Five Pounds.
	Second.—That between the 1st day of March and the 1st day of November in any year, no boat, in the said Lough of Carlingford, shall have on board any dredge or other implement for the taking of Oysters; and if, between the periods aforesaid, there shall be on board any boat any such dredge or other implement for the taking of Oysters, the master or owner of such boat shall, for each such offence, forfeit and pay a sum of Five Pounds.
	Third.—All persons engaged in fishing for or taking Oysters in said Lough of Carlingford, shall cull all such Oysters as may be taken or caught, and shall not remove from any Fishing Ground or Oyster Bed any Oyster of less dimensions than two inches and one half, at the greatest diameter thereof, and shall immediately throw back into the Sea all Oysters of less dimensions than aforesaid, as well as all gravel and fragments of shells as shall be raised or taken while engaged in such fishing; and no person shall take from any rock, strand, or shore of said Lough of Carlingford, any Oyster of less dimensions than two inches and one-half, at the greatest diameter thereof; and any person offending in any respect against this By-Law, Rule, or Regulation shall, for each offence, forfeit and pay a sum of Two Pounds.
	Fourth.—All persons are hereby prohibited from throwing into the Sea, on any Oyster Bed, or Oyster Fishing Ground in the said Lough of Carlingford, the ballast of any boat, or any other matter or thing injurious or detrimental to the Oyster Fishery; and all persons acting contrary hereto shall, for each offence, forfeit and pay a sum of Two Pounds.
Galway Bay. (18th March, 1860.)	First.—All persons engaged in fishing for or taking Oysters in Galway Bay shall, on the Fishing Ground, cull all such Oysters as may be taken or caught, and shall not remove from any Fishing Ground or Oyster Bed any Oyster of less dimensions than two inches and one-half at the greatest diameter thereof, and shall immediately throw back into the Sea all Oysters of less dimensions than aforesaid, and all such gravel and fragments of shells as shall be raised or taken while engaged in such fishing, and any person offending in any respect against this By-Law, Rule, or Regulation shall, for each offence, forfeit and pay a sum of Two Pounds.
	Second.—All persons are hereby prohibited from throwing into the Sea on any Oyster Bed or Oyster Fishing Ground the ballast of any boat, or any other matter or thing injurious or detrimental to the Oyster Fishery; and all persons acting contrary hereto shall, for each such offence, forfeit and pay a sum of Two Pounds.
	Third.—No person shall, between Sunset and Sunrise, dredge for, take, or catch any Oysters within said Bay, or any of the Estuaries of the Rivers flowing into the same; and every person acting contrary hereto shall, for each offence, forfeit and pay a sum of Five Pounds.

* These By-Laws are only passed by the Inspectors of Irish Fisheries, but are not yet approved of by the Lord Lieutenant in Council.

APPENDIX, No. 18.—*continued.*

Appendix, No. 18.
Abstract of By-Laws, Orders, &c.

ABSTRACT of BY-LAWS, ORDERS, &c., in force on 1st January, 1873, relating to the FISHERIES of IRELAND.

Place affected by By-Law, and Date thereof.	Nature of By-Law.
Galway Bay—con.	Fourth.—That between Nine o'clock in the Evening of any day and Six o'clock in the Morning of the following day, no boat shall have on board any dredge or other implement for the taking of Oysters; and if, between the hours aforesaid, there shall be on board any boat any such dredge or other implement for the taking of Oysters, the Master or Owner of such boat shall, for each such offence, forfeit and pay a sum of Five Pounds.
South-east Coast of Ireland, from Wicklow Head to Carnsore Point. (1st Sept., 1865.)	That the Close Time, during which it shall not be lawful to dredge for, take, catch, or destroy any Oysters or Oyster Brood, in or off the South-east coast of Ireland, between Wicklow Head and Carnsore Point, shall be between the 30th April and the 1st September in each year.
Coasts of Dublin, Wicklow and Wexford. (22nd April, 1869.) Approved by Her Majesty in Council, 29th April, 1869.	Prohibiting between the 30th April and 1st September in each year the dredging for, taking, catching, or destroying any Oyster or Oyster Brood in or off any part of the East and South-East Coast of Ireland, within the distance of Twenty Miles measured from a straight line drawn from the Eastern point of Lambay Island, in the County Dublin, to Carnsore Point, in the County Wexford, outside the exclusive Fishery Limits of the British Islands.
Kinsale Harbour* and Bandon River. (22nd August, 1872.)	That all persons fishing for or taking Oysters in any part of the Fishing Grounds or Oyster Beds situated in Kinsale Harbour and Bandon River, in the County of Cork, shall cull all such Oysters as may be taken or caught, and shall not remove from such Fishing Grounds or Oyster Beds any Oyster of less dimensions than three inches at the greatest diameter thereof, but shall immediately throw back into the water all Oysters of less dimensions than aforesaid; and any person offending in any respect against this By-Law shall for each such offence forfeit and pay a sum of Two Pounds.
	SALMON AND TROUT.
Teelin Estuary, (24th Feb., 1869.)	Prohibiting the use of Nets for the capture of Fish of any kind, with meshes of less than one inch from knot to knot (to be measured along the side of the square, or four inches to be measured all round each such mesh, such measurements being taken in the clear when the Net is wet), on that part of the coast of the County of Donegal inside, or to the North-east and North of lines drawn from Rossan Point to Teelin Head, and from Teelin Head to Carrigan Head, and from Carrigan Head to Muckross Point, all in the Barony of Banagh, and County of Donegal.
River Liffey, (19th Jan., 1865.)	Prohibiting the catching, or attempting to catch, Salmon with any Net of greater length than 320 yards, in that part of the River Liffey which is situated between the Weir known as the Island Bridge Weir and a line drawn due North from Poolbeg Lighthouse.
River Slaney, Co. Wexford. (25th March, 1854, and 4th March, 1862.)	Prohibiting, during the Close Season for Salmon, the use of Nets of any kind whatsoever, between Ferrycarrig Bridge and the Town of Enniscorthy.
	Prohibiting, during the Open Season for Salmon, the use of Nets with meshes of less size than one and three-quarter inches from knot to knot, between Ferrycarrig Bridge and the Town of Enniscorthy.
Bessborough Demesne, Co. Kilkenny. (9th May, 1866.)	Permitting the use of Nets for the capture of Fish with Meshes of one inch from knot to knot (to be measured along the side of the square, or four inches to be measured all round each such Mesh, such measurements being taken in the clear, when the Net is wet,) within the Waters in, and Rivers running through the Demesne of Bessborough, in the County of Kilkenny: Provided that no Net having a less Mesh than one inch and three-quarters from knot to knot, shall be used in the said Rivers during the Months of April, May, and June.
Cork District. (11th Sept., 1864.)	Prohibiting the catching or attempting to catch Salmon or Trout in any Tidal Water in the Cork District with a Spear, Lyster, Otter, Strokehaul, Dree Draw, or Gaff, except when the latter instrument may be used solely as auxiliary to angling with Rod and Line, or for the purpose of removing Fish from any legal Weir or Box by the Owner or Occupier thereof.
	Prohibiting the snatching or attempting to snatch Salmon or Trout in any Tidal or Fresh Water in the Cork District with any kind of Fish-hook, covered in part or in whole with any matter or thing, or uncovered.
River Lee, Co. of the City of Cork (7th January, 1863.)	Prohibiting, during the Close Season for Salmon the use of Draft Nets, or any other Net or Nets used as a Draft Net, having a foot-rope and leads or weights affixed thereto, within the following limits, viz.:—in that part of the River Lee, situate between Patrick's Bridge, in the City of Cork, and a line drawn across the said River Lee, from Blackrock Castle, on the south, to the Western extremity of the Townland of Dunkettle, on the North.
Argideen River, (24th Feb., 1869.)	Prohibiting the use of Nets of any kind whatsoever in the tidal part of the river known as the Argideen River, in the County of Cork, situated between the junction of the Owenkeagh or Blind River with the said Argideen River and the Bridge of Timoleague, all in the Barony of the East Division of East Carbery, and County of Cork.
Bandon River.* (2nd Nov., 1869.)	Extending for a further period of three years the By-Law (bearing date 4th December, 1866), and prohibiting the use of all Nets, except Landing Nets as auxiliary to angling with Rod and Line for the capture of Salmon or Trout, in any part of the Bandon River or its Tributaries, above a line drawn across said River at right angles with the River's course from the northern point of the quay at the mouth of the Creek between the Townlands of Rock House and Kilnaganan to a point on the opposite shore in the Townland of Ahern.
River Shannon, (5th Feb., 1856.)	Prohibiting Net Fishing in that part of the River Shannon between Wellesley Bridge and the Railway Bridge, between 1st June and 12th February.
River Shannon, (22nd Nov., 1862.)	First.—Prohibiting, between the 20th day of July and 1st day of November in each year, the use of Draft Nets, or any other Net or Nets used as a Draft Net, having a foot-rope and leads or weights affixed thereto, within the following limits, viz.:—In that part of the River Shannon situate between the Fishing Weir known as the Lax Weir, and a line drawn due North and South across the said River Shannon at the Western extremity of Graigue Island.
	Second.—Prohibiting Draft Nets for the capture of Fish of any kind, of a mesh less than one and three-quarter inches from knot to knot, to be measured along the side of the square, or seven inches to be measured all round each such mesh, such measurements being taken in the clear when the Net is wet, in the tidal parts of the River Shannon, or in the tidal parts of any of the Rivers flowing into the said River Shannon.
Rivers Shannon and Maigue. (5th June, 1867.)	Prohibiting the Shooting of Fish in that part of River Shannon between Portumna Bridge and Shannon Bridge, and also in River Maigue.
River Shannon, (8th May, 1866.)	Prohibiting the Fishing for Salmon or Trout by any means whatsoever, within a space of Twenty Yards from the Weir Wall of Tarmonbarry, on the River Shannon.
Lough Ree, River Shannon. (27th August, 1858.)	Permitting the use of Nets in Lough Ree, having a mesh of five inches in the round, measured when the Net is wet.
River Fergus, (26th June, 1865.)	Prohibiting the Fishing for Salmon or Trout by any means whatsoever, within a space of Twenty Yards from the Weir Wall of Ennis, on the River Fergus.

* This By-Law is now before the Privy Council in order to be extended for a further period of two years.

Appendix, No. 18.

Abstract of By-Laws, Orders, &c.

Appendix, No. 18—*continued.*

Abstract of By-Laws, Orders, &c., in force on 1st January, 1873, relating to the Fisheries of Ireland.

Place affected by By-Law, and Date thereof	Nature of By-Law.
River Maigue, . (17th Oct., 1864.)	Prohibiting the use of Draft Nets between Ferry Drawbridge and the old Bridge of Adare.
Killarney District, (8th Feb., 1865.)	Prohibiting the catching, or attempting to catch, Salmon in any tidal water with a Spear, Lyster, Otter, Strokehaul, Cross-Draw, or Gaff, except when the latter instrument may be used solely as auxiliary to angling with rod and line, or for the purpose of removing fish from any legal Weir or Box by the owner or occupier thereof.
Castlemaine Estuary, (27th Oct., 1858.)	Prohibiting, during the Salmon Close Season, the use of Draft Nets having a foot-rope and leads or weights affixed thereto, in the Estuary of Castlemaine inside the Bar of Inch.
Lough Neagh, . (22nd April, 1846, and 24th Feb., 1860.)	Permitting Pollen to be taken by Trammel or Set Nets composed of Thread or Yarn of a fine texture, not less than ten hanks to the pound weight, doubled and twisted with a mesh of not less than one inch from knot to knot, from the 1st of March to the 29th September.
Lough Neagh, . (25th Feb., 1867.)	Prohibiting the use of Draft Nets for the capture of Pollen.
Galway River, Lough Corrib, &c. (24th July, 1848.)	Prohibiting the use of the Instrument, commonly called Strokehaul or Snatch, or any other such instrument, in River Galway, Loughs Corrib or Mask, or their Tributaries.
Galway District, . (11th Sept., 1866.)	Prohibiting the snatching or attempt to snatch Salmon in any Tidal or Fresh Water in the Galway District with any kind of Fish-hook, covered in part or in whole with any matter or thing, or uncovered.
Clare and Clare-Galway or Turloughmore Rivers, Co. Galway. (22nd Dec., 1862.)	Prohibiting the use of Nets of any kind whatsoever in any part of the Rivers known as the Clare and the Clare-Galway or Turloughmore Rivers, in the County of Galway, above the junction of the said Rivers with Lough Corrib, in the County of Galway.
Owenmore River, Co. Mayo. (8th May, 1868.)	Prohibiting the removal of gravel or sand from any part of the bed of the Owenmore River, in the County of Mayo, where the spawning of Salmon or Trout may take place.
Owenduff or Ballycroy, Owenmore and Munhim Rivers. (11th Sept., 1868.)	Permitting the use of Nets with Meshes of one and a-half inches from knot to knot (to be measured along the side of the square, or six inches to be measured all round each such Mesh, such measurements being taken in the clear, when the Net is wet.) within so much of the said Rivers Owenduff or Ballycroy, Owenmore and Munhim, as lies above the mouth as defined, during so much of the Months of June, July, and August, as do now or at any time may form part of the Open Season for the capture of Salmon or Trout, with Nets, in the said Rivers.
Sligo River, . (1st March, 1870.)	Prohibiting the snatching or attempting to snatch, Salmon in Sligo River, with any kind of Fish-hook covered in part or in whole, or uncovered.
Currane or Waterville River—Waterville Weir. (7th March, 1870.)	Permitting the space between the Bars or Rails of the Inscales and of the Heck or upstream side of the Boxes or Cribs of the Waterville Weir to be one and a quarter inches apart.
Bush River, . (28th Feb., 1870.)	Repealing Definition of Bush River Estuary as fixed by the late Special Commissioners on 8th February, 1854.
Rivers in Bantry District. (7th March, 1870.)	Permitting use of Nets of a Mesh of one and a quarter inches from knot to knot (to be measured along the side of the square, or five inches to be measured all round each such Mesh, such measurement being taken in the clear when the Net is wet), in the tidal waters of the Bantry District, which comprises the whole of the sea along the coast between Mizen Head in the County Cork and Crow Head in the same County, and around any Islands or Rocks situate off same, with the whole of the Tideways along said Coast and Rivers, and the whole of the tidal portions of the several Rivers and their Tributaries flowing into said Coast.
Ballina District, . (21st May, 1870.)	Permitting use of Nets with Meshes of one and a quarter inches from knot to knot (to be measured along the side of the square, or five inches to be measured all round each such Mesh, such measurements being taken in the clear, when the Net is wet).
Waterford District, Clodagh River. (7th July, 1870.)	Permitting use of Nets with Meshes of one inch from knot to knot (to be measured along the side of the square, or four inches to be measured all round such Mesh, such measurements being taken in the clear when the Net is wet).
Coleraine District, (17th Oct., 1870.)	Prohibiting snatching or attempting to snatch Salmon in any of the tidal or fresh waters of District.
Wexford District, Derry Water, and River Derry. (26th Oct., 1870.)	Permitting use of Nets for the capture of Fish, having Meshes of one inch from knot to knot (to be measured along the side of the square, or four inches, to be measured all round each such Mesh, such measurements being taken in the clear when the Net is wet), in the rivers and streams following, that is to say, in the Derry Water, from its source near Kilcavan to Annacurragh Bridge, with the stream flowing into same from Moyne Church through Ballinglen, and the Tomnaskela River; and in the Greenisland, Shillelagh, and Derry River, from the bounds of the County Carlow, flowing past Tinahely by Shillelagh to the bounds of the County Wexford, with the small streams flowing into that portion of the said river, all said rivers and streams being in the County Wicklow, for and during the months of May, June, July, and August, in each year.
Wexford District, Potter River. (26th Oct., 1870.)	Permitting use of Nets for the capture of Fish with Meshes of one inch from knot to knot (to be measured along the side of the square, or four inches to be measured all round each such Mesh, such measurements being taken in the clear, when the Net is wet), in the tidal portion of the Potter River, situated below Bertine Bridge in the County of Wicklow.
Lismore District, River Blackwater (2nd Nov., 1870.)	Prohibiting the catching or attempting to catch Salmon, with any Drift Net of greater length than 240 yards in the tidal portion of the River Blackwater, situated in the Counties of Waterford and Cork.
Fergus River, (16th Dec., 1870.)	Prohibiting the use of Drift Nets in the Tidal parts of River Fergus, County Clare.
Erne River, . . (15th Feb., 1871.)	Permitting use of Nets with meshes of one inch from knot to knot in tideway of River Erne.
Waterville River, . (18th Feb., 1871.)	Prohibiting use of Nets between Waterville Weir and mouth of River as defined, between twelve o'clock noon on Friday and six o'clock on Saturday morning, and between six o'clock Monday morning and twelve o'clock noon same day in each week during Open Season.
Lough Neagh, . (28th Feb., 1871.)	Permitting pollen to be taken by trammel nets of one inch from knot to knot, between 1st February and 31st October.
River Foyle, . (28th Feb., 1871.)	Permitting the use of Nets with meshes of one inch from knot to knot in Lough Foyle and tidal parts of River.
Baronscourt Lakes and Streams. (22nd April, 1871.)	Permitting the use of Nets for the capture of fish, other than Salmon and Trout, with meshes of half an inch from knot to knot.
Suave or Coomhola, Mealagh, or Dunnamark, Ouvane, and Carrigboy Rivers. (21st June, 1871.)	Prohibiting use of all Nets, save Landing-Nets, as auxiliary to rods and lines in fresh-water portions of said Rivers.
Lee River, . . (21st April, 1871.)	Prohibiting use of all Nets except Landing-Nets, as auxiliary to rods and lines in part of South Channel between George IV Bridge and Friar's Weir.
Moy River and Tributaries (11th Feb., 1871.)	Prohibiting angling for Trout during April and May in each year—Loughs Conn and Cullen excepted.

Appendix, No. 18. — Abstract of By-Laws, Orders, &c.

Appendix, No. 18—*continued.*

Abstract of By-Laws, Orders, &c., in force on 1st January, 1873, relating to the Fisheries of Ireland.

Place affected by By-Law, and Date thereof.	Nature of By-Law.	Place affected by By-Law, and Date thereof.	Nature of By-Law.
Maigue River, . (1st March, 1871.)	Prohibiting use of all Nets, except Landing-Nets as auxiliary to rod and line, above Railway-bridge below Adare.	Erne River, . (1st June, 1872.)	Prohibiting the capture of Fish of any description with the instrument commonly called and known by the name of the Spearbeat, or any other instrument of the like nature or device during the months of January, February, and March in each year, in that part of the River Erne situated between the Falls of Belleek and a line drawn due-south across the River, from the point of Castlecaldwell Demesne, by the Eastern point of the Muckinish, or White Island, to the opposite Bank, all in the County of Fermanagh.
Lough Dunn, . (26th March, 1872.)	Permitting use of Nets with meshes of half an inch from knot to knot, for capture of Fish		
River Shannon, . (1st March, 1872.)	Prohibiting having Nets for capture of Salmon or Trout on board any Cot or Curragh between mouth of Shannon and Wellesley Bridge, in the city of Limerick, or in tidal parts of any rivers flowing into the said River Shannon between said points between the hours of Nine o'clock on Saturday morning and Three o'clock on Monday morning; or between Wellesley Bridge and the Navigation Weir at Killaloe, in the County of Clare, between Eight o'clock on Saturday morning and Four o'clock on Monday morning	Eany Water, or Inver River. (26th June, 1872.)	Permitting use of Nets for the capture of Fish with Meshes of one inch from knot to knot (to be measured along the side of the square, or four inches to be measured all round each such Mesh, such measurements being taken in the clear when the Net is wet), within so much of the River Eany Water, or Inver, in the County of Donegal, as lies above the mouth of said river as defined.
Dundalk District, . (29th April, 1872.)	Prohibiting to catch or attempting to catch Salmon or Trout with any Net of greater length than 600 Yards on that part of the Sea Coast situated between Clogher Head and Ballaghan Point, in the County of Louth.		

Appendix, No. 19.

Appendix, No. 19.

Rivers, the Tidal and Fresh Water Boundaries of which have been defined.

River.	Boundary.	Date.	
Suir, . . .	A line drawn across river at and opposite to the most up-stream part of the Coolnamuck Weir,	10th March,	1864.
Nore, . . .	The Inistiogue Bridge, ...	10th March,	1864.
Barrow, . .	The lowest Weir or Dam used for navigation purposes, near St. Mullins, in county Carlow, .	10th March,	1864.
Shannon, . .	The Weir or Dam known as the Corbally Mill Weir, ...	9th April,	1864.
Fergus, . . .	The Bridge commonly known as the New Bridge, immediately below the Club House, at Ennis,	9th April,	1864.
Liffey, . . .	The Weir or Dam on said river known as the Island Bridge Weir, ...	12th August,	1864.
Maigue, . . .	The Bridge across river immediately outside and seaward of the Adare Demesne, . .	12th August,	1864.
Lee, . . .	The Weir or Dam at the Water Works of Cork, known as the Water Works Weir, . .	12th August,	1864.
Bandon, . .	The Bridge at Innishannon, known as the Innishannon Bridge, ...	19th January,	1865.
Caragh, . .	The Caragh Bridge, being the bridge immediately seaward of the Salmon Weir, . . .	19th January,	1865.
Laune, . . .	The shallow at the head of the Pool, commonly called the Cat Pool, ...	26th July,	1865.
Maine, . . .	A straight line drawn across river at right angles with its course at the boundary between the townlands of Coolaliervo and Ballyfinnane, ...	26th July,	1865.
Moy, . . .	The foot of the falls immediately below the Weirs at Ballina, ...	26th July,	1865.
Inch, . . .	Adare Bridge, ...	1st February,	1866.
Slaney, . . .	Enniscorthy Bridge, ...	1st February,	1866.
Boyne, . . .	Eastern Point of Grove Island at Oldbridge, ...	9th April,	1868.
Eask, . . .	Foot Bridge above Donegal Bridge, ...	17th July,	1868.
Shimna, . .	The Castle Bridge near Newcastle, ...	25th August,	1869.
Deel or Askeaton, .	Askeaton Bridge, ...	26th September,	1870.
Sligo or Garvogue,	The Mill Dam above Victoria Bridge, in town of Sligo, ...	11th February,	1871.
Feale, . . .	The Railway Bridge across said River, ...	16th May,	1871.
Owvane or Ballylickey, . .	The Ballylickey Bridge on the High Road, ...	10th June	1871.
Glengariffe, . .	Cromwell's Bridge, ...	10th June,	1871.
Mealagh or Dunnemark, . .	Wooden Bridge at Dunnemark Mill, ...	10th June,	1871.
Snave or Coomhola,	Snave Bridge, ...	10th June,	1871.
Carrigboy, . .	Carrigboy Bridge, ...	10th June,	1871.
Adrigole, . .	Adrigole Bridge, ...	10th June,	1871.
Glyde, . . .	Lynn's Weir, ...	28th May,	1872.
Dee, . . .	Willistown Weir, ...	28th May,	1872.

Appendix, No. 20.

List of Licences Granted to Plant Oyster Beds up to 31st December, 1872.

Date of Licence.		Persons to whom Granted	Locality of Beds.	Area of Beds.		
				A.	R.	P.
1846,	5th November,	W. H. Carter, esq.	Tramore Bay, county Mayo,	19	1	11
1848,	9th June,	F. H. Downing,	Off Daurus Point, county Kerry,	3	2	28
1849,	24th February,	R. T. Evanson,	Dunmanus Bay, county Cork,	19	0	10
1851,	5th February,	John Mahony, esq.	Estuary of Kenmare River, county Kerry,	165	2	0
	5th February,	Rev. Denis Mahony,	Estuary of Kenmare River, county Kerry,	147	2	0
1852,	17th November,	Thomas White, esq.	Ballisodare Bay, county Sligo,	132	1	26
	17th November,	John C. Garvey, esq.	Clew Bay, county Mayo,	108	3	33
1853,	22nd September,	J. O. Woodhouse, esq.	Mulroy Bay, county Donegal,	68	0	26
1854,	1st July,	Burton Bindon, esq.	Carlingford Lough, county Louth,	81	3	10
	15th November,	Hon. David Plunket,	Killary Harbour, county Mayo,	288	0	0
	15th November,	J. K. Boswell, esq.	Ballyconnelly Bay, county Galway,	233	0	0
1855,	18th July,	John Richards, esq.	Blacksod Bay, county Mayo,	90	0	0
1856,	30th July,	Lord Charles P. P. Clinton,	Bear Haven, county Cork,	45	0	0
	21st August,	William Foreman, esq.	Ardbear Bay, county Galway,	90	2	0
1857,	7th August,	Thomas Eccles, esq.	Glengariffe Harbour, county Cork,	9	1	0
1858,	15th February,	Rev. A. Magee,	Streamstown and Cleggan Bays, co. Galway,	277	0	0
	15th February,	A. C. Lambert, esq.	Killary Harbour, county Galway,	114	0	0
1860,	3rd February,	Rev. R. H. Wall,	Mannin and Ardbear Bays, county Galway,	346	0	0
	3rd February,	Knight of Kerry,	Valentia Harbour, county Kerry,	76	0	0
	3rd February,	Captain W. Houston,	Killary Harbour, county Mayo,	43	0	0
	13th February,	William M'Cormick, esq.	Achill Sound, county Mayo,	149	0	0
	11th May,	Edward Browne, esq.	Ballinakill Harbour, county Galway,	223	0	0
	4th October,	M. C. Cramer, esq.	Oyster Haven, county Cork,	20	0	0
	9th October,	Ebenezer Pike, esq.	Lough Mahon, Estuary of Lee, county Cork,	47	0	0
	14th November,	William Pike, esq	Achill Sound, county Mayo,	1,670	0	0
1861,	10th January,	William Forbes, esq.	Mornwish Bay, county Galway,	225	0	0
1862,	14th February,	Robert W. C. Reeves, esq.	Clonderlaw Bay, county Clare,	112	0	0
	3rd March,	James Walker, esq.	Belfast Lough, Carrickfergus,	137	0	0
	6th March,	Edmund Power, esq.	Tramore Bay, county Waterford,	270	0	0
1863,	29th May,	George Clive, esq., M.P.	Achill Sound, county Mayo,	469	0	0
1864,	2nd February,	Lord Fortescue,	Tramore Bay, county Waterford,	83	0	0
	5th April,	Lord Wallscourt,	Galway Bay, county Galway,	1,770	0	0
	10th June,	Colonel C. M. Vandeleur, M.P.	Poulnasherry Bay, county Clare,	190	0	0
	10th June,	A. W. Wyndham, esq.	Newport Bay, county Mayo,	80	0	0
	30th September,	Captain George Austin,	Westport Bay, county Mayo,	194	0	0
	31st October,	John Kendall, esq	Ardbear and Mannin Bays, county Galway,	236	0	0
	31st October,	Robert T. Atkins, esq.	Lough Hyne, county Cork,	25	0	0
	31st October,	R. E. L. Athy, esq.	Galway Bay, county Galway,	100	0	0
	31st October,	P. M. Lynch, esq	Galway Bay, county Galway,	320	0	0
	11th November,	A. Boate, esq	Dungarvan Harbour, county Waterford,	66	0	0
	11th November,	J. R. Power, esq.	Dungarvan Harbour, county Waterford,	27	0	0
	31st December,	Captain W. F. Barry,	Glandore Harbour, county Cork,	68	0	0
	31st December,	C. P. Archer, esq.	Ballinakill Harbour, county Galway,	46	0	0
	31st December,	T. Young Prior, esq.	Ballinakill Harbour, county Galway,	90	0	0
	31st December,	P. Macauley, esq	Ballinakill and Barnaderg Bays, co. Galway,	130	0	0
	31st December,	Colonel F. A. K. Gore,	Killala Bay, county Mayo,	275	0	0
1865,	13th April,	Marquess of Sligo,	Clew Bay, county Mayo,	190	0	0
	13th April,	Sir Robert Gore Booth,	Drumcliff Bay, county Sligo,	146	3	0
	12th May,	Lord Baron Ventry,	Dingle Harbour, county Kerry,	130	0	0
	2nd November,	Law Life Assurance Society,	Clew Bay, county Mayo,	118	0	0
	2nd November,	Marquess of Sligo,	Clew Bay, county Mayo,	25	0	0
	1st December,	Most Rev. Dr. M'Hale,	Shores of Achill Island, county Mayo,	125	0	0
	1st December,	Thomas M'Carthy Collins, esq	Roaringwater Bay, county Cork,	75	0	0
	1st December,	Marquess of Sligo,	Clew Bay, county Mayo,	26	0	0
	1st December,	John Obins Woodhouse, esq.	Carlingford Lough, county Louth,	54	0	0
	1st December,	Captain Acheson,	Ballinakill Harbour, county Galway,	18	0	0
	1st December,	Richard J. Verschoyle, esq.	Ballisodare Bay, county Sligo,	54	0	0
	1st December,	Richard Mahony, esq.	Kenmare Estuary, county Kerry,	30	0	0
	1st December,	Mr. Robert M'Keown,	Killary Harbour,	61	0	0
1866,	20th April,	William Dargan, esq.	Wexford Harbour,	70	0	0
	20th April,	Marquess of Sligo,	Clew Bay, county Mayo,	270	0	0
	21st April,	Miss Anne Fowler,	Blacksod Bay, county Mayo,	11	0	0
	4th June,	John Obins Woodhouse, esq.	Carlingford Lough, county Louth,	42	0	0

APPENDIX, No. 20—*continued.*

APPENDIX, No. 20.

LIST of LICENCES GRANTED to Plant OYSTER BEDS up to 31st December, 1872.

Date of Licence.		Persons to whom Granted.	Locality of Beds.	Area of Beds A.	R.	P.
1867,	15th June,	Sir Robert Gore Booth, bart.	Drumcliff Bay, county Sligo,	87	0	0
	10th July,	Horatio Hamilton Townsend, esq.	Skull Harbour, county Cork,	230	0	0
	10th July,	Thomas Sandes, esq.	River Shannon, county Kerry,	760	0	0
	10th July,	Mrs. Elizabeth Atkinson,	Blacksod Bay, county Kerry,	100	0	0
	10th July,	M. J. C. Longfield, esq.	Roaringwater Bay, county Cork,	810	0	0
	10th July,	Thomas Kirkwood, esq.	Saleen Harbour, county Mayo,	17	0	0
	10th July,	Richard D. Kane, esq.	Howth Strand, county Dublin,	36	0	0
	10th July,	Christopher T. Redington, esq.	Galway Bay, county Galway,	650	0	0
	10th July,	Mrs. Elizabeth Bury,	Lough Mahon, county Cork,	70	0	0
	10th July,	Rev. Nicholas Martin,	Trawbreaga Bay, county Donegal,	90	0	0
	15th July,	John Smyth, esq.	Midleton River, county Cork,	10	2	0
	15th July,	Stephen E. Collis, esq.	River Shannon, county Kerry,	212	0	0
	15th July,	Thomas Hicks, esq.	Roaringwater Bay, county Cork,	45	0	0
	16th July,	Robert W. C. Reeves, esq.	River Shannon, county Clare,	30	0	0
	24th July,	Francis J. Graham, esq.	Bertraghboy Bay, county Galway,	90	0	0
1868,	31st January,	William Hart, esq.	Lough Swilly, county Donegal,	790	0	0
	11th February,	Richard Lyons, esq.	Midleton River, county Cork,	15	0	0
	11th February,	Charles Sandes, esq.	River Shannon, county Kerry,	56	0	0
	13th March,	Stephen Browne, esq.	Dunmanus Bay, county Cork,	9	0	0
	13th March,	Colonel Edward Cooper,	Ballisodare Bay, county Sligo,	190	0	0
1869,	13th February,	Henry Herbert,	Kenmare Bay,	20	0	0
	13th February,	Earl of Bantry,	Adrigole Harbour,	18	0	0
	13th February,	Earl of Bantry,	Glengariff Harbour,	60	0	0
	4th March,	John P. Nolan,	Ard Bay,	290	0	0
	11th March,	Richard J. Mahony,	Kenmare Bay,	46	0	0
	11th March,	Thomas Kingston Sullivan,	Kenmare Bay,	193	0	0
	15th March,	John W. Payne,	Bantry Bay,	51	0	0
	14th June,	John W. Stratford,	Killala Bay,	31	0	0
	14th June,	Mrs. Catherine Browne,	Courtmacsherry Bay,	60	0	0
	14th June,	William Little,	Killala Bay,	190	0	0
	10th September,	Lord Clermont,	Carlingford Lough,	46	0	0
	10th September,	Henry W. Meredith,	Sligo Bay,	20	0	0
	10th September,	Owen Wynne,	Sligo Bay,	77	0	0
	10th September,	Owen Wynne,	Sligo Bay,	83	0	0
1870,	12th March,	R. J. Verschoyle,	Ballisodare Bay,	13	2	0
1871,	22nd March,	Earl of Bantry and T. J. Leahy,	Berehaven,	122	0	0
	27th March,	Earl of Bantry,	Ardgroom Harbour,	240	0	0
	27th March,	Thomas Hicks,	Roaringwater Bay, county Cork,	30	0	0
	22nd April,	Agnes M. Nicholson,	Sligo Bay,	32	2	10
	24th April,	Ed. Park,	Milk Haven, county Sligo,	21	0	0
	24th April,	Martin Commane,	Milk Haven, county Sligo,	2	2	10
	24th April,	Michael Commane,	Milk Haven, county Sligo,	2	1	10
	1st July,	Arthur Hamill, esq., &c.	Carlingford Lough, county Louth,	144	0	0
	18th July,	Sir James Stewart, bart.	Lough Swilly, county Donegal,	106	2	21
	27th July,	F. Mansfield, esq.	Lough Swilly, county Donegal,	23	1	0
	9th October,	Marquis of Downshire,	Dundrum Bay,	32	0	2
	26th December,	Major Scott,	Bertraghboy Bay,	390	3	0
	26th December,	Colin Hugh Thomson,	Killary Bay,	201	2	0
1872,	9th February,	W. and J. St. George,	Galway Bay,	510	0	0
	25th May,	W. Pike,	Achill Sound,	308	3	20
	21st June,	Lord Bandon,	Dunmanus Bay,	182	3	31½
	3rd July,	J. Rowan,	Achill Sound,	43	3	0
	16th December,	W. O. M'Cormick,	Rashfran Bay,	95	1	32
			Total,	17,694	1	0½

Appendix, No. 22.

Certificates granted up to 31st December, 1872, for Fixed Engines for fishing for Salmon or Trout.

No.	Place.	Name of Person to whom Certificate granted.	Date of Certificate.	District in which Engine placed.	Description of Fixed Net.	Particulars of Net, &c.	Observations.
[illegible]	[illegible]	Henry D. [illegible]	[illegible]	[illegible]	[illegible]	[illegible]	[illegible]
[illegible]	[illegible]	[illegible]	[illegible]	[illegible]	[illegible]	[illegible]	[illegible]
19	Lough Foyle	The Irish Society.	1 January	Londonderry,	[illegible]	[illegible]	[illegible]
20	Ditto,	Ditto,	Ditto,	Ditto,	1 [illegible]	[illegible]	[illegible]
21	Ditto,	Ditto,	Ditto,	Ditto,	1 Do.,	[illegible]	[illegible]
[illegible]	[illegible]	[illegible]	[illegible]	[illegible]	[illegible]	[illegible]	[illegible]

APPENDIX, No. 21—continued.

CERTIFICATES granted up to 31st December, 1873, for Fixed Engines for fishing for Salmon or Trout—continued.

No.	Place.	[illegible]	[illegible]	[illegible]	[illegible]	[illegible]	[illegible]
[illegible]	[illegible]	[illegible]	[illegible]	[illegible]	[illegible]	[illegible]	[illegible]

Appendix, No. 22.

A Summary of Certificates for Fixed Engines issued by the late Special Commissioners for Irish Fisheries and the Inspectors of Irish Fisheries, up to 1st January, 1873.

Certificates.	Stake Nets.	Bag Nets.	Fly Nets.	Head Weirs.	Stone Walls or Beulks.	Fixed Draft Nets.	Total.	Remarks.
Total issued to 1st January, 1872,	–	–	–	–	–	–	137	These 117 certificates issued up to 1st January, 1872, represent—
Issued by Special Commissioners,	6	22	1	3	2	–	34	44 stake nets. 38 bag nets. 1 fly net. 3 head weirs. 2 beulks. 58 fixed draft nets.
" Inspectors of Irish Fisheries for Engines declared legal by Special Commissioners,	–	3	–	–	–	2	5	
" Inspectors for those declared legal by Court of Queen's Bench on appeal from decision of Special Commissioners,	24	6	–	–	–	–	27	
" Inspectors for Engines declared legal by Court on appeal from decision of Magistrates,	–	–	–	–	–	1	1	Total, 146 fixed engines, for which certificates have been sanctioned.
" Inspectors for Engines found by them to be legal,	12	7	–	–	–	51	60	
Total,	42	35	1	3	2	54	117	

Appendix, No. 23.

Return of the Number of Prosecutions and Convictions for Breaches of the Fishery Laws during the year 1872.

Number.	District.	Number of Prosecutions instituted.	Number of Convictions obtained.	Offences: Poisoning rivers.	Breach of Close Season.	Fishing without Licence.	Illegally using Gaff, Spear, &c.	Obstructing and assaulting Water Bailiffs.	Having and selling unclean fish.	Using fixed net illegally.	Boats not registered.	Fishing at Mill Weirs, and obstructing water courses.	Fishing at mouths of rivers as defined.	Non-observance of gratings at mills.	Taking undersized oysters.	Illegally snatching.	Trespass on several fishery.	Fishing for Eels between certain hours.	No free gap in weir.	Offences not stated.	Amount of Fines. £ s. d.	Remarks.
1	Dublin,	–	–	–	–	–	–	–	–	–	–	–	–	–	–	–	–	–	–	–	—	Of this sum of £1,086 0s. 6d. His Excellency the Lord Lieutenant, on memorials from the persons fined, has remitted £[illegible].
2	Wexford,	8	3	–	–	–	–	–	1	–	–	–	8	–	–	–	–	–	–	1	17 3 0	
3	Waterford,	42	42	1	4	1	6	–	2	–	1	–	–	–	–	–	3	–	–	26	72 5 0	Application of Penalties for Fishery Offences.—Under the 19th section of the 32nd and 33rd Vic., cap 92, one-third of every sum of money levied as a fine in cases of breaches of the Fishery Laws shall be paid to the person bringing the offender to justice; the remainder shall be paid to the Board of Conservators of the district in which the offence was committed.
4	Lismore,	71	43	–	14	1	16	4	2	–	–	–	6	–	–	–	–	–	–	–	77 10 0	
5	Cork,	56	33	1	3	3	16	–	–	–	–	–	–	–	–	–	–	–	–	3	63 18 6	
6a	Skibbereen,	11	11	8	–	–	–	–	–	–	–	–	–	2	–	–	–	–	–	–	2 3 8	
6b	Bantry,	8	8	1	–	–	2	–	–	–	–	–	–	–	–	–	–	–	–	–	5 7 6	
6c	Kenmare,	–	–	–	–	–	–	–	–	–	–	–	–	–	–	–	–	–	–	–	—	
7	Killarney,	47	47	6	11	5	10	–	3	–	–	–	–	–	–	–	–	–	–	27	44 19 4	
8	Limerick,	79	66	3	21	3	18	–	–	6	–	6	–	–	8	–	12	–	–	10	134 5 6	
9	Galway,	9	1	–	2	–	–	–	–	–	–	–	–	–	–	–	–	–	–	–	3 6 6	
10a	Ballinakill,	3	2	–	–	–	–	–	–	–	–	–	–	–	–	3	–	–	–	–	8 0 0	
10b	Bangor,	16	16	–	7	–	4	–	–	–	–	–	–	–	8	–	–	–	–	–	31 10 6	
11	Ballina,	48	46	7	18	–	17	1	4	–	–	–	–	–	–	–	–	–	–	6	66 16 6	
12	Sligo,	19	19	–	3	1	2	–	1	–	–	–	–	–	–	–	–	–	–	6	18 10 0	
13	Ballyshannon,	38	35	26	2	–	–	–	–	–	–	–	–	–	–	–	3	–	–	4	7 1 0	
14	Letterkenny,	14	14	7	3	1	–	–	–	–	–	–	–	–	2	–	–	–	–	1	22 10 0	
15a	Londonderry,	31	26	5	6	–	16	2	–	–	–	–	–	–	–	–	3	–	–	–	78 9 0	
15b	Coleraine,	291	264	143	5	7	5	10	11	16	5	9	–	–	–	–	–	–	–	17	299 7 6	
16	Ballycastle,	90	90	80	–	–	–	–	–	–	–	–	–	–	–	–	–	–	–	–	2 8 6	
17a	Drogheda,	20	17	9	1	–	–	4	–	–	–	–	–	–	–	–	6	1	1	8	8 13 6	
17b	Dundalk,	16	13	3	3	1	–	–	–	–	–	–	–	–	–	–	–	–	–	7	16 10 0	
	Totals,	796	636	296	106	30	119	24	24	15	10	6	15	2	10	2	24	1	1	180	1,086 0 6	

Appendix, No. 24.

Table showing the Total Amount realized and the Increase and Decrease in the Amounts received in the various Fishery Districts from the sale of Licences between the years 1863 and 1872, inclusive.

Years from 1863 to 1872		Amounts received for Licence Duty			Increase over preceding year.			Decrease under preceding year		
		£	s.	d.	£	s.	d.	£	s.	d.
—	1863	5,892	7	6	475	8	10	—		
1863	1864	7,001	15	0	1,109	7	6	—		
1864	1865	6,722	16	8	—			278	18	4
1865	1866	7,098	6	8	375	10	0	—		
1866	1867	7,317	0	0	218	13	4	—		
1867	1868	7,033	10	6	—			283	9	6
1868	1869	6,700	6	4	—			333	4	2
1869	1870	7,511	13	4	811	7	0	—		
1870	1871	8,863	15	9	1,354	2	5	—		
1871	1872	8,998	1	0	133	5	3	—		

Increase in Licence Duty since 1863, £3,105 13s. 6d.

Appendix, No. 25.

Return of Fish conveyed by the Limerick and Foynes Railway Company, during the year ending 31st December, 1872.

Stations.	White or Coarse Fish		Weight			
	Boxes.	Baskets	Tons	cwt.	qrs.	lbs.
	114	—	9	18	2	0
	382	—	35	12	2	0
	206	—	17	16	8	0
	345	—	31	11	3	6
	536	—	49	14	2	0
	1,583	—	144	14	0	6

Note.—The average gross weight of each box is about 2 cwt.

Return of Fish conveyed by the Belfast and Northern Counties Railway Company, during the Year ending 31st December, 1872.

Stations.	Salmon and Trout		White or Coarse Fish.		Weight.
	Boxes.	Baskets	Boxes.	Baskets.	Tons cwt. qrs. lbs.
Belfast,	—	—	2,009	5	
Carrickfergus,	—	—	—	1,470	
Larne,	42	69	42	135	
Antrim,	700	2	—	—	
Toome,	53	137	5,344	42	
Moneymore,	—	—	185	10	
Cookstown,	—	—	21	—	
Ballymoney,	52	28	311	94	
Coleraine,	39	3	80	66	
Portstewart,	27	6	193	18	
Portrush,	494	5	702	49	
Magilligan,	09	8	47	11	
Bellarena,	—	—	—	—	
Londonderry,	887	—	16	—	
Total,	2,443	257	8,956	1,902	

Return of Fish conveyed over their Lines by the Irish North-Western Railway Company, during the Year ending 31st December, 1872.

From what Stations.	Salmon and Trout.		Weight				White or Coarse Fish.		Weight.			
	Boxes.	Baskets.	Tons.	cwt.	qrs.	lbs.	Boxes	Baskets.	Tons.	cwt.	qrs.	lbs.
Strabane,	5	5	0	12	2	0	—	—	—			
"	15	16	2	0	1	0	—	—	—			
St. Johnston,	—	1	0	0	1	0	—	—	—			
"	—	1	0	0	1	0	—	—	—			
"	—	1	0	0	1	0	—	—	—			
"	1	28	0	10	2	4	—	—	—			
Carrigans,	—	1	0	0	1	12	—	—	—			
Derry,	—	13	0	3	1	0	—	46	2	12	3	0
"	—	1	0	0	1	16	—	10	0	10	2	0
Total,	21	70	4	0	0	4	—	56	3	3	1	0

APPENDIX, No. 25—*continued.*

APPENDIX, No. 25.

RETURN of FISH conveyed by the Enniskillen, Bundoran, and Sligo Railway Company, during the Year ending 31st December, 1872.

From what Stations.	Salmon and Trout.		Weight.				White or Coarse Fish.		Weight.			
	Boxes.	Baskets.	Tons.	cwt.	qrs.	lbs.	Boxes.	Baskets.	Tons.	cwt.	qrs.	lbs.
Belleek,	—	—	—				15	—	1	2	2	0
"	—	—	—				712	—	53	5	2	0
Bundoran,	—	23	0	9	2	18	10	22	1	8	0	0
"	3	41	1	8	1	4	1	6	0	2	0	3
"	—	4	0	0	3	0	7	—	0	13	2	20
"	—	15	0	8	1	24	6	2	0	10	3	0
"	—	24	0	15	2	0	4	11	0	15	1	20
"	—	3	0	0	2	0	1	1	0	0	3	0
"	—	1	0	0	3	0	2	1	0	2	0	0
Pettigo,	—	—	—				7	9	1	6	0	0
"	—	—	—				16	25	4	1	3	0
"	—	—	—				—	10	1	0	0	0
"	—	—	—				26	6	2	9	2	0
"	—	—	—				14	1	1	1	2	0
"	—	—	—				7	—	0	12	1	0
"	—	—	—				—	3	0	3	0	0
Ballyshannon,	1,124	—	111	8	2	0	—	—	—			
Total,	1,127	111	114	12	1	18	828	107	66	15	2	15

RETURN of FISH conveyed to Dublin by the trains of the Midland Great Western Railway Company, during the Year ending 31st December, 1872.

From what Stations.	Boxes.	Baskets.	Tons.	cwt.	qrs.	lbs.
Galway,	1,850	2,027	310	14	1	0
Sligo,	117	65	9	18	2	0
Ballysadare,	84	3	5	7	3	0
Westport,	57	30	7	13	1	0
Athlone,	7	—	0	5	0	0
Foxford,	13	1	0	12	2	0
Total,	2,124	2,126	334	11	1	0

RETURN of FISH conveyed by the Dublin, Wicklow, and Wexford Railway, for the Year ending 31st December, 1872.

Description of Fish.	Boxes.	Baskets.	Tons.	cwt.	qrs.	lbs.
Salmon or Trout,	247	150	7	18	1	25
White or Coarse Fish,	5,520	1,936	779	2	1	5
Total,	5,776	2,086	787	0	3	2

RETURN of FISH conveyed to Bristol by the Bristol General Steam Navigation Company (Limited), during the Year ending 31st December, 1872.

Dates, and from what Stations.	White or Coarse Fish.		Weight.			
	Barrels.	Hogsheads.	Tons.	cwt.	qrs.	lbs.
May 7, Dublin,	20	2	6	10	0	0
June 18, Howth,	40	—	6	0	0	0
" 25, "	26	—	3	18	0	0
July 2, "	48	—	7	4	0	0
" 16, "	18	—	2	14	0	0
" 23, "	18	—	2	14	0	0
" 30, "	20	—	3	0	0	0
Aug. 6, "	24	—	3	12	0	0
" 13, "	47	—	7	1	0	0
" 20, "	43	—	6	9	0	0
Oct. 29, "	19	—	2	17	0	0
Nov. 5, "	5	—	0	15	0	0
Total,	328	2	52	14	0	0

RETURN of FISH conveyed to all Stations by the Goods and Passenger Trains of the Great Southern and Western Railway Company, during the Year ending 31st December, 1872.

From all Stations during the year 1872, . Salmon and Trout, 186 tons; White or Coarse Fish, 1,432 tons.

APPENDIX, No. 25

APPENDIX, No. 25—*continued.*

RETURN of FISH conveyed to Ardrossan by the Steamer "South-Western," of the Ardrossan Steam Ship Company, during the year ending 31st December, 1872.

Dates, and from what Station.	Fresh Herrings. Boxes.	Fresh Herrings. Barrels.	Weight. Tons.	cwt.	qrs.	lbs.	Average Gross Weight of Boxes and Barrels.
June 21, Ardglass, . .	—	6	0	12	0	0	2 cwt. each.
,, 26, do., . .	—	14	1	8	0	0	
,, ,, do., . .	—	3	0	6	0	0	
,, ,, do., . .	—	3	0	0	0	0	
,, ,, do., . .	—	1	0	2	0	0	
,, ,, do., . .	—	1	0	2	0	0	
,, ,, do., . .	—	3	0	4	0	0	
,, ,, do., . .	—	4	0	6	0	0	
,, ,, do., . .	—	5	0	8	0	0	
,, ,, do., . .	—	4	0	8	0	0	
,, 28, do., . .	—	3	0	5	0	0	
,, ,, do., . .	—	3	0	4	2	0	
,, ,, do., . .	—	4	0	0	0	0	
,, ,, do., . .	—	3	0	5	0	0	
July 3, do., . .	—	7	0	12	0	0	
,, ,, do., . .	—	4	0	6	0	0	
,, ,, do., . .	—	4	0	6	0	0	
,, ,, do., . .	—	1	0	2	0	0	
,, ,, do., . .	—	6	0	12	0	0	
,, ,, do., . .	—	2	0	4	0	0	
,, 5, do., . .	—	0	0	9	0	0	
,, ,, do., . .	—	6	0	9	0	0	
,, ,, do., . .	7	—	0	14	0	0	
,, ,, do., . .	—	5	2	8	0	0	
,, 10, do., . .	—	2	0	4	0	0	
,, ,, do., . .	—	1	0	2	0	0	
,, ,, do., . .	—	1	0	2	0	0	
,, ,, do., . .	—	40	3	9	0	0	
,, 17, do., . .	—	20	1	10	2	0	
,, ,, do., . .	11	—	1	3	0	0	
,, 10, do., . .	—	20	1	11	0	0	
,, ,, do., . .	5	—	0	12	1	0	
,, 24, do., . .	—	45	2	14	0	0	
,, ,, do., . .	14	—	1	1	0	0	
,, 31, do., . .	—	64	3	9	0	0	
Aug. 2, do., . .	—	28	2	1	0	0	
,, ,, do., . .	9	—	0	13	2	0	
,, 7, do., . .	3	—	0	8	0	0	
,, ,, do., . .	—	1	0	2	0	0	
,, 9, do., . .	—	54	4	12	0	0	
,, ,, do., . .	15	—	1	4	0	0	
,, 14, do., . .	—	12	1	1	0	0	
,, ,, do., . .	10	—	1	11	0	0	
,, 16, do., . .	—	62	5	1	0	0	
,, 21, do., . .	—	28	2	8	0	0	
,, ,, do., . .	2	3	0	12	0	0	
,, 23, do., . .	—	49	4	15	0	0	
,, ,, do., . .	6	2	1	4	2	0	
,, ,, do., . .	1	5	0	10	0	0	
,, 28, do., . .	—	21	2	6	0	0	
,, ,, do., . .	1	—	1	6	0	0	
,, ,, do., . .	7	1	1	8	0	0	
,, ,, do., . .	2	8	1	1	0	0	
,, 30, do., . .	—	19	1	6	0	0	
,, ,, do., . .	3	1	0	12	0	0	
,, ,, do., . .	1	—	0	12	0	0	
Sept. 6, do., . .	—	18	1	0	0	0	
,, ,, do., . .	—	5	0	8	0	0	
,, 11, do., . .	—	7	0	12	0	0	
,, 13, do., . .	—	15	1	8	0	0	
,, ,, do., . .	8	—	0	12	0	0	
,, ,, do., . .	—	14	1	6	0	0	
,, 20, do., . .	—	10	1	10	0	0	
Total, . . .	105	654	67	19	1	0	

RETURN of FISH conveyed to Bristol and Whitehaven by the Belfast, Bristol, Whitehaven, and Stranraer Steamship Company, during the year ending 31st December, 1872.

Stations.	White or Coarse Fish.	Tons.	cwt.	qrs.	lbs.
Belfast to Stranraer, . .	8 bales Ling ...	0	4	0	0
	4 ,, ,, ...	0	2	0	6
	6 ,, ,, ..	0	3	0	0
	4 ,, ,, ...	0	2	0	0
,, to Bristol, . .	Nil.	—			
,, to Whitehaven, . .	Nil.	—			
Total, . . .	22	0	11	0	6

APPENDIX, No. 25—*continued.*

RETURN of FISH conveyed from Moville to Glasgow by the Steamers of Messrs. G. and J. Burns, during the Year ending 31st December, 1872.

Dates, and from what Station.	White or Coarse Fish. Boxes.	White or Coarse Fish. Baskets.	Weight. Tons.	Weight. cwt.	Weight. qrs.	Weight. lbs.	Average Gross Weight of Boxes and Baskets.
January 4th, Moville, . .	10	—	1	10	0	0	
" 8th, do., . .	25	—	3	15	0	0	
" 11th, do., . .	22	—	3	6	0	0	
" 15th, do., . .	5	—	0	15	0	0	
" 18th, do., . .	8	—	0	9	0	0	
" 22nd, do., . .	35	—	5	5	0	0	
" 25th, do., . .	28	—	4	4	0	0	
" 29th, do., . .	18	—	2	8	0	0	
February 5th, do., . .	7	—	1	0	0	0	
" 8th, do., . .	42	—	6	6	0	0	
" 15th, do., . .	15	—	2	8	0	0	
" 19th, do., . .	19	—	2	17	0	0	
" 22nd, do., . .	12	—	1	12	0	0	
" 26th, do., . .	4	—	0	12	0	0	
" 29th, do., . .	8	—	1	3	0	0	
March 4th, do., . .	8	—	1	3	0	0	
" 28th, do., . .	4	—	0	12	0	0	
April 1st, do., . .	7	—	1	1	0	0	
" 4th, do., . .	6	—	0	18	0	0	
" 15th, do., . .	4	—	0	12	0	0	
" 25th, do., . .	3	—	0	9	0	0	
" 29th, do., . .	9	—	1	7	0	0	
May 2nd, do., . .	9	—	1	7	0	0	
" 6th, do., . .	2	—	0	6	0	0	
" 9th, do., . .	1	—	0	3	0	0	
" 13th, do., . .	11	—	1	12	0	0	
" 16th, do., . .	18	—	2	7	0	0	
" 27th, do., . .	3	—	0	6	0	0	
June 3rd, do., . .	4	—	0	11	0	0	
" 6th, do., . .	2	—	0	5	0	0	
" 13th, do., . .	3	—	0	9	0	0	
" 17th, do., . .	2	1	0	7	0	0	
" 20th, do., . .	1	2	0	4	0	0	
August 1st, do., . .	1	—	0	3	0	0	
" 8th, do., . .	2	—	0	4	0	0	
" 12th, do., . .	1	—	0	3	0	0	
" 15th, do., . .	2	—	0	6	0	0	
" 19th, do., . .	3	—	0	9	0	0	
" 22nd, do., . .	3	—	0	9	0	0	
" 26th, do., . .	8	—	0	8	0	0	
September 2nd, do., . .	1	1	0	4	0	0	
" 5th, do., . .	0	—	1	7	0	0	
" 9th, do., . .	6	1	0	17	0	0	
" 12th, do., . .	2	—	0	6	0	0	
" 16th, do., . .	6	—	0	16	0	0	
" 19th, do., . .	4	—	0	12	0	0	
" 23rd, do., . .	13	—	1	19	0	0	
" 26th, do., . .	5	4	1	8	0	0	
" 30th, do., . .	8	—	0	9	0	0	
October 3rd, do., . .	3	—	0	7	0	0	
" 7th, do., . .	13	—	1	18	0	0	
" 10th, do., . .	12	—	1	15	0	0	
" 14th, do., . .	11	—	1	13	0	0	
" 17th, do., . .	4	—	0	12	0	0	
" 21st, do., . .	15	1	2	6	0	0	
" 24th, do., . .	14	—	2	2	0	0	
" 28th, do., . .	22	—	3	4	0	0	
" 31st, do., . .	2	1	0	3	0	0	
November 4th, do., . .	11	—	1	13	0	0	
" 7th, do., . .	9	—	1	5	0	0	
" 11th, do., . .	3	—	0	9	0	0	
" 14th, do., . .	26	—	3	19	0	0	
" 18th, do., . .	21	1	3	4	0	0	
" 21st, do., . .	4	—	0	12	0	0	
" 25th, do., . .	25	—	3	15	0	0	
" 28th, do., . .	43	—	5	8	0	0	
December 3rd, do., . .	26	—	3	16	0	0	
" 10th, do., . .	37	—	5	4	0	0	
" 13th, do., . .	31	—	4	10	0	0	
" 17th, do., . .	18	—	1	16	0	0	
" 20th, do., . .	21	—	3	0	0	0	
" 24th, do., . .	20	—	3	0	0	0	
" 27th, do., . .	19	—	2	15	0	0	
Total, . . .	804	12	120	6	0	0	

Appendix. No. 25.

APPENDIX, No. 25—*continued.*

RETURN of FISH conveyed to Liverpool by the Steamers of the Dublin and Liverpool Screw Steam Packet Company, during the Year ending 31st December, 1872.

From what Station.	White or Coarse Fish		Weight.				Average Gross Weight of Boxes and Baskets.
	Boxes.	Baskets.	Tons.	cwt.	qrs.	lbs.	
Dublin, ...	798	—	80	9	0	0	2 cwt. each.

Dates, and from what Stations	Salmon and Trout.		Weight.				Average Gross Weight of Boxes and Baskets
	Boxes.	Baskets.	Tons.	cwt.	qrs.	lbs.	
Feb. 2. Killarney, . .	2	—	0	4	1	14	
Aug 6. Ballina, . .	8	—	0	12	0	0	
Sept. 26. Galway, . .	—	1	0	1	1	0	
July 2. Ballysadare, . .	10	—	2	1	0	0	
" " Ballina, . .	8	—	0	16	0	0	
Total, ...	37	1	3	14	2	14	

RETURN of FISH conveyed to Liverpool by the "Emerald Isle" and "Newry," of the Dundalk and Newry Steam Packet Company, during the Year ending 31st December, 1872.

From what Stations	White or Coarse Fish.		Weight.				Average Gross Weight of Boxes and Barrels
	Boxes.	Barrels.	Tons.	cwt.	qrs.	lbs.	
Warrenpoint and Newry, . .	2,190	2,408	432	16	0	0	2 cwt. each for boxes and barrels. About one-eighth was coarse fish, the remainder herrings

RETURN of FISH conveyed to England by the Steamers of the Dundalk and Newry Steam Packet Company, during the Year ending 31st December, 1872.

Dates, and from what Station	White or Coarse Fish.		Weight.				Average Gross Weight of Boxes and Barrels.
	Boxes.	Barrels.	Tons.	cwt.	qrs.	lbs.	
Dundalk, May to December 31st,	760	200	77	0	0	0	Boxes 1¼ cwt. Barrels 2 "

Dates, and from what Station.	Salmon and Trout.		Weight.				Average Gross Weight of Boxes and Baskets
	Boxes.	Baskets.	Tons.	cwt.	qrs.	lbs.	
Dundalk, May to December 31st,	1,087	—	108	14	0	0	Boxes 2 cwt.

RETURN of FISH conveyed to Liverpool by the Steamers of the Belfast Steam Ship Company (Limited), during the Year ending 31st December, 1872.

From what station.	Salmon and Trout.		Weight.				Average Gross Weight of Boxes and Baskets.
	Boxes.	Baskets.	Tons.	cwt.	qrs.	lbs.	
Londonderry, ...	1,075	—	107	6	0	0	Each box contains 2 cwt.

RETURN of FISH conveyed by the Steamers of the Waterford and Milford Steamship Company, during the Year ending 31st December, 1872.

From what Stations.	Salmon and Trout.		Weight.				White or Coarse Fish.		Weight.			
	Boxes.	Baskets.	Tons.	cwts.	qrs.	lbs.	Boxes.	Baskets.	Tons.	cwts.	qrs.	lbs.
Waterford,	2,060	—	206	0	0	0	927	—	92	14	0	0
Ex Waterford and Limerick Railway,	2,200	—	180	9	0	0	—	—		—		
Total, ...	4,260	—	386	9	0	0	927	—	92	14	0	0

APPENDIX, No. 25—*continued*.

RETURN of FISH conveyed to England by the Steamers of the London and North-Western Railway Company, during the Year ending 31st December, 1872.

From what Station.	Salmon and Trout.		Weight.		White or Coarse Fish.		Weight.	
	Boxes.	Baskets.	Tons	cwt.	Boxes.	Baskets.	Tons	cwt.
DUBLIN.								
January,	1	–	–	2	27	1	12	15
February,	6	–	–	12	320	2	32	2
March,	11	–	1	2	583	2	58	8
April,	33	–	3	6	670	–	67	–
May,	41	–	4	2	1,307	–	130	14
June,	115	–	11	10	3,331	–	333	2
July,	199	–	19	18	3,218	–	323	12
August,	9	–	–	18	4,966	–	496	14
September,	–	–	–	–	1,152	7	105	16
October,	–	–	–	–	1,471	13	147	15
November,	–	–	–	–	510	5	51	5
December,	–	–	–	–	444	2	44	2
Total,	415	–	41	10	18,309	32	1,832	1

RETURN of FISH conveyed by the Steamers of the Waterford Steam Ship Company, during the Year ending 31st December, 1872.

From what Station.	Salmon and Trout.		Weight				White or Coarse Fish.		Weight.			
	Boxes.	Baskets.	Tons.	cwt.	qrs.	lbs.	Boxes.	Baskets.	Tons.	cwt.	qrs.	lbs.
Waterford,	20	—	2	10	0	0	—	3,518	430	15	0	0
"	252	—	31	10	0	0	—	88	11	0	0	0
Total,	272	—	34	0	0	0	—	3,606	450	15	0	0

RETURN of FISH conveyed from the undermentioned Stations of the Dublin and Belfast Junction Railway Company, during the Year ending 31st December, 1872.

From what Stations.	Salmon and Trout.		Weight				White or Coarse Fish.		Weight.			
	Boxes.	Baskets.	Tons.	cwt.	qrs.	lbs.	Boxes.	Baskets.	Tons.	cwt.	qrs.	lbs.
Dunleer,	4	—		—			—	—		—		
"	19	1		—			—	—		—		
"	17	—		—			—	—		—		
"	23	3		—			—	—		—		
"	4	—		—			—	—		—		
Total,	67	4	2	3	2	9	—	—		—		
Castlebellingham,	29	14		—			—	—		—		
"	21	12		—			—	—		—		
"	34	7		—			—	—		—		
"	40	13		—			—	—		—		
"	38	17		—			—	—		—		
"	27	—		—			—	—		—		
Total,	189	63	5	14	3	0	—	—		—		
Dundalk,	1	2		—			—	—		—		
"	7	2		—			—	—		—		
"	10	4		—			—	—		—		
"	13	2		—			—	—		—		
"	7	2		—			—	—		—		
"	2	3		—			—	—		—		
"	—	1		—			—	—		—		
Total,	40	16	2	6	3	14	—	—		—		
								Herrings.				
Drogheda,	—	—		—			3	47	3	14	2	0
Gross Total,	296	83	10	5	0	23	3	47	3	14	2	0

APPENDIX, No. 25.

APPENDIX, No. 25—*continued.*

RETURN of FISH conveyed to Dublin by the Dublin and Drogheda Railway Company, during the Year ending 31st December, 1872.

From what Stations.	Salmon and Trout.		Weight.				White or Coarse Fish.		Weight.			
	Boxes	Baskets	Tons	cwt	qrs	lbs	Boxes	Baskets	Tons	cwt	qrs	lbs
Total from all Stations, per Goods Train.	147	—	6	16	0	0	877	656	153	6	0	0
Total from all Stations, per Parcel Train.	28	393	16	7	1	0	—	12	0	13	1	6
Total, . . .	175	393	23	3	1	0	877	668	153	19	1	0

ABSTRACT of the Quantity of FRESH-WATER EELS delivered at and sold in the following places, consigned from the Irish Fisheries, from the 1st of January to the 31st of December, 1872, as far as can be ascertained:—

	No. of Boxes		No. of Boxes.
London, ...	3,703	Wolverhampton, ...	855
Liverpool, ...	2,076	Nottingham, ...	376
Leeds, ...	800	Northampton, ...	225
Manchester, ...	3,530		
Birmingham, ...	3,000	Total, ...	16,285
Bradford, ...	750		

DELIVERIES of SALMON at Billingsgate Market during 1872.

	No. of Boxes		No. of Boxes.
Scotch, ...	23,028	Norway, ...	352
Irish, ...	3,208	Sweden, ...	964
English and Welsh, ...	2,700		
Dutch, ...	852	Total, ...	33,300
		Total in 1871, ...	35,275
		Decrease, ...	1,975

ABSTRACT of the Quantity of SALMON, HERRINGS, MACKEREL, and COD, delivered at and sold in the following places, consigned from the Irish Fisheries, from the 1st of January to the 31st of December, 1872, as far as can be ascertained.

Places.	Salmon. No. of Boxes.	Herrings. No. of Boxes and Barrels.	Mackerel. No. of Boxes.	Cod. No. of Boxes.
Nottingham, ...	800	3,000	2,760	2,463
Bradford, ...	1,031	6,655	3,891	760
Manchester, ...	4,900	14,900	8,053	3,500
Sheffield, ...	926	7,703	6,000	836
Wolverhampton, ...	402½	3,338	3,300	972
Leeds, ...	1,554	5,873	3,079	2,111
Liverpool, ...	9,782	15,500	9,873	6,870
London, ...	5,298	27,264	26,500	6,755
Birmingham, ...	2,007	11,650	4,050	3,645
Total sold in 1872, . . .	27,381½	95,983	68,108	29,922
Total sold in 1871, . . .	16,340	86,373	44,632	10,172
Increase in 1872 over 1871, .	11,041½	9,610	23,476	19,750

QUANTITY of OYSTERS shipped by the City of Cork Steam Packet Company's Vessels, during the Year 1872.

46 Hogsheads, 5 Casks, and 129 Bags of Oysters. 90 Bags of Mussels.

QUANTITY of SALMON shipped by the City of Cork Steam Packet Company, during the Year 1872.

Liverpool, . . . 1,050 boxes. | Bristol, . . . 230 boxes. | Milford, . . . 40 boxes.

RETURN of FISH conveyed over the Waterford and Limerick Railway, during the Year ending 31st December, 1872.

From what Stations.	Salmon and Trout.		Weight.				White or Coarse Fish.		Weight.			
	Boxes.	Baskets.	Tons	cwt.	qrs.	lbs.	Boxes.	Baskets.	Tons.	cwt.	qrs.	lbs.
Limerick, ...	312	59	28	4	1	14						
Cahir, ...	64	5	7	6	0	16						
Clonmel, ...	38	138	5	7	2	26						
Carrick, ...	—	146	4	14	0	14						
Total, ...	414	348	45	12	2	14	11	294	37	3	2	0

APPENDIX, No. 25—*continued.*

RETURN of FISH conveyed to Bandon, in transit for Cork, by the West Cork Railway Company, during the year ending 31st December, 1872.

From what Stations	Salmon and Trout.		Weight				White or Coarse Fish		Weight.			
	Boxes	Baskets.	Tons.	cwt.	qrs.	lbs.	Boxes.	Baskets	Tons.	cwt.	qrs.	lbs.
Dunmanway, ...	72	25	6	1	2	18	83	80	8	18	2	0
Enniskean, ...	7	-	0	9	2	13	-	-	—			
Total, ...	79	25	6	11	1	3	83	80	8	18	2	0

RETURN of FISH conveyed to Cork by the Cork and Bandon Railway Company, from Kinsale Station, during the year ending 31st December, 1872.

Description of Fish.	Tons.	cwt.	qrs.	lbs.	Description of Fish.	Tons.	cwt.	qrs.	lbs.
Turbot, ...		—			Gurnet, ...		—		
Plaice, ...		—			Scad, ...	0	18	0	0
Soles, ...		—			Pollock, ...		—		
Haddock, ...	0	2	0	0	Mullet, ...		—		
Cod, ...	0	16	0	0	Sprats, ...	0	3	0	0
Whiting, ...		—			Lobsters, ...	4	5	0	7
Hake, ...	256	2	0	7	Crabs, ...	0	3	0	0
Mackerel, ...	726	18	2	0	Oysters, ...	1	15	0	0
Herrings, ...	0	10	0	0	Holybird, ...	0	1	0	0
Pilchards, ...	27	0	0	0	Winkles, ...	26	18	0	0
Ling, ...	0	4	0	0					
Bream, ...	0	15	0	0		1,046	0	2	14

RETURN of FISH conveyed to England during the year ending 31st December, 1872, as shown by the Cork Day Note of Imports and Exports.

Dates.	Salmon			Cod Fish		Trout.	Herrings.	Mackerel.	Dried Fish.		Oysters.		Winkles.	Fish not described		
	Tierces.	Boxes.	Packages.	Casks.	Cases.	Barrels.	Barrels.	Barrels.	Casks.	Cases.	Cases.	Bags.	Bags.	Hhds.	Boxes.	Bags.
January, .	-	-	-	-	-	-	-	-	-	-	-	-	-	-	-	25
February, .	-	15	-	-	-	-	-	-	-	-	-	10	-	-	3	5
March, .	-	68	-	-	-	-	-	-	-	200	-	5	-	3	20	-
April, .	-	19	-	-	-	-	-	17	-	90	2	-	-	-	127	-
May, .	-	-	-	-	-	-	92	23	1	-	-	-	10	-	646	12
June, .	-	34	30	15	-	-	250	16	-	-	-	-	13	-	227	24
July, .	-	148	-	-	-	-	-	-	-	-	-	-	-	-	109	-
August, .	-	26	-	-	-	-	-	-	-	-	-	-	-	-	-	5
September, .	-	6	-	-	-	-	-	-	-	-	-	-	-	-	-	-
October, .	-	-	-	6	-	-	-	-	-	-	-	-	50	-	8	-
November, .	-	-	-	-	-	-	4	-	-	-	-	12	-	-	-	-
December, .	30	-	-	11	350	1	-	-	-	-	-	-	-	-	-	-
Totals, .	30	315	30	32	350	1	346	56	1	290	2	28	72	3	1,236	72

RETURN OF FISH conveyed to Dublin by the Athenry and Ennis Junction Railway Company, during the Year ending 31st December, 1872.

Date, and from what Station.		Salmon and Trout	cwt.	qrs.	lbs.	
February to August, Ennis,	.	42 baskets.	9	1	16	Average weight, 26 lbs.

APPENDIX, No. 26.

KINSALE.

HIGHEST NUMBER of VESSELS or BOATS of different countries which fished off Kinsale in 1872, as furnished by Captain Carter, Inspecting Commander Coast Guard, Kinsale,

Manx.	Irish.	French.	English.	Scotch.
174	65	83	45	1

The quantity of mackerel taken amounted to 6,000 tons, or 60,000 boxes of 6 score each, the average price being 20s. per 120, or 6 score.

APPENDIX, No. 27.—ABSTRACT of

Substance of Queries issued to Boards of Conservators.	Replies received from Boards of Conservators. 1. Dublin.
1. What is the general state of the Salmon Fisheries in this District?	1. Favourable
2. Has the take of salmon throughout the district been more or less productive in 1872 than in 1871, and to what is attributed the increase or diminution?	2. Less productive, owing to unfavourable weather.
3. What was the average price obtained for salmon last year by the captors? (This has no reference to price obtained by the dealers in salmon.) What was the highest price given for salmon last season? What was the lowest price?	3. From 1s. to 1s. 6d. per lb. 4s. per lb. 10d. per lb
4. What proportion of the entire capture in your district is exported, and what proportion purchased for home consumption?	4. Rarely exported.
5. What has been the amount of protection rendered during the present close season of 1872, as compared with preceding season of 1871?	5. About the same.
6. Has the quantity of breeding fish observed in the rivers in your district been greater or less as compared with preceding year, 1871?	6. Greater.
7. About what period do the salmon commence to spawn in the several rivers in your district? What are the greatest spawning months? and when is spawning over? and generally where are the most important spawning grounds situated?	7. Latter end of October. November and December. Spawning is over about Christmas-day. The best spawning-grounds in this district are between Ballymore-Eustace and Kilcullen.
8. At what period of the year, in each river in your district, are the first clean fish taken? When do the grilse begin to run? When are the spent fish well out of the river? and when does the great bulk of the fry go to sea? Has the quantity of fry descending this year been observably greater or less than usual?	8. January. June. January. May. About the same
9. During the descent of the fry to the sea, is angling for trout prohibited by any of the proprietors of fisheries, or is it carried on during these months, and does much destruction of fry take place?	9. Angling, under pretence of perch and pike fishing, is practised throughout the year uninterfered with by the proprietors, and considerable quantities of fry are taken or destroyed, particularly in May.
10. At what period of the year do the fish begin to be discoloured, or to get heavy in spawn; and what is the general opinion as to the proper season for angling in your district?	10. The salmon begin to be discoloured in the River Liffey in October, but in the River Vartry not until November. The general opinion is that as long as angling in salmon rivers can be carried on under pretence of perch and pike fishing, by-laws having reference solely to salmon, effect very little good.
11. Have you reason to suppose that many spent fish have been destroyed hitherto in the month of February, and foul fish in the month of October by anglers?	11. No.
12. Are you aware of any change having taken place in regard to the period of the season when the salmon in your district is in best order, whether earlier or later than heretofore? If so, state particulars.	12. No.
13. Is there any increase in the average size of the spring salmon or the peals? Give average weight of salmon and peals in the season 1872, as far as practicable?	13. No. About 9 lbs.
14. Are there any pollutions or poisonous matter entering the rivers in your district? If so, state the particular cases.	14. Yes, the Gas and Chemical Works on the North and South Quays of the tideway of the River Liffey.
15. Have offences against the Fishery Laws increased or diminished?	15. Fishing for salmon without license with rods in the rivers, and nets on the sea-coast, under pretence of fishing for other fish, is on the increase.
16. What are the mill-weirs or dams, or other obstructions in each river in your district, and where have fish passes been built, when, and by whom?	16. See Appendix. Island-bridge weir, at Newbridge weir; at Lucan weir; at Salmon Leap; and at Temple Mills weir. These fish passes were constructed under the direction of the Messrs Cane & Co., as private individuals, between the years 1861 and 1862.
17. Where would fish passes be practicable and advantageous?	17. Fish-passes would be practicable in almost every weir mentioned, but their advantage is rather doubtful unless there was a sufficient staff of water-bailiffs to prevent their being used as fish-traps. A fish-pass over Poulaphouca would give the River Liffey thirty additional miles of spawning-beds; however as this cascade is 154 feet high, and is at the head of a long incline, it would probably cost £1,000 to construct it.
18. Have gratings been attached to mill-leads, or other artificial channels, in conformity with the 32 Vic., cap. 9; and, if so, specify the particular cases?	18. None.
19. Where has this provision been partially carried out, and whether at the head or tail race?	19. None.
20. What instances and nature of precautions have been adopted at mills other than that prescribed by the late Act, to prevent the destruction of fish?	20. None.
21. Where and by whom have fixed engines been used in 1872?	21. None.
22. Can you give a list of the prosecutions instituted by the Conservators during the year 1872?	22. None.
23. Can you give a list of prosecutions for fishery offences instituted by others, stating by whom?	23. No.
24. Are there any new modes of fishing for salmon adopted in your district? If so, what are they, and where used?	24. None.
25. What is the number of water-bailiffs employed by Conservators?	25. Three.
26. What is the number employed in district by private individuals?	26. One.
27. For what length of time employed?	27. The Conservators employ a water-bailiff for the year, and two for the close season. The private individual referred to in the answer to the 26th Query employs a man for a few months during the autumn to prevent anglers intruding on his portion of the river. The steward and labourers of the Island-bridge fishery prevent it being trespassed on.
28. Are there any upper proprietors who contribute towards protection, and if so, where, and how much?	28. None.
29. What is the rate of wages paid by the Conservators?	29. From £20 to £10 per annum.
30. Are there any suggestions or general observations with which the Conservators may be disposed to favour the Inspectors, with reference to the Salmon Fisheries in your district?	30. —

Statements from Boards of Conservators—*continued.*

Replies received from Boards of Conservators.	
1. Wexford.	2. Waterford.
1. Most unsatisfactory generally; while there is good water in the river in the spring, there is nothing which will take the fly but slack salmon, and by the time the new fish run into the river, the water is too low to catch them with a fly. No fish can get into the upper waters when the river is at its summer level, owing to the long stretch of netting in the narrow (so called) tidal water. If fish get up as far as Enniscorthy, they fall victims to the upper drafts in that town.	1. I consider the general state of the fisheries of this district to be satisfactory, there being a decided increase of fish.
2. In the upper waters it has been worse than ever known before in consequence of the close season not having been suitable to the river for many years past, till altered for the better in 1870, and also in consequence of the great perfection to which the system of netting in the tidal water has been brought, it has not been so good either in the tidal water.	2. The take of salmon throughout the district has been less productive in 1872 than in 1871. The cause has been attributed to the continual wet state of the weather, and the artillery practice at Duncannon fort during the summer months.
3. The price of slack salmon was lower than in former years, owing to the great difficulty of sale in the Dublin markets, the highest price being 1s. 10d. per lb.; the lowest, 10d. per lb.	3. The average price was about 1s. 6d. per lb. About 1s. About 1s.
4. All purchased for home consumption.	4. It would be impossible to say with accuracy what proportion is exported; probably 95 per cent. of the entire capture in the district, and 5 per cent. for home consumption.
5. Nearly all the protection has been concentrated on the lower waters, every old bailiff, without exception, having been dismissed, and a new set put on. The water has been so constantly high that poaching in the upper waters has been impossible.	5. The amount of protection by water-bailiffs rendered up to this has been less than last year in consequence of the constant floods in the spawning rivers.
6. The river has been too high all along for observation.	6. Greater than that of last year.
7. In November, December and January. Spawning over at the end of February or beginning of March. Spawning grounds are well distributed on the Slaney and its tributaries.	7. In the months of October, November, December, and January, are the greatest spawning months. The spawning is over about the middle of February. The most important spawning rivers are the Clodiagh, the Glasha, the Anner, the Nire, the Tar, the Aherlow, the Arglo, the Tay, the Mahon, the Colligan, and other tributaries of the Suir, Nore, and Barrow.
8. In the Slaney, though a few may be taken before, fresh fish are not general till April 1st. In August. Not till April 15th.	8. About the middle of February. In April. In April. In April and May, according to the state of the weather. The quantity of fry has been greater than usual, and appears to be increasing every year.
9. No, it is carried on; little detriment takes place, as there are but few trout anglers on the rivers.	9. Angling for trout is not prohibited, and very great destruction of salmon fry takes place thereby.
10. Towards the end of October. The general opinion is divided, the professional fishermen wishing to fish as early as possible when the largest number of spent fish can be taken. Some say, however, that the proper close season for angling is from October 15th to March 15th.	10. Salmon begin to get discoloured in the month of August, and many in spawn in October and November. It is the general opinion that angling should cease on the 15th September every year.
11. When February was in the open season many thousands of spent salmon were destroyed. Since February has been closed these are destroyed instead in March. When October was open some few full fish were caught.	11. A great number of fish (spent) are destroyed in the month of February. There are not many full fish destroyed in the month of October.
12. No change desirable.	12. I am not aware of any change having taken place.
13. No increase. Say roughly 11 lbs. for salmon, 4 lbs. for peal.	13. There has been a great increase in the size of spring fish for the last few years. Average weight of salmon about 10 lbs. Average weight of peals about 4 lbs.
14. No.	14. None.
15. They have diminished, owing to the greater efficiency of, and number of prosecutions conducted by, the lately appointed Inspector. The destruction of foul salmon continues as before.	15. Offences against the Fishery Laws have diminished.
16. At the head of the mill race at St. John's, where Mr. Davis promised to put up a fish ladder, he has not done so. Nor has he complied with the instructions as to the erection of gratings at the tail race of his mill at Fairfield.	16. Two fish passes have been built on the Suir at Cahir. A mill dam at Galbally obstructs the spawning fish passing up.
17. At Fitzgerald's mill at Ballymurphy, Tullow, county Carlow.	17. In Clonmel particularly.
18. The 32 Vic., cap. 9 has not in any case been carried out by the erection of gratings at tail race, but in most cases the head gratings have been erected.	18. Not aware of any.
19. In all cases partially carried out at the head races.	19. I cannot say.
20. None.	20. None that I know of.
21. None.	21. —
22. —	22. —
23. None that I am aware of.	23. None that I am aware of.
24. None.	24. None.
25. Four water-bailiffs and an Inspector.	25. The number of water-bailiffs vary according to the season of the year from about eighty to twenty.
26. One.	26. I don't know of any.
27. The Inspector of water-bailiffs and one bailiff permanently; the others during the close season.	27. —
28. None.	28. None.
29. The Inspector of water-bailiffs received £1 per week, the bailiffs 10s. per week each.	29. From £3 to 30s. a month.
30. The Conservators have lately passed some resolutions on these subjects, which will be brought before their notice.	30. No.

Appendix, No. 27.—Abstract of

Substance of Queries issued to Boards of Conservators.	Replies received from Boards of Conservators.
	4. Lismore.
1. What is the general state of the Salmon Fisheries in this district?	1. Good in tidal portion, exceedingly bad in upper waters.
2. Has the take of salmon throughout the district been more or less productive in 1872 than in 1871, and to what is attributed the increase or diminution?	2. More productive in tidal and lower waters, far less in upper; the early period at which the fishery opens in tidal portion of the district allowing very few spring fish to ascend the rivers. The excessive use of drift nets, and destructive mode in which they are used in the tideway.
3. What was the average price obtained for salmon last year by the captors? (This has no reference to price obtained by the dealers in salmon.) What was the highest price given for salmon last season? What was the lowest price?	3. 1s. 6d. 2s. 6d. 6d. for peale.
4. What proportion of the entire capture in your district is exported, and what proportion purchased for home consumption?	4. Nearly all from the lower waters, scarcely any from the upper or fresh-water portion above Lismore.
5. What has been the amount of protection rendered during the present close season of 1872, as compared with preceding season of 1871?	5. Ten men less than in 1871. Thirty-six extra bailiffs employed this close season.
6. Has the quantity of breeding fish observed in the rivers in your district been greater or less as compared with preceding year, 1871?	6. More breeding fish this year.
7. About what period do the salmon commence to spawn in the several rivers in your district? What are the greatest spawning months? and when is spawning over? and generally where are the most important spawning grounds situated?	7. Commences in October. November and December. About January 15th. Blackwater and its tributaries, Bride, Funshion, and Araglin.
8. At what period of the year, in each river in your district, are the first clean fish taken? When do the grilse begin to run? When are the spent fish well out of the river? and when does the great bulk of the fry go to sea? Has the quantity of fry descending this year been observably greater or less than usual?	8. In February. About 10th of June. End of February in upper waters, long in tideway some time longer. In April. No observable difference.
9. During the descent of the fry to the sea, is angling for trout prohibited by any of the proprietors of fisheries, or is it carried on during these months, and does much destruction of fry take place?	9. Trout fishing not prohibited. Not much destruction.
10. At what period of the year do the fish begin to be discoloured, or to get heavy in spawn; and what is the general opinion as to the proper season for angling in your district?	10. In October. As at present.
11. Have you reason to suppose that many spent fish have been destroyed hitherto in the month of February, and full fish in the month of October by anglers?	11. No fishing in October. Very few this season.
12. Are you aware of any change having taken place in regard to the period of the season when the salmon in your district is in best order, whether earlier or later than heretofore? If so, state particulars.	12. None.
13. Is there any increase in the average size of the spring salmon or the peale? Give average weight of salmon and peale in the season 1872, as far as practicable.	13. Salmon has increased in size in both lower and upper waters. Average weight from 12 to 12½ lbs. Peale same as usual in lower waters; average in lower about 5 lbs. Peale smaller in upper waters, average 3 lbs.
14. Are there any pollutions or poisonous matter entering the rivers in your district? If so, state the particular cases.	14. Not that I am aware of.
15. Have offences against the Fishery Laws increased or diminished?	15. Largely increased in upper waters; diminished in lower.
16. What are the mill-weirs or dams, or other obstructions in each river in your district; and where have fish passes been built, when, and by whom?	16. Mill-weirs—Fermoy, Clondulane, and Gurteen, on the Blackwater, Castletownroche, Doneraile, and Doneraile, on the Awbeg, Conna and Alern, on the Bride; Kanturk, on the Dallow. Fish passes have been built at Clondulane and Fermoy by the Board of Conservators, the former pass is now quite useless.
17. Where would fish passes be practicable and advantageous?	17. At Clondulane, Castletownroche, Alern, Gurteen, and Kanturk mill-weirs.
18. Have gratings been attached to mill-leats, or other artificial channels, in conformity with the 32 Vic., cap. 9; and, if so, specify the particular cases?	18. No gratings to the head races of any of the mills. Gratings have been erected to all the channels for irrigation.
19. Where has this provision been partially carried out, and whether at the head or tail race?	19. At the tail races—Clondulane, Fermoy, Quartertown, Gurteen, Kanturk, and Alern mills.
20. What inducements or measures of prevention have been adopted at mills, other than that prescribed by the late Act, to prevent the destruction of fish?	20. None.
21. Where and by whom have fixed engines been used in 1872?	21. —
22. Can you give a list of the prosecutions instituted by the Conservators during the year 1872?	22. —
23. Can you give a list of prosecutions for fishery offences instituted by others, stating by whom?	23. —
24. Are there any new modes of fishing for salmon adopted in your district? If so what are they, and where used?	24. No new legitimate modes in the small tributaries. Poachers are beginning to use nets to capture salmon on the spawning beds by night.
25. What is the number of water-bailiffs employed by Conservators?	25. Fifty. Eleven all the year, three during open season (in tideway), and thirty-six extra men during spawning season.
26. What is the number employed in district by private individuals?	26. Four. Two by N. T. Foley, Esq., one by R. Longfield, and one by Thomas Franks, Esq.
27. For what length of time employed?	27. Eleven all the year, three in tideway from February 14th to September 8th, and thirty-six for periods from two to four months.
28. Are there any upper proprietors who contribute towards protection, and if so, where, and how much?	28. No subscriptions.
29. What is the rate of wages paid by the Conservators?	29. One head bailiff £40 per annum. Three men 14s. per week each, the remainder 12s. per week.
30. Are there any suggestions or general observations with which the Conservators may be disposed to favour the Inspectors, with reference to the Salmon Fisheries in your district?	30. The Conservators consider the early opening of the tidal fishery most injurious to the fresh-water fishery. Since the change of close season the latter are almost worthless. The excessive fishing with draft nets in the bay and harbour of Youghal they look on as most detrimental to the lower and upper fisheries, from the number of nets used there. They think the fish are prevented entering the river, and are turned out to sea to seek some other river, and are consequently lost to the district. The law as to gaffs, spears, stroke-hauls, &c., is most defective. A penalty should be imposed upon any person having any of the above instruments on or near the banks of any river or lake at any time of the year, except when the gaff is carried by a duly licensed fisherman. A by-law, if possible to this effect would greatly facilitate the protection of the breeding fish.

STATEMENTS from Boards of Conservators—*continued.*

Replies received from Boards of Conservators.		
6. Cork.	**6¹. Skibbereen.**	**6². Bantry.**
1. A great many more fish than last year. A very good season for the net men. Very few fish taken by rods. For which reason there is no accounting 2. Much more productive in 1872 than 1871, on account of the increased preservation.	1. The quantity of fish captured by nets is below the average. The quantity of breeding fish is equal to or above the average 2. The take by nets has been less productive in the tideway, on account of the quantity of fresh water which carried the fish up the river	1. Not as good as last year in the tideway and upper waters 2. Much less productive in 1872, caused by the wet season
3. About 2s per lb. About 3s. per lb. About 1s. per lb	3. 8½d and 6d. per lb. 4d. per lb. 6d. per lb. in October	3. 5½d and 6d per lb. 4d per lb 4½d. per lb.
4. Nearly all exported.	4. A greater quantity of salmon is sent for sale out of Skibbereen than what is consumed in the neighbourhood, but the relative proportions cannot be ascertained	4. Nearly all exported.
5. Several more bailiffs were put on in 1872, both by the Board of Conservators and the Anglers' Club	5. The water-bailiffs in 1871 were dismissed on the 18th of November, this year on the 1st of November	5. Nearly double, owing to the increase of funds to pay water-bailiffs
6. Much greater.	6. The quantity of breeding fish in the Ilen is supposed to be larger this year than last year, on account of the continued floods.	6. About the same.
7. From September; and spawning goes on until the end of December. The Sullane, Laney, Foherish, Upper Lee, and Dripsey	7. In the Ilen the spawning commences about the middle of November for the early run fish. The chief spawning month is December, and the spawning ceases about the middle of January.	7. About the 1st November. November and December are the greatest.
8. Some from the 1st of February, if there is water high enough to take them up. March. March. April. Much greater.	8. A clean fish is seldom taken in May, a few in June, but not many until the first floods in July. The grilse run at the same periods. The bulk of spent fish are out of the river at the latter end of March; a few remain until the middle of April. The fry run down from the middle of February to middle of April. The quantity of fry in 1872 has been the same as in 1871	8. In May, but the great run in July. By the 1st of March. April. Much greater.
9. Trout fishing not prohibited. Much destruction is done.	9. Fishing for brown trout is not prevented during the descent of the fry; at the same time the destruction of the fry is prevented by the Conservators, and the destruction of them is trifling	9. Angling is not prohibited in this district, nor carried on during the descent of the fry to the sea
10. End of September. From about the 12th February to end of October.	10. The fish begin to be discoloured about the latter end of October, and also heavy in spawn. The proper season for angling is considered to be from the 1st of April to 1st November	10. In October. Angling may be carried on from the 1st of March to the 1st of November
11. A good many spent fish have been killed in February, but not so many of late. Not many full fish taken in October. 12. Not aware of any change. Spring fish have been running up for the last three weeks	11. It is not the practice on the Ilen to angle for rawels in spring. Few full fish are killed by rods in October. 12. Not the least	11. Spent fish have been destroyed in the month of February last year, and some full fish in October. 12. About the same.
13. Fish running much larger than formerly. Average of spring fish from 12 lbs. to 18 lbs., grilse from 3 lbs. to 4 lbs. 14. None.	13. There are no spring fish in the Ilen. The average weight of salmon is 6¼ lbs. 14. There are no pollutions entering the Ilen.	13. The same 14. None.
15. Diminished. 16. Waterworks weir, Carrigrohane weir, Ballincollig weir. There is a pass, but a bad one, on Carrigrohane, a very good one at Ballincollig. Do not know by whom they were built 17. Waterworks weir and Carrigrohane weir. 18. In no case but at the Waterworks weir	15. Considerably increased 16. There is one mill weir at Lurriga. A fish-pass has been made over it 17. There is no place where they are required. 18. Two have been erected—one at the Lurriga tail-race, another on a mill drain flowing into the river	15. Diminished. 16. None. 17. At Donemark 18. At Carrigboy.
19. Waterworks weir, at the head race.	19. See last question.	19. At Carrigboy
20. There is only one mill in the district where fry are destroyed—namely, Mr Coulihan's mill, at Carrigaline 21. See Appendix. 22. —	20. None. 21. None. 22. No.	20. — 21. — 22. None
23. There were none.	23. None.	23. No.
24. None	24. None.	24. None.
25. From eighteen to twenty bailiffs since the fish began to spawn, most of which are now put off, as spawning is all but over. 26. Anglers' Club had five or six bailiffs 27. From about 15th of October to end of December, much depends on the weather	25. Four, but not continually. 26. None. 27. About four months	25. None 26. Two, by Earl of Bantry. 27. From June to February.
28. Contributes to the Anglers' Club, can't say how much.	28. None, except anglers.	28. None.
29. 16s and 18s per week.	29. From 8s. to 10s. a week.	29. 8s. 6d. and 4s. per week
30. It is feared that the district will suffer much on account of the month of February being taken off. Poachers will go to fish in other rivers, and will take out licences in other districts. The preserving of February puts a great expense on this district, which month will cost more to preserve than three months. Spring fish going up the river, and high prices given for them. At all times there was much trouble and expense in keeping the nets off the tideway from the 12th or 15th of January, when some spring fish are running; much more will it be now that they are told they cannot fish before the 1st of March. I am of opinion myself that the funds of this district, which are far too small to preserve as I would wish, will be so much smaller the coming season that next to nothing can be done for the preservation of the winter of 1873, and January and February, 1874.	30. —	30. —

APPENDIX, No. 27.—ABSTRACT OF

Substance of Queries issued to Boards of Conservators.	Replies received from Boards of Conservators. 6°. Kenmare.
1. What is the general state of the Salmon Fisheries in this district?	1. On the whole I should consider satisfactory; but I am of opinion that the season as now fixed is injurious. The quantity of full fish destroyed towards the latter end of October is very great, and from the 1st of February till the 1st of April the unclean fish are destroyed to a great extent
2. Has the take of salmon throughout the district been more or less productive in 1872 than in 1871, and to what is attributed the increase or diminution?	2. Less productive—and I attribute it to the very wet season we have had. The continued floods caused the salmon to ascend without showing in the estuaries, and the net fishing in consequence did not pay. The rod fishing for the same cause was not good, as the fish had too much food from the continual floods and would not rise to the fly
3. What was the average price obtained for salmon last year by the captors? (This has no reference to price obtained by the dealers in salmon.) What was the highest price given for salmon last season? What was the lowest price?	3. 6½d. per lb. 8½d. per lb. 4½d. per lb.
4. What proportion of the entire capture in your district is exported, and what proportion purchased for home consumption?	4. I should say about four-fifths, and the remaining fifth for home consumption.
5. What has been the amount of protection rendered during the present close season of 1872, as compared with preceding season of 1871?	5. About the same.
6. Has the quantity of breeding fish observed in the rivers in your district been greater or less as compared with preceding year, 1871?	6. Greater
7. About what period do the salmon commence to spawn in the several rivers in your district? What are the greatest spawning months? and when is spawning over? and generally where are the most important spawning grounds situated?	7. From 20th to end of November. The whole of December to January 10th. After the 10th of January all spawning is over, as far as I can observe or get any information. The most important spawning grounds are the tributaries flowing into the rivers, and they are situated about midway.
8. At what period of the year, in each river in your district, are the first clean fish taken? When do the grilse begin to run? When are the spent fish well out of the river? and when does the great bulk of the fry go to sea? Has the quantity of fry descending this year been observably greater or less than usual?	8. May. June. About the 15th of April. From the middle of April till 1st May. Not greater, about the same as preceding year
9. During the descent of the fry to the sea, is angling for trout prohibited by any of the proprietors of fisheries, or is it carried on during these months, and does much destruction of fry take place?	9. I am sorry to say it is not; it is carried on during the whole time, and great destruction follows in consequence.
10. At what period of the year do the fish begin to be discoloured, or to get heavy in spawn, and what is the general opinion as to the proper season for angling in your district?	10. The beginning of October. As I said before the season should not open before the 1st of April, and close at latest 10th of October.
11. Have you reason to suppose that many spent fish have been destroyed hitherto in the month of February, and full fish in the month of October by anglers?	11. Yes, I am sure of great destruction taking place during these periods.
12. Are you aware of any change having taken place in regard to the period of the season when the salmon in your district is in best order, whether earlier or later than heretofore? If so, state particulars.	12. No change that I can ascertain.
13. Is there any increase in the average size of the spring salmon or the grilse? Give average weight of salmon and peals in the season 1872, as far as practicable?	13. No. Average weight of salmon from 7 to 9 lbs., and peals about 3 lbs.
14. Are there any pollutions or poisonous matter entering the rivers in your district? If so state the particular cases	14. No.
15. Have offences against the Fishery Laws increased or diminished?	15. I should say they have diminished, and I attribute it to the wet season. The most ruinous offence is that of poisoning, and the continuous floods I may say were the greatest protection.
16. What are the mill-weirs or dams, or other obstructions in each river in your district, and where have fish passes been built, when, and by whom?	16. —
17. Where would fish passes be practicable and advantageous?	17. —
18. Have gratings been attached to mill-heads, or other artificial channels in conformity with the 32 Vic., cap 9, and, if so, specify the particular cases?	18. —
19. Where has this provision been partially carried out, and whether at the head or tail race?	19. —
20. What instances and nature of precautions have been adopted as sufficient other than that prescribed by the late Act, to prevent the destruction of fish?	20. —
21. Where and by whom have fixed engines been used in 1872?	21. Eugene O'Sullivan, Esq., Westcove, bag-net.
22. Can you give a list of the prosecutions instituted by the Conservators during the year 1872?	22. —
23. Can you give a list of prosecutions for fishery offences instituted by others, stating by whom?	23. —
24. Are there any new modes of fishing for salmon adopted in your district? If so, what are they, and where used?	24. —
25. What is the number of water-bailiffs employed by Conservators?	25. Fifteen
26. What is the number employed in district by private individuals?	26. Fifteen.
27. For what length of time employed?	27. Throughout the year.
28. Are there any upper proprietors who contribute towards protection, and if so, where, and how much?	28. None.
29. What is the rate of wages paid by the Conservators?	29. From 2s. to 4s. per day.
30. Are there any suggestions or general observations with which the Conservators may be disposed to favour the Inspectors, with reference to the Salmon Fisheries in your district?	30. Not that I am aware of, unless limiting the season for rod fishing, as I have before stated, I am sure it would increase the weight of spring salmon considerably.

STATEMENTS from Boards of Conservators—*continued.*

Replies received from Boards of Conservators.		
7. KILLARNEY.	8. LIMERICK.	9. GALWAY.
1 Good	1. Satisfactory as regards the quantity of fish that enters the different rivers.	1. Upon the whole satisfactory. The capture at Galway has been less productive, while Ballinahinch has been a great success. Ballinahinch fishery had not been netted for some years, and only partially netted for the last three years.
2. More	2 I do not think the take was as good in 1872 as in 1871, certainly it was not in the fresh water. I attribute the diminution to the very severe weather that prevailed during the spring and summer months. For the past few years the salmon have not taken either fly or bait freely, in this district.	2. Less productive on the whole, the inclement season contributing largely to this result
3. About 2s. per lb in spring, and 7d. in summer	3 About 1s 7d. per lb. About 1s. 6d. About 8d	3. About 1s. per lb. 2s. 6d. per lb. 10d. per lb.
4 Nearly all exported.	4 Almost the entire is exported; very little is retained for home consumption, particularly in the earlier portion of the season	4 About nine-tenths exported and one tenth for home consumption
5 About the same.	5. The sum of £1,6[illegible] was expended in wages to water bailiffs in 1872 and £1,370 12s 6d. in 1871	5. About the same.
6 Far greater	6 It would be difficult to answer this question in consequence of the unusually swollen state of all the rivers during the present close season.	6. In some places less, and in others more. On the whole about an average. The great floods have rendered it difficult to speak with certainty on the subject.
7 Salmon generally commence to spawn early in November and end generally in the month of January. With very few exceptions the spawning ground in the district is generally good, but the [illegible] is considered the best.	7 About the middle of December. The latter part of December and the entire of January constitute the spawning season. Spawning may be said to be over about the 1st of February. The most important spawning grounds are in the Mulcaire River and its several branches, also in the Nenagh River, and at Castleconnell and Killaloe in the River Shannon	7. In November spawning commences. It is at its highest point in December, and ends in January, generally speaking about the middle of the month
8. In Waterville 1st January. Laune 15th January. Grilse generally begin to run very early in May. About the latter end of August. May, and sometimes in April. Much greater.	8 Clean fish might be taken as early as the month of November. The grilse begin to run about the last week in May. The spent fish in ordinary seasons are out of the river about the end of April. The great bulk of the fry go to sea in the same month and early in May. No fry have as yet appeared	8. In February at Galway and Ballinahinch, the two principal fisheries. In May. About the latter end of April. In May. Greater
9 No prohibition; nor is there much destruction of fry	9 Angling for trout is not prohibited during any portion of the open season. I should say that the destruction of fry is inconsiderable, as the places where they could be taken in any quantity are watched by water-bailiffs	9. It is, strictly, at Galway. I don't believe any great destruction of fry takes place.
10 The fish generally become discoloured in the month of October, at the end of which month angling should cease.	10 About the middle of August. The present season is considered the proper one for angling in this district.	10 In August. The proper period for angling in this district is that which is now sanctioned by the Inspectors' orders.
11 No. Anglers sometimes take a good many foul fish.	11. I have no reason to suppose that many spent fish have been destroyed between the month of February, but I know that great quantities of foul fish were destroyed in October, by anglers, when that was an open month.	11. Not now, but great destruction took place formerly, before the grating clause was passed by Parliament.
12 I am not aware. Salmon in prime order here as early as December.	12 I am not; but for the past few years a large run of grilse has been observed in August and September.	12 Not aware of any such change
13 An evident increase. I would say spring salmon about 12 lbs; peals, say about 7 lbs.	13 The average size both of the spring salmon and peals appears to be increasing every year. I think the average weight of the spring salmon was about 12 lbs., and of the peals about 7 lbs.	13 The average weight of spring salmon was better this year. I have no means of giving the average weight exactly, but between spring salmon and peals, the nearest approach would be about 6½ lbs.
14 No	14. No	14. Not any
15 Diminished.	15 They have diminished	15 Diminished to such an extent that we have only had two or three cases in the whole district. The high floods have been our best protectors.
16 The Flesk, near Killarney; the [illegible], the [illegible]. No fish passes have been built.	16. I could not enumerate all the mill-weirs or dams or other obstructions in so large a district as this. Very few fish passes have been built, but in very few instances are fish prevented from ascending in floods, and in most of the small rivers it is better they should not get high up early in the season, as these rivers run very low in summer	16 Galway, Abbey, Knockmoy, Milltown, Ballinrobe, Hollymount, all built by the Board of Works. There is one built at Cong by the late Thomas Ashworth, Esq., and one built at Ballygluinin by Walter Blake, Esq.
17 The Flesk	17. I cannot satisfactorily answer this query as regards any weirs, except an old one at Abington, in the Mulcaire River, which is a great obstruction to fish. A pass in this weir (not to be opened before the month of October in each year) would be of great service	17 None required.
18 One on the [illegible], one on the [illegible], and one on the Flesk.	18 So many mill-owners claim exemption on the plea of injury to the water power of their mills, that gratings have been attached to no mill heads in this district except those at Ennis mills and Ballyartella mill on the Nenagh River	18. Erected where absolutely necessary, at Galway especially.
19 [illegible], head, [illegible], dam above the wheel; Flesk, head.	19. Ennis and Ballyartella mills; at the tail races.	19. At Galway, and some tributaries of Lough Corrib
20 None	20. None.	20 —
21. No fixed engines in the district.	21. See Appendix	21 Messrs. Miller and Co., salmon cribs and eel nets, Galway. Eel nets Ballinahinch, Ballygluinin, and Tyrone.
22. —	22 I could not, within the space allowed.	22. —
23. —	23 No. In some instances the Constabulary have prosecuted on their own account, but I cannot give a list of their prosecutions.	23 Not aware of any.
24. None.	24 No	24. None.
25 Eighty-two.	25. Eighty-three men were employed in the open season of 1872, and 120 in the close season.	25 About the same as in 1871.
26 By Conservators and private individuals 32.	26 Two by Mr Malcomson, on his own fishery	26. More than 200.
27. From 8 to 12 months.	27. I cannot answer this query, as the length of time depends so much on the state of the weather, height of water, &c. About thirty-four are employed permanently, the others as required.	27 Some all the year round; others during the close season only.
28. Henry A. Herbert, £16; James Butler, Waterville, £41; Henry W. Dodd and Co., £40; Mr. Mahony, £10; John Godfrey, Esq., £10; Lord Ventry, £16.	28 No	28 None, except what is paid for a draft net at Cong and a draft net and cross lines at Oughterard.
29 From £6 to £12, according to time and work	29 From 6s. to £1 per week.	29. It varies from £2 to £20.
30 None.	30. No.	30 None

APPENDIX, No. 27.—ABSTRACT of

Substance of Queries issued to Boards of Conservators.	Replies received from Boards of Conservators.
	16°. BALLINAKILL.
1. What is the general state of the Salmon Fisheries in this district?	1. Satisfactory.
2. Has the take of salmon throughout the district been more or less productive in 1872 than in 1871, and to what is attributed the increase or diminution?	2. More productive
3. What was the average price obtained for salmon last year by the captors? (This has no reference to price obtained by the dealers in salmon.) What was the highest price given for salmon last season? What was the lowest price?	3. About 9d.
4. What proportion of the entire capture in your district is exported, and what proportion purchased for home consumption?	4. Almost all exported.
5. What has been the amount of protection rendered during the present close season of 1872, as compared with preceding season of 1871?	5. About the same.
6. Has the quantity of breeding fish observed in the rivers in your district been greater or less as compared with preceding year, 1871?	6. Much the same.
7. About what period do the salmon commence to spawn in the several rivers in your district? What are the greatest spawning months? and when is spawning over? and generally where are the most important spawning grounds situated?	7. About 20th November. December. Over about 5th January.
8. At what period of the year, in each river in your district, are the first clean fish taken? When do the grilse begin to run? When are the spent fish well out of the river? and when does the great bulk of the fry go to sea? Has the quantity of fry descending this year been observably greater or less than usual?	8. Latter end of April. June. April. March and April.
9. During the descent of the fry to the sea, is angling for trout prohibited by any of the proprietors of fisheries, or is it carried on during those months, and does much destruction of fry take place?	9. Not prohibited. Very little angling so early.
10. At what period of the year do the fish begin to be discoloured, or to get heavy in spawn, and what is the general opinion as to the proper season for angling in your district?	10. September
11. Have you reason to suppose that many spent fish have been destroyed hitherto in the month of February, and red fish in the month of October by anglers?	11. Very few.
12. Are you aware of any change having taken place in regard to the period of the season when the salmon in your district is in best order, whether earlier or later than heretofore? If so, state particulars.	12. —
13. Is there any increase in the average size of the spring salmon or the peale? Give average weight of salmon and peale in the season 1872, as far as practicable.	13. 12 lbs. to 14 lbs. 4 lbs. to 7 lbs.
14. Are there any pollutions or poisonous matter entering the rivers in your district? If so, state the particular cases.	14. —
15. Have offences against the Fishery Laws increased or diminished?	15. About the same
16. What are the mill-weirs or dams, or other obstructions in each river in your district, and where have fish passes been built, when, and by whom?	16. Louisburgh river and Belclare.
17. Where would fish passes be practicable and advantageous?	17. —
18. Have gratings been attached to mill-heads or other artificial channels, in conformity with the 12 Vic., cap 57 and, if so, specify the particular cases.	18. On the Belclare river by Wm. Livingston, esq.
19. Where has this provision been partially carried out, and whether at the head or tail race?	19. On head and tail races by Wm. Livingston, but not by the parties higher up the Belclare river.
20. What instances and nature of precautions have been adopted at mills, other than that prescribed by the late Act, to prevent the destruction of fish?	20. —
21. Where and by whom have fixed engines been used in 1872?	21. —
22. Can you give a list of the prosecutions instituted by the Conservators during the year 1872?	22. —
23. Can you give a list of prosecutions for fishery offences instituted by others, stating by whom?	23. —
24. Are there any new modes of fishing for salmon adopted in your district? If so, what are they, and where used?	24. —
25. What is the number of water-bailiffs employed by Conservators?	25. Twenty-eight.
26. What is the number employed in district by private individuals?	26. Fourteen.
27. For what length of time employed?	27. Five all the year; the others for close season.
28. Are there any upper proprietors who contribute towards protection, and if so, where, and how much?	28. —
29. What is the rate of wages paid by the Conservators?	29. One £10, £4, £3, £2, and £1 10s
30. Are there any suggestions or general observations with which the Conservators are disposed to favour the Inspectors, with reference to the Salmon Fisheries in your district?	30. —

STATEMENTS from Boards of Conservators—*continued.*

Replies received from Boards of Conservators		
10b. Newport.	11. Ballina.	12. Sligo.
1. Satisfactory.	1. Satisfactory.	1. Satisfactory.
2. Much the same as in 1871.	2. Less productive in 1872 than in 1871, attributed altogether to unfavourable weather.	2. About the same.
3. About 6d. per lb. 2s. 6d. per lb. 6d. per lb.	3. Cannot say. 2s per lb. 6d. per lb.	3. Various prices; from 2s. down to 6d. per lb. Cannot say further than the above.
4. All are exported.	4. Cannot say.	4. Almost all exported.
5. The same number of water bailiffs are employed this year as in 1871.	5. By Conservators in 1871, £397 10s. By Conservators this year, £747 9s. By lessees of Moy Fishery, some £700.	5. Rather better.
6. Greater.	6. The quantity of breeding fish observed this year much less than last, owing, very possibly, to the constant floods preventing their being seen in the early part of the season; but since the floods have fallen, the quantity of fish seen is quite equal to last year.	6. Much the same.
7. In November, December, and January. Spawning is over towards the latter end of January. The spawning grounds have no particular location.	7. Salmon commence to spawn in the end of October. November and December are the greatest months for spawning. Swinford, Crossmolina, Curry, Tubbercurry, Belaghy, Turlow, Rathbran, and Easky are the most important districts.	7. November. The last fortnight in December. In January. In the upper tributaries.
8. The first clean fish are taken in the Lake Carramore on the 14th February. June. Early in March. April and May.	8. May, February. Easky, June. Rathbran and Ballycastle, September. End of April. April. April and May. Much as usual.	8. Sligo River, January; Ballisodare River, April; Drumcliff River, May. In May. In April. In April and May. Much the same.
9. Angling for trout is prohibited by all the proprietors during the months of April and May.	9. Angling for trout is prevented by a recent by-law of the Inspectors during the months of April and May, otherwise much destruction of fry would take place.	9. Not prohibited. Little or no destruction of fry.
10. September 20th. The general opinion is that the present season for angling is proper.	10. Salmon in the Moy begin to become discoloured in August, and in the other rivers in this district in September. The general opinion as to angling is, that the season should commence (as it does now) on 1st February and end on 15th September.	10. In the inland waters begin to get discoloured in May. The present season fixed for angling a fair one.
11. I have not.	11. I believe a great many.	11. Not many—well protected. Angling in October stopped.
12. I am not aware of any such change.	12. No.	12. No observable change.
13. There has. 12 lbs., 19 lbs.	13. Cannot say.	13. There is an increase in weight of spring fish. Peals about the same.
14. None.	14. None.	14. None, unless a little flax water now and again, but well looked after.
15. Increased.	15. Fishing with rods increased during close season. Not so much by candle and gaff. The former much more destructive and more difficult to detect.	15. Diminished.
16. The only mill weir of any importance is on the Newport River, where also there is a fish ladder above the old salmon weir.	16. There are several mill weirs upon the Gladagh River, near Castlebar, in which there are no fish passes or ladders, and are a great obstruction to fish passing up, as also one upon the Ballinrobe River, erected in 1846 or 1847, and one upon the Curry River, at Curry. The only fish pass or ladder in this district is upon the Moy River, near Turlow, put up by the Board of Works.	16. Fish passes have been built in Ballisodare and Sligo by private individuals.
17. —	17. Upon the mill weirs on the River Gladagh.	17. None required.
18. Yes, at the Newport Mills.	18. To nearly all. Those that have not have promised to do so.	18. All where required.
19. —	19. Too numerous to mention.	19. None.
20. No instances of this nature.	20. None in this district.	20. None.
21. See Appendix.	21. See Appendix.	21. See Appendix.
22. See Appendix.	22. All prosecutions are, in this district, I may say, done by the lessees of the Moy Fishery.	22. Cannot.
23. See Appendix.	23. Nearly all done by Mr Little, manager of Moy Fishery, who had some seventy-five cases last winter.	23. Cannot.
24. None.	24. Leaching in the fresh water since passing of the Fishery Act of 1842.	24. None.
25. Eighty.	25. Fifty-five.	25. Twenty-five.
26. —	26. Over 300.	26. About sixty.
27. Sixty are employed during the close season, along with twenty that are employed for the year.	27. November, December, and January for the protection of the salmon; April and May for the fry; some for the entire year.	27. Mostly during the close season, and a few in the open season.
28. —	28. No.	28. None.
29. From £30 to £5, according to the duty to be performed.	29. £3 to £20.	29. From £15 down to £2.
30. —	30. None.	30. None.

APPENDIX, No. 27.—ABSTRACT of

Substance of Queries issued to Boards of Conservators.	Replies received from Boards of Conservators. — 3 Ballyshannon.
1. What is the general state of the Salmon Fisheries in this district?	1. In a fair state.
2. Has the take of salmon throughout the district been more or less productive in 1872 than in 1871, and to what is attributed the increase or diminution?	2. Diminished, the reason cannot well be assigned.
3. What was the average price obtained for salmon last year by the captors? (This has no reference to price obtained by the dealers in salmon.) What was the highest price given for salmon last season? What was the lowest price?	3. From 9s 6d. to 7d per pound 1s 6d. 7d.
4. What proportion of the entire capture in your district is exported, and what proportion purchased for home consumption?	4. Nearly all exported.
5. What has been the amount of protection rendered during the annual close season of 1872, as compared with preceding season of 1871?	5. Slight increase.
6. Has the quantity of breeding fish observed in the rivers in your district been greater or less as compared with preceding year, 1871?	6. Less.
7. About what period do the salmon commence to spawn in the several rivers in your district? What are the greatest spawning months? and when is spawning over? and generally where are the most important spawning grounds situated?	7. November. November and December January. The Erne, Maguire's-bridge, Arney, Swanlinbar, Killeshandra, and Ballyconnell; the Drowes, at Bellaghamahon and Rossinver; the Bundrowes at Conwell; the Donegal, at Corrober and Barnesmore.
8. At what period of the year, in each river in your district, are the first clean fish taken? When do the grilse begin to run? When are the spent fish well out of the river? and when does the great bulk of the fry go to sea? Has the quantity of fry descending this year been observably greater or less than usual?	8. Bundrowes, in February, Erne, in April and May. In May In April. In April
9. During the descent of the fry to the sea, is angling for trout prohibited by any of the proprietors of fisheries, or is it carried on during those months, and does much destruction of fry take place?	9. Prohibited in the Erne only
10. At what period of the year do the fish begin to be discoloured, or to get heavy in spawn, and what is the general opinion as to the proper season for angling in your district?	10. End of August discolouring. In the Bundrowes from 1st February to middle of September: some of the Conservators think it should begin earlier in this river. In the rest of the district from middle of May to middle of September.
11. Have you reason to suppose that many spent fish have been destroyed hitherto in the month of February, and full fish in the month of October by anglers?	11. In former years there was considerable destruction, but, owing to recent prohibitions, it is almost ceased.
12. Are you aware of any change having taken place in regard to the period of the season when the salmon in your district is in best order, whether earlier or later than heretofore? If so, state particulars.	12. Not aware of any.
13. Is there any increase in the average size of the spring salmon or the peale. Give average weight of salmon and peale in the season 1872, as far as practicable?	13. Not aware of any difference. Average about 7 lbs. for the peale, and 10 lbs. for salmon.
14. Are there any pollutions or poisonous matter entering the rivers in your district? If so, state the particular cases.	14. A considerable amount of flax-water.
15. Have offences against the Fishery Laws increased or diminished?	15. Diminished.
16. What are the mill-weirs or dams, or other obstructions in each river in your district, and where have fish passes been built, when, and by whom?	16. See last year's Report. No changes or additional obstructions made since.
17. Where would fish passes be practicable and advantageous?	17. At Ballyconnell and Littlemount, on the Erne. At Bruckless, on the Oily.
18. Have gratings been attached to mill-heads or other artificial channels, in conformity with the Act 32 Vic. cap. 9, and, if so, specify the particular cases?	18. Yes, at Pettigo; but not aware of any other.
19. Where has this provision been partially carried out, and whether at the head or tail race?	19. Head and tail at Pettigo.
20. What instances and nature of precautions have been adopted at mills other than that prescribed by the late Act, to prevent the destruction of fish?	20. None whatever.
21. Where and by whom have fixed engines been used in 1872?	21. See Report of 1871.
22. Can you give a list of the prosecutions instituted by the Conservators during the year 1872?	22. None ordered by the Conservators.
23. Can you give a list of prosecutions for fishery offences instituted by others, stating by whom?	23. See Appendix.
24. Are there any new modes of fishing for salmon adopted in your district? If so what are they, and where used?	24. A drift net in the Bay of Donegal, at St. John's Point.
25. What is the number of water-bailiffs employed by Conservators?	25. Two hundred.
26. What is the number employed in district by private individuals?	26. Eight.
27. For what length of time employed?	27. Yearly.
28. Are there any upper proprietors who contribute towards protection, and if so, where, and how much?	28. None whatever.
29. What is the rate of wages paid by the Conservators?	29. From £1 to £7.
30. Are there any suggestions or general observations with which the Conservators may be disposed to favour the Inspectors, with reference to the Salmon Fisheries in your district?	30. It is necessary to call your Board's attention to the eel fishery established and carried on contrary to the statute, at Messrs. Mahon's mills, Belturbet, which, it is feared, is no solitary case of infraction of the law against fisheries, attached to mills.

STATEMENTS from Boards of Conservators—*continued*.

Replies received from Boards of Conservators.

14. Letterkenny.	15. Londonderry.	16. Coleraine.
1 Satisfactory.	1. Satisfactory.	1. Much the same as in former years; on the whole very satisfactory.
2 The take of salmon has not been more productive in 1872 than in 1871. The supposed cause of diminution being too many salmon up the river in 1871 for breeding, viz., one salmon destroying the other's spawn.	2 The take in 1872 not so good as in 1871. No cause can be assigned.	2 Less productive in 1872 than 1871. It is believed that there is some obstruction at the mouth of the Bann, which prevented them from entering as freely as in former years.
3 9d. At the commencement of season, 2s. 6d. 7d. as the lowest price.	3 8d. per lb. 1s. 6d. per lb. 9d. per lb.	3. About 1s. per lb. 2s. 6d. per lb. 10d. per lb.
4 Ninety out of every hundred exported.	4 Nearly all exported.	4. About two-thirds are exported, and one-third for home consumption.
5 Same as in preceding season of 1871.	5. About the same.	5 Much the same as last year.
6 Breeding fish were not more plentiful in 1872 than in 1871.	6. Considerably less.	6 In the Loughinsholin or upper part of the district the quantity of breeding fish has been less than 1871, but in the lower or Bann division greater than in 1871.
7. End of November and December. December to January the greatest spawning months. Spawning is over about end of January. The important spawning beds are from Ballydoon Bridge to upper sources of River Lennan.	7 Late in November. December and January. Spawning over in February. Rivers Derg, Strule, Glenelly, Finn, [illegible], and Faughan.	7 About the middle of November. November and December. Beginning of January. Ballinderry River, ford below Coagh; Main River ford at Randalstown Bridge, and ford below it; Moyola River, the ford up the park, the Bann River, Taylor's ford, one ford above and one below Portglenone Bridge; one ford above [illegible] Ferry; Kells, Connor, and Cullybackey.
8 Early in February. In May. All gone by end of March. In months of April and May. Not greater.	8 In May. End of May. End of March. In April. Greater.	8 In the month of April. June and July. During February the salmon go to the sea. In the month of May and June. Rather less than 1871.
9 Angling is not prohibited during these months; but there is not much destruction of fry, as angling is carried on by the very few who have permission to fish.	9 No prohibition to angling during the term mentioned, angling is carried on, and considerable destruction of fry takes place.	9. No. Angling is carried on during the descent of the fry; but little injury takes place, as anglers generally avoid destroying them.
10 Those in sea show discolouration slightly in August, those in fresh water earlier. Heavy in spawn end of October and November.	10 Discoloured in end of August, and get heavy in spawn towards the end of September. From 15th March to the 15th October.	10. About the latter end of October. The general opinion of the majority of anglers is, that angling should commence about the 1st March, and end on the 1st November.
11 I do not hear of any destruction taking place in these months.	11. Often large numbers of spent fish are captured in February, and full fish in October, by anglers.	11 Very few spent fish are destroyed in February; but there are more full fish killed in the month of October, by anglers, than in any other month of the year.
12 I believe salmon to be in best order in the early part of the season.	12. Not aware of any change.	12 I am not. Salmon in this district are always best in season in June and July.
13 No increase in size.	13 Spring salmon were larger than usual in 1872. Average weight of salmon 12 lbs., and of grilse 5 lbs.	13 No increase. I think the average weight of the salmon in 1872 would be about 10 lbs. each.
14 Flax-water, towards the close of the season, is the only pollution, which was not at all so destructive as last season, owing to the circulation of circulars, by order of Fishery Inspectors, as to penalties for flax-steeping in small rivers.	14. Flax-water only.	14 Yes. In the flax season some of the poisonous matter is allowed to flow into the streams through the district, but invariably the parties are brought before the magistrates and punished. At Ballyclare, in the county Antrim, there is a paper mill, and the matter flowing from it poisons the Sixmilewater for miles. The owners were summoned by Mr Shell, the late Inspector, and by the police subsequently, but on both occasions the cases were dismissed.
15. Undiminished.	15. Decreased.	15 In the upper division of the district diminished. In the lower division rather increased.
16 Fish passes were built at Ramelton, by Mr Kelly, some years ago. One by Lord Hill at Gweedore, and two on the Gweebarra River by Lord Clon[illegible].	16 The only fish pass in this district is at Sion Mills, on the Mourne River.	16 No change since last season, except two mills in county Derry, one at Innisrush and the other at Glenone, the property of Mr Courtney; however, Mr Blake, one of the Inspectors, visited both, and directed gratings to be put up, but the great floods this season have prevented that gentleman doing so up to the present. It will be put up as soon as the state of the river will allow of it.
17 Have not heard where such would be necessary.	17 At Ballyarton, on the Faughan River.	17 Cannot suggest any at present, except over the Ballymena Spinning Company's mill-dam.
18 At Ramelton and Tully gratings are erected in conformity with orders.	18 Some were erected in conformity with Act, but in many cases, through wear and neglect they have been rendered useless. In one case, that of the Messrs. Ballantine, at Ardmore, on the Faughan River, gratings were ordered by the Inspectors to be erected during the months that the salmon frequent the river, but as yet no steps have been taken to carry out these instructions.	18. None within the last two years, see reply to No. 16, except at Randalstown, [illegible], Kilrea, Kells, Lisnafillan, [illegible], and Drum[illegible].
19 At Ramelton and Tully this provision was carried out at the head race. No necessity for such at tail race, as fish could not ascend by mill wheels.	19. See Report for 1863.	19 At the tail races.
20 None, that I am aware of.	20. None.	20 No precautions, except where gratings are erected.
21 A sweep net, used by Mr. Kelly, at Ramelton.	21. See Appendix.	21 See Appendix.
22 See Appendix.	22. Cannot.	22 Total amount received for the Board of Conservators during the year 1872, £40 12s. [illegible]
23 —	23 The Constabulary have instituted several prosecutions for allowing flax-water to flow into several breeding rivers, and also for other offences.	23 In a few instances the police were the complainants, but very few.
24 No new modes of fishing adopted in the Letterkenny district.	24 None.	24 None that I can hear of.
25 Seventy.	25. About 100.	25. Sixty-one.
26 About twelve.	26 About ninety by the Lessees of the Irish Society Fishery in the Foyle.	26 About ten at present.
27 Usually by the year; some by three or six months, according to the season.	27. Generally from the 1st November till the 1st April; in a few cases for the whole year.	27 The whole year.
28. None.	28 In one case the Duke of Abercorn supplements the salary of the Conservators' bailiff at Sion mills, but cannot say as to what amount.	28 No.
29 Head keepers are paid £20 per year, others £15, and some £6 per year.	29. From £20 to £3.	29 From £5 to £10.
30 No.	30 The Conservators would strongly recommend that the close season for angling be extended from the 15th October till the 15th March.	30 None.

APPENDIX, No. 27.—ABSTRACT of

Substance of Queries issued to Boards of Conservators.	Replies received from Boards of Conservators — 16 BALLYCASTLE.
1. What is the general state of the Salmon Fisheries in this district?	1. Satisfactory
2. Has the take of salmon throughout the district been more or less productive in 1872 than in 1871, and to what is attributed the increase or diminution?	2. The take in 1872 was not so good as in 1871. This is attributed to the heavy floods in the rivers.
3. What was the average price obtained for salmon last year by the captors? (This has no reference to price obtained by the dealers in salmon.) What was the highest price given for salmon last season? What was the lowest price?	3. 1s. 4d. per lb. 3s. 6d. per lb. In spring months 6d. per lb.
4. What proportion of the entire capture in your district is exported, and what proportion purchased for home consumption?	4. Almost all exported.
5. What has been the amount of protection rendered during the present close season of 1872, as compared with preceding season of 1871?	5. Much the same as in 1871.
6. Has the quantity of breeding fish observed in the rivers in your district been greater or less as compared with preceding year, 1871?	6. About the same rivers are well stocked with fish.
7. About what period do the salmon commence to spawn in the several rivers in your district? What are the greatest spawning months? and when is spawning over? and generally where are the most important spawning grounds situated?	7. 1st November. From 1st November till 20th December. 1st January. All River Bush contains good spawning ground.
8. At what period of the year, in each river in your district, are the first clean fish taken? When do the grilse begin to run? When are the spent fish well out of the river? and when does the great bulk of the fry go to sea? Has the quantity of fry descending this year been observably greater or less than usual?	8. Believe a clean fish can be got in the Bush any day in the year. 20th June. 15th April. During April, and until 15th May. Much the same as last year.
9. During the descent of the fry to the sea, is angling for trout prohibited by any of the proprietors of fisheries, or is it carried on during these months, and does much destruction of fry take place?	9. It is prohibited in upper waters. Where salmon angling is, little damage is done.
10. At what period of the year do the fish begin to be discoloured, or to get heavy in spawn; and what is the general opinion as to the proper season for angling in your district?	10. Fish don't become discoloured until they are some time in the river. They get heavy in spawn towards end of August. The general opinion is angling is carried on too long.
11. Have you reason to suppose that many spent fish have been destroyed hitherto in the month of February, and full fish in the month of October by anglers?	11. Has never known any spent fish being destroyed except by accident or mistake. Full fish are often killed in October by legitimate anglers and poachers.
12. Are you aware of any change having taken place in regard to the period of the season when the salmon in your district is in best order, whether earlier or later than heretofore? If so, state particulars.	12. None.
13. Is there any increase in the average size of the spring salmon or the peals. Give average weight of salmon and peals in the season 1872, as far as practicable?	13. —
14. Are there any pollutions or poisonous matter entering the rivers in your district? If so, state the particular cases.	14. Nothing except flax-water.
15. Have offences against the fishery laws increased or diminished?	15. Diminished.
16. What are the mill-weirs or dams, or other obstructions in each river in your district, and where have fish passes been built, when, and by whom?	16. No fish passes required.
17. Where would fish passes be practicable and advantageous?	17. None necessary in this district.
18. Have gratings been attached to mill-races, or other artificial channels, in conformity with the 32 Vic., cap. 9, and, if so, specify the particular cases?	18. Yes, generally.
19. Where has this provision been partially carried out, and whether at the head or tail race?	19. On both.
20. What instances and nature of precautions have been adopted at mills other than that prescribed by the late Act, to prevent the destruction of fish?	20. —
21. Where and by whom have fixed engines been used in 1872?	21. —
22. Can you give a list of the prosecutions instituted by the Conservators during the year 1872?	22. —
23. Can you give a list of prosecutions for fishery offences instituted by others, stating by whom?	23. —
24. Are there any new modes of fishing for salmon adopted in your district? If so, what are they, and where used?	24. None.
25. What is the number of water-bailiffs employed by Conservators?	25. On Bush 12 permanent men, 20 during spawning season. On Ballycastle Sub-district, 4 permanent men, and 7 in spawning season.
26. What is the number employed in district by private individuals?	26. One.
27. For what length of time employed?	27. See answer to No. 25.
28. Are there any upper proprietors who contribute towards protection, and if so, where, and how much?	28. —
29. What is the rate of wages paid by the Conservators?	29. Permanent men from 8s. to 10s. per week, watchers at spawning season, 10s. to 12s. per week.
30. Are there any suggestions or general observations with which the Conservators may be disposed to favour the Inspectors, with reference to the Salmon Fisheries in your district?	30. Several proprietors and occupiers of fisheries are anxious to have the open season extended to 1st September.

STATEMENTS from Boards of Conservators—*concluded.*

Replies received from Boards of Conservators.	
17. DROGHEDA.	18. DUNDALK.
1. Satisfactory. The improvement alluded to last year continues.	1. Satisfactory.
2. The take of fish was very good in the tidal waters in the early part of the season, perhaps a little in excess of former years. The late fishing here was somewhat under the average. In the upper waters the fishing was not so good in the beginning, but improved steadily as the season advanced, caused, no doubt, by the continuous rainfall.	2. Less in number, but greater in weight. Can give no reason.
3. About 1s. 1d. Prices opened somewhat lower than usual, but did not fall in proportion. 7d. 10d.	3. 1s. 3d. per lb. Highest price 2s. 6d. per lb. Lowest price 6d. per lb.
4. Almost the entire is exported, very little local consumption, certainly not more than one-tenth, if so much.	4. About nine-tenths sent to Dublin and Belfast, and one-tenth purchased for home consumption.
5. Very great attention has been paid to protection of fish this season. In the lower waters this has been attended with more than usual difficulties, owing to some parties having, on a supposed point of law, neglected to remove their nets at the close of the season, on the excuse of capturing white fish. In the upper waters offences have been comparatively rare.	5. The same.
6. Greater than for many years past, the heavy rainfall having enabled fish to ascend with facility.	6. They seem to be greater this year.
7. Spawning commences early in October and closes in January, about the first week of both months. The Boyne and Blackwater and their tributaries are all good breeding grounds.	7. In the Dee and Glyde in October and November, the greatest spawning month in these rivers is November. In the Fane in November, and the greatest spawning months are November and December. In all the rivers north of this in November and December, and their greatest spawning months are December and January. The most important spawning beds are as follow:—On the Dee—at Dromore, Cappagh, Drumgoolstown, Richardstown, and Ardee. On the Glyde—at Castlebellingham Wood, Dunnleck, Mountstown, Corballis, Tallanstown, Tiragha, and Cookleary. On the Fane—at Stephenstown, Knockgrange, Lisnaboy, Clonmacnoe, Drumcah, Inishkeen, Moyles, Blacksmiff [illegible], Collon, and Ballinacarry. On the Castletown River, Phillipstown branch—at Castletown, Tateetra, Kilkea, Phillipstown, Dungooly branch—at Dromiskin and Falmore. Forkhill branch—at Scotchgreen and Whitemill. On the Flurry River—at Ballaragan and Ravensdale Park. On the Pinfold River—at Faldmount and Mountbagnal. All the rivers north of this are not sufficiently well known to be able to note the most important spawning beds.
8. When the season opens; but clean fish are numerous before that, say early in January. About 10th June. Early in April, about the first week. April and May. Much greater. There were several new spawning beds formed last season; and some of the riparian proprietors also fixed fish, and turned down large quantities.	8. In the Glyde and Dee on the 1st day of February. In the month of June. In March. In April and May, about a month or six weeks later in all rivers north of these. About the same.
9. No prohibition generally; some breeders did so this year in their own localities. Much fry is destroyed in the lower part of the fresh water by anglers.	9. Angling for trout is not prohibited by any of the proprietors of fisheries. There is some destruction by young boys, but not to a great extent.
10. Some are found in the latter end of August, but after 1st September the very great majority are gravid. Opinions are divided as to the proper season, but the great majority are in favour of commencing and closing earlier.	10. On the Glyde and Dee the fish begin to get discoloured in the latter end of July, and to be heavy in spawn in September. In the Fane they begin to be discoloured in August, and to get heavy in spawn in October. In all rivers north of this a month later.
11. Certainly, in the upper waters, spent fish do not show in the tidal waters till April, and gravid fish are seldom seen there, as they have passed up before they are found in that condition, except during the last few days of August.	11. A considerable number of spent fish have been destroyed in the River Fane, and all rivers north of it, in February, and in all rivers in the month of October.
12. Fish are now admittedly "in condition" at an earlier period than was formerly supposed, hence, probably, the wish for an earlier opening of the season.	12. No.
13. The size of fish has varied less than usual this season, medium sized fish have been rather in excess, say about 14 lbs., some large, from 30 to 50 lbs., were taken in the early season. The size of peals seldom varies, from 5 to 8 lbs. may be taken as the average.	13. There has been an increase in the average size of the spring salmon and peals, the average weight of salmon being 17 lbs. or 18 lbs., and that of peals 7 lbs.
14. Cloudy Sea-water.	14. In the Dundalk River spent wash is allowed to flow from the distillery through the town sewer, causing great destruction to all kinds of fish when the water is low in the river.
15. Offences have been comparatively rare this season. Poaching has not been practised to any great extent, owing probably to the flooded condition of the land along the rivers preventing approach to the haunts of the fish.	15. Diminished.
	16. Glyde and Dee or Annagassan River. There is a dam on each river to supply Delany's mill at Annagassan. Fish passes have been built in each of these by the Board of Works in 1848 and 1850. On the Dee River, the Whitemill weir and fish pass, built at or about the same time by the Board of Works. At Julianstown, on the river, a fish pass was built by the Board of Works or Drainage Company, under the superintendence of Mr Manning, engineer, which is repaired useless. Glyde River—Castlebellingham mill weir, where fish pass was built by the Board of Works in 1847–48. Braggenstown threshing mill weir, at which fish pass was built at same time. At Killeeny mill weir, on the Ballymakenny River, fish pass built by the Board of Works in 1868. On the River Fane—Clonmacnoe mill weir, where there is no fish pass, but some sluices put up by Colonel Fortescue and the late Mr Sutton are very useful. At Inishkeen mill there is no fish pass, but fish can cross in high water. Moyles mill weir and Collon the with the same. There are other mills, but their dams offer no obstruction on these rivers. The Dundalk River at Phillipstown mill a complete barrier. Dungooly and Balriggan mills the same. On the Flurry River there are O'Hare's several factories, at Dubergy, Wynn's several bleaching factories, Thompson's bleaching mill, and M'Connell's corn mill, at Ravensdale. The obstructions caused by these mills are, that they take all the water of the river, so that unless in very high and constant floods no fish can pass them. The Pinfold River has M'Ardle's mill weir at Riverstown; but it appears the salmon only go there at spawning time.
16. There are numerous weirs on all the rivers in the district, both navigation, malting, and fishing; all the latter have good passes, and several have been lately erected or improved on navigation weirs by the Board of Conservators. Many of the mill weirs are altogether without passes, and where such do exist they are very defective.	17. Fish passes would be practicable and advantageous at Clonmacnoe's Inishkeen, and Phillipstown mill weirs, on Dee, at Whitemills, present pass being useless; and at Julianstown, where pass also useless, being partly carried away, on Glyde also, at Braggenstown, where pass is very inefficient.
17. On three navigation weirs on Boyne now without them, and on several mill weirs on all the rivers.	18. Gratings have been placed as follow:—On the River Fane, at Mr M'Cann's mill, Knockbridge, head and waste races; Mr Kieran's mill, Clonmacnoe, head and tail race, Mr Kelly's, Balriggan mill, tail race; Mr Dougherty's Scotchgreen mill, tail race, Mr O'Hare's Barleyfield mill, tail race, Mr. O'Hare's waste race, Dubergy. Mr. Wynn's bleach mill, at Ravensdale, on tail race and waste race; and at the head race of Mr. Thompson's bleach mill, at Ravensdale.
18. In the great majority of instances exemptions were granted. In those cases "ordered" gratings have been put up, except at Kennedy's mill, at Trim. Notice calling for erection has been served in this case.	19. See No. 18.
19. One on tail race of Courtney's mill on the Boyne.	20. None.
20. None whatever, except that in a few instances mill owners endeavour to prevent malpractices.	21. See Appendix.
21. See Appendix.	22. See Appendix.
22. See Appendix.	23. See Appendix.
23. None.	24. No.
24. None; but there is great destruction of trout by night lines in inland waters, and large quantities of both salmon and trout are taken by stake-nets on the coast, used during the entire year under the pretence of taking white fish.	25. Six, including inspector.
25. Twelve.	26. Two.
26. Two.	27. Permanently.
27. Permanent.	28. The Conservators—namely, Colonel Fortescue and others—contribute by paying two water-bailiffs, but I cannot state the amount.
28. Yes. The Marquess of Headfort, J. L. W. Naper, Esq.; on the Blackwater; £18 per annum.	29. Three at £18; two at £10, and one, who is also inspector, at £36, and salary increased to £40 on 1st December, 1872.
29. Five at £1 10s. per month; seven at £1 per month.	30. The Board of Conservators suggest and strongly recommend, that the necessary steps be taken by the Inspectors of Irish Fisheries, with the least possible delay, to have an Act passed authorising and requiring the Royal Irish Constabulary to enforce the provisions of the 14th section of 5 & 6 Vic., cap. 106, so as to prevent the pollution of rivers by flax water, &c.
30. —	

OYSTER

APPENDIX No. 28.—ABSTRACT of Replies to Queries received

Queries Issued.	Licence No 1—24th November, 1846. Tranmore Bay, County Mayo. Granted to W. H Carter. Lessee—James Gallagher.	Licence No. 2—7th December, 1846. Sabron Harbour, County Mayo. Granted to Luke Lyons.	Licence No 3—6th June, 1848. Of Dawros Point, County Kerry. Granted to F. H Downing. Present owner—Marquess of Lansdowne.
1. At what time after the above date were steps taken to cultivate the bed?	1. In 1847	This is the same bed as that for which a licence was granted to John Townsend Kirkwood, Luke Lyons being only agent.—See No. 71.	1. 1852.
2. What was the nature of the steps taken by you then to cultivate the bed?	2. To dredge oysters and replant same on the bed.		2. —
3. What quantity of oysters were put down by you, and were they small or full grown oysters?	3. About 100,000; both large and small oysters.		3. About 80,000 or 100,000 oysters.
4. Were any collectors used for catching spat, and if so, of what description?	4. None.		4. No.
5. What was the result of your first operations?	5. Favourable.		5. The oysters grew and were sold.
6. What quantity of oysters were put down each year since, and were they small or full-grown oysters?	6. About 50,000; small oysters.		6. None.
7. Have you ever collected spat on your bed; and if so, when and in what quantity?	7. None.		7. No.
8. What amount of oysters has been sold off your bed annually since the licence granted?	8. About 100 barrels.		8. Nothing worth talking of, these ten years past.
9. How many people are employed on your bed? At what season are they so employed, and at what work?	9. Thirty to fifty in March and during the spring time of the year, dredging and cleaning oysters.		9. One.
10. What is the stock of oysters and oyster spat at present on your bed, as near as you can calculate?	10. About 100,000 oysters.		10. None.
11. Was the spatting this year good?	11. Very bad.		11. None.
12. If your undertaking has not proved satisfactory, to what cause do you attribute its non-success?	12. The public oyster beds being over-dredged by day and night.		12. That the brutes won't breed.
13. Any general observations or statements you wish to make.	13. Several strangers come into the bay and buy the oysters, large and small.		13. Young oysters are now so costly that it does not pay to import them from other beds; and until the oysters on the bed take to breeding, as they used of old, the oyster farming will not pay.

Queries Issued.	Licence No. 8—17th November, 1852. Clew Bay, County Galway. Granted to John O. Garvey. Lessee—Captain George Austin.	Licence No 9—22nd September, 1853. Mulroy Bay, County Donegal. Granted to John O. Woodhouse.	Licence No 10—1st July, 1854. Carlingford Lough, County Louth. Granted to Barton Blacker. Present owner—Lord Clermont.
1. At what time after the above date were steps taken to cultivate the bed?	The operations under this licence are carried on conjointly with those under the licence granted to myself. All replies to the queries as to the latter are equally applicable to this.—See Licence No. 72.	1. About six months.	See No. 17.
2. What was the nature of the steps taken by you then to cultivate the bed?		2. Mark the beds.	
3. What quantity of oysters were put down by you, and were they small or full-grown oysters?		3. About 10,000. They were small.	
4. Were any collectors used for catching spat, and if so, of what description?		4. Beds of stones.	
5. What was the result of your first operations?		5. Not favourable.	
6. What quantity of oysters were put down each year since, and were they small or full-grown oysters?		6. —	
7. Have you ever collected spat on your bed; and if so, when and in what quantity?		7. Did not collect the spat.	
8. What amount of oysters has been sold off your bed annually since the licence granted?		8. No oysters were sold.	
9. How many people are employed on your bed? At what season are they so employed, and at what work?		9. —	
10. What is the stock of oysters and oyster spat at present on your bed, as near as you can calculate?		10. —	
11. Was the spatting this year good?		11. —	
12. If your undertaking has not proved satisfactory, to what cause do you attribute its non-success?		12. —	
Any general observations or statements you wish to make.		13. —	

FISHERIES.

from Owners, Occupiers, or Lessees of Oyster Beds.

Licence No. 4—24th February, 1869. Dunmanus Bay, County Cork. Granted to R. B. Evanson. Present owner—R. H. Morris	Licence No. 5—4th February, 1861. Estuary of Kenmare River, County Kerry. Granted to John Mahony. Present owner—Joseph Goff	Licence No. 6—4th February, 1861. Estuary of Kenmare River, County Kerry. Granted to Rev. Denis Mahony.	Licence No. 7—17th November, 1863. Ballisodare Bay, County Sligo. Granted to Thomas White. Present owner—James Chas. Whyte Douglas.
1. Immediately, by the late Mr. R. T. Evanson. 2. I believe nothing more than laying down oysters. 3. Generally small oysters picked up on the shores of Bantry Bay and Dunmanus Bay; I believe about 300,000. 4. None were used. 5. They increased well in size and gave good quality. 6. None. 7. No. 8. Probably 30,000 would be the limit of the entire sales. The bed was used for private consumption, and I should say the amount taken off the bed annually since 1869 would not average more than 3,000. 9. None. 10. Oysters nearly all. Never observed spat. 11. — 12. First, want of culture and collectors; 2nd, constant growth of short sea-weed (black weed); also deposit of marine vegetable matter in the channels and sheltery nooks, where oysters would best thrive; it does not come to the surface, but is deposited in from three to twelve feet water. I fear this is a great obstacle to growth of oysters here. I have also removed great numbers of fresh opened oyster-shells and the fish abstracted. 13. —	1. In the year 1866 Mr. John Mahony sold this estate to Mr Joseph Goff, and I can furnish no information prior to that date. Mr Goff subsequently leased this oyster bed to a Mr Mathews, who in April, 1866, took steps to cultivate it. 2. A cargo of oysters was imported from Arklow by Mr Mathews, at a cost of £300, as he stated. 3. I cannot state the exact quantity. They were chiefly small oysters. 4. No, except a pond was formed by mason-work, over which the tide ebbs and flows. 5. Most of the oysters imported died, and there was not much result from the operations. 6. In 1866–67 Mr Mathews brought oysters from Tralee and also purchased some from local fishermen—chiefly small oysters—and laid them down, but I can't say what quantity. 7. No. 8. In the year 1868 Mr Mathews died, and after his death his executors sold about 20,000 oysters from the bed, and the lease of the bed was subsequently evicted by Mr. Goff for non-payment of the rent. 9. There was one boatman employed all the year by Mr Mathews. 10. There are but few oysters on the part of the bed which strips at low water, but there are some on the remainder of it, although I cannot say what quantity. 11. I cannot say. 12. So many of the oysters imported having died, and so the oysters having been stolen and dredged by night; but since the bed came into Mr Goff's possession I have had some persons fined who were caught dredging, which, I trust, has put a stop to it. 13. I should like to be referred to some book of instructions for cultivating the bed.	This oyster bed is worthless. Although partly protected, it has not improved. Nobody thinks of dredging it. There are but few oysters in it.	Owing to my absence in France, and having a law-suit with the late tenant of the oyster bed, (which is now settled,) I have been unable to cultivate it, but intend now to commence, and hope to send you results next year.

Licence No. 11—18th November, 1864. Killery Harbour, County Mayo. Granted to Hon. David Plunket. Present owner—E. C. MacDonnell	Licence No. 12—18th November, 1864. Ballyconneely Bay, County Galway. Granted to J. A. Boswell. Lessee—William Young	Licence No. 13—16th July, 1865. Blacksod Bay, County Mayo. Granted to John Richards.	Licence No. 14—30th July, 1866. Bear Haven, County Cork. Granted to Lord C. P. P. Clinton.
Could not state positively what steps were taken to cultivate the bed, but I am aware of the Hon. David Plunket having taken steps to cultivate the beds and of his having brought skilled persons from Westport for that purpose.	1. Mr. Boswell planted seed oysters in the year 1866, and Mr Young on subsequent occasions—in 1867 and 1868—to the value of about £100. 2. The beds were kept clean from sea-weed and star-fish, the oysters shifted about as necessary, and the large ones selected and sold. The most difficult thing was watching the beds against poachers and persons stealing oysters. 3. The oysters were very small, and two hooker loads were put down; but of the numbers I can give no approximate figure. 4. There were no collectors used, there being plenty of stones, old oyster-shells, &c., on the beds. 5. The oysters grew in size rapidly, and were sold off as they became marketable. 6. There were no oysters put down since 1868, as it became practically impossible to purchase small oysters in that neighbourhood. 7. No. 8. The amount is very irregular, not exceeding £30 in any one year. 9. There is no regular staff kept; one man watches the beds; but people are employed when required. 10. I can give no correct reply to this. 11. I do not know. 12. The chief reasons for its not paying better are—its distance from market; the heavy run of sea-weed which covers the oysters, and is expensive to remove; and the difficulty of protecting the oysters from the kelp and sea-weed gatherers. 13. —	1. I think from October, 1866, to March, 1867. 2. I had the shore above low water, where I found it hard, divided into beds or parks. 3. I put down about £150 worth of oysters, most of them full size. 4. Stones and oyster-shells. 5. I was disappointed in the quantity of spat. 6. I put on no fresh oysters. 7. I have collected small oysters and spat from time to time. 8. Out of about £100 worth of oysters put on the bed, after being one year there I sold about £40 worth, and since, up to this date, £10 worth. 9. I have two persons, man and wife, who inhabit a house on the shore of the bed, caretakers. 10. Perhaps £10 worth—may be more. 11. I should think not. 12. Seasons cold and ungenial, and difficulty of protecting the oysters from being stolen by night. 13. —	1. I cannot answer this question with any accuracy, as I was not then connected with the estate, but I believe that steps were taken immediately after the grant of the licence. 2. I cannot say. 3. Since I became agent I put down no oysters; but I took very few from the old bed, hoping that the oysters on the bed would propagate. 4. No. 5. — 6. No oysters put down. 7. No. 8. None sold or taken off the bed, except very few for immediate use, when I am on the estate. 9. One man employed to watch the bed, to prevent it from being trespassed on, or the oysters stolen. 10. I cannot say. 11. I heard the spatting was good this season. 12. I believe the bed has not improved, owing to the floods from the mountains flowing on the beach, and bringing with them rubbish of all sorts, which choke the oysters. 13. I am not acquainted with the proper culture of oysters, and I should feel grateful for any hints likely to improve this bed, and would carry them out.

APPENDIX No. 28.—ABSTRACT of Replies to Que[ries]

QUERIES ISSUED.	Licence No. 15—21st August, 1866. Ardbear Bay, County Galway. Granted to William [illegible]. Lessee—John Kendall.	Licence No. 16—?th August, 1867. Glengarriff Harbour, County Cork. Granted to Thomas Frake. Present owners—[illegible] & Curtis.	Licence No. 17—[illegible] Streamstown and Clegga[n] Granted to Rev. A[illegible] —
1. At what time after the above date were steps taken to cultivate the bed?	See Licence No. 37, the replies to which equally refer to this bed, as both are worked conjointly.	1. 1867, 1868, 1869.	1. On the 10th May, 1[illegible]
2. What was the nature of the steps taken by you then to cultivate the bed?		2. Placed a large quantity of small oysters on it.	2. We endeavoured [illegible] the bay, and clean[ed] weed off it.
3. What quantity of oysters were put down by you, and were they small or full-grown oysters?		3. Cannot tell accurately; several hundreds, small, about half-grown.	3. Three hooker load[s] running about [illegible] large tar-barrels
4. Were any collectors used for catching spat, and if so, of what description?		4. None.	4. We employed [illegible] furze bushes, an[d] certain distances but our endeavou[rs]
5. What was the result of your first operations?		5. Good.	5. First May, 1861, [illegible] nation all over th[e] greatly disappoin[ted] [illegible], finding shells, but very [illegible]
6. What quantity of oysters were put down each year since, and were they small or full-grown oysters?		6. Cannot tell exactly, half-grown.	6. May, 1864, we plac[ed] bank some forty and in 1867 we [illegible] barrels. The oy[sters] about the size of
7. Have you ever collected spat on your bed, and if so, when and in what quantity?		7. No.	7. We have collected
8. What amount of oysters has been sold off your bed annually since the licence granted?		8. None, the local supplied: a large quantity used every year.	8. To the best of my [illegible] sold about eight [illegible] since. I have [illegible] them sent to [illegible] present, some six
9. How many people are employed on your bed? At what season are they so employed, and at what work?		9. None regularly.	9. I employ but two [illegible] my [illegible]
10. What is the stock of oysters and oyster spat at present on your bed, as near as you can calculate?		10. Cannot tell.	10. I cannot say, b[ut] oysters greatly [illegible]
11. Was the spatting this year good?		11. Very bad.	11. I cannot say, [illegible] looked after the[m]
12. If your undertaking has not proved satisfactory, to what cause do you attribute its non-success?		12. The strand is very muddy. A sort of stuff called weed, which is used here as manure, collects on the strand in the early spring, and is most destructive to the oysters. The bed is not good this year.	12. I do not consid[er] made as good as [illegible] might, considera[ble] and outlay I hav[e]
13. Any general observations or statements you wish to make.		13. —	13. —

QUERIES ISSUED.	Licence No. 22—12th February, 1868. Achill Sound, County Mayo. Granted to William M'Cormick. —	Licence No. 21—?th May, 1869. Ballynakill Harbour, County Galway. Granted to Edmund Brown. —	Licence No. 24—[illegible] Oyster Haven, C[illegible] Granted to M. —
1. At what time after the above date were steps taken to cultivate the bed?	No replies received.	1. I do not know anything about the beds before October 4th, 1871. Since that time the West of Ireland Oyster and Fish Company have held a lease from Mr. G. W. Hart.	1. In 1862 I had dre[dged] and [illegible] a the foreshore
2. What was the nature of the steps taken by you then to cultivate the bed?		2. Young oysters were placed on clean parts of bed.	2. —
3. What quantity of oysters were put down by you, and were they small or full-grown oysters?		3. Estimated by Mr. Hart at 300,000 small and spat shells.	3. Six few hundreds full-grown.
4. Were any collectors used for catching spat, and if so, of what description?		4. A few tiles and some lumps of chalk.	4. I did not use any.
5. What was the result of your first operations?		5. Nothing was obtained on either tiles or chalk, as far as yet examined.	5. The oysters wer[e] the rough stones and below low-[water] covered with sa[nd] severe gale fro[m] covered the oy[sters] fully six inches and destroyed [illegible] them.
6. What quantity of oysters were put down each year since, and were they small or full-grown oysters?		6. None.	6. A few baskets fr[om] an experiment, ground must be [artifi]cially prepared
7. Have you ever collected spat on your bed, and if so, when and in what quantity?		7. Not any.	7. —
8. What amount of oysters has been sold off your bed annually since the licence granted?		8. None since our possession.	8. —
9. How many people are employed on your bed? At what season are they so employed, and at what work?		9. I cannot answer this; so far, I have not employed my boats on this bed except for a few days this spring.	9. —
10. What is the stock of oysters and oyster spat at present on your bed, as near as you can calculate?		10. I cannot tell.	10. —
11. Was the spatting this year good?		11. No.	11. —
12. If your undertaking has not proved satisfactory, to what cause do you attribute its non-success?		12. 1872 was a very wet, cold year, and, I fancy, we got no spat in consequence.	12. —
13. Any general observations or statements you wish to make.		13. —	13. —

FISHERIES.

from Owners, Occupiers, or Lessees of Oyster Beds—*continued.*

Licence No. 18—18th February, 1868. Killery Harbour, County Galway. Granted to A. C. Lambert.

1. About two years.
2. Replanting it where it had failed, and throwing out old oyster-shells and such things as I was told spat would stick to.
3. A sixteen ton boat load, containing, I think, 60,000 or 70,000—some full-grown, half-grown, and small, just as I was informed they were taken out of the beds in Clew Bay.
4. No collectors were used. I never heard of them, or that they could be used in such a place as the Killeries.
5. A failure. The places I replanted in failed entirely. The small sheltered bay (a very small one) was successful.
6. I can't say; but they were both large and small. In dredging where they succeeded, I put most of them back repeatedly where they had failed.
7. Whenever, in dredging, small oysters have been taken up, they have been put back again, or into the places where they had before failed.
8. None.
9. None, continually. The bed, both as to character and extent, is very limited—quite small—and all in deep water.
10. My oysters can in no way be raised, except by dredging.
11. Not good.
12. Not satisfactory, owing to the strong tides in the Killeries, except in deep water. The tide completely swept them away where it was shallow.
13. Except in one particular small bay (which is sheltered and the tide checked)—all have failed practically.

Licence No. 19—3rd February, 1868. Mannin and Ardbear Bays, County Galway. Granted to Rev. R. H. Wall. Present owner—Walter B. Wall.

I cannot let you have any answers to your queries. I have been very busy and greatly put about, in consequence of family affairs, and have done nothing in the way of oyster culture.

Licence No. 20—3rd February, 1869. Valentia Harbour, County Kerry. Granted to Knight of Kerry.

I have already replied more than once, that finding that the bottom was not of a nature suitable for oysters, I had not done more than place a not large quantity of full-grown oysters imported from Smerwick, in River Kenmare.

Licence No. 21—1st February, 1869. Killary Harbour, County Mayo. Granted to Captain W. Houstoun.

1. Two years.
2. Oysters were bought and put down.
3. I cannot say what quantity were put down. They were of different sizes.
4. —
5. —
6. None were put down since.
7. —
8. None.
9. —
10. The stock of oysters is very small, but as large as usual.
11. —
12. —
13. The oysters will only do on a very small piece of ground, and the available portion of the bed is only large enough to supply the wants of the table.

Licence No. 25—6th October, 1869. Lough Mahon, Estuary of Lee, Co. Cork. Granted to Ebenezer Pike.

The railway bridge has caused the channel to be changed, which has prevented the oysters doing any good, from the quantity of mud moved on the bed.

Licence No. 26—14th November, 1869. Achill Sound, County Mayo. Granted to William Pike.

1. At once.
2. Laying oysters on various parts of the bed.
3. Many boat-loads of large and small oysters.
4. No.
5. I have found that there has been a great increase of oysters on some parts of the grounds, over fourteen young oysters adhering to some of the old shells. In other places they did not breed so well.
6. I did not keep an exact account of this. No oysters were removed for several years, but were spread on the beds.
7. A fall of spat takes place on this bed every year.
8. —
9. —
10. Cannot at present say the beds having been leased for the last three years.
11. Cannot say.
12. The undertaking has proved satisfactory to me.
13. From what I have seen from the fall of spat on the bed, I believe when fully cultivated it will be one of the best in the kingdom.

Licence No. 27—10th January, 1870. Mannin Bay, County Galway. Granted to William Forbes.

I have to inform you that I have now no oyster beds. They were robbed during my long absence of nearly two years, from sickness. There are some rock oysters still to be had.

Licence No. 28—16th February, 1869. Clonderlaw Bay, County Clare. Granted to Robert W. C. Reeves.

1. In 1864.
2. I brought over a Frenchman from the Ile de Ré, who laid down flags and hurdles to collect the spat. There are a good many oysters now on the flags, but the hurdles were all pulled up by the different fishermen, and I have consequently given them up, although they were most successful.
3. I put down 170,000 oysters in 1864 and 1865; they were a good-sized oyster.
4 and 5. I have already described them.
6. The oysters from the natural bed in Clonderlaw Bay supply spat to the collectors.
7. I collected a very considerable quantity of spat, but I find great difficulty in detaching it from the flags, as a great number of oysters are broken in taking them off, and the hurdles were pulled up.
8. None have been sold.
9. From time to time I have had from six to twenty persons employed.
10. About 10,000.
11. Yes.
12. The soil being mud, there is a tendency for slime to form over the collectors, but the great difficulty I have is in trying to detach the young oyster without breaking or injuring it.
13. —

Oyster

Appendix No. 28.—Abstract of Replies to Queries received

Queries Issued.	License No. 23—3rd March, 1862. Belfast Lough, Carrickfergus, Co. Antrim. Granted to James Walker	License No. 29—6th March, 1863. Tramore Bay, County Waterford. Granted to Edmund Power	License No. 31—20th May, 1863. Achill Sound, County Mayo. Granted to George Clive.
1. At what time after the above date were steps taken to cultivate the bed?	I am sorry I cannot answer any of these questions, as Mr. James Walker, who obtained the grant, went to Natal in 1864, and I know nothing about what he did in the way of developing the oyster bed.	1. Immediately after.	1. Winter, 1863.
2. What was the nature of the steps taken by you then to cultivate the bed?		2. I formed parks, and also laid down small oysters in the channels included in my license. I also, at considerable expense, in 1867, formed 4 reservoirs or tanks inside my embankment.	2. Put out some few bushels of oysters.
3. What quantity of oysters were put down by you, and were they small or full-grown oysters?		3. From the commencement to the present time I put down at least 700,000 small oysters about one year old.	3. Mixed.
4. Were any collectors used for catching spat, and if so, of what description?		4. In the parks I used stones, tiles, and hurdles, as collectors.	4. None.
5. What was the result of your first operations?		5. In the parks I had a fall of middle or grown oysters, and in the deep part of one of the channels some spat was found attached to pebbles and shells, but in a small quantity.	5. —
6. What quantity of oysters were put down each year since, and were they small or full-grown oysters?		6. From 20,000 to 50,000 small oysters each year, until they became scarce and dear.	6. None put down since first year.
7. Have you ever collected spat on your bed, and if so, when and in what quantity?		7. Not more than is mentioned in answer to No. 5.	7. No.
8. What amount of oysters has been sold off your bed annually since the license granted?		8. From 8,000 to 10,000 up to 1871.	8. Some thirty bushels sold in 1868; about the same in 1870, and sixty bushels in 1872.
9. How many people are employed on your beds? At what season are they so employed, and at what work?		9. When making the parks and tanks I had seven or eight labourers employed, and afterwards one permanent caretaker.	9. One to watch the bed, and six at the time of dredging.
10. What is the stock of oysters and oyster spat at present on your bed, as near as you can calculate?		10. It is impossible to tell, as a large quantity have been smothered by shifting sands, as to spat there is none.	10. About twenty bushels.
11. Was the spatting this year good?		11. No spatting this year.	11. —
12. If your undertaking has not proved satisfactory, to what cause do you attribute its non-success?		12. The undertaking so far as collecting spat, has not proved satisfactory, and I attribute this to the strong currents and shifting sands in the channels, but with regard to feeding, some of my ground is, I can say from experience, invaluable.	12. The chief part of the water granted to Mr. Clive has mud bottom, therefore not worth going to expense; and only a few were put out on a small spot for private use; but almost every second or third year the above quantity is sold off the bed.
13. Any general observations or statements you wish to make.		13. —	13. —

Queries Issued.	License No. 36—19th September, 1864. Westport Bay, County Mayo. Granted to Captain George Acklin.	License No. 37—21st October, 1864. Ardbear and Mannin Bays, County Galway. Granted to John Kendall.	License No. 38—21st October, 1864. Lough Hyne, County Cork. Granted to R. T. Atkins.
1. At what time after the above date were steps taken to cultivate the bed?	1. Immediately.	1. —	1. On getting the license I applied to several persons to get seed oysters, but up to the present without success.
2. What was the nature of the steps taken by you then to cultivate the bed?	2. Cleaning and preparing the beds for oysters, also bought lumber and sent them round the bay collecting oysters.	2. —	2. —
3. What quantity of oysters were put down by you, and were they small or full-grown oysters?	3. About 13,444 baddigans of oysters, of all sizes, shells and culch, &c., &c., with spat on it.	3. —	3. —
4. Were any collectors used for catching spat; and if so, of what description?	4. Dredgers were employed to catch and clean bed.	4. No, except shells.	4. —
5. What was the result of your first operations?	5. Most unsatisfactory, there was so much poaching.	5. —	5. —
6. What quantity of oysters were put down each year since, and were they small or full-grown oysters?	6. —	6. Having stocked the beds, I have not put down more oysters lately.	6. —
7. Have you ever collected spat on your bed; and if so, when and in what quantity?	7. Yes, in small quantities culled out when cultivating oysters and cleaning the bed. This spat was re-laid on part of the bed prepared for it.	7. Yes, every year, but not in large quantity, except in one little spot where the water is calm.	7. —
8. What amount of oysters has been sold off your bed annually since the license granted?	8. —	8. I have only sold in one year. I am endeavouring to get up a stock.	8. —
9. How many people are employed on your bed? At what season are they so employed, and at what work?	9. Six men are employed constantly; sixteen employed at weekly wages during the months from October to April, and as many as from 100 to 200 men and women are engaged about the oysters during the months from December to April, chiefly employed sorting the different sizes, dredging the bed, cleaning away weeds, and parting the clusters of brood, &c., to enable them to be culled out each year, saleable oysters for market. The six men are watchmen, 15 are buyers and collectors of oysters from surrounding islands in the bay.	9. Two constantly as watchmen; and in the spring I employ several boats and men to dredge and clean the ground.	9. —
10. What is the stock of oysters and oyster spat at present on your bed, as near as you can calculate?	10. As nearly as can be calculated there should be about 27,400 baddigans of oysters, spat, shells, culch, &c., on the beds, but of this quantity it is calculated that at the present time only 5,000 or more baddigans are oysters and spat, as a very large allowance must be made for 10 years' death rate, and for the number of shells, culch, dirt, &c., bought with the spat and oysters from year to year.	10. I cannot calculate such a matter; but the stock has cost me many hundreds of pounds.	10. There are a few oysters on the bed at present; I cannot say what number.
11. Was the spatting this year good?	11. No, the spatting was very bad.	11. I have been unable to examine personally, but there are good reports.	11. —
12. If your undertaking has not proved satisfactory, to what cause do you attribute its non-success?	12. It has not proved as satisfactory as we expected.	12. Robbery and laziness.	12. —
13. Any general observations or statements you wish to make.		13. That the sale of small oysters should be made illegal, and that the gentry should not buy oysters for the table from thieves.	

FISHERIES.

from Owners, Occupiers, or Lessees of Oyster Beds—*continued.*

Licence No. 33—2nd February, 1864. Tramore Bay, County Waterford. Granted to Lord [illegible].	Licence No. 35—8th April, 1864. Galway Bay, County Galway. Granted to Lord Wallscourt.	Licence No. 36—10th June, 1864. Poulnasherry Bay, County Clare. Granted to Colonel C. M. Vandeleur, M.P.	Licence No. 38—10th June, 1864. Newport Bay, County Mayo. Granted to A. W. Wyndham.
1. The winter of the year 1864. 2. An oyster park was made on the foreshore just above low water mark of spring tides, which was stocked the following spring with oysters from Wexford, and a man placed in charge of them. The year following a second oyster park was made near the other. 3. I cannot say exactly; ten or fifteen tons. In the most part small oysters. 4. Only some rough stones. 5. A certain percentage of oysters perished by their usual enemies. The remainder developed into oysters of excellent flavour. 6. In 1867 ten tons mixed oysters laid down, from Wexford. 7. No spat has ever been collected, and hardly any, if any, observed in the bed, or on the stones, or the oysters placed in the adjoining channel. 8. In 1866 500 sold at 6s. per 100; in 1868 between 7,000 and 8,000 sold at 5s. per 100; in 1869, to the value of £11 14s. 6d., and a small quantity in 1870. 9. No one at the present date. 10. None at present. 11. — 12. I attribute the loss of spat, if the oysters ever spatted at all, to the exposure of the oysters to the rapid tidal current in the foreshore, from which they could only be protected by costly masonry works. 13. I have noticed the great change produced in the shell of the oysters by their transfer from the muddy banks near Wexford to the clean shingle of this foreshore.	1. Oysters were purchased in years 1862, 1863, and 1864—*Vide* late Commissioners' Report Book, 1866, pages 39 and 40, and Report Book, 1867, pages 54, 59, 60, 61, and 62. 2. See Report Book, 1867, page 6, per Mr John P Brophy. 3. See Report Book, 1867, pages 59, 60, 60, 61, and 62. See John Keevan's sworn information. 4. As many oyster and other shells as could be procured in this locality were strewn on the beds for clutch to catch spat. 5. Answered in Report Books, as above. 6. All the oysters that could be found above low water each year from 1861 to present date have been put below low water, leaving above low water, scars and shores, which is sold each year to different parties, who would deprive us of any that might be above low water. 7. I refer to above answers. 8. In the years 1869 and 1870 sold to Mr Owen Pees, St. Johns Market, Liverpool, and in the year 1872, to Mr John Armstrong, 130 Mount-street, Grosvenor-square, London, 148,000 (a five score to each hundred). 9. There are eight men employed during the oyster season at such work as cleaning beds, clearing rocks, dredging, &c., and many women and children occasionally, picking oysters above low water mark. Have watchmen in Ardgay and Galway. 10. Have fished at large and 72 smaller oysters in six hauls of dredge, on different parts of the beds. 11. No, nor since the year 1867, near as good as previous to that year. 12. — 13. Lord Wallscourt has had an interview with Mr Brady on the subject of his oyster fishery.	1 to 4. Steps were immediately taken to protect the grounds included in the licence, which had been completely exhausted, and to lay down about ten thousand oysters, to form a breeding bed, and have since depended on the natural course, which has been most successful, the spat extending both up and down the bay, and large numbers of young oysters were collected and placed in parks at low water spring tides by the caretaker and his family, who complain very much of the injury committed by women gathering periwinkles in the season, by turning over the stones and disturbing the young oysters. I had faggots and hurdles tried, but found small stones answer best, and propose removing the breeding beds out of the strong tideway. 5. Having left my bed to recover there has been no result, and as yet have not heard of any reports been made in the Shannon. 6. None. 7. Spat is deposited by nature on the beds. Quantity depends on the state of the tide and weather and is very uncertain. 8. None. 9. One man, his wife, and four children. 10. I am told we have from ten to twenty thousand young and old, but have my doubts. 11. I hear it was good; a great portion goes into deep water with the tide. 12. My oyster bed, like many others, was worked out before I took it up, and will take a great many years to recover. 13. —	1. The following winter. 2. Laying down oysters. 3. About 200 stone weight of large and small mixed. 4. Tiles; the ground under them being previously made firm by putting gravel thereon. This was done last year. 5. Oysters sunk in the sand and lost. 6. None since. 7. No. 8. None. 9. None now. 10. None at all worth mentioning; may be a few. 11. Don't know. 12. To the ground being unfit for oyster culture. 13. —

Licence No. 39—21st October, 1864. Galway Bay, County Galway. Granted to R. N. L. Athy.	Licence No. 40—31st October, 1864. Galway Bay, County Galway. Granted to P. M. Lynch. Present Owner—J. W. Lynch.	Licence No. 41—8th November, 1864. Dungarvan Harbour, County Waterford. Granted to A. Boate.	Licence No. 42—11th November, 1864. Dungarvan Harbour, County Waterford. Granted to J. B. Dower.
I have many times informed the Board of my having abandoned all idea of forming an oyster bed in New Harbour, as competent judges recommended me not, the harbour being too exposed to the westerly gales.	I have to state that before and since the licence was granted to my late father, Mr P. M. Lynch, a considerable quantity of oysters were put out on the beds in question, but owing to the exposure to the north and west, from which there is no protection whatever, the oysters have drifted away and are not now recoverable. I do not, therefore, think it advisable that any further outlay be incurred on these beds, as the return from them is nil. The old oyster bed which faces the south, and is well protected from the north, produces the finest oysters; for this no licence was required.	1. The ground, being very foul, was partly cleared by hand labour in 1865-6, and again in the spring of 1867. This could only be done at low water spring tides. 2. To remove the stones and weeds, of which there was a considerable accumulation, the latter growing again annually in the summer season. The ground was marked off by means of suitable buoys, and some small brood oysters placed on the most eligible parts of the ground. 3. Several thousand small brood oysters. 4. None, except the local shells, &c. 5. None, if inquiry refers to question No. 4. 6. Having stocked the cleanest part of the ground, I have not laid down more oysters, and am waiting the result of an experiment with some American oysters in Devonshire waters. 7. Yes, annually. 8. The stock is increasing, and I am desirous of a considerable accumulation for a regular annual supply for market. 9. In the spring several women and boys, one man regularly. 10. The depth of water varying from one to six feet at low water, cannot estimate. 11. Have reason to believe of an average production. 12. The undertaking seems to have been as satisfactory as most of the others on the coast. 13. More protection might be desirable from persons who pick seaweed and perrywinkles in the spring and summer months on the adjoining strand.	1. I took no steps to cultivate them. 2. None. 3. None. 4. None. 5. — 6. — 7. — 8. — 9. — 10. — 11. — 12. — 13. —

OYSTER

APPENDIX No. 28.—ABSTRACT of Replies to Queries received

QUERIES ISSUED.	LICENCE No. 43—31st December, 1864. Glandore Harbour, County Cork. Granted to Captain W. F. Barry.	LICENCE No. 44—31st December, 1864. Ballyvaghan Harbour, County Galway. Granted to C. F. Archer. Lessee—West of Ireland Oyster & Fish Co.	LICENCE No. 45—31st December, 1864. Ballyvaghan Harbour, County Galway. Granted to T. Young Prior. Lessee—West of Ireland Oyster & Fish Co.
1. At what time after the above date were steps taken to cultivate the bed?	Up to this I have done nothing in reference to cultivation of oysters, but hope to do so shortly; and with this object I intend applying for renewal of license granted in 1864.	1. October, 1871.	Nothing has yet been done on this bed, except that Mr. Prior has year after year taken what oysters he could get off it.
2. What was the nature of the steps taken by you then to cultivate the bed?		2. Oysters laid down and ground cleared.	
3. What quantity of oysters were put down by you, and were they small or full-grown oysters?		3. About 100,000; all sorts.	
4. Were any collectors used for catching spat; and if so, of what description?		4. No.	
5. What was the result of your first operations?		5. Nothing.	
6. What quantity of oysters were put down each year since, and were they small or full-grown oysters?		6. 250,000; all sizes.	
7. Have you ever collected spat on your bed; and if so, when and in what quantity?		7. No.	
8. What amount of oysters has been sold off your bed annually since the license granted?		8. None since I have had the beds, October, 1871.	
9. How many people are employed on your bed? At what season are they so employed, and at what work?		9. None.	
10. What is the stock of oysters and oyster spat at present on your bed, as near as you can calculate?		10. Cannot tell; perhaps half a million.	
11. Was the spatting this year good?		11. No.	
12. If your undertaking has not proved satisfactory, to what cause do you attribute its non-success?		12. —	
13. Any general observations or statements you wish to make.		13. —	

QUERIES ISSUED.	LICENCE No. 50—25th April, 1865. Sligo Bay, County Sligo. Granted to Right Hon. John Wynne.	LICENCE No. 51—29th May, 1865. Dingle Harbour, County Kerry. Granted to Lord Baron Ventry.	LICENCE No. 52—2nd November, 1865. Clew Bay, County Mayo. Granted to Law Life Association.
1. At what time after the above date were steps taken to cultivate the bed?	This license withdrawn, and a new license, with altered boundaries, issued to Owen Wynne (See No. 106).	1. No steps have been taken to cultivate the bed.	I have to apologize for not answering your letters referred to in yours of the 3rd [illegible]. In reference to same, I beg leave to inform you, for the information of the Commissioners, that the Law Life Society did not consider it prudent to go to any expense in making an oyster bed on Licence No. 52, owing to the limited extent of ground granted by the Commissioners in 1865. At the inquiry I was led to suppose a much greater area would have been given under the license, when, no doubt, it would have been well worth an outlay to make a good oyster bed, but nothing been done it was hopeless to think anything could be done.
2. What was the nature of the steps taken by you then to cultivate the bed?		2. —	
3. What quantity of oysters were put down by you, and were they small or full-grown oysters?		3. —	
4. Were any collectors used for catching spat; and if so, of what description?		4. —	
5. What was the result of your first operations?		5. —	
6. What quantity of oysters were put down each year since, and were they small or full-grown oysters?		6. —	
7. Have you ever collected spat on your bed; and if so, when and in what quantity?		7. —	
8. What amount of oysters has been sold off your bed annually since the license granted?		8. —	
9. How many people are employed on your bed? At what season are they so employed, and at what work?		9. —	
10. What is the stock of oysters and oyster spat at present on your bed, as near as you can calculate?		10. —	
11. Was the spatting this year good?		11. —	
12. If your undertaking has not proved satisfactory, to what cause do you attribute its non-success?		12. The site proposed for bed on further investigation proved unsuitable, as requiring too large an outlay. The bottom consists of soft sandy mud, covered, for the most part, with a rank growth of sea-weeds.	
13. Any general observations or statements you wish to make.		13. It would, in my opinion, be much easier to form a bed to the east of the site included in the license, as there the character of the bottom is more suitable, and there are already a few oysters on the ground.	

FISHERIES.

from Owners, Occupiers, or Lessees of Oyster Beds—*continued.*

Licence No 46—31 Dec., 1864. Ballyvaghan and [illegible] Bays, Co Galway. Granted to F. M'Namara. Lessee—West of Ireland Oyster and Fish Company.	Licence No 47—31st December, 1864. Killala Bay, County Mayo. Granted to Colonel Sir F. A. Knox Gore, Bart.	Licence No. 48—19 April, 1865. Clew Bay, County Mayo. Granted to the Most Hon. Marquess of Sligo. Lessee—Lord John Browne.	Licence No. 49—19th April, 1865. Drumcliffe Bay, County Sligo. Granted to Sir Robert Gore Booth, Bart.
1. October, 1871. 2. Laying down oysters and clearing bed. 3. One million; large and small. 4. Chalk from Isle of Wight, in lumps, and tiles coated with cement. 5. Nothing. 6. None. 7. No. 8. This year 148,000. 9. Sometimes 10. Summer and spring. 10. A million. 11. No. 12. Bad year. 13. —	1. The following season. 2. Agents were employed to collect and buy brood oysters wherever obtainable. These were laid down on those parts of the bed which apparently were suitable, after the places had been carefully examined and cleaned. 3. All I could obtain was, as well as I now remember, about £30 worth, in several cart-loads and one boat-load; all being size-sized brood oysters. 4. Yes, pieces of tiles, clean shells, and stones as large as a man's hand. 5. The oysters grew and fattened well in some spots, and in others completely failed. 6. From £10 to £15 worth. This season I have been unable to obtain brood from the sources I previously drew from, viz.—Blacksod and Clew Bay. 7. No. 8. None, having a large home consumption otherwise, and the parts of the beds suitable for oysters very limited in extent. 9. The caretaker and his family are always employed—others at intervals, as found requisite, from a couple to a crew upon it—chiefly dredging for use or for the purpose of examining, separating, and relaying first brood, and cleansing beds from weed and noxious fish, &c. 10. Difficult to estimate, as the water is deep; but on those spots where the oysters thrive, a fair quantity. 11. Good, as far as my observation goes. 12. The beds would be more prosperous but for the following reasons:—1st, a great portion of the beds appear quite unsuitable for oyster culture, owing to unforeseen causes, such as shifting sand and mineral exudations, which in places destroy all shell fish; 2nd, depth of water, which makes it difficult to be cultivated for oysters, and sweeps away by a very strong current a vast proportion of the spat shed; 3rd, extreme difficulty in obtaining brood oysters, and its cost. 13. My experience goes to say that the bed, where suitable, is excellent for rearing oysters of excellent flavour, but quite unsuitable for a breeding ground.	This ground was leased to Leonard Wray, Esq., of Eagle House, Ramsgate. He was bound to clean, plant, buoy, and preserve it, but he has entirely neglected to do so. The ground has been virtually abandoned by him.	1. The May following (1866). 2. Employed thirty men for quarrying, breaking, carting, and boating stones to form bed, which were planted between 19th April, 1865, and May, 1866. 3. 180,000 small oysters. 4. None. 5. Prosperous. 6. At an average of 150,000 per year. 7. Removed no spat from beds. 8. In the year 1867, sold 180,000; in 1869, 170,000; in 1870, 141,000; in 1871, 142,000; in 1872, 132,000. 9. Fifteen men employed throughout the year, dredging in winter and making bed in summer. 10. As near as can be calculated, 2,000,000. 11. Very good. 12. Satisfactory. 13. I should have preferred to have waited another year before I sent a report upon the state of my oyster beds, for it is impossible to give an exact account of the new one, as large quantities of small and 3-year-old oysters during the dredging season have been placed on the new bed out of the boats, and as the two beds lie together and are dredged together, it would be impossible to keep the numbers separate. I have imported large quantities of fine young oysters and they have done well, and the quantity of spat this season is so very great, I have not been able to dredge any oysters on either bed—not even for use of my house—even small oysters having 5 to 6 spat on them. On the whole I think I can give a favourable report; but in this bay we have an increase of sand, which possibly may overwhelm all our oysters—18 to 10 feet increase in many places. Before 1867 many acres of the new bed were quite overwhelmed, and the channel sent far to the northward. In fact, the only place where the oysters can live is in the channel. We had 4 or 5 acres planted with stones to prevent the oysters moving away, and many thousands doing well; one night a frost at low spring tide killed them all. This portion of the bed north of channel has too much sand on it to think of replanting it, the sand must ever prevent the use of walls or fences to keep up the water at low tide, but the new bed is perfectly stocked, having been just formed with broken stones as far as the deep water reaches; and my manager, who has given me the returns, states that he considers the bed doing well and ought next season to be very productive, far more so the following season.

Licence No 71—2nd November, 1865. Clew Bay, County Mayo. Granted to the Most Hon. Marquess of Sligo.	Licence No 64—1st December, 1865. Sherwood Achill Island, County Mayo. Granted to Most Rev. J. M'Hale, D.D.	Licence No. 65—1st December, 1865. Roaringwater Bay, County Cork. Granted to Thomas M'Carthy Collins.	Licence No. 66—1st December, 1865. Clew Bay, County Mayo. Granted to the Most Hon. Marquess of Sligo. Lessee—Lord John Browne.
This piece of ground was leased to Messrs. Baxter and Co., (county Kent,) who cleaned and planted it immediately with a very large quantity of oysters. Mr. Barry (Fishery Inspector), when on a similar inquiry at Westport less than a year afterwards, took evidence in writing on this point, and the result of his inquiry was, that the Board of Works, by letter dated January 16, 1866, certified that the ground had been properly planted, buoyed, and marked in due time. Unless I am much mistaken, Mr. Barry also took a boat and examined the ground personally, but I am not sure of this. Messrs. Baxter (large London oyster merchants) purchase every year any quantity of oysters they can get in and near Clew Bay. These oysters are placed on this bed immediately. The best of these are taken to England early in the spring. The smallest and poorest are left on the bed for the following year. I cannot give details, but have no doubt that the undertaking is successful. The men employed on the bed are also engaged in other places. I understand that the oyster spat frequently to some extent every year in Clew Bay. I believe that no tiles or artificial collectors have been used.	1. Early in February, 1866. 2. Chains were purchased and buoys were laid down to mark the boundaries of the bed, while the firm portions of the bed were seen to be cleared for laying down oysters. 3. About 2,250 stones of full-grown oysters. 4. Shells strewn on the bed, and a long sedgy grass to the north of the bed, were the collectors used. 5. At the close of September, 1866, I found the oyster laid down in February to grow a rich, fat, and well-flavoured oyster. 6. The quantity was variable, and generally small-grown oysters. 7. Yes, in July and August and other months of the year, in fair quantity. 8. None. 9. One family constantly employed in watching the bed, in having the weed cut off it, and seeing to the securing of the spat. 10. 12,880 stones. 11. Yes. 12. It has been highly satisfactory, and the bed being a natural one, and having a first-class position, is of itself very prolific, and well calculated to supply a superior oyster. 13. The Commissioners should see that the Government authorities keep poachers off the beds at night.	No replies received.	This piece of ground was leased to Messrs. Dalmon and Co., (county of Kent,) who were bound to clean, plant, and buoy it. They did so, but it was found unsuitable for the purpose; the oysters did not breed, but died on it. Believing that they made a very fair effort to carry out their engagements, the lessee thereupon released them from the lease, the buoys were taken up, and the ground abandoned.

OYSTER

APPENDIX No. 28.—ABSTRACT of Replies to Queries received

Questions Issued.	Licence No. 27—1st December, 1858. Carlingford Lough, County Louth. Granted to John Obins Woodhouse.	Licence No. 16—1st December, 1868. Ballinakill Harbour, County Galway. Granted to Captain Ashworth.	Licence No. 28—1st December, 1868. Ballysadare Bay, County Sligo. Granted to E. J. Verschoyle.
1. At what time after the above date were steps taken to cultivate the bed?		1. In 1866 and 1867.	1. In 1868. Did not commence sooner because it was so uncertain that my property in oysters would be secured by the law.
2. What was the nature of the steps taken by you then to cultivate the bed?		2. From the nature of the coast where the bed was made, I could do no more than lay down the oysters, large and small, when the tide was out, in the interstices of the rocks and rocky bed.	2. Put out stones expecting to catch spat, but failed; also put out gravel on sandy places to make a firm bottom.
3. What quantity of oysters were put down by you, and were they small or full-grown oysters?		3. The ground for which the licence was granted is very small, and only on a part of it could oysters be laid, and the quantity put down was in proportion to the ground.	3. In the year ending May, 1869, put out 42,900, principally three-year old oysters. See No 6.
4. Were any collectors used for catching spat; and if so, of what description?		4. Collectors on this particular ground would be useless unless fixed in a permanent and solid way to the rock, owing to the violence of the tides at certain times.	4. Stones only.
5. What was the result of your first operations?		5. I could not ascertain.	5. No spat on stones; but where gravel had been thrown the ground much improved, and in consequence less loss of oysters.
6. What quantity of oysters were put down each year since, and were they small or full-grown oysters?		6. No oysters were put down since the year I mentioned, when both small and full-grown oysters were put down.	6. Year ending May, 1869, 46,896; 1870, 98,400; 1871, 224,360; 1872, 361,628—different sizes.
7. Have you ever collected spat on your bed; and if so, when and in what quantity?	This bed is included in that granted by Licence of 5th June, 1868.—See No. 59.	7. No.	7. In 1871 I tried a few collectors made of hurdles, with oyster shells placed on top, and got some spat on both hurdles and shells.
8. What amount of oysters has been sold off your bed annually since the licence granted?		8. None, but I believe the oysters are found by the country people and taken off the bed.	8. Year ending May, 1870, 41,720; 1871, 33,396; 1872, 64,640.
9. How many people are employed on your bed? At what season are they so employed, and at what work?		9. None at present.	9. Two watchmen constantly; four men picking for three or four days each spring, and sorting oysters for market.
10. What is the stock of oysters and oyster spat at present on your bed, as near as you can calculate?		10. I do not know.	10. About 600,000, exclusive of some brought from breeding pond for trial and not yet counted against this bed. See No 13.
11. Was the spatting this year good?		11. I do not know.	11. I have not seen any on my bed, but am informed there was spat on the public bed adjoining.
12. If your undertaking has not proved satisfactory, to what cause do you attribute its non-success?		12. My absence from home, attending to a fishery case, which has extended over six years and prevented my giving that attention which I otherwise would have done to oyster culture under the above Section.	12. Tolerably satisfactory so far, but would be much more so if I was sure my oysters would not be stolen unless watched.
13. Any general observations or statements you wish to make.		13. —	13. In No. 10 I have referred to breeding ponds. The stock in them is hard to estimate, but perhaps 546,000 would not be excessive for this year's crop.

Questions Issued.	Licence No. 64—21st April, 1869. Blacksod Bay, County Mayo. Granted to Miss Anne Fowler. Lessee—James Gallagher.	Licence No. 59—5th June 1868. Carlingford Lough, County Louth. Granted to J. O. Woodhouse.	Licence No. 52—25th June, 1867. Drumcliffe Bay, County Sligo. Granted to Sir Robert Gore Booth, Bart.
1. At what time after the above date were steps taken to cultivate the bed?	1. In the year 1867.	1. The following September.	1. December, 1866 up to end of April, 1867, recommencing in December, 1867.
2. What was the nature of the steps taken by you then to cultivate the bed?	2. To dredge oysters and replant same on the bed.	2. After preliminary marking and buoying, a large part of the bed was hollowed out, enclosed with sea walls and fitted with a sluice, in order the better to preserve the oysters and to have access to them at any time by letting off the water.	2. Cleaning the bed for the purpose of planting.
3. What quantity of oysters were put down by you, and were they small or full-grown oysters?	3. About 700,000, both in size large and small.	3. About 4,000, including three sizes, the larger number were full-grown.	3. About 1,100,000 small, and about 2,065,000 large.
4. Were any collectors used for catching spat, and if so, of what description?	4. None.	4. Yes, square beds of large stones.	4. No.
5. What was the result of your first operations?	5. Very good.	5. Favourable.	5. —
6. What quantity of oysters were put down each year since, and were they small or full-grown oysters?	6. About 902,000 oysters, in size large and small.	6. In the second year (1867) a much lead of full-grown oysters; in the third and following years the number varied. Average about 30,000, per annum, half-grown.	6. The oysters I have planted were put down in 1867, 1868, and 1870.
7. Have you ever collected spat on your bed; and if so, when and in what quantity?	7. None.	7. The spat was never gathered from the collectors.	7. The oysters did not spat until this year.
8. What amount of oysters has been sold off your bed annually since the licence granted?	8. About 130 barrels.	8. About 60,000.	8. About 80,000 in 1870 and 1871, and about 100,000 in 1872.
9. How many people are employed on your bed? At what season are they so employed, and at what work?	9. Thirty to Fifty in March and during the springtime of the year, dredging and cleaning oysters.	9. Four men constantly employed, sometimes during the season thirty men. Turning the oysters; cleaning the beds.	9. About twenty between September and May, dredging, carting, &c.
10. What is the stock of oysters and oyster spat at present on your bed, as near as you can calculate?	10. About 200,000 oysters.	10. The stock at present has not been calculated, but is small.	10. Cannot say.
11. Was the spatting this year good?	11. Bad.	11. Yes.	11. Yes.
12. If your undertaking has not proved satisfactory, to what cause do you attribute its non-success?	12. The public beds being over dredged by day and night.	12. The undertaking has been satisfactory.	12. So far it has been successful.
13. Any general observations or statements you wish to make.	13. Several strangers coming into the bay, lifting the oysters large and small.	13. —	13. I fear I have been seriously robbed by poachers, and this is the only unsatisfactory statement I can make.

FISHERIES.

from Owners, Occupiers, or Lessees of Oyster Beds—*continued.*

Licence No 60—1st December, 1866. Kenmare Estuary, County Kerry. Granted to Richard Mahony.	Licence No 61—1st December, 1866. Killary Harbour, County Galway. Granted to Robert M'Keown.	Licence No. 62—28th April, 1868. Wexford Harbour. Granted to William Dargan.	Licence No 63—28th April, 1868. Clew Bay, County Mayo. Granted to Most Hon. the Marquess of Sligo. Lessee—Lord John Browne.
1 The spring of 1867.	1. November, 1871.		
2 Clearing the bed and planting oysters.	2. Clearing the beds by dredging.		
3 About 20,000, about 2½ to 3 inch oysters, some smaller.	3. About 20,000, both small and full-grown.		
4 No collectors used, except shells which were strown over the bed.	4. Small branches were used, bound together by wires and anchored down with stones.		
5 Could not observe much spat.	5. —		
6 About 5,000 small, have not put in any last three years, very difficult to get small oysters at anything like a reasonable price.	6. —		
7 No. I have not dredged it last two years, I have observed some spat.	7. —	In consequence of the prolonged absence of Mr Wray, I am instructed by his family to inform you that he gave up, many years ago, the oyster fisheries to which you allude, and has had nothing—had nothing whatever to do with such matters for several years past.	This ground was leased to Leonard Wray, Esq., of Eagle House, Ramsgate. He was bound to clean, plant, buoy, and preserve it, but he has entirely neglected it, and it is not in any way now preserved.
8 I have sold altogether about 11,000.	8. None, only what has been used in the hotel.		
9 I had four men occasionally in autumn and winter cleaning the bed.	9. Four persons from March till July, dredging.		
10 I would say about 40,000 to 50,000.	10. 10,000.		
11 No.	11 Considered fair, but very late.		
12 There is only a small part of the licensed shore available for growing oysters, the rest is rock and mud. I attribute the want of better success to the scarcity of spat and the difficulty to get small oysters at a fair rate.	12. —		
13 —	13. —		

Licence No 67—10th July, 1867. Scull Harbour, County Cork. Granted to Horatio Hamilton Townsend.	Licence No 68—10th July, 1867. River Shannon, County Kerry. Granted to Thomas Sandes.	Licence No 69—10th July, 1867. Blacksod Bay, County Mayo. Granted to Mrs Elizabeth Atkinson. Lessee Capt. M. W. Davis.	Licence No. 70—10th July, 1867. Roaringwater Bay, County Cork. Granted to M. J. C. Longfield.
I have been unable to carry out the intention of laying down the beds, as the gentleman (Mr. Wray), on whose behalf I may say I obtained the license, left the neighbourhood immediately almost afterwards, and did not, therefore, carry out his agreement as to laying down the beds, and I have since then been unable to get anyone willing to do so. I should be most happy to give assistance to any person wishing to lay them down, and any right I may have for almost a nominal consideration, as I should very much like to see them established, but could not undertake doing so myself, as I know nothing about the business.	No steps have been taken to cultivate the bed.	1 In March, 1872. 2 Clean the bed by dredging, and planting oysters. 3. About 1,600 oysters, large and small, principally the latter. 4 No 5 Satisfactory 6. A sub-lease of this bed was given for five years from 1872. I am therefore unable to state what has been done. 7. Not any collected. 8. I let this bed in the year 1871. I cannot say what quantity of oysters were taken off it. This was the only year it was dredged since I became lessee. 9. One man employed yearly to protect the bed. 10. See observations and statements, query No 6. 11. See observations and statements, query No. 6. 12. — 13. This bed being covered at lowest spring-tides, and in the most shallow parts, with from one and a-half to two feet of water, it is difficult to ascertain with any amount of certainty the results of your operations. On the best parts of the bed very strong tides run, which I should think would prove fatal to the collection of spat in any quantities. From the few opportunities I have had of judging, I fancy this ground is more adapted for fattening than for breeding purposes, the oysters I have seen that were taken off it were in fine condition and first-rate quality. I would strongly recommend to the favourable consideration of the Commissioners, private enterprise in oyster culture as being one of the best means of increasing our supply of these bivalves. From personal observation, I have remarked the law for prohibiting the sale of undersized oysters to be a dead letter. On the public beds on the west coast of Ireland—Blacksod Bay—there is a total disregard as to the size of the oysters taken, they are sent off from an oyster eight inches in diameter, to a spat not larger than a threepenny piece. The poor hard-working dredger does not see at present the harm he is doing himself and the public by this wholesale destruction, therefore the Government should step in for the public and his (the dredger's) good, and prevent dredging on beds that are now nearly cleared out, say from one to three years, according to the evidence, inquiries made, and from personal inspection of the Commissioners themselves.	The person who had agreed to become tenant for the oyster layings at Long Island has declined to go on with his engagement, and I do not think it advisable to attempt to enforce it.

OYSTER

APPENDIX No. 28.—ABSTRACT of Replies to Queries received

Questions Issued.	Licence No. 71—13th July, 1867. Saleen Harbour, County Mayo. Granted to John Townsend Kirkwood. Lessee—James Gallagher.	Licence No. 73—16th July, 1867. Howth Sound, County Dublin. Granted to Richard D. Kane.	Licence No. 75—20th July, 1867. Galway Bay, County Galway. Granted to William and J. St. George.
1. At what time after the above date were steps taken to cultivate the bed?	1. Immediately.	1. I cannot now state the exact time, but as soon as I was able to get young oysters.	
2. What was the nature of the steps taken by you then to cultivate the bed?	2. Had the bed properly buoyed, and then collected all small oysters on the outskirts of the bed and placed them	2. I got young oysters from different places and put them on the bed.	
3. What quantity of oysters were put down by you, and were they small or full grown oysters?	3. None.	3. Several thousand, but chiefly small young oysters.	
4. Were any collectors used for catching spat, and if so, of what description?	4. No.	4. Yes, I put down several long posts and fenced the bed with stones.	
5. What was the result of your first operations?	5. Good.	5. I found that the tide and storm carried off a large quantity of the oysters I put down.	
6. What quantity of oysters were put down each year since, and were they small or full-grown oysters?	6. None	6. I cannot state the exact quantity. I have put down several thousand young oysters from Clare and Arklow every year	
7. Have you ever collected spat on your bed, and if so, when and in what quantity?	7. No	7. I cannot say that I have; but I frequently see young oysters on the beds and near them.	
8. What amount of oysters has been sold off your bed annually since the license granted?	8. Very few oysters were sold off the bed (which is a small one) until 1870, when it was then leased for twenty-one years to a Mr James Gallagher, for £20 a year, which I consider a very good rent, as we never got £5 worth of oysters off it.	8. I have never sold any	Licence revoked by order, dated 19th January, 1871.
9. How many people are employed on your bed? At what season are they so employed, and at what work?	9. —	9. From eight to twelve people are employed in the summer time cleaning the beds and collecting the oysters that have been scattered by the tide.	
10. What is the stock of oysters and oyster spat at present on your bed, as near as you can calculate?	10. I believe good.	10. I cannot now state the exact quantity, as the weather is too severe to go near the bed.	
11. Was the spatting this year good?	11. Yes.	11. Very bad.	
12. If your undertaking has not proved satisfactory, to what cause do you attribute its non-success?	12. —	12. I attribute the want of success to the strength of the current along the estuary, which carries the spat and oysters to sea, and the difficulty of putting down collectors, owing to the rocky foundation of the place.	
13. Any general observations or statements you wish to make.	13. —	13. —	

Questions Issued.	Licence No. 78—13th July, 1867. River Shannon, County Kerry. Granted to Stephen E. Collis.	Licence No. 79—15th July, 1867. Roaringwater Bay, County Cork. Granted to Thomas Hicks.
1. At what time after the above date were steps taken to cultivate the bed?	1. Immediately after the license was granted.	1. I believe in the course of ensuing autumn.
2. What was the nature of the steps taken by you then to cultivate the bed?	2. Buoys were fixed defining the limits of the grant. A slated house for the caretaker was commenced and finished adjoining the shore or strand, in which he has since resided, to protect the place from trespassers.	2. Laying down some oysters in eligible places.
3. What quantity of oysters were put down by you, and were they small or full-grown oysters?	3. One hundred thousand oysters were purchased in Arklow, brought thence by train, &c., and laid on the beds in the early part of 1869; the average size of these oysters was two inches. One hundred thousand more of small oysters were purchased from different beds in the Shannon and laid down during 1869 and 1870, and in 1871 50,000 more were planted	3. In the first year from time of granting license, dated 15th July, 1867, to 14th July, 1868, I put down all the oysters I could obtain—some by purchase, others as presents from friends, but the numbers were not recorded, as I was not then aware I should have to make a return of them.
4. Were any collectors used for catching spat, and if so, of what description?	4. Hurdles were put down in June, 1869, but whether they have been successful or not in catching spat it is difficult to say. It is believed, from the partial dredging made this present season, that the stock of oysters has increased. I believe a good deal of spat has flowed from my beds to those of Mr Charles Lawlor, of Carrig	4. Yes, several thousands. They were of slate about the size and thickness of tiles. I have also laid down a quantity of oyster-shells.
5. What was the result of your first operations?	5. —	5. I left all the oysters undisturbed, to breed, but I did not observe any spat floating on the surface
6. What quantity of oysters were put down each year since, and were they small or full-grown oysters?	6. Since 1871 no oysters have been laid. The quantity (250,000) already put having been placed on old beds of great repute, although almost worn out, it is believed will be sufficient to restock the beds, which have been carefully preserved since the license was granted.	6. In second year—from 14th July, 1868, to 15th July, 1869—I put down over 11,000 oysters, some hundreds being large or adult oysters for immediate breeding, and the remainder, I believe, about two years old. I also put down this year a boat-load of oyster-shells, with some spat on and amongst them. In the third year—to 14th July, 1870—I put down 2,772, two years old. Lastly, in 1871 I laid down 408 oysters, some adults or half-grown, and some two years old.
7. Have you ever collected spat on your bed, and if so, when and in what quantity?	7. No.	7. None collected.
8. What amount of oysters has been sold off your bed annually since the license granted?	8. None.	8. Not one, as I wished them to breed.
9. How many people are employed on your bed? At what season are they so employed, and at what work?	9. The caretaker, permanently. Other hands have from time to time been employed, as required, putting down buoys, forming new bed, clearing sea-weed, &c.	9. I have three boatmen and a boat. I have employed them to lay down the oysters, to dredge over beds to see how the bottom was as to weeds, also to dredge in the summer, to drive away the star-fish, or five-fingers, as commonly called; also to put down and remove the buoys for tarring and painting, and in replacing them
10. What is the stock of oysters and oyster spat at present on your bed, as near as you can calculate?	10. Cannot say.	10. The water being for the most part deep, I cannot say.
11. Was the spatting this year good?	11. Cannot say.	11. Being absent at the time, I cannot say; but I fear not.
12. If your undertaking has not proved satisfactory, to what cause do you attribute its non-success?	12. Hitherto it has only involved outlay; but there is fair reason to hope the adventure will prove successful in a moderate degree. The coast is exposed, and we often experience very severe gales and wild weather, which brings in enormous quantities of sea-weed.	12. Should it not eventually do so, I should attribute it to the wildness of this coast interfering with the spatting, and to the five fingers, which unfortunately abound, and, possibly, to some incompatibility of the ground.
13. Any general observations or statements you wish to make.	13. Any advice the Commissioners can give—especially as to the retention of the spat on the beds, which appears to be the greatest difficulty the lessee has to contend with—will be thankfully received.	13. I would have put down more of late had it not been for the Divisions named in Survey of Licences, 1871 (No.), and the almost impossibility of getting oysters for the purpose during last two years, from scarcity and dearness

FISHERIES.

from Owners, Occupiers, or Lessees of Oyster Beds—*continued.*

Licence No. 74—30th July, 1867. Galway Bay, County Galway. Granted to Christopher T. Redington.	Licence No. 75—30th July, 1867. Lough Mahon, County Cork. Granted to Mrs. Elizabeth Bury.	Licence No. 76—10th July, 1867. Trawbreaga Bay, County Donegal. Granted to Rev. Nicholas Martin.	Licence No. 77—19th July, 1867. Midleton River, County Cork. Granted to John Smyth.
1. Immediately. 2. The sea-weed was removed from the bed, which was thus cleared and prepared for the oysters. 3. About 100,000 medium-sized oysters were put down. 4. No. 5. — 6. — 7. No; we prefer leaving it there. 8. Twenty-four thousand annually. 9. About six men are continually employed clearing the bed of sea-wrack driven in after the winter storms in large quantities. The dredging is done in December and January. 10. The stock has not diminished since it was put out; but the exact amount is not known. 11. Not so good as last year. 12. The undertaking has proved satisfactory, but entails a good deal of trouble throughout the winter, owing to the storms driving in the sea-wrack. 13. —	1. Immediately. 2. Brought oysters chiefly from county Kerry. 3. About £400 worth. Large and small. 4. No. 5. A good amount of spat. 6. Annually about £10 worth. Chiefly large. 7. No. 8. Hardly any; have used them for my own consumption, but wished to give the bed time to improve. 9. Two always, assisted at times by labourers from the estate. 10. I can hardly say, the bed has been so robbed. One night alone about £36 worth were taken. 11. Yes. 12. To repeated poaching; poachers coming in such force it is almost impossible to capture or identify them. Sometimes they are armed, and always carry large stones for aggressive purposes. 13. Without the aid of a gun boat or coastguard station, I fear it is impossible to stop the poaching.	I have never had anything to do with the oyster beds constructed by the Rev. Mr. Martin, and I am aware there is not a trace remaining of them for some time past. Should you wish to communicate with the Rev. Mr. Martin, his address is Belmont, Ontario, Canada.	1. Immediately. 2. Oysters were purchased and laid down when the foreshore was cleared of stones and rocks. 3. About 200,000 were laid by my father. In point of size those put down were about two inches in diameter, with about 2,000 full-grown oysters. 4. A few tiles only. 5. A small take of spat, the greater part of which dies off again. 6. Few oysters were laid since the first year, on an average about 10,000 each year, small size. 7. No, but see it on large oysters, shells, &c., but in small quantity. 8. Not more than 10,000 per annum, that only for the last three years. 9. Three; one watchman and two men dredging for the bed. That being a shore laying, nothing can be done except at low tides, when they are employed clearing the ground of weeds, and placing down oysters that have been thrown up by the sea. 10. Would not put them down at more than 120,000, as quantities were destroyed through having been placed too high on the strand. 11. I count it bad, having seen very little spat this year. 12. The bed was not, in my opinion, properly managed. The oysters were too high on the strand, consequently too long exposed to the action of either sun or frost, so that they did not grow or thrive as they should have done. 13. —

Licence No. 80—18th July, 1867. River Shannon, Co. Clare. Granted to Robt. W. C. Reeves.	Licence No. 81—26th July, 1867. Bertraghboy Bay, County Galway. Granted to Francis J. Graham. Lessees—West of Ireland Oyster and Fish Company.	Licence No. 85—31st January, 1868. Lough Swilly, County Donegal. Granted to William Hart.
1. In 1868. 2. I put oysters in beds on the French principle of claires, and they fattened very well and grew fine. 3. About 800, they were not quite full-grown. 4. No, but the spat grew on all the stones. 5. — 6. — 7. — 8. — 9. — 10. — 11. — 12. — 13. In order to make this bed as it ought to be I must bring out a small river at a higher level. This I am doing, but it is a very heavy job.	1. By West of Ireland Oyster and Fish Company (Limited), in October, 1871. 2. Ground cleaned and oysters laid. 3. Five hundred thousand large oysters. 4. Lumps of chalk, tiles coated with rough cement. 5. Nil. 6. — 7. None. 8. Since October, 1871, 72,080. 9. Twenty or thirty all the year, except March and April, when they will not work, and July and August, when the beds are left quiet. 10. About 200,000. 11. No. 12. Season very wet sends a great deal of cold fresh water into the land-locked bays; perhaps, too, the oysters do not spat till acclimatised to the new beds. 13. —	1 and 2. Immediately on receipt of the licence I employed men to clean the portions of the foreshore best suited for occupation, and commenced the construction of small tanks or ponds within the range of neap tides, and of a larger pond of about two acres, cut off from the sea by a railway embankment, a culvert through which enables me to regulate the supply of water to the pond, so as to use it either for breeding—on the plan which has in several years proved very successful in the beds of the South of England Oyster Company—or as a fattening bed. The ponds were not completed until June, 1869, but during March and April, 1868, I laid down on the cleared parts of the foreshores several beds of oysters, in places where there was the greatest abundance of natural cultch, and about these I suspended, on stakes and cocoa-fibre cords, small faggots of twigs. 3. By the 1st of May, 1868, I had laid down about 77,000 full-grown oysters, and about 208,800 small oysters, spatted in 1866. 4 and 5. The first artificial collectors tried by me were small faggots, or rather bunches of twigs, principally birch, beech, and whitethorn. I did not find them answer, as on the foreshore they gathered masses of drift-weed, and seemed likely to afford shelter to sea-urchins and other vermin, and no oyster-spat settled on them, but I obtained on the natural shell cultch a small crop of spat, from two beds of about 10,000 oysters imported from Sligo. There was also a slight fall of spat on other parts of the shore. The young oysters laid down grew very fast during the summer of 1868, forming remarkably fine shell—as I have since found to be the case with all the young oysters that I have laid upon my ground. 6. The following is a statement of the number of oysters laid down by me in each year since I commenced operations:—In 1868, mixed, 1,468,060; in 1869, mixed, 690,000; in 1870, mixed, 264,000; in 1871, mixed, 71,300; in 1872, mixed, 30,100; in 1873 (to January 31), mixed, 3,166; total, 2,515,690. 7. In 1868 there was a small fall of spat on two of the beds. In 1869 a large proportion of oysters spawned; but the fall was not much greater. In 1870 spat appeared at greater distances from the layings, but the fall was very scanty in proportion to the number of oysters apparently in spawn. In 1871 I obtained an encouraging fall of spat—some on the foreshore, but the largest and of most rapid growth in the pond inside of the railway embankment, which had previously shown remarkable fattening properties, but had failed to secure a fall of spat. The collectors which were most successful in 1871, were slates laid on wire netting frames. In 1872, my health was not such that I could personally examine the beds, but I believe that if there was any fall of spat it must have been an insignificant one. 8. The following is a statement showing the number of oysters sold by me in each year since commencing operations:—In 1868, none; in 1869, 63,800; in 1870, 218,800; in 1871, 178,500; in 1872, 164,800; in 1873 (until 31st January), 15,000; total, 640,300. 9. I employ regularly at present an overseer and five men, who have to watch and work on the beds, to keep the ponds in repair, and the banks, &c., in order. They have also to aid and direct extra hands employed during the ebbs of spring tides. These are women and boys (paid by tide work), who have to clean the beds when requisite, and keep the oysters laid on them in order; to lift and sort oysters for the market; to separate the small ones and relay them on the beds, &c. 10. My reply to this question must be of a conjectural nature. If the loss by casualties be taken to be equal to the amount sold off the beds, the number of oysters remaining of those laid down by me would be about 1,231,228. I can make no reasonable guess as regards increase by spat on the ground, and should not be inclined to take it into consideration. It would probably raise the total to above a million and a quarter. 11. I believe the spatting of the year 1872 to have been very scanty. 12. I undertook my operations in oyster culture solely with the view of establishing breeding beds, the success of which, in such a position as that of my licensed oyster ground, must altogether depend on the occurrence of a general spat on this coast. Such spats are said to occur, on an average, about every seventh year, and the last two occurred in 1848 and 1858.

OYSTER

APPENDIX No. 28.—ABSTRACT of Replies to Queries received

Queries Issued.	Licence No. 83—11th February, 1868. Middleton River, County Cork. Granted to Richard Lyons.	Licence No. 84—11th February, 1868. River Shannon, County Kerry. Granted to Charles Sandes.
1. At what time after the above date were steps taken to cultivate the bed?	1. In March, 1868.	1. Immediately.
2. What was the nature of the steps taken by you then to cultivate the bed?	2. I had a boat of my own worked by two men, and during each season kept her continually dredging and putting down the oysters; and bought a good quantity of small ones from other parties.	2. I formed out beds and laid oysters on them, also put down posts to slacken the run of the tide and cause an eddy. I also made an artificial pond and laid oysters in it, but this was a failure.
3. What quantity of oysters were put down by you, and were they small or full-grown oysters?	3. I could not exactly say, but I think from 40,000 to 50,000 middling size, and some small ones.	3. Altogether about 150,000. These oysters were of all sizes, but more small than large.
4. Were any collectors used for catching spat, and if so, of what description?	4. No, but I find a good quantity of spat on the strand.	4. I used boards and faggots, also poles, tiles, and stones.
5. What was the result of your first operations?	5. The oysters I put down first have grown to a good size, and are of excellent quality.	5. I did not find any însuccess until last year when we had a quantity of spat deposited on the stones and slates, but I cannot say to what amount.
6. What quantity of oysters were put down each year since, and were they small or full-grown oysters?	6. About 10,000 middle size.	6. I cannot say, almost all small oysters.
7. Have you ever collected spat on your bed, and if so, when and in what quantity?	7. No, I leave the spat to nature; some attach themselves to stones and grow well on them.	7. I have a man constantly looking after the bed at low water spring tides, and sometimes a good many hands employed replacing any oysters that may have been moved by storms, &c., but I cannot say how many as it is only at low water that they can work on the beds.
8. What amount of oysters has been sold off your bed annually since the licence granted?	8. The first year none, and say about £20 worth each year since.	8. I have scarcely sold any as I want to stock the bed thoroughly in the first place.
9. How many people are employed on your bed? At what season are they so employed, and at what work?	9. I have a man and his family all the year; they keep the seaweed from growing too much.	9. I cannot say.
10. What is the stock of oysters and oyster spat at present on your bed, as near as you can calculate?	10. My former answers would be the only criterion to judge by. There is a great growth in the spat, which vary in size from a fourpenny bit to half a crown.	10. I could not come yet at this, there was a large quantity of spat deposited last year, but none this season.
11. Was the spatting this year good?	11. I do not consider this was a good year; the year before last was excellent.	11. No.
12. If your undertaking has not proved satisfactory, to what cause do you attribute its non-success?	12. I consider that the oysters thrive wonderfully well on my bed.	12. I think I am too much in the fairway to catch the quantity of spat that I ought, and want of funds hinders me from doing what is required as quickly as I could wish, but it may succeed in time. This year, I think, was too cold and wet for a good spatting season. I find that they do not spat with me until very late in the season, August and September.
13. Any general observations or statements you wish to make.	13. None.	13. —

Queries Issued.	Licence No. 88—12th February, 1869. Ardgroom Harbour, County Cork. Granted to Right Hon. the Earl of Bantry.	Licence No. 89—12th February, 1869. Glengarriff Harbour, County Cork. Granted to Right Hon. the Earl of Bantry.	Licence No. 90—4th March, 1869. Ard Bay. Granted to Captain John P. Nolan.
1. At what time after the above date were steps taken to cultivate the bed?	1. Immediately.	1. Immediately.	
2. What was the nature of the steps taken by you then to cultivate the bed?	2. Collected as many oysters as possible and put them on the bed.	2. Putting down oysters.	
3. What quantity of oysters were put down by you, and were they small or full-grown oysters?	3. Good sized oysters, but cannot say what quantity.	3. From 54,000 to 60,000; many of them large oysters. All the oysters that could be got were put into the beds.	
4. Were any collectors used for catching spat, and if so, of what description?	4. No.	4. A quantity of empty oyster-shells were thrown on the beds.	
5. What was the result of your first operations?	5. None as yet.	5. There appears to be a number of small oysters on the beds, but the continued floods this year have destroyed quantities of the oysters, and makes it very difficult to ascertain the state of the beds. There is no doubt Glengarriff Harbour is good breeding ground.	
6. What quantity of oysters were put down each year since, and were they small or full-grown oysters?	6. None put down since, they are not to be got.	6. From 10,000 to 15,000 one year.	Owing to the election petition and prosecutions, Captain Nolan and I have been unable to procure oysters for stocking the beds laid out at [illegible] [illegible]. The agent for the Law Life refused to sell us any, and it would have required much time to get them from elsewhere. If you will extend the time so as to allow me to lay down the beds in March and April, I shall do so.
7. Have you ever collected spat on your bed, and if so, when and in what quantity?	7. No.	7. Have not taken any off these beds.	
8. What amount of oysters has been sold off your bed annually since the licence granted?	8. None.	8. None.	
9. How many people are employed on your bed? At what season are they so employed, and at what work?	9. A caretaker.	9. Merely a caretaker.	
10. What is the stock of oysters and oyster spat at present on your bed, as near as you can calculate?	10. Cannot tell.	10. Cannot tell. The weather has been such it has been impossible to make a satisfactory inspection of the beds for some time.	
11. Was the spatting this year good?	11. Cannot tell. An inspection will be made the first favourable weather and strand.	11. See No. 5.	
12. If your undertaking has not proved satisfactory, to what cause do you attribute its non-success?	12. It is too soon to expect any return, but I have no doubt the bed will be a good one.	12. I expect it will be successful.	
13. Any general observations or statements you wish to make.	13. The difficulty of getting oysters to lay down is very great; the beds in Glengarriff are the only source I can rely on for getting oysters, and I hope to stock all my beds from them by degrees.	13. —	

Fisheries

from Owners, Occupiers, or Lessees of Oyster Beds—*continued.*

Licence No 83—18th March, 1869. Dunmanus Bay, County Cork. Granted to Stephen Browne.	Licence No. 85—18th March, 1869. Ballysadare Bay, County Sligo. Granted to Colonel Edward Cooper.	Licence No. 87—12th February, 1869. Kenmare Bay. Granted to Henry Herbert.
1. In a short time after I received my license I commenced to mark out my bed with poles and buoys. Some of the owners of land in the neighbourhood opposed my doing so, in consequence there were cross-summonses to Durrus Petty Sessions Court, where judgment was given against me. I appealed to Quarter Sessions Court at Skibbereen, where the judgment of Petty Sessions Court was reversed in October, 1869. It was now too late to do anything this year.	1. At once.	1. March, 1869.
2. In June, 1869, having marked the boundaries of my bed, I laid down a small bed about one and a half feet deep, and protected it with a fence of large rough stones all round, and placed hurdles over part of it, and fascines of furze and boughs of trees over other parts of it.	2. Putting down spat and full-grown oysters.	2. Had the ground cleaned and protected.
3. In this bed I placed 1,540 large oysters for the purpose of spatting, and at Christmas, 1869, there appeared a great promise of spat both on the stones in the bed and round it, and also on the hurdles, but the rough dark stones promised most. I also laid down several thousand young oysters on other parts of the bed for the purpose of growing. In the spring of 1870 there came a great land swell, called by the people in the neighbourhood an "out-all" to which this bay is exposed, and covered all my bed with gravel, sand, and weed, and destroyed my expectation of a crop.	3. —	3. The bed being small, about 10,000 small oysters were put down.
4. I used hurdles, fascines, and large stones placed together.	4. Weir net on posts, and old shells.	4. The natural collectors are large stones and rocks with sea-weed.
5. I beg to refer to answer to question No. 3.	5. None.	5. Found that oysters did badly.
6. In 1870 I made another bed in what I consider a more protected part of the foreshore, and placed in it about 1,800 large oysters for the purpose of breeding spat, also a considerable quantity of seed oysters, but these also were covered with gravel, &c., as the former, by the swell and scour from the bay.	6. 4,000 full-grown put in a pond last year; some spat, but not as much as pay.	6. —
7. I have not—for the causes assigned—in any considerable quantity, but I gather some spat every year.	7. None.	7. Never saw any sign of spat.
8. I have not sold any.	8. None.	8. None sold or taken off.
9. Three of my tenants occupy the land adjoining my bed and look after it. I have also employed a caretaker to prevent trespass and protect the bed.	9. Two all the year.	9. —
10. I cannot give even an approximate answer to this question at present.	10. —	10. They seem to be getting less each year.
11. I cannot at present say.	11. No.	11. I hear very bad everywhere in this estuary.
12. From my experience, since I obtained my license, I would say that Dunmanus Bay, from its open and exposed nature and the swell or out-all to which it is exposed, cannot be depended on as affording promising oyster farms; and I also consider from the observations I have made that the last few years have been exceptional against the production of spat, at least in shallow waters.	12. —	12. —
13. —	13. —	13. I am afraid oysters will not do on the small bed that I have got; there is mud near, which may be the cause.

Licence No 84—17th March, 1869. Kenmare Bay, County Kerry. Granted to Richard J. Mahony.	Licence No. 82—17th March, 1869. Kenmare Bay, County Kerry. Granted to Thomas Kingston Sullivan.	Licence No. 89—18th March, 1869. Bantry Bay, County Cork. Granted to John W. Payne.	Licence 96—14th June, 1869. Killala Bay, County Mayo. Granted to John W. Broadhead.
1. April, 1869.	1. April, 1869.	Some time previous to the application for this license I had put down on portion of this bed about 120,000 oysters, small size; they grew to a fair size, and were very good, but the ground is evidently not breeding ground and they did not increase, it is also much exposed, so on the whole they have disappeared from the bed, and I fear there is not any use in my trying to cultivate it any further; however, I should like to make another small trial during the next three months if the Commissioners will allow me, and I will let them know the result.	1. In the following year a beginning was made by clearing the beach of obstructions, removing stones and sea-weed.
2. Clearing the bed, and then planting oysters.	2. Clearing the bed, and then planting oysters.		2. In the beginning of 1871 twenty-eight and a half barrels of oysters were purchased at Belmullet, and planted out on the beach.
3. 20,000 in April, 1869; about three to three and a half inches.	3. 20,000 in April, 1869, about three to three and a half inches.		3. Of the above about one-fourth were full-grown and the remaining three-fourths were small.
4. Yes; fascines were used without success. Oyster-shells were scattered over the bed.	4. Yes; fascines were used without success. Oyster-shells were scattered over the bed.		4. No.
5. Did not observe any spat on the collectors put down, but observed a good deal on the oyster-shells scattered over the bed.	5. Did not observe any spat on the collectors put down but observed a good deal on the oyster-shells scattered over the bed.		5. The oysters appeared healthy, but there was no natural increase such as to encourage a large outlay.
6. Planted in this bed in 1870, 1871, and 1872, about 130,000 oysters, and 20,000 in 1869, in all about 150,000 oysters; about two and a half inches, some more.	6. Planted in this bed in 1870, 1871, and 1872, about 130,000 oysters, and 20,000 in 1869, in all about 150,000 oysters; about two and a half inches, some more.		6. None in 1872.
7. Never collected any spat by artificial means, but the spat cast outside the bed has been dredged and planted in the bed.	7. Never collected any spat by artificial means, but the spat cast outside the bed has been dredged and planted in the bed.		7. This year the bed looked more promising, as there was a better spatting.
8. Sold altogether about 26,000.	8. Sold altogether about 26,000.		8. None.
9. Sometimes eight men clearing weeds, &c., off the bed, and dredging outside the bed and replanting.	9. Sometimes eight men clearing weeds, &c., off the bed, and dredging outside the bed and replanting.		9. A caretaker employed constantly.
10. I should say, as far as I can form an opinion, that there are about 130,000 oysters.	10. I should say, as far as I can form an opinion, that there are about 130,000 oysters.		10. About thirty-eight and a half barrels.
11. More spat this year than in previous years.	11. More spat this year than in previous years.		11. Better.
12. The undertaking promises to be very successful. The proprietors are protecting it carefully, and are annually putting in stock, and have not dredged any last two years.	12. The undertaking promises to be very successful. The proprietors are protecting it carefully, and are annually putting in stock, and have not dredged any last two years.		12. —
13. This bed and the bed granted to T. K. Sullivan, Esq., same date, are worked in partnership by Messrs. Richard Mahony and T. K. Sullivan.	13. This bed and the bed granted to Richard J. Mahony, Esq., same date, are worked in partnership by Messrs. T. K. Sullivan and Richard J. Mahony.		13. In consequence of the better appearance of the bed a quantity of additional oysters has been lately purchased and will be planted this spring.

Appendix No. 28.—Abstract of Replies to Queries received

Queries Issued.	Licence No. [illegible]—14th June, 1869. Courtmacsherry Bay. Granted to Mrs. Catherine Bourne.	Licence No. [illegible]—14th June, 1869. Killala Bay. Granted to William Little.	Licence No. [illegible]—20th September, 1869. Carlingford Lough, County Louth. Granted to Lord Clermont.
1. At what time after the above date were steps taken to cultivate the bed?		1. In spring of 1871.	1, 2, and 3. Lord Clermont having in 1866 purchased the interest in a licence granted to the late Burton Bowdon for an oyster bed in Carlingford Lough, the site of which is included in that of the licence of 1869, he began operations by engaging a competent caretaker, and employing hands to collect and settle in the most suitable places the oysters that were scattered about; and in 1867 he purchased and laid down 68,000 small oysters, with small large intermixed.
2. What was the nature of the steps taken by you then to cultivate the bed?		2. Putting down seventeen and a half barrels of oysters.	
3. What quantity of oysters were put down by you, and were they small or full-grown oysters?		3. Seventeen and a half barrels, small size.	
4. Were any collectors used for catching spat, and if so, of what description?		4. None.	4. Some large pipe-drain tiles were placed on the bed.
5. What was the result of your first operations?		5. A great disappointment.	5. The oysters were taken care of.
6. What quantity of oysters were put down each year since, and were they small or full-grown oysters?	In consequence of the death of a relative who had undertaken to establish the fishery for Mrs Bourne, no steps have been taken to cultivate what is believed to be a good shore for the purpose.	6. Have not put down any since March, 1871.	6. In 1871 there were laid down 35,000, and in 1872 11,500 small oysters.
7. Have you ever collected spat on your bed, and if so, when and in what quantity?		7. Never collected any spat.	7. No.
8. What amount of oysters has been sold off your bed annually since the licence granted?		8. Nil.	8. In 1869 sold 21,300; in 1870, 14,600; in 1871, 27,278; in 1872, 10,000.
9. How many people are employed on your bed? At what season are they so employed, and at what work?		9. Nil.	9. One caretaker, at regular weekly wages, who employs extra hands when required.
10. What is the stock of oysters and oyster spat at present on your bed, as near as you can calculate?		10. Cannot say.	10. Having laid down 114,000 oysters and sold 86,375, there ought to be between 40,000 and 50,000 on the bed, without reckoning spat.
11. Was the spatting this year good?		11. Cannot say.	11. No.
12. If your undertaking has not proved satisfactory, to what cause do you attribute its non-success?		12. To over-current.	12. Unless the oysters on this bed prove productive of spat, so as to keep up a stock without bringing oysters from other places, the undertaking is not likely to prove satisfactory as an investment of money.
13. Any general observations or statements you wish to make.		13. —	13. —

Queries Issued.	Licence No. [illegible]—22nd April, 1871. Cullenamore Strand, County Sligo. Granted to Miss Agnes Mary Nicholson.	Licence No. [illegible]—27th March, 1871. Ardgroom Harbour, County Kerry. Granted to Right Hon. the Earl of Bantry.	Licence No. [illegible]—23rd March, 1871. Berehaven, County Cork. Granted to Right Hon. the Earl of Bantry and T. J. Leahy.
1. At what time after the above date were steps taken to cultivate the bed?	1. In November, 1872, the principal improvements took place.		
2. What was the nature of the steps taken by you then to cultivate the bed?	2. By putting on small oysters purchased at Belmullet, county Mayo, to the amount of £45.		
3. What quantity of oysters were put down by you, and were they small or full-grown oysters?	3. Seventy-five thousand, mixed, small, and full-grown.		
4. Were any collectors used for catching spat; and if so, of what description?	4. There were, for gathering some washed to shore by the storm.		
5. What was the result of your first operations?	5. Not very successful.		
6. What quantity of oysters were put down each year since, and were they small or full-grown oysters?	6. Nil.		
7. Have you ever collected spat on your bed; and if so, when and in what quantity?	7. I have—any that could be picked up. Cannot say what quantity, but were very few.	Has not been able to get any oysters to lay down on this bed, but hopes that as the beds at Glengarriffe and Adrigole are now very fairly stocked, to get a supply from them.	Have not been able to get any oysters to lay down on this bed, but hope that as the beds at Glengarriffe and Adrigole are now very fairly stocked, to get a supply from them.
8. What amount of oysters has been sold off your bed annually since the licence granted?	8. On an average, for the years 1871 and 1872 there has been a profit of £22 12s.		
9. How many people are employed on your bed? At what season are they so employed, and at what work?	9. I cannot give a direct answer to this query, as I call upon my labourers at times when the tides answer in the winter and spring of the year.		
10. What is the stock of oysters and oyster spat at present on your bed, as near as you can calculate?	10. One hundred thousand in spat, including large and small, as far as I can judge.		
11. Was the spatting this year good?	11. No, and has been bad for the last ten years.		
12. If your undertaking has not proved satisfactory, to what cause do you attribute its non-success?	12. The seasons have been bad for spawning. Also the drifting sands coming on the beds occasionally.		
13. Any general observations or statements you wish to make.	13. I have put out on the bed from time to time a large quantity of stone, gravel, and shell.		

FISHERIES.

from Owners, Occupiers, or Lessees of Oyster Beds—*continued.*

Licence No. 98—16th September, 1869. Sligo Bay, County Sligo. Granted to Henry W. Meredith.

1. November, 1869.
2. Clearing the bed of stones, and paving it with cockle shells and oyster shells.
3. Seventy thousand of small oysters.
4. No.
5. Favourable.
6. About 22,000 small oysters.
7. None.
8. Two thousand five hundred.
9. Six persons, in winter, keeping the bed cleared of weeds and stones, and keeping the spat in their proper place when removed by tidal action.
10. Oysters, 190,000; oyster spat, cannot calculate.
11. Yes.
12. —
13. To enlarge the bed in the south direction, the southern limit of the present bed being the most successful.

Licence No. 99—18th September, 1869. Sligo Bay. Granted to Owen Wynne.

Have not been able to proceed with any cultivation on this bed, from different causes—Difficulty of procuring hands at the season when weather would best admit of buoying the boundaries, except at an exorbitant rate of wages, and of getting hands to clean the bed (requiring much careful handwork to remove stones and sea-weed, &c., growing on same, so as to form a tolerably smooth surface), which work can only be done with advantage after ebb of spring tides, and for but two to three hours at a time; and while the Harbour Commissioners continue to carry on their operations of depositing between the inside boundary wall of their channel and the shore (where the bed is situate,) barge-load after barge-load of sand dredged from the bed of their channel, it would be almost useless to deposit or lay young oysters, which must be destroyed by this loose sand being carried over them with the action of the tide.

Licence No. 100—18th September, 1868. Sligo Bay, County Sligo. Granted to Owen Wynne.

1. The beginning of November, 1868.
2. A number of buoys were placed at a measured distance of 200 feet northward of the channel wall, to define the part licensed between the said line of buoys and high-water mark.
3. From close observation, noted each day, we compute that from 10th December, 1868, to 20th April, 1871, we laid down 121,500 oysters, at a cost of £384 18s. 10d.
4. Not any.
5. No results were noted.
6. Answered under query No. 3. Some of the oysters measured from one and a half to two and a half inches, and a few nearly three inches in diameter.
7. Never.
8. A few hundred were selected during the spring of 1872 for private use, but were not found to be very good. In December we sold 11,968.
9. One superintendent and one watchman, who share the labour day and night, and a standing crew of five men, ready at all times when called upon.
10. At low water of ordinary spring tides, there being about three feet of water on the bed, it would be very difficult to ascertain the stock.
11. Cannot say.
12. Very well satisfied with the prospect of success, from the results of a few days' dredging.
13. —

Licence No. 104—19th March, 1870. Ballysadare Bay, County Sligo. Granted to R. J. Verschoyle.

The answers given to queries for Licence No. 99 apply also to this, as both licences now form one bed.

Licence No. 105—27th March, 1871. Roaringwater Bay, County Cork. Granted to Thomas Hicks.

1. On the 14th April, 1871.
2. I laid down some adult or full-grown oysters fit for breeding at once; also some collectors for the spat to fall on.
3. In the year from March, 1871, to 27th March, 1872, I laid down between 900 and 800 oysters, the greater part of them full-grown, for breeding.
4. Yes; they were of slate, about the size and thickness of common tiles, and many of them were coated on both sides with rough lime wash for the spat to adhere to the more firmly. I also with these collectors threw amongst them a collection of pieces of old iron of various kinds.
5. I don't know at present.
6. In the second year—counting from 27th March, 1872, up to 4th January, 1873—I have laid down 4,378, being seed or young oysters mostly apparently over two years old—a very good sort, from Cork Harbour.
7. I have not.
8. None.
9. I have three boatmen and a boat. I have employed them to lay down the oysters, and to dredge over the beds to see how the bottom was as to weeds.
10. I cannot say, as it is chiefly deep water.
11. I don't know, having been absent in the summer, but I fear it was not.
12. Should it not eventually do so, I should attribute it to the wildness of this coast, and to the five-fingers, which unfortunately abound, and, possibly, some incompatibility of the ground.
13. —

Licence No. 106—24th April, 1871. Off the lands of Moneygold, County Sligo. Granted to Edward Parke.

At the time I got my licence there were some oysters on the bed attached to rocks. I had a number of them removed and placed on the strand, but found the current so strong that it carried off the lighter ones. I am at present making embankments of stones as breakwaters. The oysters have increased considerably. There is about £40 worth, but all attached to rocks, with few exceptions. I would have purchased and put down some, but Mrs. Eccles and I had arranged to charter a vessel when she got her license, which we still purpose doing. I may add, her bed adjoins mine.

Licence No. 107—24th April, 1871. Off the lands of Moneygold, County Sligo. Granted to Martin Connors.

1. Since above date no steps taken to cultivate the bed.
2. None.
3. None.
4. None.
5. None.
6. None.
7. Yes; in May, 1871, 200.
8. None.
9. None but myself.
10. Two hundred.
11. It was not.
12. I was waiting for Mrs. Eccles and Mr. Parke till we should plant the shore in oyster beds together.
13. None.

Licence No. 108—24th April, 1871. Off the lands of Moneygold, County Sligo. Granted to Michael Connors.

1. Since above date no steps taken to cultivate the bed.
2. None.
3. None.
4. None
5. None.
6. None.
7. Yes, in May, 1871, 200.
8. None.
9. No one but myself.
10. Two hundred.
11. It was not.
12. I was waiting for Mrs. Eccles and Mr Parke till we should plant the shore in oyster beds together.
13. None.

OYSTER

APPENDIX No. 28.—ABSTRACT of Replies to Queries received

Queries Issued.	Licence No. 109.—18th July, 1871. Off the Lands of Killydonnell, Co. Donegal. Granted to Sir James Stewart, Bart.	Licence No. 1[illegible]0.—27th July, 1871. Off the lands of [illegible], Co. Donegal. Granted to Francis Mansfield.	Licence No. 1[illegible]1.—1st July, 1871. Carlingford Lough, County Louth. Granted to [illegible] Hamill, q.c.
1. At what time after the above date were steps taken to cultivate the bed?	1. Immediately.	1 & 2. Shortly after receiving the licence I wrote to various persons both in Ireland and America to try and procure oysters to plant on my beds, but could not procure any. This year I sent a special messenger to Arklow, and although a considerable quantity of oysters were taking, there was such difficulty in obtaining a smack to bring them round, that I was obliged to give up thinking of it at present.	1. I was not, until after November, 1871, able to procure brood oysters anywhere.
2. What was the nature of the steps taken by you then to cultivate the bed?	2. Laying for the purpose of planting the bed.		2. In January, 1872, I procured a quantity, I cannot say how much, from the south of Ireland, and in March or beginning of April, 1872, I got 4,000 brood oysters from an oysterman in [illegible] upon the Carlingford Lough.
3. What quantity of oysters were put down by you, and were they small or full grown oysters?	3. About 400,000, large and small.	3. 21,[illegible] The greater part small and the remainder tolerably large.	3. The total quantity of brood laid down by me might be [illegible] about [illegible] oysters, averaging in size about an inch and a half in diameter.
4. Were any collectors used for catching spat, and if so, of what description?	4. No.	4. The only collectors employed were women. If any artificial collectors are ever used, I shall be much obliged if the Inspectors will render me any information they may have on the subject.	4. I have not as yet made use of any artificial collectors.
5. What was the result of your first operations?	5. —	5. —	5. Nil.
6. What quantity of oysters were put down each year since, and were they small or full-grown oysters?	6. The whole of the oysters were planted between May and September, 1872.	6. In 1872, 19,100[illegible] were put down; in 1873, 6,200[illegible] were put down, partly small and partly large, but not to any considerable extent.	6. See my first answer.
7. Have you ever collected spat on your bed, and if so when and in what quantity?	7. None as yet.	7. No spat has been collected on my bed.	7. I am not able to speak of this as yet, as I have not had time to secure or know results.
8. What amount of oysters has been sold off your bed annually since the licence granted?	8. None as yet.	8. None.	8. None.
9. How many people are employed on your bed? At what season are they so employed, and at what work?	9. Not having yet commenced dredging, I have merely a caretaker at present.	9. Three persons have been employed in planting oysters and watching the bed.	9. None. I have a man to watch what I have put down, or rather to have a guard upon what I have put down.
10. What is the stock of oysters and oyster spat at present on your bed, as near as you can calculate?	10. I have not yet worked the bed to ascertain what quantity of spat there might be.	10. It would be impossible to tell or give any guess of what quantity of oysters or spat there may be on my bed.	10. This I cannot answer with any certainty or satisfaction.
11. Was the spatting this year good?	11. Cannot say at present.	11. Very remarkably good.	11. —
12. If your undertaking has not proved satisfactory, to what cause do you attribute its non-success?	12. I have every hope of the bed turning out a success.	12. For so far I have every reason to hope that at the end of the next year there will be a very satisfactory return.	12. I am not able to say whether my undertaking might not have proved satisfactory, if disturbing and exceptional causes of a temporary nature did not exist to retard it.
13. Any general observations or statements you wish to make.	13. It is my intention to complete the stocking of the bed during 1873.	13. It would be very important if the Inspectors would be so kind as to permit my having the beds inside my present bed, as I find it very difficult to prevent trespassers.	13. —

FISHERIES.

from Owners, Occupiers, or Lessees of Oyster Beds—*continued.*

Licence No. 112—8th October, 1871. Dundrum Bay, County Down. Granted to the Most Hon. the Marquess of Downshire.	Licence No. 113—[illegible] December, 1871. Ballynakill Harbour, County Galway. Granted to Major Henry Scott.	Licence No. 114—[illegible] December, 1871. Killary Bay, Leenane, County Galway. Granted to Colin Hugh Thomson.
1. Immediately.	1. The cultivation commenced before the above date.	1. Fifteen years previous to the above date.
2. Two enclosures, formed by embankment; one seawards, supposed favourable for breeding, the other inshore, more for fattening; the former contains about three acres, the latter one acre.	2. Cleaning the bed.	2. Cleaning it with a dredge.
3. On 11th November, 1871, 7,000 small oysters laid down from Lough Swilly, and in same month 4,000 from Carlingford, and on December 17th 6,700 same size from Lough Swilly.	3. 300,000 mixed, most of them small.	3. Never counted the number that were put down, but they were full-grown oysters, a few thousand.
4. No. From the smallness of the fish laid down, it would have been a useless expense.	4. None on some parts, except the culch thrown back on beds; about 1,000 tiles on one part.	4. Put down several collectors for catching spat, both trees and tiles.
5. They have grown very much—increased in size from one and a quarter inches diameter to two and a half inches during the season, and are healthy and thriving. It is to be observed, those inshore were larger and plumper.	5. Do not yet know.	5. The tiles did very well, but the trees did nothing.
6. 20,000 from Lough Swilly in November last, small, one and two years old, and 5,000 same time from Carlingford, small.	6. This is the second year; cannot answer till the season is over.	6. I cannot say the number.
7. No. The fish growing so much, not likely.	7. No.	7. —
8. None.	8. None.	8. Never sold any, except one year, about 20,000.
9. The men are taken from other works, and employed, when necessary, in repairing the embankments, from April to November; one man say constant for 6 months.	9. About twenty on an average all the year round, dredging, cleaning, and shifting oysters, except during June and July.	9. Don't give people constant employment. I employ about eight men dredging for three months, January, February, and March; but this year I have not done, as the weather has been so bad, it was impossible.
10. Over 10,000.	10. Do not know.	10. Have not the most remote idea.
11. None.	11. No.	11. No.
12. Satisfactory. The fish are thriving and very healthy, and hopes are entertained of spat being obtained in the course of the next two years.	12. Ignorance and laziness and extravagance.	12. Cannot state.
13. Collectors will be placed the ensuing season, the beds properly cleaned, and it is intended to put a sluice for regulating the in and out flow of the water. Oysters are very difficult to be got, only the smallest can be obtained, at a cost of over 30s. per 1,000.	13. —	13. —

Appendix, No. 29.

Appendix No. 29.

Registry of Fishing Vessels.

115. Regulations for the Lettering, Numbering, and Registering of British Sea-Fishing Boats under Part II. of the Sea Fisheries Act, 1868 (31 & 32 Victoria, Chapter 45.)

[Note.—The Regulations approved by Her Majesty in Council on the 4th day of February, 1869, are REVOKED by the Order in Council of the 18th day of June, 1869, and the following Regulations are now in force].

1. The following Regulations shall be in future observed by owners and masters of all British boats or vessels hailing from, or belonging to any port or place in the United Kingdom, the Islands of Guernsey, Jersey, Alderney, Sark, or Man, of whatever size, and however propelled or navigated, which find any portion of their ordinary employment in sea fishing, or oyster or mussel dredging, for purposes of sale; subject, however, to the following qualifications:—

(1). Yachts, vessels, or boats not usually employed in fishing or dredging for purposes of sale shall not be subject to the following Regulations when they are not so employed.

(2) If a boat or vessel employed in fishing or dredging for purposes of sale is also used as a pilot boat, and is marked and numbered as such, under any laws or regulations governing such pilot boat, such boat or vessel shall not be subject to the following Regulations;

(3). Boats employed in the pilchard seyn fishery on the coasts of Cornwall shall, if otherwise duly marked to the satisfaction of the officers of Customs or Coast Guard, be exempt from the necessity of having letters and numbers painted on their sails, bows, or sterns, as required by the following Regulations.

2. Every sea fishing vessel or boat, whether registered under any other Act or not, shall, except as hereinbefore provided for, be lettered, numbered, and have a certificate of registry, and shall for that purpose be entered or registered in a Register of Sea Fishing Boats to be kept at the principal office of Customs in each collectorship. Application, as hereafter prescribed, for letters, numbers, and certificates of Registry shall be made by all owners of fishing boats to the Officer of Coast Guard or Fishery Officer in charge of the Station at or near the place where the boat may for the time being be employed. In any case where a boat belongs to a place situated at a distance from a Coast Guard Station, such application may be delivered to the principal Officer of Customs or to any Fishery Officer at the creek or station at or nearest to the place to which the boat belongs, or at which she may be temporarily employed in fishing. And such application upon being received by any such Officer, shall be forthwith forwarded to the Collector of Customs of the Port in which the place to which the boat belongs is situated, who, upon the receipt of such application, shall cause the boat to be registered and numbered, and grant the certificate of such registry, and forward the same to the Officer through whom the application was received, who is to deliver such certificate to the applicant.

3. The port or place at which any British vessel or boat is registered under the provisions of "The Merchant Shipping Act, 1854" (17 & 18 Vict., c. 104), shall be considered the port or place to which she belongs.

4. In Scotland the Officers of the Board of British White Herring Fishery shall assist the Officers of Customs and of Coast Guard in the performance of the duties imposed by these Regulations; and shall in places where there are no Coast Guard, themselves discharge the duties hereby imposed upon the Coast Guard.

5. If, in the opinion of the Collector of the Port to which any boats belong, or of the Inspecting Commander, or Divisional Officer of the District, it is desirable from local circumstances or otherwise, that the mode of application prescribed in the second article of these Regulations should be partially modified or altered, such Collector, Inspecting Commander, or Divisional Officer shall make a special report to the Board of Trade, setting forth the reasons for and particulars of such modification or alteration.

6. There shall be series of numbers and distinguishing letters for the boats belonging to each collectorship of customs.

7. For purposes of numbering, lettering, and registration, boats shall be divided into three classes, as follows.—

1st Class—Boats of 15 tons burthen and upwards.

2nd Class—Boats of less than 15 tons burthen, navigated otherwise than by oars only.

3rd Class—Boats navigated by oars only.

Provided that the officer to whom the application to register is made may, if he think proper, place any small boat occasionally navigated or propelled by sail in the third instead of the second class.

8. For boats of the above classes the positions and dimensions of the letters and numbers shall be as follows:

1st Class—For the hulls, 18 inches in height, and 2½ inches in breadth, and for the sails one-third larger every way.

2nd Class—For the hulls, 10 inches in height, and 1¾ inches in breadth, and for the sails, one-third larger in every way.

3rd Class—Three inches at least in height, and half an inch in breadth.

Provided that in boats that have a "band piece" or "rubbing streak" the letters and numbers shall be as high as the space above the "band piece" or "rubbing streak" will admit. In boats where the space between the gunwale and water-line is not sufficient in size for the prescribed letters and numbers, the letters and numbers shall be as high as the size of the boats will admit.

9. In boats of the 1st and 3rd class the number will follow, and in those of the 2nd class precede the distinguishing letter or letters.

10. When vessels carry, or have attached to them, small boats as tenders or otherwise, such boats must be marked with the same numbers and letters as the vessels to which they belong. Such numbers and letters may be of the size appropriate to the class to which the boat would belong according to its own size and means of propulsion, but in position and precedence according to the class of the vessel to which the boat is attached.

11. In sailing boats, and boats navigated by the occasional use of sails, the letters and numbers shall be placed on each bow, three or four inches below the gunwale, and on each side of the mainsail, except for lug-sail boats, in which the letters and numbers may be placed on the foresail or mizen instead of the mainsail. For boats of the third class, the letters and numbers shall be placed on the outside of the stern of the boat immediately under the name. On the hulls all letters and numbers shall be painted in white oil colour on a black ground; and on sails, in black oil colour on white or gray sails, and in white oil colour on tanned or black sails. Except in the case of vessels only occasionally engaged in fishing for purposes of sale, hereinafter in the thirteenth article of these Regulations specially provided for, the letters and numbers of sails shall be painted on each side of the cloth forming the substance of the sail, and not upon any cloth or other thing sewn or otherwise attached to it; and shall be placed on each side of the centre cloth or cloths of the mainsail, clear of and immediately above the close reef, and so as to be at all times conspicuous whether the sail be reefed or not.

12. All boats of whatever class shall have their names, and those of the ports to which they belong, painted in white oil colour on a black ground on the outside of the sterns, in letters which shall be at least 2 inches in height and ½ an inch in breadth.

13. In the case of any vessel or boat only occasionally engaged in fishing for purposes of sale, and not usually so employed, the letters and numbers prescribed by these Regulations may be temporarily affixed by pieces of canvas or board attached to the mainsail and bows, but of the same dimensions as those specified in the eighth article of these Regulations.

14. The letters, numbers, and names placed on boats and on their sails shall not be effaced, covered, or concealed in any manner whatsoever.

15. All the buoys, barrels, and principal floats of each net, and all other implements of fishery, shall be marked with the same letters and numbers as the boats to which they belong, so as to be easily distinguished. The owners may further distinguish them by any private marks they think proper. Provided that this Regulation shall not apply in the case of boats employed,

(1) In the Scotch herring fishery;
(2) In the drift net and seyn fisheries in Cornwall,
(3) In such other drift net and seyn fisheries (if any) as the Board of Trade may direct.

In the above-mentioned cases it will be held sufficient that the nets and buoys be numbered, so as to identify their true owners; but in all cases of doubt it will devolve upon the masters of buoys and nets to satisfy Sea Fishery officers, (as defined by the 8th section of the Sea Fisheries Act, 1868), that the said buoys and nets properly form part of the trains of the boat with which they may be found, or that they belong to the fishermen of other boats temporarily fishing in it.

16. The owner and master of any boat not having all its nets, buoys, and other implements duly marked in the manner above directed, shall be liable to a penalty not exceeding five pounds.

17. A register of sea-fishing boats, in the form contained in Table A. hereto annexed, shall be kept by the Collector of Customs at each collectorship, which shall contain the date of registry, name of the vessel or boat, and of the port or place to which she belongs, names of owner and master, description of her rig and of her ordinary mode of fishing, her registered number, class, tonnage, and length of keel, and number of crew usually employed.

18. Certificates of Registry in the above register shall be issued by the respective Collectors of Customs, on application being duly made as directed by the second article of these Regulations; and such certificate shall be in the form contained in Table B. hereto annexed, and when necessary shall be transmitted to the Officer of Coast Guard or Customs or other Fishery Officer through whom the application may have been transmitted for delivery by such Officer to the owner. The Certificates of Registry shall contain the name of the collectorship and the distinguishing letters, the name and description of boat, the name of the owner and master, the registered number and class, and the date of entry.

19. All applications for letters, numbers, and registration of fishing boats must be in writing, and according to the form contained in Table C. hereto annexed, and in duplicate if they are to be forwarded from a distant station as provided by the second article of these Regulations; and the duplicate copy is to be retained and filed by the Officer of Coast Guard or Customs at the station to which the boat belongs.

20. Whenever the owner of any registered vessel or boat proves to the satisfaction of the proper Officer of Customs or Coast Guard or any Fishery Officer that he has lost or been deprived of any Certificate of Registry already granted to him, the proper Officer may cause a copy of such Certificate of Registry to be made out and delivered to such owner; and such copy, duly certified by the proper officer, shall have all the effect of the original.

21. Once in every year the owner of every boat shall submit his Certificate of Registry for examination, either at the head office in each collectorship or at the station through which it was originally obtained, and the proper officer shall sign his name on the back of the said Certificate, together with the date of examination, as a record of its authenticity and correctness.

22. In the first week of every year each officer of Customs or of Coast Guard and each Fishery Officer shall forward to the Collector of Customs of the district a list, showing the numbers and classes of all boats whose Certificates of Registry have been presented for examination and endorsed in the preceding year, and a notation of all inspections of Certificates shall be made in the Register against the name of each boat. On a change of ownership, or on removal to another collectorship, of any boat registered under these Regulations, a fresh Certificate of Registry must be applied for, and the former Certificate be given up, in order that the same, together with the former Registry, may be cancelled, and on a *change of Master* due notice shall be given of such change, which shall be duly noted in the Register, *and be endorsed on the Certificate of Registry*.* A failure on the part of the owner of any boat to comply with these Regulations shall subject the owner and master to the same penalties that they would have incurred if the Certificate of Registry had never been applied for.

23. If any boat required to be registered, lettered, and numbered in pursuance of these Regulations, and not being so registered, lettered, and numbered, in the manner prescribed, is used as a fishing boat, the owner and the master shall each be liable to a penalty not exceeding twenty pounds. Any Sea Fishery officer may seize and detain such boat, and prevent it from going to sea and from sea fishing until it is duly registered, lettered, and numbered, and may for that purpose, if it is at sea, take it back into the nearest or most convenient British port. Such boat shall not be entitled to any of the privileges or advantages of a British Sea Fishing Boat, but all obligations, liabilities, and penalties with reference to such boat shall be the same as if it had been duly registered.

24. The master of every boat registered under these Regulations shall have on board his boat at all times the Certificate of Registry hereby required to be obtained; and any master not having such Certificate shall, in the absence of any reasonable cause for the same, (proof whereof shall lie on him,) be liable, together with his boat and crew, to be taken by any Sea Fishery officer, without warrant, summons, or other process, into the nearest or most convenient port, and there to be ordered by the Court, on any proceeding in a summary manner, to pay a penalty not exceeding twenty pounds. Provided that the masters of boats employed in the pilchard fishery in Cornwall, or in such other fishery (if any) as the Board of Trade shall direct, shall be exempt from this Regulation.

25. After registration no change shall be made in the name of any Sea Fishing Boat.

* NOTE.—Where a change of Master occurs, the Lords of the Admiralty, by letter dated 11th April, 1876, have authorized officers of the Coast Guard in Ireland, in all cases where they feel satisfied that delay in Fishing would be caused by forwarding the Register for endorsement to the Collector and waiting till it is returned, may themselves make the endorsement, notifying the same as early as possible to the Collector at the Head Port of Registry.

TABLE A.

SEA FISHERIES ACT, 1868, 31 & 32 Vict. Cap. 45.

Port of ____________________

REGISTRY of VESSELS and BOATS ENGAGED in FISHING.

Date of Registry.	Name of Vessel.	Port or Place to which belonging.	Name of Owner.	Name of Master.	Description		Registered No.			Size.		No. of Crew usually employed.		Remarks.
					Of Vessel or Boat, how rigged, what Sails used, &c.	Ordinary Mode of Fishing.	1st Class.	2nd Class.	3rd Class.	Tonnage.	Length of Keel.	Men.	Boys.	

APPENDIX, No. 29

TABLE B.

SEA FISHERIES ACT, 1868.—31 & 32 Vict. Cap. 45.

Port of ——————

CERTIFICATE OF REGISTRY.

of ——————, named ——————
of ——————
Owner ——————
Master ——————

Registered No. ——— of ——— Class ———

Signature of Registering Officer } ——————

Date ——————

TABLE C.

SEA FISHERIES ACT, 1868.—31 & 32 Vict. Cap. 45.

Application to Register a Vessel or Boat.

Port of ——— ——— Letter ———

The ——————
Port or place to which belonging } ——————
Owner ——————
Master ——————
Description of vessel or boat, how rigged, what sails used, &c. } ——————
Mode of fishing ——————
Tonnage ——————
Length of keel ——————
No. of men ——————
No. of boys —————— } usually employed.
Signature of applicant ——————
Residence ——————

NOTE.—The Act does not require that Boats *engaged exclusively* in Salmon Fishing should be registered; but the 81st section of 5 & 6 V. c. 106, further directs that every Boat, Cot, or Curragh, shall have, upon some conspicuous place thereof, the Name of the Owner, or of one of the Owners, where more than one, and of his Place of Residence, painted in clear, legible characters or letters, of not less than Two Inches in length. Penalty for non-compliance, *Two Pounds*.

DUBLIN: Printed by ALEXANDER THOM, 87 & 88, Abbey-street,
For Her Majesty's Stationery Office.

www.ingramcontent.com/pod-product-compliance
Lightning Source LLC
Chambersburg PA
CBHW031343160426
43196CB00007B/725